Network Analysis and Troubleshooting

J. Scott Haugdahl

ADDISON–WESLEY

Boston • San Francisco • New York • Toronto • Montreal
London • Munich • Paris • Madrid
Capetown • Sydney • Tokyo • Singapore • Mexico City

Many of the designations used by manufacturers and sellers to distinguish their products are claimed as trademarks. Where those designations appear in this book, and
we were aware of a trademark claim, the designations have been printed in initial
capital letters or all capital letters.

The author and publisher have taken care in preparation of this book, but make no
expressed or implied warranty of any kind and assume no responsibility for errors
or omissions. No liability is assumed for incidental or consequential damages in connection with or arising out of the use of the information or programs contained
herein.

The publisher offers discounts of this book when ordered in quantity for special sales.
For more information, please contact:

Pearson Education Corporate Sales Division

One Lake Street

Upper Saddle River, NJ 07458

(800) 382-3419

corpsales@pearsontechgroup.com

Visit Addison-Wesley on the Web: www.awprofessional.com

Library of Congress Cataloging-in-Publication Data

Haugdahl, J. Scott.
    Network analysis and troubleshooting / J. Scott Haugdahl
        p.   cm.
    Includes bibliographical references and index.
    ISBN 0-201-43319-2
    1. Computer networks—Maintenance and repair. 2. Computer networks—
Management. I. Title.
    TK5105.5 H374 2000
    004.6—dc21   99-049134

ISBN 0-201-43319-2
Text printed on recycled paper.
3 4 5 6 7 8 9—BM—07060504
Third printing, August 2003

Contents

Chapter 5   Analyzing and Troubleshooting the Transport Layer   177

Chapter 6   Analyzing and Troubleshooting the Session Layer   215

Preface

Introduction

What qualifications do you need to become a good network analyst? Numerous Engineering or Computer Science degrees? A vast knowledge of UNIX or Windows 95/98/NT/2000/...? Fifty years of industry experience? Being able to recite the OSI seven-layer reference model?

The best qualification is to simply have a real passion for problem solving. Sure it helps to have a background in data communications, but nothing beats logical thinking with a "detective" bent when it comes to analyzing and troubleshooting networks.

To identify the culprit, you need to be resourceful and sift through clues provided by cable testers, protocol analyzers, Simple Network Management Protocol (SNMP) probes and consoles, router tables, switch and hub statistics, network documentation, and even empirical observations from end-users.

In my eighteen years in the networking industry, I have learned far more over the past six years by "doing" rather than "observing" and critiquing (a.k.a. my early consulting years). The insights and case studies presented in this book are based on my experiences and adventures in solving real problems on real networks, mainly at Fortune 1000 companies with large networks. Although there is no substitute for hands-on experience, this book is intended to help you learn the operational details of many of today's popular protocols and enhance your skills in troubleshooting networks using proven protocol analysis techniques.

Sometimes working with networks can be hazardous to your health. My favorite story of all time is from a network support person working with me at an on-site troubleshooting job. As I recall, it went something like this:

We had completed an upgrade of our workstation wiring, making sure that Category 5 cable ran everywhere. During the process, we found a large wooden spool (like the kind the Telcos would discard and you could turn into a cheap table) containing several hundred feet of the old thick Ethernet coax. Unlike a spool of Cat 5, this baby was big and heavy. In the process of moving the spool of cable from one of our wiring closets to permanent cold storage, we proceeded to load it into the back of a pickup truck. Needless to say, the spool slipped off and began rolling down an incline. Imagine the look on the face of one of my colleagues who was approaching the truck and saw this big spool of wire hurtling down on him!

True story. Or so I've been told.

I should note that even though I mention a few commercial products from time to time, the emphasis of this book is on learning analysis fundamentals as well as techniques in solving problems. To avoid bias, I've intentionally used screen shots from a variety of protocol analyzers to show that the techniques can be applied using different analyzers. While conducting training classes, I really don't care what analyzer is used as long as there's some flexibility in the tool.

Who Should Read This Book

This book is aimed at those responsible for maintaining the efficiency and integrity of their network infrastructure on a day-to-day basis. This includes:

- **Network Engineers:** These are professionals involved in the analysis and troubleshooting of problems that escalate beyond the help desk. This includes network analysts, support specialists, senior technicians as well as independent consultants who are called in to assist in troubleshooting their client's networks. This book teaches a proven approach to troubleshooting and will help these users to become more comfortable and proficient when using the protocol analyzer to help solve those tough networking problems as well as to proactively analyze their networks.

- **Technical Managers:** Managers will benefit from reading this book in that they will gain a better understanding of the kinds of problems that their network support staff can diagnose with the help of protocol analyzers. Such information can be used to better allocate tasks ranging from identifying the reason for poor response time or throughput to baselining the current network infrastructure for future expansion and rearchitecting.

The reader is assumed to have a basic understanding of data communications, especially in local area networks. Rather than simply rehash standards information and packet formats, this book presents the most pertinent information contained in packets along with the protocol operation details necessary to understand how to troubleshoot and optimize mission-critical networks. Even the "seasoned pro" will benefit from the generous analysis and troubleshooting tips, diagrams, and trace file snapshots that accompany the text throughout the book.

Although not covering every conceivable networking topology and protocol, the book offers a general approach for readers to focus on to identify and solve problems at the various layers of infrastructure. This book uses a "bottom-up" approach structured around the seven-layer OSI model that can be generalized and applied to many different situations.

A Brief Organization of This Book

Network Analysis and Troubleshooting begins with a look at the layered methodology to network analysis and why a protocol analyzer is the tool of choice for solving complex problems.

Chapter 2 looks at issues specific to the physical layer, including cabling types, Time Domain Reflectometry (TDR), and transmission encoding techniques.

Chapter 3 focuses on the data link layer. Topics covered include details on the IEEE 48-bit address format, the impact of different types of broadcast traffic, the role of the Cyclic Redundancy Check (CRC), operational details and analysis consideration for layer 2 switches, Ethernet and Token Ring operation and troubleshooting, and an in-depth look at the IEEE 802.2 Logical Link Control (LLC) protocol.

Chapter 4 concentrates on the network layer, beginning with a discussion of datagram concepts and router operation. The addressing schemes of various protocols are discussed, including details on IP classes and subnetting. IP specifics such as the role of the Internet Control Message Protocol (ICMP) are analyzed. Other topics include IPX operation and analysis, and local routing problems.

Chapter 5 analyzes the transport layer by examining the operation of the NetWare Sequenced Packet Exchange (SPX), SPX II, User Datagram Protocol (UDP), and the Transmission Control Protocol (TCP). Specifically for TCP, the concepts of block size, segment size, and sliding window are covered in detail.

Chapter 6 covers the session layer, including how some session services are actually embedded in other layers, how different protocols operate to find resources via DNS, NetWare Service Advertising Protocol (SAP), or NetBIOS. The three major NetBIOS implementations—NetBIOS over LLC (NetBEUI), NetBIOS over IPX, and NetBIOS over TCP/IP—are covered.

Chapter 7 covers the presentation layer by examining presentation protocols that are specific to certain protocol families and why there is no general-purpose presentation protocol in widespread use today.

Chapter 8 examines the application layer, beginning with a discussion of networked application characteristics, followed by a discussion of logon sequencing for different protocol stacks. Then specific protocols are covered in depth, including the Dynamic Host Control Protocol (DHCP), NetWare Core Protocol (NCP), Microsoft/IBM Server Message Block (SMB) Protocol, Sun Network File System (NFS), and the File Transfer Protocol (FTP). As a bonus, the NT Browse protocol (not to be confused with Internet browsing!) is discussed.

Chapter 9 shows how to use your protocol analyzer to measure and baseline throughput and latency, identify bottlenecks in your network, and determine server and client response times.

> **!**
>
> Throughout these chapters you'll find many helpful Tips that will be presented in this format.

Acknowledgments

Several reviewers provided excellent technical feedback from the rough draft. These people include Robert Bullen, Phil Koenig, Phillip Scarr, Howard Lee Harkness, Ehud Gavron, Glen Herrmannsfeldt, Louis Breit, Doug Hughes, Bob Vance, Barry Margolin, and William Welch.

I'd also like to thank those wonderful folks at Addison Wesley Longman who worked with me during the various stages of developing this book, including Mary Hart, Karen Gettman, Lorraine Ferrier, and Tracy Russ.

And last, but not least, my family, Nancy, Daniel, and Matthew. I love you guys!

Have any great troubleshooting experiences? Feel free to drop me a line at scott@net3group.com.

All the best,

J. Scott Haugdahl

August 1999

I can do all things through Him, who strengthens me. *Philippians 4:13.*

Customer:

Internet Archive Reno NS 3

Travel + Leisure's Unexpected France (Travel + Leisure Unexpected) (Travel + Leisure Unexpected)

Novogrod, Nancy

6B-08-07-D2

No CD

Used - Good

W2-CRE-234

9780756624972

Picker Notes:

M _____ 2 _____

WT _____ 2 _____

CC _____

79120881

[DirectSales] IA - Reno: 999-0000000-0385507

2149 Items

1086227172

Reno Internet Archive 2

Ship. Created: 1/19/2022 12:53:00 PM

Date Ordered: 1/19/2022 3:48:00 PM

Chapter 1

Introduction

1.1 Building a Foundation

I'm truly amazed at how many people jump right into network analysis without a basic understanding of network communications. Although you don't need to understand how bits are encoded into electrical signals on the cable, you do need to know how end-nodes locate and communicate with each other. The key to making this happen can be summarized in one word: protocol. Understanding protocols is the foundation of network analysis.

Microsoft Bookshelf '98 Dictionary defines a protocol as: "The forms of ceremony and etiquette observed by diplomats and heads of state; a code of correct conduct." Imagine two end-nodes on a network that didn't observe the correct code of conduct for a given protocol!

A better understanding of a protocol in the context of computer networking can be found in the following process:

1. Attach end-nodes to a network that need to exchange data.
2. Break data up into units called packets.
3. Exchange packets using agreed upon conventions or *protocols*.

Protocols define the data syntax (bits) and their semantics (interpretation). Then various layers of protocol define application data, flow control, error detection, and addresses. The Open Systems Interconnect (OSI) reference model defines these layers.

Radia Perlman, inventor of the spanning tree algorithm and author of *Interconnections,* once said during a lecture: "There must be a law that says you can't present a tutorial on the subject of networking without some discussion of the OSI reference model!" Because the OSI model presents a general framework from which to develop standards and implement protocols for various layers of functionality, I'm going to extend this philosophy into network analysis as well.

Over the years, I've developed a methodology for troubleshooting networks that mirrors the OSI model: troubleshoot from the bottom up beginning with the physical layer and working up layer by layer to the application layer, if necessary. For example, it doesn't make sense to troubleshoot a low through-put problem by first looking at the file server's application layer when the client's Ethernet segment is experiencing a large number of CRC (cyclic redundancy code) errors. Although you may be able to mask the problem by tweaking upper layer protocol timers to shorten the retry intervals, the fundamental problem of CRC errors does not go away.

One of the problems in many networks today is that as performance suffers, additional bandwidth is simply added to the infrastructure without regard for the real cause. More bandwidth by reducing the number of users per network segment, often referred to as "micro segmentation"; more bandwidth by putting switches in front of routers; more bandwidth by upgrading routers or switches with more backplane speed or more powerful processing capability; more bandwidth by swapping out backbones for ATM or Gigabit Ethernet. More and *more!* Faster and *faster!*

A more intelligent approach is to troubleshoot and optimize what you already have before throwing a faster box at it. Get rid of those CRC errors. Improve the efficiency of your protocols. Tune your servers. Get rid of all that "space junk" floating around on your network, like print servers looking for servers using protocols you don't even support. And the best place to start is at the very bottom of your network, the physical media.

1.2 The OSI Reference Model Revisited

In a nutshell, the OSI reference model is a multi-layer communications model developed by the International Standards Organization (ISO). In theory, each of the seven layers has a well-defined function and is independent of the others. In practice, the real world is far from perfect. For example, the ever-popular Transport Control Protocol (TCP) and Internet Protocol (IP) are essentially implementations of OSI layer 4 (transport) and layer 3 (network), respectively, but they violate the independence principle: TCP cannot operate without IP because it borrows portions of the IP header to create a "pseudo header" when computing the TCP checksum. Ever see TCP running over IPX?

The popular User Datagram Protocol (UDP) is considered to be a transport layer protocol, but it lacks many of the requirements of a true transport layer, a topic examined in more detail in Chapter 5.

Also, some legacy protocols such as IBM's proprietary Systems Network Architecture (SNA) are very difficult to map to the OSI model because SNA has a completely different layering philosophy developed independently of OSI. This doesn't mean that you can't troubleshoot SNA in the same manner as TCP/IP, from the bottom up.

Another important aspect of the OSI layers is that each peer layer appears to be communicating directly with the same peer layer elsewhere in the network. Thus, if an application calls an API into the network layer to send a datagram to another IP address, the application need not be concerned about how it gets there.

1.2.1 The Seven Layers

Figure 1.1 illustrates the seven layers of the OSI reference model and summarizes the functionality of each layer. The summary emphasizes what you need to know when analyzing your network. Let's go through each layer.

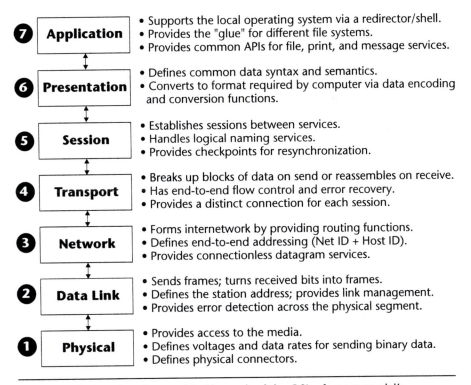

FIGURE 1.1 Functionality provided by each of the OSI reference model's seven layers.

- *Layer 1 (Physical Layer).* This layer provides the basic mechanism to encode (transmit) and decode (receive) binary data (bits) to or from physical media. It is where you'll see signaling types (the way the 1s and 0s are represented) defined, such as Manchester encoding for 10 Mbps Ethernet, differential Manchester encoding for Token Ring, or 4B/5B encoding for FDDI. The physical layer also informs layer 2, the data link layer, when it can gain access to the medium, such as the carrier sense function for Ethernet.

  The physical layer also defines the physical connection mechanism to the media, but not the media itself. In the spirit of the reference model, the actual physical media reside below the physical layer. After all, the bit stream should be independent of the media type, capable of running over copper, fiber, infrared, microwave, laser, barbed wire (but probably for a very short distance!), and so on. Standards such as the IEEE 802.x LAN standards contain detailed specifications on a variety of media types to ensure consistency and compatibility when using a particular media type.

- *Layer 2 (Data Link Layer).* Also called the data link control or DLC layer, this layer provides bit "framing" by defining a header with a beginning flag or preamble bits, addressing information, and for LANs, a 32-bit cyclic redundancy code (CRC) at the end of the frame to protect the integrity of the bits as they traverse the physical media. The DLC layer also provides link management. For Ethernet, frames are transmitted when the channel is idle and aborted when a collision is detected. In Token Ring, frames are transmitted when a free token is received.

  The CRC protects the data across the physical network segment or series of physical segments tied together with repeaters, such as a 10BASE-T Ethernet hub or a series of stations forming a ring. Repeated segments joined together by hubs in an Ethernet are collectively called a "collision domain," a subject discussed in more detail in Chapter 3.

  A recipient of a frame calculates the CRC as the frame is being received. If the CRC does not match that at the end of the frame, the DLC layer discards the frame.

  You also need to know that the IEEE has a slightly different view of the DLC layer, as shown in Figure 1.2. The IEEE DLC layer is actually made up of the Logical Link Control (LLC) and Media Access Control (MAC) layers. The MAC layer is essentially equivalent to the entire DLC layer of "old." The addition of the LLC layer was largely a contribution from IBM during Token Ring development (and concurrently with the IEEE 802.5 standards effort), in that it mimics HDLC operation in support of SNA. By adopting LLC for their LAN standards, IEEE has essentially provided a standard interface into the MAC layer. About the only upper layer protocols that use "true" LLC (LLC Type 2) protocols are SNA and NetBEUI (NetBIOS Extended User

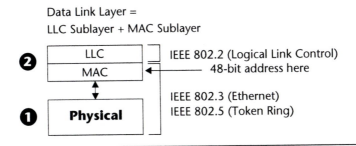

Data Link Layer =
LLC Sublayer + MAC Sublayer

FIGURE 1.2 IEEE LAN standards map to the lower two layers by breaking up layer 2.

Interface), also referred to as NetBIOS over LLC. NetWare only uses an LLC Type 1 header as a "stub" for IPX. LLC operation is covered in detail in Chapter 2, and IPX is detailed in Chapter 4.

I generally refer to a unit of information at the DLC layer as a frame (because the DLC layer truly does frame the bits it sends and receives), and above that, a packet. I like to also refer to a station's address at the DLC layer as the Media Access Control (MAC) address in keeping with the conventions of the IEEE LAN standards.

- *Layer 3 (Network Layer).* This layer forms an internetwork by provided routing functions, provides connectionless datagram services for end-nodes, and defines the end-to-end addressing across the entire inter-network. The network layer takes data from the layer above it, the transport layer, and some network layer protocols also break it up into multiple datagrams that will fit inside the payload of the DLC frame.

  The end-to-end addressing of the network layer is independent of the DLC layer. Unlike that of the DLC layer, the addressing of the net-work layer consists of network plus host identifiers. The network iden-tifier can be flat like IPX, subnetted like IP, or hierarchical like DECnet. (DECnet is unique in that the node sending the packet, such as a router, has its DECnet address mapped to its DLC address; refer to Chapter 4 for more details.) Protocols such as Routing Information Protocol (RIP) or Open Shortest Path First (OSPF) propagate information about net-work identifiers to other routers such that packets can be forwarded accordingly. The host part of the network address is always flat and designates an end-node on the specific network or subnetwork.

  The network layer may also contain a checksum, usually 16 bits. Beware, however, that this checksum may only protect the information in the network layer header and not the datagram payload. Such is the case with IP.

- *Layer 4 (Transport Layer).* This layer provides data segmentation and reassembly by breaking up blocks of data on send and reassembling them on receive, has end-to-end flow control and error recovery, and provides a distinct connection for each session required by an application. Fields like segment identifiers as well as sequence and acknowledgment numbers are in the transport layer header. The receiving side ensures that the segmented packets are reassembled in the proper order. The sending side ensures that all segments are acknowledged, and resends those that are not. It can also implement flow control when segments have to be retransmitted. Without the TCP protocol, for example, a highly congested network such as the Internet would virtually grind to a halt (although on some days, it sure seems as if it does anyway).

Without a transport layer, recovery must by done by a higher layer, such as the application layer or the application itself. In some cases, the buck is passed to the user with messages like the classic DOS "Error receiving from network. Abort, Retry, Ignore?"

The NetWare Core Protocol (NCP) over IPX does not have a separate transport layer and as such, the recovery mechanisms are built into NCP. To avoid the issue of dropped segments and acknowledgments, NCP can only send one packet at a time. By virtue of a reply to a command, the command is acknowledged. NCP also maintains its own sequence numbers.

- *Layer 5 (Session Layer).* This layer provides naming services (logical name-to-network address mapping), establishes sessions between services such as between a client and a Web server, and provides checkpoints for resynchronization in the event of a lost connection. Sessions are established using a logical name or alias. Often, a session ID is embedded in the packet after a session is established.

  Every protocol family provides its own way of finding a logical name associated with an address. For example, TCP/IP-related applications use the Domain Name System (DNS), NetWare applications use the NetWare Service Advertising Protocol (SAP), and NetBIOS uses a Naming Service (IP only) or a broadcast method to locate resources.

  Examples of session layer protocol implementations include NetBIOS, Remote Procedure Call (RPC) in IP-based applications such as Network File System (NFS), and the AppleTalk Session Protocol (ASP).

  NCP over IPX does not have a separate session layer per se, except to locate a resource using SAP. After that, the actual session is established by sending a RIP packet to find the next "hop" to the resource, followed by an exchange of NCP packets with that resource.

  Many IP applications rely on DNS to locate a resource and on TCP to establish a session. TCP does, in fact, take on some session characteristics because it sets up (SYN) and tears down (FIN) a connection, and it offers a maximum segment size (of TCP payload data) to the other side of the connection. Chapter 5 covers these critical aspects of TCP in more detail.

- *Layer 6 (Presentation Layer)*. This layer manages abstract data structures. Common data syntax and semantics are defined and data types are converted, where needed, for layer 7, the application layer. Except for certain applications such as SNMP or XWindows, the presentation layer is usually not present when you go to analyze traces; that is, there is no widely implemented session layer protocol for all applications. The overhead required for such data conversions would be too high. Simple conversions, like EBCDIC-to-ASCII character set conversion, are done by the application itself. More complex operations, like byte ordering, are also usually done by the application.

- *Layer 7 (Application Layer)*. This layer supports the local operating system via a shell or redirector mechanism. It provides the glue for differing operating systems by converting APIs for file, printing, and messaging services into a common language such as NetWare Core Protocol used in NetWare client/server environments or Server Message Block (SMB) used in OS/2 and Windows environments.

Figure 1.3 illustrates how many of the popular protocols map to the layers of the OSI reference model. Subsequent chapters cover most of these protocols.

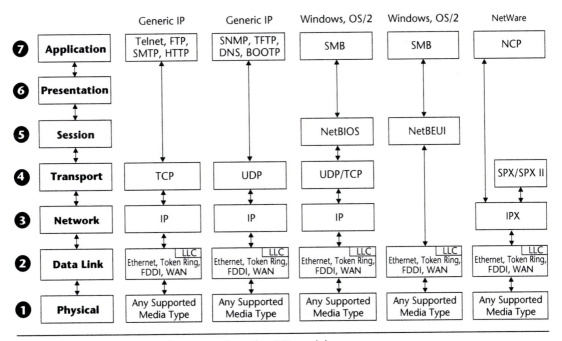

FIGURE 1.3 Mapping popular protocols to the OSI model.

1.2.2 Packet Construction

Beginning with a small or large amount of data at the application layer, headers are added as the data is passed down the stack. Figure 1.4 illustrates this concept. Note that depending on the application and the protocols, the format header or session ID header may not be presented. If only the datagram services of the network layer are used with no transport layer, sequencing information may be absent as well. Keep in mind that some upper layer protocols such as NCP have their own sequencing information.

> ❗ When analyzing any application, always ask yourself if the amount of data being transferred makes sense for this application. If there's only one byte of application data, the protocol header overhead is tremendous, especially in a minimal-sized Ethernet packet of 64 bytes. If the application is a user running Telnet, that's probably okay because most users can't type more than about 10 packets per second. If the application is reading or writing a file one byte at a time, then you've got a real problem!

In the end, the packet is packaged as a frame at the DLC layer and then transmitted to the media when access is available. For full-duplex LANs or WANs, this is almost immediate. For standard Ethernet and Token Ring LANs, the DLC layer must wait its turn to access the shared media.

At the peer end (which could be on another subnet), the headers are stripped until the data reaches the application layer, assuming there are no CRC or checksum errors along the way.

1.3 Identifying Problems by Layer

Figure 1.5 contains a summary of common problems seen at various layers. The problems are described generically here and later chapters specific to each layer provide examples.

Bad wiring is probably the number one cause of problems at the physical layer. Although I've never done a study to confirm this, it's been said that somewhere in the neighborhood of 90 percent of all networking problems are cabling related. This is a good reason to start at the physical layer and have access to a high-quality cable tester. Cable testing is fast and accurate. Too bad I can't say the same for the other 10 percent of the problems that take 90 percent of your time!

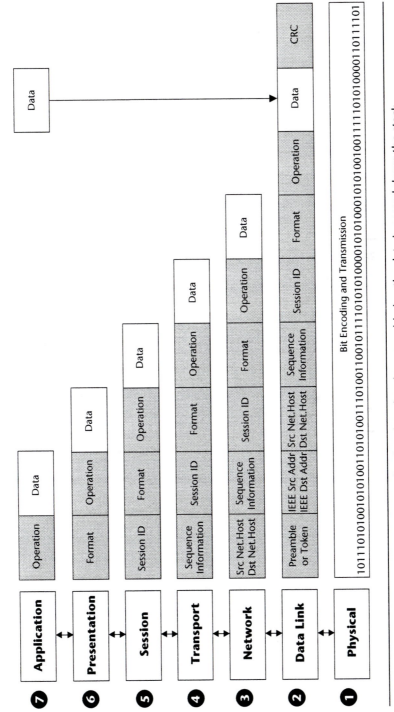

FIGURE 1.4 Beginning with a unit of application data, headers are added as the data is passed down the stack.

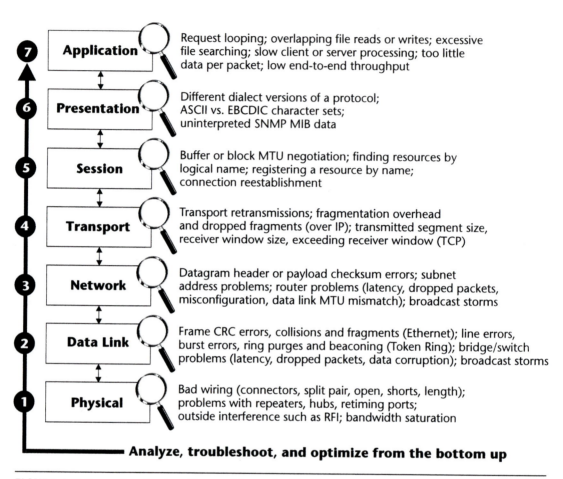

7 **Application** — Request looping; overlapping file reads or writes; excessive file searching; slow client or server processing; too little data per packet; low end-to-end throughput

6 **Presentation** — Different dialect versions of a protocol; ASCII vs. EBCDIC character sets; uninterpreted SNMP MIB data

5 **Session** — Buffer or block MTU negotiation; finding resources by logical name; registering a resource by name; connection reestablishment

4 **Transport** — Transport retransmissions; fragmentation overhead and dropped fragments (over IP); transmitted segment size, receiver window size, exceeding receiver window (TCP)

3 **Network** — Datagram header or payload checksum errors; subnet address problems; router problems (latency, dropped packets, misconfiguration, data link MTU mismatch); broadcast storms

2 **Data Link** — Frame CRC errors, collisions and fragments (Ethernet); line errors, burst errors, ring purges and beaconing (Token Ring); bridge/switch problems (latency, dropped packets, data corruption); broadcast storms

1 **Physical** — Bad wiring (connectors, split pair, open, shorts, length); problems with repeaters, hubs, retiming ports; outside interference such as RFI; bandwidth saturation

Analyze, troubleshoot, and optimize from the bottom up

FIGURE 1.5 Examples of networking problems classified by OSI layer.

Errors associated with the data link layer include CRC errors, collisions and fragments (Ethernet only), line errors, burst errors, ring purges and beaconing (Token Ring), insufficient buffers causing packet loss in a switch or bridge, data corruption in a bridge or switch, and broadcast storms as identified by a data link with a destination address of all 1s (FFFFFFFFFFFF in hex).

Because routers rely on information contained in the network layer header, many problems associated with the network layer can be attributed to routing. Examples included dropped packets, queuing and filtering latency, misconfiguration of the router, MTU mismatch between incoming and outgoing router ports, Routing Information Protocol (RIP) packet route time-outs received from other routers, and multiple subnets assigned to a port. Although a rare problem in my experience, a router could corrupt a network layer header as a packet is forwarded, as evidenced by a bad checksum inside the header.

The number one symptom of problems with packets in transit—transport retransmissions—surfaces at the transport layer. This symptom tells us that packets are lost or delayed in transit. In many cases, the client does not allow enough time and unnecessarily does a transport retransmission. Problems specific to the TCP protocol include large TCP data blocks that are fragmented by the IP layer, small TCP segment sizes that don't take advantage of the DLC layer's MTU, and a TCP window into the receiver's buffer that is too small (or too large!). Chapter 5 covers TCP in detail.

The problems in the session layer are often associated with mapping a logical name or alias to a network address. Conversely, registering logical names such as with a Domain Name System (DNS) server or a Windows Internet Naming Service (WINS) server can present problems. Another critical area in the session layer is how a client and server negotiate the session buffer size for sending and receiving data. The session layer is also responsible for reconnecting a dropped session so that the user doesn't have to log back in to the resource and start a new session from the beginning.

As I mentioned earlier, the presentation layer is usually specific to a given application such as SNMP, or it doesn't exist at all. Because no general-purpose presentation layer is in widespread use today, data conversion and representation are usually handled by the end-application itself. Thus not too many problems are associated with this layer, and data presentation problems can be deferred instead to the end-application such as a MIB browser or database front-end.

The application layer presents several challenges to the analyst. Request looping is when the application asks for and receives data, then asks for the exact same data (i.e., the same file, offset into the file, and amount of data) in succession. Another example would be repeated directory listings for the exact same path. Overlapping file reads or writes occur when a portion of the data being read or written has already appeared in a previous read or write request. Excessive file searching can lead to excessive packets and server utilization. Slow clients that receive data from a server and take too long to process that data can lead to a perception that "the network is slow." Conversely, a server that takes too long to crunch on a request from a client can lead to the same perception.

Thus many of the application layer problems that you see with your analyzer can be traced back to the behavior of the end-user application itself, yet the end-users will blame the underlying network infrastructure. If the application is written in house, great. If, on the other hand, the application is written by a third party, you may have a tough time proving that the application is beating up your network without supporting proof shown in analyzer traces.

1.4 The Protocol Analyzer

Many excellent tools are available for troubleshooting very specific problems ranging from checking the integrity of a station's cable by using a cable tester to verifying a printer driver version on a client via a central administration console. It's all the complexity in between that requires a protocol analyzer to see exactly what transpires between a client and server, bit by bit. You can observe the external symptoms—slow user response, high network utilization, sessions being dropped—but you can't see inside without something akin to an x-ray machine or CAT scanner.

So, before throwing more bandwidth at the problem, why not investigate with a protocol analyzer?

1.4.1 Basic Protocol Analyzer Operation

The operation of a protocol analyzer is actually quite simple:

1. Receive a copy of every packet on a piece of wire by operating in a promiscuous capture mode (a mode that captures all packets on the wire, not just broadcast packets and packets addressed to the analyzer's adapter).
2. Timestamp the packets.
3. Filter out the stuff you're not interested in.
4. Show a breakdown of the various layers of protocol, bit by bit.

These packet traces can be saved and retrieved for further analysis. The basic analyzer capture flow is illustrated in Figure 1.6.

Protocol analyzer packaging varies widely. Sometimes all that's needed is a protocol analyzer executable that runs like any other application on the desktop, using the network interface controller (NIC) that is already installed. Examples of these kinds of analyzers include Microsoft Network Monitor, AG Group EtherPeek/Tokenpeek, Network Instruments Observer, Novell's LANalyzer for Windows, Solaris "snoop," tcpdump (for UNIX), and so on. The biggest concern is with performance because other applications may be contending for resources in the workstation, namely, the bus, CPU, and NIC. Usually the NIC drivers themselves are not optimized for continuous packet capture.

In other cases, the analyzer is packaged as a complete "high performance" platform, such as an HP Internetwork Advisor or Wavetek Wandel Goltermann DA-30. Another option is to provide a separate NIC card or pod that works in conjunction with an existing workstation or laptop. The Network Associates (formerly Network General) Sniffer is an example of the latter, and the Wavetek Wandel Goltermann Domino is an example of the former.

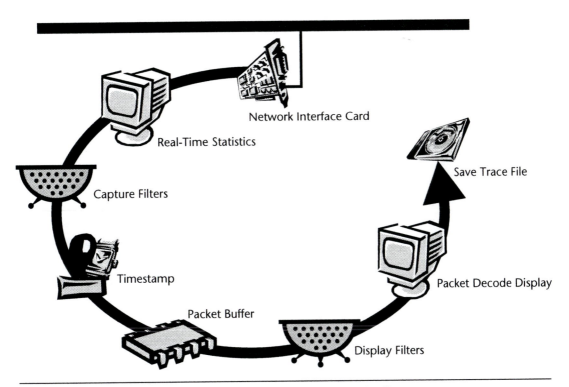

FIGURE 1.6 The basic protocol analyzer packet capture and display flow.

Once a packet is captured from the wire, the analyzer breaks down the headers and describes each bit of every header in detail. A sample breakdown of an NT logon packet is illustrated in Figure 1.7, showing the detail and raw hex data of the packet for the various layers of protocol.

1.4.2 Analysis Essentials—What Differentiates One Analyzer from Another?

The analyzer marketplace is becoming very competitive, especially the analyzer executables for 32-bit Windows 95/98 and NT platforms. I continue to be amazed, however, that many of the offerings lack basic functions that are often overlooked in favor of more decodes, esoteric packet filters, lackluster expert systems, and other bells and whistles.

Naturally, every analyzer filters packets while capturing and displaying. Every analyzer displays your basic packet summary, protocol details, and raw packet data in hexadecimal and ASCII format. Every analyzer timestamps the packet

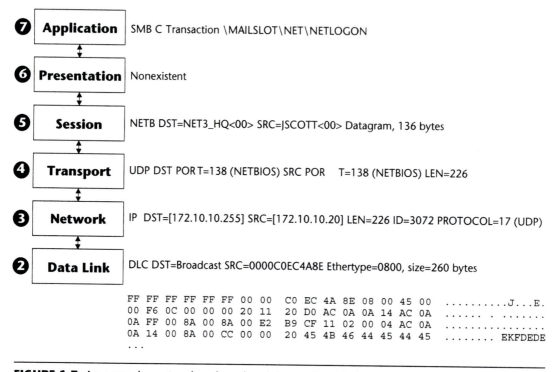

FIGURE 1.7 An example protocol analyzer breakdown of an NT logon packet, showing the hex and detail for various layers of protocol.

and shows you the addresses of who is sending and (should be) receiving that packet at both the data link and network layers.

Although this is all good for basic packet exploring, a few essentials are missing. For example, if I can set the analyzer to display two additional metrics—cumulative time and cumulative bytes—in the summary display by setting the appropriate filters, I can more easily perform throughput analysis for a given application such as a file transfer. Only a few high-end units such as the Sniffer and Domino have this capability. The low-end analyzers have no excuse for not including this basic but essential capability (maybe, by the time you read this, they will have these features).

The resolution of a timestamp can also vary from analyzer to analyzer. Many Windows-based analyzers only show the absolute time of a packet arrival or delta time between packets down to 1 millisecond due to Windows timing limitations. (Timing down to a frequency of 1,193,182 ticks per second or 0.838 microseconds is possible, but the accuracy is somewhat suspect depending on how quickly the NIC interrupts and drivers are processed.) Showing more accurate information usually requires another time source, such as an external analyzer pod.

> ❗ Keep in mind that the delta time of a packet in your analyzer's packet buffer includes not only the "gap" since the previous packet was received, but also the *transmission time of the current packet*. For example, a 1,518-byte packet takes approximately 0.0012 seconds (1.2 milliseconds) to transmit on a 10 Mbps Ethernet. Thus a packet's delta time of 0.0012 seconds means that the packet was sent with virtually no delay after the previous packet.

Having only a 1-millisecond timestamp makes it difficult for precise timing measurements even at only 10 Mbps. For example, a minimum-sized Ethernet packet (64 bytes, including CRC) takes only 48 microseconds to transmit, excluding the preamble. Thus, a lot of packets will be stamped with the same value before incrementing to the next millisecond.

Packet filters are extremely useful, especially if the analyzer lets me filter down to a specific bit within a packet, a feature that seems to only be available in the upper bracket analyzers. I can also specify a bit pattern with "don't care" bits, such as 101*xxxxx*. This tells the analyzer to match on the bit pattern 101 at the beginning of the byte, but to ignore the remaining 5 bits (they can be set to anything) of that byte.

On some analyzers, you can also start the offset from the end of the DLC encapsulation header as well as from the beginning of the frame. Being able to filter "DLC relative" is an essential feature for Token Ring users due to the variable routing information field (RIF) that can follow the destination and source addresses in source-routed networks.

Another little essential that makes a big difference in troubleshooting is the ability to display a user-selectable layer of protocol in the summary. As an example, I may want to study the TCP transactions for an application using the Server Message Block (SMB) application layer protocol to communicate with an NT server. By setting the summary to display only up to the TCP layer, I can quickly see the ports in use, the TCP handshaking, the amount of TCP payload during data transfer, and the TCP sequence and acknowledgment numbers. Although some analyzers have this capability, they may only show part of the critical information I need to know about the TCP layer. Perhaps the port numbers are present but not the sequence or acknowledgment numbers.

The ability to summarize each layer is a subtle, yet important, part of network analysis. It's painful to have to rely on the detail window to glean more than the very basic information about a protocol. You may want to consider comparing the analyzers of choice side by side and see for yourself what critical summary information is missing about the layers of protocol in use in your network. The more mature analyzers show this information very well because they know many of the key elements to extract from the detail for displaying in the summary.

To me, having in-depth and accurate protocol decodes is the most important criterion for any analyzer. What good is it if the lower layers are decoded very well, but not the mission-critical upper layer protocols used in your network? How good is your analyzer of choice in decoding required protocols above the IPX or TCP/IP layers? Does your network use NetWare Directory Services (NDS)? NT Network Neighborhood browsing? SQL client/server database applications? How well does your analyzer support these protocols? In many cases, the vendor's marketing hype will indicate that certain upper layer protocols are decoded by saying "our analyzer decodes 350 protocols," but you'll be surprised at how many of them only provide superficial high-level information like "SMB MAILSLOT/NETLOGON" with no underlying details.

Analyzer capture performance is also a growing concern, especially as backbones and even desktop network segments become faster, reaching into the gigabit-per-second range. Many desktop-based analyzers drop packets even on 10 Mbps Ethernet segments, so you can imagine what happens when you use them to analyze at speeds upwards of 100 and 1000 Mbps (1 gigabit per second).

One solution for handling higher speeds is for the analyzer vendor to provide a proprietary driver that bypasses the standard desktop NIC driver. For example, the vendor may offer a driver that is designed to work with a specific NIC, such as a DEC-chip PCI card for 10/100 Mbps Ethernet. Regardless, the bottleneck still lies with the limited NIC buffering (usually with 32 to 64 Kbytes of packet buffer) designed for workstation usage and data transfer efficiency over, say, the PCI bus to the real packet buffer contained in main memory in the workstation. Add to that the fact that capture filtering chews up additional CPU cycles, which further increases the likelihood of dropped packets.

With network topologies like ATM, FDDI, and synchronous WANs, you have no choice but to buy a pod-based analyzer or an analyzer with a vendor-supplied NIC designed to work in your standard desktop slots. If you have Token Ring segments to analyze, special adapters may be required if you are using IBM or third-party "true blue" Token Ring NICs because these adapters can't be placed in promiscuous capture mode. If you have Madge or Olicom cards, you're probably okay.

Speaking of desktop NIC drivers, there's one caveat you need to be aware of: virtually all Windows workstation NDIS drivers do *not* pass packets with CRC errors! Thus any Ethernet packets with CRC errors or collision fragments (a packet less than the 64-byte minimum size and an invalid CRC) will not be passed to the analyzer capture buffer. You may get a CRC indication, that is, a count of CRC errors, but you will not be able to examine the packets for any potential clues to the problem. Once again, proprietary vendor drivers come to the rescue.

1.4.3 Packet Filtering, Slicing, and Triggering Tips and Tricks

All too often I see those that are new to network analysis and even a few pros capture *every* packet on a segment when trying to troubleshoot a specific problem. If the problem only affects users communicating with a certain server, put an analyzer on that segment and filter on traffic to and from the server. If the problem only affects users who go through a router, start by putting an analyzer on one of the routed segments and filter on traffic to and from the router's MAC address. If you are troubleshooting a slow login process, why not start by analyzing from the client's segment and putting a filter on the client's MAC address?

Carry a 10/100 Mbps pocket hub and microtransceiver to complement your portable analyzer. This will allow you to temporarily "share" a drop next to a workstation with a half-duplex Ethernet connection so you can coordinate with a user whose application you are trying to troubleshoot. For Token Ring users, use a station lobe wiring port "multiplier."

Beware, however, that sometimes you will need to filter on more than just a specific workstation or server address when troubleshooting a problem. For example, if you are analyzing DHCP, a process where a workstation obtains or renews an IP address from a DHCP server at startup, the response to a DHCP request from a workstation is usually sent back on a DLC broadcast address. Thus, you wouldn't see the response if you had a filter for only packets to and from that workstation's specific MAC address. Keep in mind that you can still apply a display filter to the packets in the capture buffer. Filtering can help you focus on the problem at hand, not to mention get more packets into the capture buffer.

Another way to squeeze more packets into your capture buffer is to use a feature known generically as packet slicing. Some analyzers describe this feature as "Capture only the first nnn bytes of a packet." I recommend capturing at least the first 128 bytes of each packet to ensure that you get the most critical part of the packet—the protocol headers. The analyzer still remembers the original size of the packet, but only uses 128 bytes plus some housekeeping overhead to store each packet. If you need to capture more of the packet, such as when looking at route information contained in an IP or IPX Routing Information Packet (RIP), by all means, increase the slice size or capture the entire packet.

> ❗ Have you ever wondered how many packets in an analyzer's capture buffer pass a display filter? Simply write the buffer to a file with the "Save Filtered Packets Only" option selected. Watch for the total packet count as the analyzer writes the file, or read the filtered data back in (be sure to save the original trace if you need to look at other packets later).

Sometimes you need to look for an unknown traffic event that triggers a certain problem. In this situation, you may need to capture "wide open." If you know what the end-result of the event is, you may want to apply a trigger to look for that event. For example, you may want to look for an abnormal message aging in a spanning tree bridge protocol data unit (BPDU) packet where the analyzer triggers on a bit pattern in the packet at a given offset not equal to, say, 1 second. Then, when a BPDU packet is delayed, the analyzer will trigger. Because analyzers are continuously capturing packets looking for the trigger, you can specify when you want the analyzer to stop—for example, right at the trigger or continuing for a while afterwards until the triggered packet is at the midway point in the capture buffer.

You also need to capture all packets if you want a detailed breakdown of protocols, top talkers, top destinations, and so on. Even though many of these features are oriented toward probes and SNMP consoles, by taking several snapshots of all the packet traffic, you can save and analyze the traffic in detail at a later time. Just be aware of rapidly filling up your hard drive, especially if the analyzer supports a real-time capture to disk or a periodic snapshot to disk feature. If such is the case, you may want to limit the total amount of space on your hard drive that the analyzer can use.

> ❗ When your analyzer asks for numerical input such as for a filter or trigger or data offset for a filter, be mindful of whether you need to input a decimal or a hexadecimal value. Sometimes an analyzer displays an offset in hex, but requires you to enter the value in decimal, or vice versa. Invest in an inexpensive calculator capable of binary/hex/decimal conversion to carry with you at all times in your analysis "bag of tricks."

> ❗
>
> A good way to learn complex pattern match filtering for capturing packets is to first experiment with display filters, then apply them to a capture filter.

1.4.4 Proactive Performance and Upgrade Analysis

Protocol analyzers can be used for more than just troubleshooting. You may want to baseline the throughput of a particular application. By doing so you become proactive. That way, you can develop baselines of key applications when users are happy and the applications are presumably working the way they should. Basic operations such as logging on (including running a logon script), loading applications or parts of an application off a file server, querying and updating a database, and transferring a file via drag-and-drop should all be traced with a protocol analyzer and stored for future reference. Problem areas can be more rapidly pinpointed if you can compare a "normal trace" to an abnormal trace, for example, if you compare a fast login with a slow one.

> ❗
>
> Work proactively with your protocol analyzer when not working reactively! In other words, understand the protocol transactions for different applications for TCP/IP, ARP, DHCP, NCP, IPX, NetBEUI, and so on when your network is working normally. Take some snapshots of your workstation boot sequences and applications running over the network. Then, when something slows down or breaks altogether, you can compare the bad trace with the normal and more easily identify the problem.

In the absence of a good working trace of an application, you can often find packet anomalies by comparing them to successful packets of the same type elsewhere in the trace. In one such analysis of a file transfer that was slow, but eventually completed, I noticed that the analyzer was saying "normal end of packet" in each decoded packet. In reality, two extra bytes were in request packets that had no reply. I noted this by comparing a previous command of the same type (a read file command) and seeing that it was two bytes shorter than the suspect packet.

You can also baseline your file transfers to compare differences in drivers, NIC upgrades, platform upgrades, and so forth. If you arbitrarily upgrade a workstation, server, or part of the network itself, how do you know if performance is improved other than empirical observations from end-users?

As another example, you could compare various operations of, say, two workstations with identical hardware and applications, but one with a Microsoft IPX client and the other with Novell's Client 32. You may be surprised at the difference between the two in operation and how they recover from errors.

> **(!)**
>
> Only change one variable at a time when tuning a protocol stack, server, or workstation for optimal network performance. Use your protocol analyzer to verify the change and effect. If no improvement is noted, set the parameter back to its original value, change a different setting, and reanalyze.

You've probably guessed by now that I'm a big fan of making the best of what you have in terms of fixing problems and tuning where possible. By baselining, tweaking, and re-baselining, you can often avoid costly upgrades. At one major university, slow response time complaints from end-users were addressed by repeatedly dividing existing Ethernet segments with switches until the complaints went away.

1.4.5 Multi–LAN/WAN Analysis

Analyzing multiple LAN and/or WAN segments simultaneously raises several considerations. First off, you don't necessarily need an analyzer on every network segment. It may not be practical in terms of number of analyzers or accessibility to the segments. I've solved many WAN problems without a WAN analyzer by tracing packets at the LAN router ports on both sides of the WAN. Latency and throughput across a WAN can also be estimated very closely when measured by taking traces from the client side on a LAN. Chapter 9 shows you how in detail.

Having multiple analyzers, however, can definitely be advantageous, especially if you are looking for certain traffic events or patterns from one segment that trigger a problem on another. WAN analyzers also make it a lot easier to characterize WAN traffic, especially if the router has multiple WAN ports or is connected to a frame relay network.

WAN analyzers are great in the case of frame relay where you have potentially dozens of remote sites (virtual circuits) feeding a single router port (one physical circuit) at a main site. With a WAN analyzer, you can filter on all

> **❗** In the absence of a WAN analyzer, filtering on the source and destination IP or IPX network addresses on the LAN side makes it possible to capture traffic that you know is being routed across a WAN. With some protocols, such as SNA and NetBEUI, it is difficult to sort out the WAN traffic from the LAN side because there are no end-to-end network addresses to filter on; that is, the protocols are bridged.

traffic to and from any remote site by merely pattern matching on the Data Link Connection Identifier (DLCI) in the frame relay header.

1.4.6 Remote Analysis

Speaking of WAN analysis, wouldn't it be great if you could analyze any network segment in your infrastructure from the comfort of your cubicle? Fortunately you can, but with a few caveats.

I always question what impact remote monitoring has on the traffic being monitored to begin with and what impact getting the information back has on the rest of the network. Some remote analysis products require packet collection from an RMON II agent/probe, without any sophisticated filtering capabilities to speak of and having to effectively transfer all of the packets captured remotely back to a local site for analysis. Others, such as the Distributed Sniffer System (DSS), keep traffic to a minimum by emulating the screen and keyboard of a remote machine and doing the analysis remotely as well.

Such a setup works great for minimizing data transfer over problem or bottlenecked links, or low bandwidth situations such as a dial-up connection over the Internet. Where congestion or reliability in getting to the remote analysis device is questionable, many analyzers support access via a dial-up port, also known as an out-of-band connection.

An example of the RMON approach to remote analysis is to use a probe such as NetScout to collect packets from a remote segment, transfer them back to a local workstation, and convert them for analysis on a Sniffer. The advantage to this approach is that it's standards based; in theory, you should be able to use any standards-based RMON II probe to gather your packets. On the minus side, reasonable bandwidth is required to retrieve a modest-sized packet buffer, making it unsuitable for direct dial-up access or dial-up access over the public Internet. It doesn't take long to collect megabytes of packets from a remote LAN segment. Further, if you rely only on standards-based features, you won't find the complex filtering capabilities of a stand-alone protocol analyzer. The bottom line is that you have a standards-based way of collecting packets, at the expense of flexibility and interactiveness of your analysis.

The remote screen/keyboard emulation approach is very popular as exemplified by the Sniffer. In the case of the DSS, screen updates from a remote Sniffer are sent via a proprietary IP-based protocol to a Windows or UNIX "SniffMaster" console. Being IP-based like the RMON approach, this approach requires that you have a bridged or IP-routed network to get to the remote DSS or that you use a serial port and modem for direct dial-up access.

Because only screen updates and keystrokes are sent over the network, DSS works well over low-speed links and even 28.8 dial-up Internet connections. Traces can be saved at the remote Sniffer for later analysis, avoiding the need to transfer packets before the next analysis session. Of course, if you want to analyze the data on a local Sniffer, you need to transfer the packets. If such is the case, you should use the remote Sniffer to display, filter, and save only what you need before packet retrieval.

The remote Sniffer also has two NICs: one for the actual packet capture and one for communicating with the remote console. This allows you to place the communicating NIC on a different segment so you can get to the remote analyzer even if the segment you are capturing on is in bad shape.

Windows-based analyzers can usually be controlled via a commercial remote control Windows program such as Closeup or pcAnywhere. Like DSS, these programs only transfer screen and keyboard updates, keeping traffic to a minimum. There's a version of LANalyzer that can run on a NetWare server, but for maximum performance and reliability, you'll want to dedicate a server for this purpose.

Yet another approach to remote analysis is implemented by Microsoft's Network Monitor (NetMon) protocol analyzer. By running a NetMon agent in a remote Windows workstation or server, you can gather statistics and packets from a remote segment. NetBIOS is required to communicate with the remote agent, allowing remote access over TCP/IP, IPX, or bridged NetBEUI.

As for remote packet retrieval, NetMon has a clever compromise between the two previous approaches. While monitoring a remote segment, you can specify the statistics display update at periodic intervals, with the default at 2 seconds. All of the capturing packets are contained remotely until you actually view them.

In an interesting case study, I actually used another protocol analyzer to monitor a protocol analyzer!

By attaching a protocol analyzer to the same segment as the local NetMon, I was able to see the impact on the network while viewing the remotely captured packets. I could see that on the second analyzer, NetMon only transfers packets that are viewable in the capture display of my local NetMon. Not until I scrolled down were more packets actually transferred from the remote agent. In fact, grabbing the scroll bar and moving it all the way to the end of the buffer only transferred the last few packets that were in the remote buffer. Thus, in many situations, you really only end up transferring a small portion of the remote capture buffer that you need to examine. Of course, as with all of the approaches to remote analysis, if you want to save the entire trace, the remainder of the remote buffer must be transferred.

If you have a large number of network segments to support, you may want to invest in an electronic A/B switch for the analyzer. This way, you can remotely control which segment you are monitoring, not to mention cut down on the number of analyzers required.

Analyzing remote segments can be very cost effective in terms of not having to be at the remote location physically—be it on another floor in a building, across a campus, or across the country. At times, however, you can't solve everything remotely—when you don't have physical access to the wiring closets, can't make direct contact with support personnel and end-users, or are blind to physical equipment configurations and real-time status indicators. Often times I pick up important clues pertaining to the problem by physically being on location.

1.4.7 Traffic Generation

Many of the available protocol analyzers contain traffic generators. Typically you can edit your own packet for transmission, replay one or more packets you previously captured, or modify a packet you captured for replay. The flexibility and performance of traffic generators vary widely, so consult each product if this feature is important to you.

An analyzer with a traffic generator can be a useful tool or an A-bomb. You don't want to transmit the wrong kind of traffic and bring down your network. For example, in a bridged or switched environment, you could flood the network with all kinds of nasty stuff with a DLC broadcast address of all 1s (FFFFFFFFFFFF in hex). Networks with bridge groups or VLANs contain these broadcasts to some extent. In a routed environment, replaying an IP or IPX RIP packet on a different segment from which it was captured may cause router table updates and packets to be sent to the wrong segments.

It's generally not a good idea to arbitrarily replay a packet trace for the sake of "loading your LAN" to see how it responds under additional load. Some analysts are tempted to play it safe by sending traffic with a destination address of the analyzer itself, but in my opinion, this is not a very realistic loading that emulates the real world. So what good is a traffic generator? If you are in a closed network, such as a detached network for training purposes, trace replays are great for educational purposes. I use them all the time for this reason. Replays are also useful for testing equipment in a lab setting.

An interesting feature of such analyzers as the Sniffer is the ability to replay the trace from a capture file to yourself, without even touching the network. This is a feature I'm surprised that other vendors haven't picked up on. You can do some cool things like test a capture filter or trigger to make sure it works before you go "live." You can study the statistics a second time and observe those broadcast peaks in "real time." You can take a large trace and replay it with a more refined filter to see the amount of traffic generated by, say, a single workstation.

> **❗**
>
> A few analyzers allow you to edit the data in the capture buffer. What I find most interesting about this feature besides editing data for replay is that the analyzer reinterprets the packet, allowing you to experiment and learn about various bit settings in different protocol headers.

There have been times when I have replayed traffic back onto a live network with extreme caution and a thorough understanding of where the packets were destined. In other words, rather than "let's throw out this random trace and see what happens," they are controlled tests. As an example, I may send out a short burst of packets that follow a specific route in a source-routed Token Ring environment to measure packet loss across a series of switches.

1.4.8 Expert Systems—Helpful or Hindrance?

When you think of expert systems, what comes to mind? One of my favorite definitions of an expert system comes from the *Microsoft Bookshelf '98 Dictionary:* "A program that uses available information, heuristics, and inference to suggest solutions to problems in a particular discipline." Do expert systems in protocol analyzers deserve such a high honor?

One of the biggest problems with network analysis expert systems is that you have to be an expert to use one. Always get a second opinion—usually from yourself! Make sure you understand the underlying reasoning for the suspected "problem" and verify it by carefully scrutinizing the packet details and transactions. I have encountered more than one situation in which expert systems have misdiagnosed problems. In one case, a misdiagnosis on spanning tree data led to a manual bridge reconfiguration that ended up crippling the whole network.

Although expert systems usually provide a brief explanation with each diagnosis, they fail to mention *all* of the packets involved. For example, a packet may be flagged as a "transport retransmission," but the user has to backtrack and match the sequence numbers to find the original packet. A packet flagged as "missing reply" could mean that the analyzer is simply dropping packets under heavy load, one of the explanations *not* given in the expert help.

A "misrouted packet" diagnosis can also be misleading because the analyzer is basing the diagnosis on the fact that it didn't see the route for that IP address being advertised by a router. Perhaps the route is static or a link state protocol is in use as well as RIP. The link state protocol doesn't advertise routes unless there's an update.

I recently looked at an entry into the low-end expert system fray that contained a very rudimentary set of alleged "top nine" TCP/IP-related problems that the expert checks for. The problem is that the expert doesn't look for slightly more complex situations of the simple cases.

Take, for example, a trace of a Windows 95 workstation booting up on the network, getting its address via DHCP. The expert system complained about a duplicate IP address for that workstation. The expert should know that a workstation that's never had an IP address before uses 0.0.0.0 as its source address in its initial DHCP broadcast packet when looking for a DHCP server. As any experienced analyst knows, 0.0.0.0 is not a duplicate address for that workstation!

Many of the expert systems in protocol analyzers rely heavily on "one shot" events or statistical thresholds. One shot events are those that can be derived from a single packet, such as a packet with a CRC error or a packet containing an Internet Control Message Protocol (ICMP) message.

For example, 22 of the TCP/IP "events" in one such analyzer are errors already reported by ICMP packets. Because ICMP is inherently designed to report problems and the packets are decoded by virtually *every* analyzer on the market today, do you really need an expert system to tell you that you have ICMP packets in your buffer? Perhaps, but a more compelling argument for an ICMP "expert" notification to the user would be to present possible reasons behind the ICMP packet such as why the ICMP packet is telling you that a route is unreachable. Fortunately this additional information is usually obtainable via an on-line help file.

As for thresholds, every analyzer expert system will say something along the lines of "You have a broadcast storm because the broadcast packets per second exceeded 100." You can also get these kinds of alerts from SNMP consoles and probes, so do they fall in the category of expert systems?

You could "smarten" the statistics by providing a window, instead of knee-jerk responses to short bursts of broadcasts, a brief spike in network utilization, and so on. Instead of a broadcasts-per-second threshold, how about broadcasts per second over a 10-second period exceeding a user-definable threshold?

> **!**
>
> Keep in mind that all protocol analyzers install with default threshold settings, including the expert thresholds. Is there such a thing as a "typical" network? No! Therefore, the analyzer's defaults must always be changed manually on a segment-by-segment basis. Perhaps a better way is to put the analyzer in a "learn" mode where it can analyze the traffic patterns during a busy period on a segment that the network analyst believes is functioning normally, with no throughput or response time problems being reported. Then, the analyzer can set "suggested" levels of thresholds for future analysis of that segment. Vendors take note!

Expert systems are not a panacea for discovering all of your network problems. Protocol analysis expert systems can, however, be tremendous time savers and spot problems you may overlook, especially when you are under pressure to quickly put out a fire.

No matter what, you will always find yourself looking for other hints to your problems in the traces. You may also find yourself gathering data with other tools, such as SNMP console and probes, tables from switches and routers, and even poring over your network documentation for clues.

1.5 Last But Not Least: Document Your Network!

I'm going to wrap this chapter up with an important but often neglected tool that can actually be quite helpful in troubleshooting problems: network documentation.

I used to joke that the extent of one's network documentation can often be found on the back of a napkin. Not far from the truth, I often encounter organizations that maintain their network documentation in bits and pieces—essentially scraps of information—that must be pieced together to see the big picture and overall flow. In some situations, I end up documenting the network in my mind or jotting down a skeletal picture by reverse engineering protocol traces.

I've also seen the pretty pictures complete with a minutely detailed graphic of the actual vendor's hub in use or where actual cubicle furniture is depicted. Dumb and dumber.

Figure 1.8 is an example of clean, highly readable, and highly useful network documentation that works in successfully managed networks. As with any documentation, keeping it up to date and accurate is critical, making for a good proactive project in your "spare time." I can certainly empathize with the lack of spare time that many of you don't have, but I'd really push for resources to get a project like this going and maintained. I will briefly discuss some of the fundamentals of a useful network documentation project that are representative of proven techniques, and you're certainly welcome to try variations of them.

The key to good documentation is not to become bogged down in documenting every workstation attached to every segment (imagine trying to keep that up to date), but rather concentrate on the network interconnectivity (topology, switches, and routers) plus servers, gateways, and firewalls. Routers and switches don't have to be represented by fancy graphics that mimic what the device looks like. Use simple geometric shapes like octagons, circles, squares, and rectangles. Be consistent. For example, always use an octagon to represent a router and a square to represent a switch.

By using a geometric shape instead of a detailed graphic, you can put valuable information *inside* the shape, such as router port designators. Immediately outside the shape next to a port designator, document the IP and/or IPX address of the router port. Optionally, you could document the IP subnet mask. The example in Figure 1.8 uses all class B IP addresses, with an 8-bit subnet mask, so I chose not to document the mask.

When documenting information common to a given protocol, be sure to color code that information. For example, use red for IP, purple for IPX, orange for DECnet, green for AppleTalk, blue for bridging, and so forth.

The example shows all protocol information on one drawing. In a more complex drawing, you may want to draw a base layer, then multiple layers showing connectivity by protocol. For example, one layer might show all the IP connectivity, another IPX, and yet another where bridging is enabled. Be sure to color code the connecting lines between devices per the protocol.

The graphic tool of choice is mostly a matter of personal preference. Choosing a tool with layers, grids, and a "snap to connector" feature (for joining lines to shapes) makes your task easier. Examples of such tools that meet these criteria include CorelDRAW 8, AutoCAD Lite, and Visio.

Documenting your servers and gateways by using a horizontal shape such as a rhombus minimizes the space required to place them on the drawing. Be sure to name the server by its DNS or logical name, along with its IP, IPX,

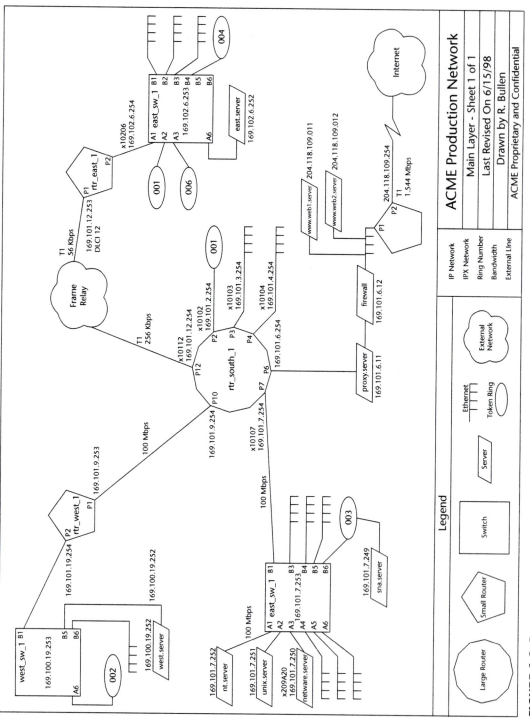

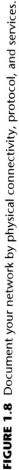

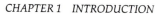

FIGURE 1.8 Document your network by physical connectivity, protocol, and services.

AppleTalk, or DECnet address. For SNA controllers, document their local administered address (LAA).

If you have remote analyzers or probes, you should show them as well and identify the segments to which they connect. In the case of an analyzer or probe connected to an electronic A/B switch, document which segments they can connect to using a dotted line coming off the data switch.

Well-maintained documentation can be a powerful aid in troubleshooting and maintaining networks. Use it often to trace the flow of packets when analyzing problems.

Chapter 2

Analyzing and Troubleshooting the Physical Layer

2.1 Introduction

As noted in Chapter 1, bad wiring is one of the leading causes of problems at the physical layer. One such source of problems is at the connector itself. For the older coaxial-based Ethernet 10BASE5 (10 Mbps with a maximum of 500 meters per coaxial segment) networks, a.k.a. "thick Ethernet," loose Attachment Unit Interface (AUI) connections at workstations or transceivers were problematic, especially those wonderful sliding/locking gizmos that often got bent or twisted, causing intermittent connections. If you've been around in networking since the 70s (oops, I'd better say 1970s to make this book Y2K compliant!), you had to deal with "state-of-the-art" technology like attaching a bulky transceiver by coring the coax or using vampire taps.

10BASE2 (10 Mbps with a maximum of 185 meters per coaxial segment), a.k.a. "thin Ethernet" or "thin net," was the next big advancement. You then had to deal with issues like users inadvertently disconnecting a segment of coax from one side of the "T" connector at the back of their personal computers, causing the Ethernet to be improperly terminated and bringing down everyone on the network. Of course, cutting the coax anywhere along the line had the same effect.

Speaking of termination, both 10BASE5 and 10BASE2 require 50-ohm termination at both ends of the coax, with grounding at one end. Not grounding at all can lead to an undesirable charge in the coax, whereas grounding at both ends can lead to a difference in ground potential, causing an undesirable current on the coax.

> **❗**
>
> Fiber optics saved the day for many Ethernet installations. By using fiber to extend segments between buildings in a campus environment, you don't have to worry about the difference in ground potential between buildings.

When the IBM cabling system, a structured wiring system to support existing IBM equipment as well as the new Token Ring, was announced in the early 1980s, IBM jumped all over Ethernet saying how unreliable and inflexible the cabling was. IBM was right in more ways than one, which set off a war in cabling strategies. IBM pushed the use of shielded twisted pair wiring. The original thick Ethernet cable was so stiff you could hardly bend it. And with both the thick and thin coax, you had to be really careful about the maximum bending radius and spacing of attached transceivers.

The IBM cabling system also had centralized hubs with one port per attaching device to the Token Ring. The original wiring system hub, or "multistation access unit (MAU)" as IBM called it, was also passive (no power is required) for enhanced reliability, or so IBM claimed at the time.

The whole issue of centralized wiring forced the Ethernet camp to hash out a new standard once they figured out how to send 10 Mbps over widely installed telephone wire. (The telephone wire is often referred to as Category 3 wire, although some earlier telephone wiring does not meet the Category 3 specifications.) Multiport repeaters with RJ-45 receptacles were also developed and specified in the 10BASE-T portion of the 802.3 standard. The introduction of "repeaters on a chip" led to low-cost, high port density Ethernet hubs.

Meanwhile, IBM had to scramble to figure out how to send 4 Mbps Token Ring over telephone wire because the IBM cabling is basically a system built around proprietary shielded twisted pair wire. Later, support for 16 Mbps over Category 5 UTP was officially added by all the hub vendors. Category 5 also supports 100 Mbps Ethernet, but only for relatively short distances, as discussed later on in this chapter.

In the end, Category 5 cable with RJ-45 connectors and receptacles became the de facto LAN wiring standard. The Ethernet workstation wiring rules follow the EIA 568-A cabling standard. For example, the maximum end-to-end cabling distance between a hub port and a workstation NIC is 100 meters.

The problem with longer distances in Ethernet is twofold: The likelihood of collisions (two stations transmitting simultaneously) increases as the wiring radius increases and the likelihood of CRC errors increases as the signal degrades (due to attenuation) over longer distances. Going to 101 meters doesn't mean that your network will no longer work, but you shouldn't go much beyond that, especially if you plan to upgrade to data rates higher than 10 Mbps.

2.2 The EIA 568-A Wiring Standard

The 568-A standard specifies a generic voice and data cabling system to support a multi-product, multi-vendor environment. Its roots can be found in decades of experience in wiring telephones in corporations. Early telco studies revealed that the majority of telephones were wired within 100 meters of a wiring closet. When you think about it, this is an area close to the size of four football fields (assuming the wiring closet is in the middle of the four quadrants).

The 568-A standard provides for a structured cabling system that specifies performance and technical criteria for various cabling types and connecting hardware. The life span of the system is expected to be about ten years. The cabling infrastructure is highlighted in Figure 2.1 and described as follows:

- *Work Area*. The work area includes the station equipment, patch cable, and adapters (such as a media filter). The maximum recommended patch cable length is 3 meters.
- *Telecommunications Closet*. The telecommunications closet is considered to be the floor serving facilities for horizontal cable distribution and can be used for intermediate and main cross-connects. The closet must be designed with minimal cable stress from bends, cable ties, and tension (there's actually a standard for this: ANSI/EIA/TIA-569-A).
- *Equipment Room*. The equipment room is the area in a building where telecommunications equipment is located and the cabling system terminates.
- *Horizontal Cabling*. The horizontal cabling covers from the work area receptacle to the horizontal cross-connect in the telecommunications closet, including the receptacle, optional transition connector (such as undercarpet cable connecting to round cable), horizontal cable (maximum of 90 meters), and patch cables. The maximum end-to-end distance is 100 meters, making for a maximum of 10 meters of patch cables.

  Two outlets are required at the work area: 100-ohm Unshielded Twisted Pair (UTP) and 100-ohm UTP, Shielded Twisted Pair (STP-A) or 62.5/125 µm multimode fiber. The two outlets allow for both a data and voice connection. Grounding needs to conform to applicable building codes.

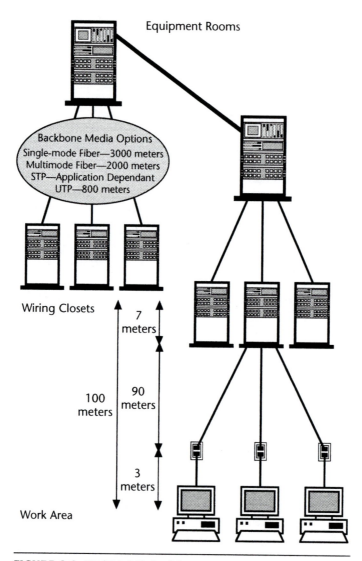

FIGURE 2.1 EIA/TIA 568-A wiring summary.

- *Backbone Cabling.* The backbone cabling provides interconnections between telecommunications closets, equipment rooms, and entrance facilities and includes the backbone cables, intermediate and main cross-connects, terminations, and patch cords for backbone-to-backbone cross-connections. Cabling should be 30 meters or less for connection equipment to the backbone. If there are no intermediate cross-connects, a maximum of 90 meters is allowed. Hierarchical cross-connections cannot exceed two levels.

TABLE 2.1 Summary of 568-A UTP Cabling Types

Cable Type	Maximum Frequency	Example Application
Category 3	16 MHz	10BASE-T, 100BASE-T4, and 4 Mbps Token Ring
Category 4	20 MHz	10BASE-T, 100BASE-T4, and 4 Mbps Token Ring
Category 5	100 MHz	10BASE-T, 100BASE-TX, 4 and 16 Mbps Token Rings, and Copper FDDI (CDDI or FDDI TP-PMD)

- *Entrance Facility.* The entrance facility is defined as where the outside telecommunications service enters the building and interconnects with the building's telecommunications systems. In a campus or multi-building environment, it may also contain the building's backbone cross-connections.

Table 2.1 summarizes the 100-ohm UTP cabling types.

Additional cabling characteristics are as follows:

- The characteristic impedance is 100 ohms ± 15 percent from 1 MHz to the highest referenced frequency (16, 20, or 100 MHz) of a particular category.
- The recognized shielded twisted pair (STP) cables are IBM type 1A for backbone and horizontal distribution and IBM type 6A for patch cables with 2-pair, 22 AWG solid with a characteristic impedance of 150 ohms ± 10 percent (3 MHz–300 MHz).
- The optical fiber medium for horizontal cabling is 62.5/125 μm multimode optical fiber (with a minimum of two fibers), and for backbone cabling it is 62.5/125 μm multimode and single-mode optical fiber.

A good cable tester will have the various 568-A parameters programmed in to ensure that the various cable types you test are up to spec.

2.3 An End to Wiring Problems?

Does a standards-based wiring system built largely around Category 5 and hubs end the wiring problems? Nope.

In theory, a multi-hub wiring structure is more fault tolerant than sharing a series of coax segments strung together. Hub-based wiring also allows us to build some cool management features right into the hubs. Problems still exist, but they tend to be more isolated to individual workstation connections, to a "slot" or "blade" of ports in a hub, or worst case, to the entire hub itself.

With UTP wiring, you must be very careful about the quality of the RJ-45 connector crimping and to use the proper pairs within the Category 5 bundle—typically a set of 4-pair, or eight wires total. Bad crimping can lead to intermittent connections or pulled out wires altogether. You also must make sure that the pairs stay twisted right down to the connector.

2.4 Basic Cable Testing

One of the really cool things I like about a cable tester is its high degree of portability—a device that you can hold in one hand, runs on batteries, and doesn't take up much room in your network analysis bag of tricks. If there are media problems on a segment as noted on your analyzer or SNMP probe such as CRC errors (on Ethernet) or line errors (on Token Ring), the cable tester becomes invaluable in helping you pinpoint the problem.

> **❗**
>
> Even though a cable may test well, it does not guarantee reliability in actual operation due to Radio Frequency Interference (RFI) noise from outside sources. UTP is more susceptible to noise than STP or coax.

Basic cable testers check for shorts, opens, and split pair, and they calculate the length of a cable based on Time Domain Reflectometry (TDR) tests. Some of the more advanced features include the ability to measure a cable's near-end crosstalk (NEXT), to detect split pair (which usually requires NEXT capability), and to measure cable noise or the signal-to-noise ratio.

A cable that is shorted will have one or more wires crossed with another inside the cable. An open cable is not terminated at both ends, such as a missing terminator on an Ethernet coax, or an RJ-45 Category 5 cable unplugged from a hub port.

When using 10BASE-T or 100BASE-T transceivers or NIC cards with built-in transceivers, you will notice a "link integrity" indicator, usually a green LED. A transceiver sends a periodic link pulse down the transmit pair for detection at the other end.

A more sophisticated test, the TDR, measures the time delay between a pulse and its reflection in a wire that has no termination to absorb the signal. Obviously this test requires that you unplug the far end of a Category 5 wire from the hub, or if using coax, remove the terminator at the other end. TDR

> When the link LED is on, it means that only the receive side of the link is good. You also need to check the other end of the wire and its connection to make sure that the link LED is on there as well. Chances are pretty good that if the link is okay on one end, it will be okay at the other end, too, but why take the chance when troubleshooting a station that doesn't receive a response to anything it transmits? Checking the LED at both ends is a simple continuity check for the cable.

tests are usually accurate to within a couple of feet, provided you tell the cable tester what type of cable is being tested. This information is necessary to set the velocity of propagation (how fast the signal travels in relation to the speed of light) for that particular cable type. The results can vary somewhat from one vendor's tester to another. There can also be slight variances in the "same" cable type (such as Category 3) between different vendors. The idea of a TDR test is to get a ballpark figure so that you know whether or not you are exceeding the maximum recommended distances in your cable drops. TDR tests are also handy when you need to document cable lengths.

Split pair is when a transmit or receive signal is carried on a single wire with no opposing wire (i.e., the second wire of a pair twisted around the first) to help filter out unwanted noise from the outside world and crosstalk from a neighboring pair. Split pair is common when incorrectly wiring a punchdown block or when crimping those RJ-45 connectors onto the wrong wires. 568-A certified Category 5 wiring should always be wired straight through—that is, the same color of wiring to the same pin at both ends. A NEXT that fails badly is usually an indication of split pair.

Figure 2.2 illustrates the correct pair wiring for various topologies and standards using the RJ-45 connector. Once again, the 568-A is the industry standard. The AT&T Premises Distribution Standard (PDS) is accommodated by the 568-B addendum. The older Universal Systems Ordering Code (USOC) is provided for reference.

Note that pair 2 always goes to pins 3 and 6. This is the receive pair for Ethernet and the transmit pair for Token Ring (obviously we cannot support both an Ethernet and Token Ring connection on the same connector and still meet the standard). A common mistake is to use pair 1 on pins 1 and 2 (okay so far), then pair 2 on pins 3 and 4 (a mistake), and so on. This leads to a split pair situation in Ethernet or Token Ring, as illustrated in Figure 2.3.

In my experience, I've noticed that half-duplex Ethernet is more tolerant than Token Ring of split pair. Why? Think about how Token Ring works—there's always a signal on the receive and transmit pairs, even when data is not

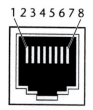

1 2 3 4 5 6 7 8

RJ-45 Receptacle

Ethernet	**Token Ring**	**FDDI**
transmit pair	transmit pair	transmit pair
1 2 3 4 5 6 7 8	1 2 3 4 5 6 7 8	1 2 3 4 5 6 7 8
receive pair	receive pair	receive pair

EIA/TIA	**AT&T PDS**	**USOC**
pair 2		pair 2
pair 1	pair 2 pair 1	pair 1
1 2 3 4 5 6 7 8	1 2 3 4 5 6 7 8	1 2 3 4 5 6 7 8
pair 3 pair 4	pair 3 pair 4	pair 3
		pair 4

Color-Coding

Pair	Colors	EIA/TIA	PDS	USOC
1	W/B & B/W	4&5	4&5	4&5
2	W/O & O/W	3&6	1&2	3&6
2	E/G & G/W	1&2	3&6	2&7
4	W/BR & BR/W	7&8	7&8	1&8

FIGURE 2.2 Common RJ-45 wiring terminations and wire color coding.

being sent. If no frame is present, a token is traversing the ring with special symbols known as "idle" bits being transmitted right behind it.

Because there is always a signal on both pairs in Token Ring, there's a greater chance for interference between the two pairs and an even greater chance for interference in split pair, where you don't have an opposing wire wrapped around the actively transmitting wire.

With half-duplex Ethernet, the receive side is always quiet, unless there's collision. With full-duplex Ethernet, proper wiring is more critical because you will likely be sending and receiving frames at the same time, using both pairs.

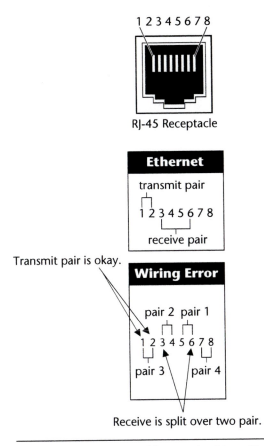

FIGURE 2.3 Incorrect wiring can lead to split pair problems.

> ⚠️ Even with the proper pairing, some crosstalk is inevitable, especially at the higher data rates such as 100 Mbps Ethernet. Therefore, being able to measure near-end crosstalk (NEXT) is important. NEXT needs to be measured at different frequencies for different LAN speeds and cable types, so make sure your cable tester has this flexibility.

NEXT is measured by sending a signal on one pair and measuring how much of this signal, or crosstalk, is picked up by a passive pair. The difference between the two is the NEXT value, which is usually given in decibels (dB). The bigger the value, the better. If the measurements were the same for a given pair (resulting in a 0 dB difference), the passive pair would be picking up 100% of the sending signal!

You should also measure NEXT at both ends of the cable because the signal is affected by attenuation (loss) as it travels down the cable. A weaker signal is less likely to be picked up by another pair as it travels down the wire, hence the reason for measuring NEXT where the signal is strongest, at the near end where the cable tester is attached.

If there is interference in the transmission of these bits, such as excessive cable noise, you may encounter CRC (also known as FCS, or Frame Check Sequence) errors on Ethernet or line errors on Token Ring (a line error is a CRC mismatch detected by a station inserted into the ring). If you suspect noise on the cable, a cable tester with noise measurement capability is invaluable. Otherwise, you can try to correct the problem by replacing a suspect cable or by routing the cable on a different path. As always, be sure to check the CRC counts on a good cable tester or protocol analyzer before and after correcting the problem.

Interference is not always the culprit with CRC errors. Ethernet collisions often show up as CRC error packets whenever the collision extends beyond the preamble of an Ethernet frame—that is, into the header of a packet. Chapter 3 covers CRC errors in more detail.

2.5 Smart Cable Testers

No one can argue that cable testers and protocol analyzers are essential network troubleshooting tools. Other tools such as SNMP-based management platforms and probes/agents are also important because they can alert us to problems like excessive packet errors or bandwidth overload on a segment. These tools can also be used to perform simple baselining, such as computing packets per second vs. collisions per second on an Ethernet segment.

A new breed of troubleshooting tools is emerging known as "hand-held network testers" or "smart cable testers." Lacking the packet capture and decode capabilities found in protocol analyzers, these new tools are really a cross between cable testers and SNMP consoles.

Because the cable tester is a no-brainer carry-around, why not add some additional testing capabilities to its small form factor? For the most part, this is exactly what many of the leading vendors of these testers have done.

By adding a microprocessor, some memory, and firmware to a cable tester, it now has the capability to transmit and receive packets. The diminutive processing capability, screen size, and limited keyboard prevent the cable tester from becoming a full-blown protocol analyzer, but it can perform proactive testing and data querying—something most protocol analyzers don't perform. The testers typically allow you to perform Ping tests, identify active servers, display network utilization and error counts, and show top senders.

> ❶
>
> Beware that some Windows-based protocol analyzers that rely on stock NDIS NIC drivers are not capable of showing frames with CRC errors—they are discarded by the NDIS drivers. To correct for this deficiency, look for special NDIS drivers that work with certain NICs.

Smart cable testers have added monitoring and additional testing capabilities beyond the physical layer. Typical passive monitoring functions include overall network utilization, CRC errors and collisions for Ethernet, soft errors for Token Ring, and individual station frame counts including broadcasts.

These functions are essential to network troubleshooting, especially if they provide additional clues about the error. For example, if you see high CRC counts, it is convenient to know the Media Access Control (MAC) source address(es) of the error packets. Then you can test the cable and hub to which that station is connected. If the cable tester shows only CRC counts, you'll have to break out another tool such as your protocol analyzer to see the station addresses.

Many cable testers also have proactive testing capabilities such as Ping to check responsiveness of remote IP addresses. Some meters, such as the Fluke One-Touch and MicroTest Compass, also include an "IPX Ping" function. Actually, nodes are queried using the NetWare Diagnostic Responder (NDR) protocol. One caveat is that, unlike IP where virtually every IP client in the world responds to a PING request, an IPX client must have its Diagnostic Responder enabled or you won't see it.

There is a true IPX Ping protocol, but only NetWare 4.1x, Novell Multiprotocol Router 3.x, and Client 32-based workstations respond to it. Thus, for now, NDR is more widely recognized.

Other proactive functions include querying a workstation or server for more information. For example, the One-Touch can tell you if an NT Server is a primary or back-up domain controller. The Compass can query NetWare servers for information such as connections in use or number of packet receive buffers.

2.6 The Cable Tester as a Mini-SNMP Console and Mini-Web Server

There are still two largely untapped market opportunities for hand-held network testers—providing mini-SNMP console and Web server functions. The mini-SNMP console and mini-Web server approaches are exemplified by the Fluke LANMeter series that can query SNMP agents for statistics such as utilization on a router's LAN or WAN port. You can also use your desktop browser to access logs and screens. The LANMeter pushes the limit of a hand-held tester, however, by being about half the size of a notebook, but you can still hold it in one hand!

How can these mini-SNMP consoles add value to your troubleshooting efforts? After troubleshooting some problems at a client's network recently, I decided to do a little proactive analysis by probing their routers in various locations around the campus and throughout the country.

Armed with network documentation, but not the SNMP community name, I decided to obtain the community name the lazy way—by waiting for an SNMP trap packet captured by the protocol analyzer. It only took a minute or two to get one, so I set the community name in the LANMeter and was able to query the SNMP MIB information from any router on the network.

Some of the more useful statistics are the traffic and error counts for each router port. By sorting on error counts, I was able to quickly determine if the error-to-traffic count ratio was high. In one instance, a router's T1 port was experiencing a moderate rate of packet errors, prompting us to open a trouble ticket for the T1.

2.7 Ethernet Wiring Issues

Remember the old 5-4-3 rule for coax-based baseband Ethernet? Basically you could have five segments of coax, four repeaters, and three of the segments populated with data terminal equipment (DTE) devices. Using all 10BASE5 coax, you could basically have a total of 5 segments × 500 meters/segment, or 2.5 kilometers, end to end. Using all 10BASE2 or "thin" coax limits you to a total of 5 segments × 185 meters/segment, or about 1 kilometer, end to end. With the addition of fiber and twisted pair media types, however, the wiring rules have gotten more complicated.

The physical size of an Ethernet is limited by several factors, including:

- The media lengths and their propagation delay
- Repeater and hub delay
- The reduction in minimal packet spacing (gap) due to repeaters
- Delays in the DTEs due to the carrier sense mechanism
- The response time of collision detection

These components boil down to two main factors: round-trip collision delay and interpacket spacing. The IEEE 802.3 standard provides two simplified models for computing the maximum physical size (collision domain) of your Ethernet. A collision domain is such that if two or more stations were to transmit at the same time, a collision would occur. This is likely to happen when multiple stations share a common hub or set of hubs.

> Devices that connect to a dedicated bridge or switch port still have two devices sharing a common collision domain—the station itself and traffic coming from the switch. Having only two devices on an Ethernet, however, dramatically cuts down on the likelihood of collisions. Going one step further, you could reduce collisions to zero by operating the two devices in full-duplex mode, where one pair is used exclusively for transmitting packets from the switch to the station and the other pair is for transmitting packets from the station to the switch.

In the 802.3 standard, the first model assumes certain simplifications that if followed, allow you to build an Ethernet within spec. The second model is more complex, in that you need to compute the worst-case path delay.

The first model actually follows the 5-4-3 rule quite nicely, once you get used to some basic Ethernet wiring terminology. For example, a link segment is a point-to-point connection between two medium-dependent interfaces—the fiber, twisted pair, or coax interfaces. A mixing segment is one that can connect more than two medium-dependent interfaces—your stations.

Mixing segments can only be coax or fiber (with a passive star hub). Link segments can be fiber or twisted pair. Bear in mind that link segments can only have two devices attached to them. Because all 10BASE-T segments are link segments, the maximum number of stations on a 10BASE-T segment is two—a station to a repeater or a repeater to a repeater. Once again, you need a multiport 10BASE-T repeater/hub to attach more than two 10BASE-T stations to a physical Ethernet.

In the simple 802.3 model, you can still have up to five segments and four repeaters. If fiber is used as a link segment between repeaters, the fiber can be up to 500 meters in length. Coaxial link segments or mixing segments can be up to 500 meters for 10BASE5 and 185 meters for 10BASE2. 10BASE-T link segments between repeaters or from a repeater to a workstation are limited to 100 meters in length.

Figure 2.4 gives an example of a maxed-out Ethernet with multiple media types. Notice the worst-case scenario of five segments and four repeaters

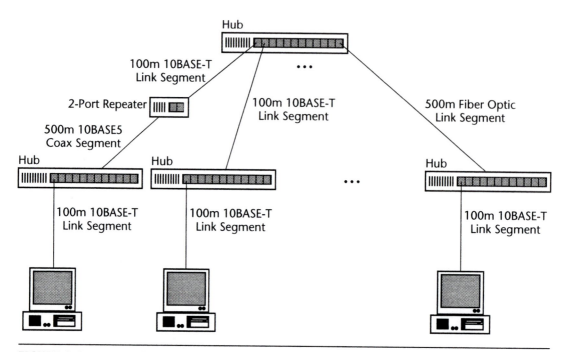

FIGURE 2.4 An example of maximum repeater and cable distances for mixed media Ethernet.

between any stations. Chapter 3 looks at what happens when you exceed the maximum recommended Ethernet wiring specifications.

Referring back to Figure 2.2, the receptacle is from the view of looking straight into a hub port. If you are looking at a NIC, the transmit and receive pair are actually crossed over internally. Thus, a frame is repeated by a hub on pair 1, the transmit pair, and received on pair 1 at the NIC. Likewise, the NIC actually transmits on pair 2 and the hub receives on pair 2. To expand a nonstackable hub (hubs with no external bus system), a crossover cable or a hub with internal crossover is required to go from one hub port to another.

> **❗**
>
> If you connect a crossover cable from a hub to a NIC card, you won't see the link indicator LED turn on for either side unless you cross over a crossover port on a hub. So when wiring crossover cables, make sure they are marked as such!

One of the disadvantages to expanding hubs using crossover cables is that the second hub counts as another repeater in the Ethernet segment/repeater calculation. Stackable hubs usually cost more because they stack and count as one unit and usually contain SNMP management features as well.

2.7.1 Case Study: An Ethernet Wiring Violation

One site I visited had a "hub and spoke" wiring architecture consisting of a centralized fiber optic hub with 10BASE-T hubs strategically placed in user work areas. An AUI-to-fiber micro transceiver attached to an AUI port on each work area hub, which in turn connected the fiber to the central hub.

The network ran quite well until the work areas began expanding and additional hubs were added. Some of the hubs were daisy chained off an existing work area hub using a crossover cable. It wasn't long before the Ethernet wiring rules were violated, as illustrated in Figure 2.5. There were now up to five repeaters between two stations on the Ethernet. Worse, one of those stations happened to be a router connected to one of the daisy chained hubs. As traffic increased to and from the router, collisions were as high as 30 percent—about 1 in 3 frames collided.

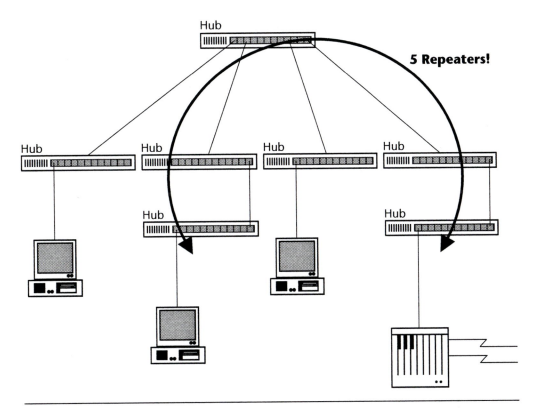

FIGURE 2.5 An Ethernet with a worst-case scenario of five hubs between two stations.

This problem has several solutions, short of breaking up the collision domain with switching.

One solution is to move the router to the centralized fiber hub, reducing the repeater counts that the majority of the traffic has to traverse. This is a short-term solution that actually does help to reduce the collision count, but the system still has too many repeaters. Another solution is to replace the work area hubs with higher port density hubs, eliminating the daisy chaining. Finally, you could replace the work area hubs with stackable or modular hubs so you don't chew up your repeater budget as you add more ports.

In the actual case study, I ended up installing a higher density hub as a temporary solution until I could study the feasibility of breaking up the busy segment with switching.

Sometimes you can still have a high collision count with a wiring system within spec. Part of the reason for this is the nature of the beast: Ethernet is a contention-based system that has collisions no matter what (short of a dedicated full-duplex connection). The trick to running an efficient Ethernet is to keep collisions to a minimum. Chapter 3 discusses what acceptable levels of collisions should be. For now, assume that 30 percent is definitely a little high.

> ❗ The keys to keeping Ethernet collisions to a minimum are to keep your wiring distances and repeater counts in any given path to a minimum and to optimize your applications and protocols to keep the average frame size up.

If you look at your cable testers, RMON probes, or protocol analyzers and see that average frame size is only 80 bytes, that's not good. It's not the average frame size per se that's the problem. It's the fact that you can send more of them in a given amount of time, increasing the likelihood of collisions. It's all in the law of probability.

For example, if all of your frames were only the minimum size of 64 bytes including the CRC, you could theoretically send up to 14,880 frames per second on a 10 Mbps Ethernet. In practice, this never happens unless only one station is transmitting. At the maximum frame size of 1518 bytes, you can send a maximum of 812 frames per second. Therefore, there's a 14,880/812, or an 18×, more likely chance of collisions per second when sending small frames. Ideally your average frame size should be around 300 bytes or higher.

At another site, I observed an Ethernet with collisions often hitting the 35 to 40 percent range. The wiring appeared to be within spec. In a nutshell, there was a hub in the computer center that served one level of workgroup hubs from the outside and a direct fiber link to a router located in the telecommunications closet in the far corner of the facility (see Figure 2.6). There were only two repeaters maximum between any two stations, and the fiber run to the router was long but within the 1000-meter limit.

The traffic to and from the router steadily increased over time because it was the primary link to the Internet. As traffic increased and shifted (as a percentage of total frames) to the router, the collision percentage got worse. Upon closer examination, I noted that the workgroups were concentrated in a corner of a large warehouse-like facility, not far from the computer room. The router, on the other hand, was at the end of a long fiber link to a far

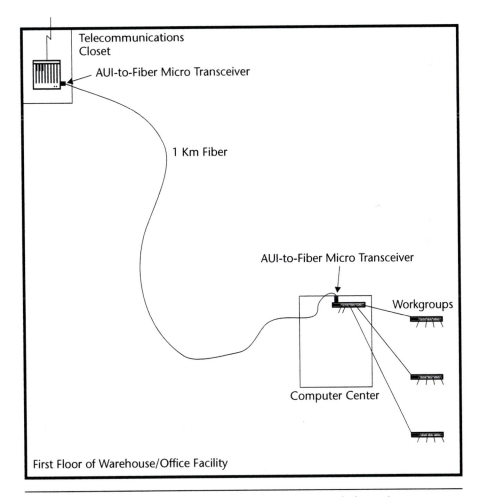

FIGURE 2.6 An Ethernet within spec, but not a recommended practice.

> **❗**
>
> A small frame size has nothing to do with "reaching the end of the wire" before another station starts transmitting, thus causing a collision. The 56-bit preamble and 8-bit start-of-frame delimiter that precede every frame always propagate throughout the entire wiring structure before a station even transmits the first bit in the frame.

corner of the building. In addition to the propagation delay of the signal through the repeaters and over the fiber, there was additional delay in the micro transceivers located at both ends of the fiber.

Stations that needed to transmit within the workgroup at very close to the same moment would sense each other quicker (in the neighborhood of nanoseconds) than the router at the far end, decreasing the likelihood of collisions.

The solution here is to move the router to the computer center and extend the telco CSU/DSU T1 connection, thereby eliminating the long fiber run. For political reasons, this wasn't possible. After all, the router belonged to the telecommunications group that ran the phone system that terminated in the room in the corner of the building. I suggested a closed rack with ventilation and a lock if the telecom folks didn't want the datacom folks to touch the router, but to no avail.

What I just described isn't rocket science (certainly not the politics), but small packets and long wire runs definitely increase the likelihood of collisions.

> **❗**
>
> Does your protocol analyzer accurately count Ethernet collisions? Don't be so sure. Always verify a suspect segment with a cable tester that can count collisions. Some low-end analyzers only indicate collisions if they see a runt packet with a CRC error, usually the result of a collision fragment. However, the most common type of collisions—those that occur in the preamble of a packet—go totally undetected. I've even seen this problem on a high-end analyzer (with PCMCIA adapters in laptops). Finally, do not rely on Windows-based analyzers that use "stock" NDIS drivers. Forget about collisions. They won't even tell you about CRC errors.

One of the neat things about 10BASE-T wiring is that you can now have dedicated full-duplex Ethernet links. What used to be a shared single conductor (coax) for both transmitting and receiving has been split into a separate transmit and receive pair. All you have to do is turn off the collision detection mechanism, which is precisely what 10/100 Mbps Ethernet NICs or switch/ router ports do when operating in full-duplex mode. Of course, you no longer have a shared Ethernet, but rather a high-speed point-to-point link such as between two routers or from a server to a switch. Because the link is full duplex just like a WAN link, you no longer have to worry about collisions.

2.7.2 How Collisions Are Detected

Collisions are detected differently for connections to UTP as opposed to coaxial segments. For UTP, separate wires are used for sending and receiving frames, making the collision detection mechanism very simple. Because you cannot send data and receive data at the same time, any activity on the receive side while you are sending will assert the collision detect signal to the DLC layer. The transmitter then backs off and retries the transmission a short time later (more on this in Chapter 3). If you are operating in point-to-point full-duplex mode (like a server to a dedicated switch port), the collision detect circuitry is disabled, allowing simultaneous sending and receiving of frames.

Because fiber optic transceivers have two fibers, one for send and one for receive, the collision detection and full-duplex operation is very similar to that for UTP.

With coax, there is only one conductor and full duplex is not possible. The collision detection mechanism is only slightly more complicated than that for UTP. A transceiver simply watches for transitions in the Manchester encoding (this signaling technique is explained later in this chapter) that are not within the bit timings of the currently transmitting frame. If abnormal transitions are noted, the collision detection is once again asserted to the DLC layer.

As coaxial-based Ethernet evolved to UTP, a few wiring compatibility problems developed along the way. One such problem involved an AUI feature called Signal Quality Error, or SQE. The AUI consists of a DB-15 receptacle on the attaching station's (or Data Terminal Equipment (DTE) in IEEE terminology) interface that connects to a multiconductor cable with an external transceiver at the other end, up to 50 meters away. This was essentially the way all Ethernet devices were connected in the early 1980s.

SQE is asserted under the following conditions:

1. As a signal integrity check immediately following a frame transmission (sometimes referred to as a "heartbeat")
2. To indicate a collision during a transmission
3. Improper signals on the wire such as those caused by a break or short in the AUI-to-external transceiver cable.

In short, the station is ensured of a successful, collision-free transmission.

As Ethernet migrated to Category 5 cable, AUI-to-Cat 5 micro transceivers included a switchable on/off SQE. The reason for this is that the 802.3 standard specifically reminds us that the SQE function "shall not be performed by MAUs [Medium Attachment Unit] that are attached to repeaters."

In other words, SQE should be switched off whenever a micro transceiver (i.e., the MAU) is connected to a hub. Otherwise, the SQE will assert at the end of every frame passing through the micro transceiver, making the hub think that there's been a collision! A cable tester connected to one of the ports on the hub will actually detect these "faux" collisions.

Imagine connecting two hubs via two micro transceivers as shown in Figure 2.7 and having SQE enabled at *both* ends. In this scenario, frames traveling in both directions will have faux collisions generated by the SQE test. Believe it or not, throughput can drop by as much as an order of magnitude between devices communicating across these two hubs.

In addition to repeating bits, converting between different media types, and extending the reach of Ethernet, repeaters also detect collisions and perform "collision reinforcement" by propagating their own "jam" signal on all the ports in that repeater. For example, the hub in Figure 2.8 detects a collision on port 3. That collision is reinforced by simultaneously sending a jam signal to all of the other ports.

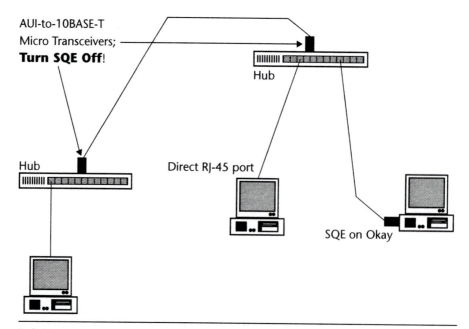

FIGURE 2.7 A case where you should turn off the SQE function.

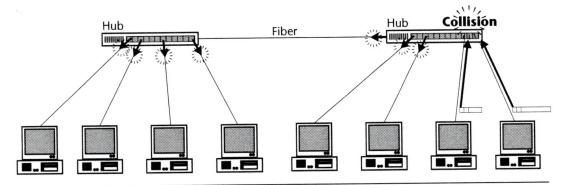

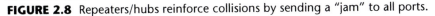

FIGURE 2.8 Repeaters/hubs reinforce collisions by sending a "jam" to all ports.

> **❗**
>
> Some cable testers and analyzers differentiate between a collision that actually occurred on the cable segment you are monitoring versus one that was reinforced by a repeater. These are often called "local" vs. "remote" collisions. If you hook up a cable tester to a 10BASE-T hub, every collision is remote because a hub is a repeater and you are the only device attached to that port.

The usefulness of differentiating local versus remote collisions is diminished as the industry does away with coax, but it is obviously very useful if you have any coax segments in your Ethernet. Then you can run a quick test to see if most of the collisions originate on the coaxial segment or are "remote."

2.8 Fast Ethernet Wiring

100 Mbps Ethernet, a.k.a. "Fast Ethernet" or 100BASE-T, has its own wiring rules. At 100 Mbps, the timing is a lot tighter and so is the maximum physical size of the Ethernet.

Unlike 10 Mbps Ethernet, Fast Ethernet has different classes of repeaters/ hubs: Class I and Class II. Class I hubs have relaxed timing, which allows mixing 4-pair (100BASE-T4) and 2-pair (100BASE-FX fiber or 100BASE-TX twisted pair) wiring. 100BASE-T4 supports Category 3, 4, or 5 wiring, but requires 4-pair wiring. You can only have one Class I hub in an Ethernet collision domain.

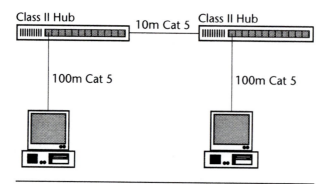

FIGURE 2.9 Maximum wiring for Fast Ethernet with Class II repeaters and Category 5 wire.

With Class II hubs, timing is tighter and only 2-pair wiring is supported. Category 5 wire or Type 1 and 2 IBM STP wire or fiber is required. Because most newer Ethernet installations already have Category 5 wiring, Class II is the more popular of the Fast Ethernet hubs. An advantage over the Class I hub is that you can have two Class II hubs in a single Ethernet collision domain.

Like the 10 Mbps 802.3 standard, the IEEE 100 Mbps 802.3u standard contains a simplified model for wiring. If you are just wiring point to point between two stations (which could be a station to a switch or router port, router to router, etc.), 100 meters is the maximum distance for copper and 412 meters is the maximum for fiber.

With two Class II hubs, the maximum end-to-end wiring for copper is 205 meters as shown in Figure 2.9. If station wiring is 100 meters on both hubs, you can have only 5 meters of patch cable between the two hubs. If you're willing to do some bit-budget calculations involving the velocity of propagation of copper wire, you can buy wire that exceeds the Category 5 specification and obtain a few more meters. If fiber is used throughout, a maximum of 228 meters is allowed end to end. For a mixture of copper and fiber, I recommend studying the 802.3u standard in detail.

2.9 Token Ring Wiring

When IBM first introduced its structured wiring system for Token Ring, it was entirely passive, including the hubs. Token Ring hubs are also called multistation access units, or MAUs, by IBM and concentrators in the IEEE 802.5 Token Ring standard. I prefer the term "hub" because it's more generic.

IBM even has a device called the Controlled Access Unit, or CAU, which is a powered and managed MAU. There's also an accessory for the CAU called the Lobe Access Module, or LAM. So your Token Ring could have MAUs, CAUs, and LAMs—a total farm!

In the original passive wiring system, the maximum number of stations supported on one physical ring depended on the number of hubs, distance between hubs, and type of wiring used. Paradoxically, the bigger the ring (in terms of number of attached devices), the smaller it got (in terms of cabling distance between the hub and the attached devices).

For example, if you are supporting 12 stations on one passive hub running at 16 Mbps, the maximum recommended IEEE 802.5 station wiring distance is 107 meters for Category 5 wiring and 196 meters for STP wiring. On the other hand, if you are supporting 84 stations with seven passive hubs, the maximum recommended station wiring distance is 74 meters for Category 5 wiring and 135 meters for STP wiring.

For active hubs, the maximum station distance stays constant just like Ethernet. With Category 5 wiring, the maximum recommended distance is 195 meters and 356 meters for STP Type 1.

Regardless of the hub technology, Token Ring is limited to 250 stations maximum for both 4 Mbps and 16 Mbps rings, which is now what both IBM and IEEE recommend.

> **❗**
> Wiring for Token Ring networks can be tricky. Always check with the vendor for rules when using their hubs. For example, hubs that retime every port reduce the maximum IEEE 802.5 recommended station count to 180 for 16 Mbps and 144 for 4 Mbps rings.

There are a lot of great stories about the early IBM wiring system, which is still in use in many places today. The data connector is this big old ugly hermaphroditic plug that could mate with itself. The idea was to have the same connector anywhere in the system—at the hub, the patch panel, the receptacle, and so on. The connector also wraps the transmit and receive pair when unplugged, allowing a station to self-test its own wiring (also known as the lobe wiring) right up to the hub port before inserting into the ring.

One of the problems IBM engineers encountered was that the connector was too fat to couple with a Token Ring NIC card out the back of the IBM personal computer. Thus, for PCs, there's actually a male DB-9 connector for the PC at one end and the hermaphroditic plug at the other.

At the time, the monochrome display adapters were popular. Problem was, they had the same DB-9 connector type as the Token Ring NIC. So users were plugging Token Ring cables into their display adapters and bringing down the whole network. This occurred because commonly used pin outs activated the insertion relays inside the hubs, causing the ring to go into a beaconing state.

When RJ-45 connectors became the Ethernet standard, Token Ring was quick to follow. This also reduced the cost of the connector from $10 down to $1. RJ-45 connectors can't auto-wrap themselves when unplugged from a hub, so you do lose that advantage. When the RJ-45 connectors are plugged into a hub, however, the hubs are designed to wrap the transmit and receive pair of that port, allowing a station to self-test before inserting. Some of the earlier RJ-45 Token Ring hubs also required RJ-45 wrap plugs in the ring-in and ring-out ports of the hub.

Token Ring NICs that don't have UTP connections require a media filter to go from the standard DB-9 connector on the back of a NIC to UTP. These are usually referred to as "Type 3" media filters, that function as a balun to match the 150 ohm impedance of STP to the 100 ohm impedance of UTP.

One problem I've seen involves a neat little converter plug that has an RJ-45 connector on one side and the hermaphroditic connector on the other, allowing you to plug a UTP cable into a port on the old 8228 passive hubs. Conversely, you could also connect an IBM 3745 Front End Processor Token Ring Interface Card (TIC) or a router to an RJ-45 Token Ring hub. The only problem is that the neat little converter plug doesn't contain a media filter. This causes many line errors (Token Ring line errors are covered in detail in Chapter 3) due to the impedance mismatch between the STP interface (150 ohms) of the adapter and the UTP cable (100 ohms). There are converters that *do* have a built-in media filter, so be careful as to which one you use.

2.10   Encoding the Bits onto the Media

Every network topology must have some method of turning the bits of a frame into a physical signal for transmission as electrical signals on a piece of wire or light pulses on a fiber. Conversely there must be a way to receive these signals or pulses to put the frame back together, bit by bit.

Different topologies have different encoding and signaling techniques as summarized in Table 2.2.

10 Mbps Ethernet uses a binary signaling mechanism that combines data and clocking into bit-symbols. Each bit is split into two halves, the second half being the inverse of the first. In other words, there is always a transition of

TABLE 2.2 Encoding and Signaling Techniques for Various Topologies and Media

Topology	Cable Type	Encoding/Signaling Technique
Ethernet	All supported cable types	Binary/Manchester
Token Ring	All supported cable types	Binary/Differential Manchester
Fast Ethernet (100BASE-TX)	2-pair copper	4B5B/MLT-3
Fast Ethernet (100BASE-FX)	Fiber	4B5B/NRZI
Fast Ethernet (100BASE-T4)	4-pair copper	8B6T/MLT-3
FDDI	Copper	4B5B/MLT-3
FDDI	Fiber	4B5B/NRZI

the signal in the middle of a bit. For a binary 0, the first part of the signal is hi and the second part lo. Conversely, a binary 1 is represented by a signal transitioning from lo to hi in the middle of a bit. An example of Manchester encoding for various bit patterns is shown in Figure 2.10.

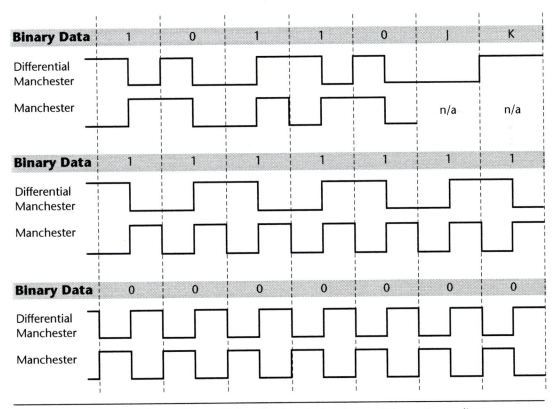

FIGURE 2.10 Differential Manchester (Token Ring) and Manchester (Ethernet) encoding.

What happens if there are consecutive 0s or 1s? As you can see in Figure 2.10, there is a transition at the beginning of the first half of the signal to set up for proper signaling in the middle of the bit.

The neat thing about Manchester encoding is that it guarantees at least one signal transition, and maybe two, for every bit. This allows the receiving side of an Ethernet transceiver to lock onto the signal and derive the receiving clock. Thus it's not super-critical that all stations send at *exactly* 10 Mbps.

A major drawback to Manchester encoding is that when several binary 0s or 1s are sent consecutively (like 48 binary 1s in a broadcast address), the signal is effectively 10 MHz. This doesn't scale well for higher speed signaling because higher frequencies lead to higher attenuation of the signal in copper, not to mention higher potential for causing radio frequency interference (RFI) to outside devices. This is why higher speed networks such as 100 Mbps Ethernet or FDDI use a different encoding and signaling technique for copper.

Token Ring uses a variation on Manchester encoding called differential Manchester. You still have clocking at every bit, but with one important difference: The bit is determined by the presence or absence of a transition at the beginning half of the signal. If there's a transition from hi to lo *or* from lo to hi, you have a binary 0. Conversely, no transition means a binary 1. Like the Ethernet Manchester, transitions still occur in the middle of a bit for binary 1s and 0s.

Unlike Ethernet Manchester, however, two new symbols—Non-data J and Non-data K—are introduced in addition to the 0 or 1. A Non-data J is essentially a violated 1; i.e., neither the beginning half nor the middle of a signal has a transition. Likewise, a Non-data K is a violated 0, where there *is* a transition at the beginning but none in the middle. To preserve the integrity of the clocking, there can never be two consecutive J's or two consecutive K's. Chapter 3 shows how J's and K's come in handy to indicate the start and end of a token or frame.

As transmission rates increased, new encoding signaling techniques were developed. The simple on/off or two-level binary encoding was no longer adequate.

Fast Ethernet over 2-pair copper wiring (e.g., Category 5 cable) or fiber actually breaks an 8-bit character into two 4-bit "nibbles" that are in turn encoded as two 5-bit "symbols," also known as 4B5B. If this sounds like FDDI to you, you're right—the technique was indeed borrowed from the proven FDDI standard. For fiber media, the bits are then transmitted using the Non-Return to Zero or NRZI signaling technique. For copper, the bits are transmitted using MLT-3, a technique where actually *three* voltage levels are present on the wire, not just two as with Manchester.

Using NRZI effectively reduces the transition rate from 200 MHz to 125 MHz because, unlike Manchester encoding, NRZI does not require two transitions per bit, but only one. However, one bit is wasted for every four, thus the transition rate of 125 MHz instead of 100 MHz.

Why waste a bit? The extra bit is necessary because NRZI doesn't transition when you have consecutive 0s or consecutive 1s. By using an extra bit, you guarantee that there is always a zero in the bit stream at least every nibble. From Table 2.3, you can see that the binary value of 1111, or hex F, will be encoded as 11101. This ensures that the NRZI signal will always have transitions even if you sent all hex F's (or all 0s for that matter) so that the receiving end can recover the data and clocking, just as Manchester encoding does.

TABLE 2.3 4B/5B Encoding

	5B Encoding	Code Name	Meaning
Binary Data			
0000	11110	0	Data 0
0001	01001	1	Data 1
0010	10100	2	Data 2
0011	10101	3	Data 3
0100	01010	4	Data 4
0101	01011	5	Data 5
0110	01110	6	Data 6
0111	01111	7	Data 7
1000	10010	8	Data 8
1001	10011	9	Data 9
1010	10110	A	Data A
1011	10111	B	Data B
1100	11010	C	Data C
1101	11011	D	Data D
1110	11100	E	Data E
1111	11101	F	Data F
Control Symbols			
	11000	J	Start-of-Stream Delimiter, Part 1—Paired with K
	10001	K	Start-of-Stream Delimiter, Part 2—Paired with J
	01101	T	End-of-Stream Delimiter, Part 1—Paired with R
	00111	R	End-of-Stream Delimiter, Part 2—Paired with T

TABLE 2.3 *(continued)*

	5B Encoding	Code Name	Meaning
Invalid Symbols			
	00100	H	Transmit Error; used to force signaling errors
	00000	V	Invalid Code
	00001	V	Invalid Code
	00010	V	Invalid Code
	00011	V	Invalid Code
	00101	V	Invalid Code
	00110	V	Invalid Code
	10000	V	Invalid Code
	01100	V	Invalid Code
	10000	V	Invalid Code
	11001	V	Invalid Code

The Fast Ethernet over 4-pair wiring standard takes this concept one step further by encoding 8 bits into a pattern of 6 ternary symbols called a 6T code group. Each 8 bits is sent out over three wire pairs in a rotating fashion, for a total bandwidth of 33.3 Mbps per wire, or 25 MHz (8/6 of 33 Mbps). The fourth wire pair is used for collision detection. Because only one wire pair is left over while transmitting, full-duplex operation is not possible using 100BASE-T4. Coincidentally, 100BASE-T4 is not very popular in the marketplace.

It's time to stop right here before I go too far with this cable "technophobia." In fact, it's not even necessary to understand the level of detail presented here for troubleshooting physical layer problems. It is useful to know some level of detail, however, so that you understand why there are certain cabling restrictions for different transmission rates and topologies.

The bottom line is this: As networks get faster, pay very close attention to cabling details. Don't exceed the *standards* recommendations (note that I said standards, not vendor) to accommodate multi-vendor hub and cable compatibility and to ensure growth into the future.

Chapter 3

Analyzing and Troubleshooting the Data Link Layer

3.1 Introduction

The Data Link Layer, or Data Link Control (DLC), has a very critical role in networking in that it provides the final envelope or encapsulation of upper layer data before it is passed to the physical layer. To provide these services, two elements must be defined:

1. The format of the frame
2. The access technique for transmitting or receiving the bits that make up the frame to or from the physical layer

The DLC frame contains the addressing fields and information necessary to detect errors.

Frames on networks usually begin with some type of preamble to delimit the beginning of the frame. For example, Ethernet uses a 64-bit preamble, Token Ring and FDDI have a Starting Delimiter, and HDLC contains an 8-bit "Start-of-Frame" flag.

Point-to-point networks such as frame relay and ATM contain only circuit information in their frame or cell headers. A frame relay frame contains a 10-bit connection identifier for a switched virtual circuit (SVC) or permanent virtual circuit (PVC), whereas the ATM cell has an 8-bit or 12-bit virtual path identifier plus a 16-bit virtual circuit identifier for multiplexing within a virtual path. For error detection, a frame relay frame contains a 16-bit Frame Check Sequence (FCS), and ATM cells contain an 8-bit Header Error Control (HEC) field.

Local area networks (LANs) have a 48-bit destination address, immediately followed by a 48-bit source address. All LAN frames also contain a 32-bit Cyclic Redundancy Check (CRC).

This chapter covers error detection in a generic sense, discusses details of the 48-bit IEEE MAC addressing format, looks at how bridges and switches use the MAC address to forward frames, examines the spanning tree operation in detail, delves into details specific to Ethernet and Token Ring, and finishes by looking at the logical link control (LLC) sublayer of layer 2.

3.2 Error Detection

When a frame is passed from one device to another via a piece of wire, there must be some way of protecting the integrity of the bits during transmission. For a LAN frame, this is accomplished by including a 32-bit CRC at the end of each frame. The CRC is also referred to as a Frame Check Sequence, or FCS, because a CRC is the *technique* for generating a bit pattern called the FCS.

A chip at the DLC layer computes the CRC on the fly as the bits are being transmitted. At the receiving end, a chip generates a polynomial from the received bits and divides by the received CRC. If a remainder is left over, there has been a transmission error and the frame is discarded. All single bit, double bit, and burst errors that are no longer than 32 bits can be detected. The probability of longer burst errors or a series of short burst errors escaping error detection is very low, around 1 in 2^{32}. So, as you can see, a 32-bit CRC protects the frame quite well.

> **!**
>
> It is important to realize that the CRC at the DLC layer only protects the bits of a frame over a physical segment, as illustrated in Figure 3.1. Because the CRC is always calculated by a transmitting DLC layer, it is recalculated whenever the frame goes through a bridge, switch, or router for retransmission on another port. Thus, the data is subject to corruption in the store-and-forward memory of a transferring device. To truly protect your data from corruption *end to end*, you must implement checksums in the upper layers of protocol.

The DLC layer does, however, note that a CRC error has occurred, and many devices such as routers, switches, or managed workstation network adapters can store this information for later retrieval via proprietary or SNMP-based management consoles.

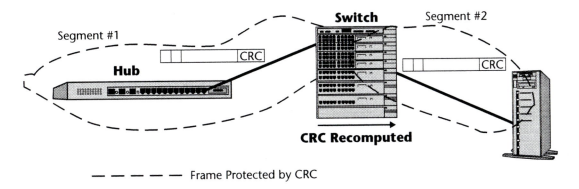

FIGURE 3.1 The DLC layer CRC protects a frame on the local segment only.

> ❗ When checking a 10BASE-T or 100BASE-T collision domain for CRC errors with an analyzer or cable tester, be sure to check the segment from a port on *every* hub module (in a chassis or stack). I have seen CRC errors that don't propagate across the entire collision domain. That, is they only emanate from a certain hub module, so a quick check from an arbitrary hub port may not show any CRC errors!

3.3 IEEE MAC Layer 48-Bit Addressing

Ethernet, Token Ring, and FDDI LANs all rely on the IEEE 48-bit addressing scheme at the MAC layer (the "lower" part of the DLC layer, as discussed in Chapter 1). For historical purposes, note that ARCNET LANs had an 8-bit address, and at one time, 16 bits were an IEEE option for MAC addressing, but this was never widely adopted.

As shown in Figure 3.2, the first bit of an IEEE MAC layer destination address is known as the I/G, or Individual/Group, bit. I like to call it the broadcast bit. (In the case of a source address, the first bit has a special meaning known as the Source Route Indicator. The meaning of this bit is covered in detail in the discussion on Token Ring later in this chapter.) If this bit is not set (i.e., there is a 0 in the destination address), the frame is destined for an individual station. If it is set (i.e., there is a 1 in the destination address), it is a *broadcast* frame. If all the remaining bits are set to 1, the address is an

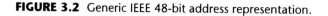

| I/G | U/L | 46 Remaining Address Bits |

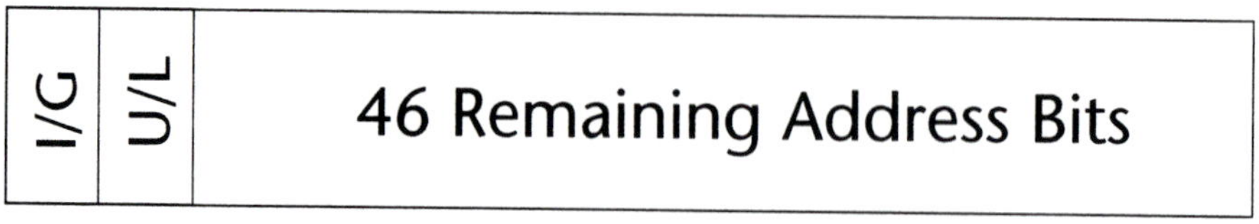

I/G = Individual 0 or Group (Broadcast) 1 Address bit
U/L = Universally Administered 0 or Locally 1 Address bit

FIGURE 3.2 Generic IEEE 48-bit address representation.

all stations broadcast; otherwise, it is *multicast-group* address intended for a select subset of stations. In this case, a station's adapter must be programmed to recognize a multicast address.

3.3.1 Functional Addresses

On a Token Ring, *functional* addresses are usually used in place of multicast addresses. A functional address is a set of locally administered group addresses. Functional addresses always begin with hex C0, with the next bit set to 0 (the Functional Address Indicator), and the lower 31 bits are mapped one to one to a specific function. Because each of the lower 31 bits represents a specific function, there can only be a total of 31 functional addresses. A list of functional addresses, in hex, is as follows:

```
C0-00-00-00-00-01    Active Monitor
C0-00-00-00-00-02    Ring Parameter Server
C0-00-00-00-00-04    Network Server Heartbeat
C0-00-00-00-00-08    Ring Error Monitor
C0-00-00-00-00-10    Configuration Report Server
C0-00-00-00-00-40    Directory Server
C0-00-00-00-00-80    Synchronous Bandwidth Manager
C0-00-00-00-01-00    Bridge
C0-00-00-00-02-00    LAN Manager
C0-00-00-00-04-00    Ring Authorization
C0-00-00-00-08-00    LAN Gateway
C0-00-00-00-08-00    Appletalk Zone Multicast
C0-00-00-00-10-00    Ring Wiring Concentrator
C0-00-00-00-10-00    Appletalk Zone Multicast
C0-00-00-00-20-00    IBM LAN Manager
C0-00-00-00-20-00    Appletalk Zone Multicast
C0-00-00-00-40-00    Appletalk Zone Multicast
C0-00-00-00-80-00    Appletalk Zone Multicast
C0-00-00-01-00-00    Appletalk Zone Multicast
C0-00-00-02-00-00    Appletalk Zone Multicast
C0-00-00-04-00-00    Appletalk Zone Multicast
```

```
C0-00-00-08-00-00          Appletalk Zone Multicast
C0-00-00-10-00-00          Appletalk Zone Multicast
C0-00-00-20-00-00          Appletalk Zone Multicast
C0-00-00-40-00-00          Appletalk Zone Multicast
C0-00-00-80-00-00          NetWare
C0-00-00-80-00-00          Appletalk Zone Multicast
C0-00-01-00-00-00          Appletalk Zone Multicast
C0-00-02-00-00-00          Appletalk Zone Multicast
C0-00-04-00-00-00          Appletalk Zone Multicast
C0-00-08-00-00-00          Appletalk Zone Multicast
C0-00-10-00-00-00          Appletalk Zone Multicast
C0-00-20-00-00-00          Appletalk Zone Multicast
C0-00-00-FF-FF-FF          Ring Broadcast
```

You may have noticed a conflict with some of the AppleTalk addresses. If you use AppleTalk over Token Ring, I recommend avoiding the use of AppleTalk Zone Multicast addresses that conflict with other multicast addresses, such as those for IBM LAN Manager and NetWare.

The usage of various functional addresses such as Active Monitor, Ring Parameter Server, and Ring Error Monitor is discussed in more detail later in this chapter. Also note in the list the special functional address of hex C00000FFFFFF, which denotes a broadcast to every station on the local ring and should not cross a bridge or a switch.

One exception to the rule of "multicast addresses as functional addresses" are layer 2 bridges operating the spanning tree algorithm. These bridges send out periodic bridge configuration packets to the Token Ring group address of hex 800143000000.

If you look at the generic IEEE address format in Figure 3.2 and compare it to an Ethernet multicast address from an analyzer, you may notice that the broadcast bit seems out of place. For example, a bridge sends on the multicast address of hex 0180C2000000 or binary 00000001 10000000 00000000 11000010.... Ethernet addresses are always represented with the broadcast bit as the right-most bit in the first byte of the address (the underlined bit in the multicast example). On Token Ring, the broadcast bit is the left-most bit. Figure 3.3 shows representations of addresses in Ethernet and Token Ring formats.

> **❗**
>
> When analyzing both Token Ring and Ethernet, don't forget that the MAC address bits are swapped bit for bit on a byte-by-byte basis between the two networks. Thus, on Token Ring, the very first bit you see in an address is the broadcast bit, whereas on Ethernet, the broadcast bit is the eighth bit in from the left.

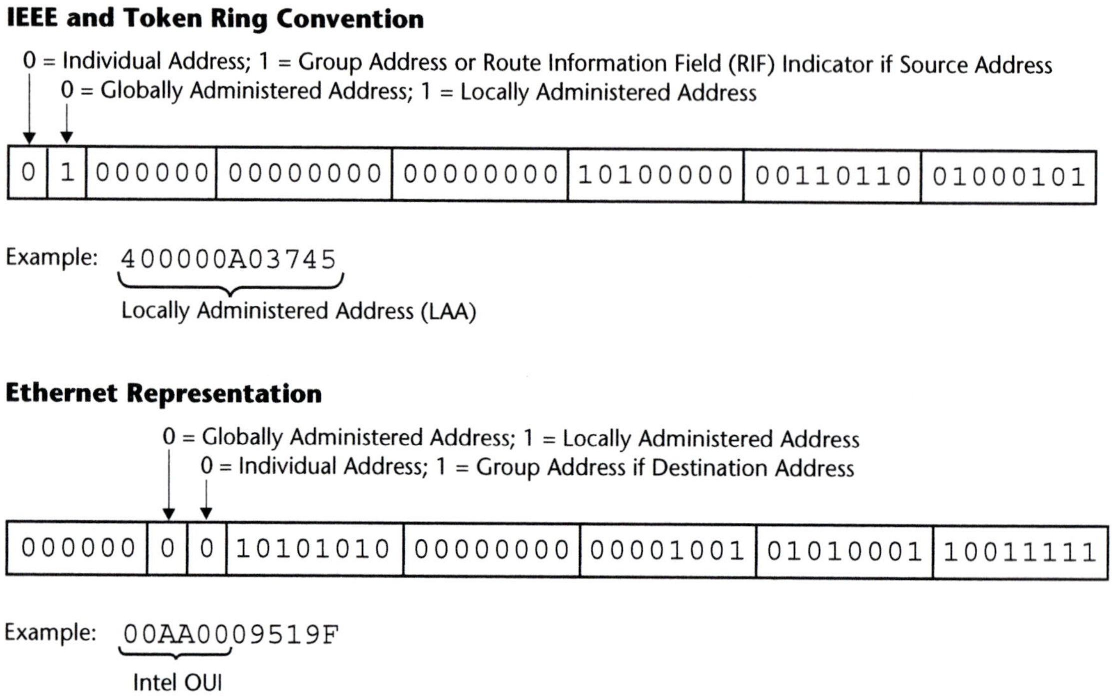

IEEE and Token Ring Convention

0 = Individual Address; 1 = Group Address or Route Information Field (RIF) Indicator if Source Address
  0 = Globally Administered Address; 1 = Locally Administered Address

| 0 | 1 | 000000 | 00000000 | 00000000 | 10100000 | 00110110 | 01000101 |

Example: 400000A03745

Locally Administered Address (LAA)

Ethernet Representation

0 = Globally Administered Address; 1 = Locally Administered Address
  0 = Individual Address; 1 = Group Address if Destination Address

| 000000 | 0 | 0 | 10101010 | 00000000 | 00001001 | 01010001 | 10011111 |

Example: 00AA0009519F

Intel OUI

FIGURE 3.3 Representing the IEEE 48-bit address on Ethernet and Token Ring.

One could argue that Ethernet is technically correct because it was the first to define DLC addressing back in the days of Xerox PARC where Ethernet was developed and adopted by the DEC Intel Xerox (DIX) Ethernet "blue book" standard prior to the IEEE standards. On the other hand, the first bit on the wire is always the broadcast bit, so on Token Ring, the bits are truly represented in the order in which they were transmitted; the Ethernet DLC chips are actually bit swapping the address bits. This bit swapping must also be performed by a bridge or switch that joins Ethernet to Token Ring in order to keep the broadcast bit definitions intact.

To make matters worse, the upper three bytes of the DLC address (sometimes called the Burned in Address, or BIA) burned into every NIC that ships from the factory represents the manufacturer of the NIC and is represented in Ethernet format. Another name for these three bytes is the Organizationally Unique Identifier (OUI). OUIs used to be assigned by Xerox, the inventors of Ethernet. When IEEE took over the task, they kept the OUIs in the Ethernet format, not bothering to swap the bits to conform to their own MAC address representation in the Ethernet (IEEE 802.3) and Token Ring (IEEE 802.5) standards.

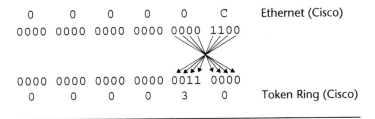

FIGURE 3.4 Bit-swapping a Cisco OUI.

Virtually every protocol analyzer comes with a table that maps OUIs to vendor names. Because OUIs are always represented per the Ethernet convention, you have to provide a bit-swapped entry into your OUI table for your Token Ring analyzers. For example, the Cisco-assigned OUI of 00000C appears as 00000C in the upper three bytes of an address on Ethernet and 000030 on Token Ring. Figure 3.4 illustrates how to bit-swap the OUI.

Not all MAC addresses contain an OUI. Note the second bit from the left in Figure 3.2. This is known as the Locally Administered bit and if it is set to 1, the address has been locally set to an address that overrides the factory setting. If it is set to 0, the address has been set to the factory default, which is also known as a Universally or Globally assigned address. These addresses are the OUIs now assigned by IEEE. For a mere $1000, you can purchase your very own OUI.

IBM introduced LAA addresses such that users could move around with one address in an SNA network. This way, SNA administrators didn't have to reprogram a Front End Processor (FEP) with the new address.

You can have LAAs on Ethernet because most Ethernet NICs have a configurable MAC address. Obviously one of the drawbacks to LAAs is that it's possible to have duplicate addresses in a LAN. On the other hand, if you'd like to manage user's MAC addresses, there are some clever ways to encode the address. For example, a typical LAA in a Token Ring might be something like hex 400000374501 to indicate FEP #1 or 400001000222 to indicate a user on the first floor with extension 222.

3.3.2 Impact of Different Types of Broadcast Traffic

Thinking back to the different types of MAC broadcast addressing, you may be wondering what impact all these broadcast addresses have on your network. With multicast or functional addresses, a station has to be programmed to recognize the specific multicast or functional address. If the address is not recognized, the NIC will throw it away without bothering the CPU.

With an all stations broadcast (hex FFFFFFFFFFFF), however, a NIC receives the frame and interrupts the CPU in order for the NIC driver to process the frame and decide which upper layer protocol (IPX, IP, etc.), if any, needs to process the frame. Thus a "broadcast storm" of several hundred broadcasts per second can impact the CPU of a workstation (or server), potentially slowing down any foreground applications. In some cases, users have noticed a significant slowdown in application processing, not realizing that a broadcast storm was the culprit.

This can also be a problem with network segments connected to a layer 2 bridge or switch because broadcast packets are forwarded to all ports. Virtual LANs, or VLANs, that group switch ports together can contain broadcasts, but they have some drawbacks as we'll see Chapter 4. Routers, on the other hand, block DLC layer broadcasts unless either a bridging function is turned on within the router or the network layer also contains a broadcast address, in which case the router forwards the frame.

3.4 Transparent Bridging and Switching Operation and Troubleshooting

3.4.1 Switches as Multiport Bridges

Remember, all LAN bridges (and routers) are packet switching devices. It seems that when bridges gained more than two ports, they became known as switches. These "multiport bridges" became a popular way to collapse backbones into a box and to break up busy segments, or "microsegment" a network.

Switches operate at the data link layer by looking at MAC addresses and blocking or forwarding frames to other ports. They are sometimes called layer 2 switches to differentiate them from layer 3 switches or routers. In a layer 2 switch, a frame is passed through unaltered. For this reason, this type of switching is also called transparent bridging.

The standard for transparent bridging is IEEE 802.1D, which not only describes how bridges learn MAC addresses and forward frames, but also provides an algorithm to ensure that bridges that operate in parallel do not loop packets, called spanning tree.

Switches are constantly "learning" MAC addresses as frames are received. In the 802.1D standard, there is also a brief learning period after an incoming port becomes active in which addresses are learned but not forwarded. This learning period is either at power-up of the switch or when a backup switch takes over for a failed switch that's in parallel with a primary switch.

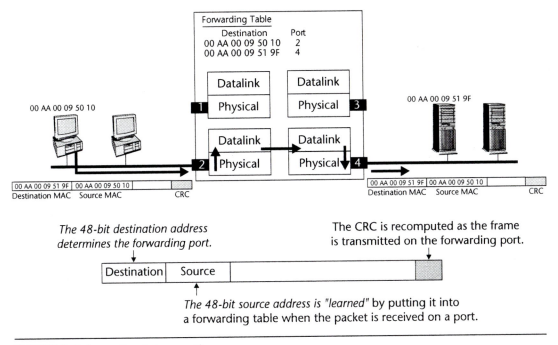

FIGURE 3.5 Layer 2 switch operation.

Figure 3.5 illustrates the various steps in learning a MAC address. The way a switch learns, or associates a MAC address with a given port, is straightforward. A switch looks up the source address of a frame when it arrives. If it is not in the internal switch table, it is added along with the port number. If it is already in the table, the port is checked and updated in case a station was moved from a different segment. Table entries are also cleared after a certain aging period, such as 15 minutes.

Once an address is learned, all packets destined for that address are simply forwarded to that port. If a destination address is a broadcast, multicast, or unknown address, it is flooded to every port on the switch or every port within a given VLAN.

3.4.2 Spanning Tree

Most layer 2 bridges and switches offer spanning tree operation, which ensures that no loops are created in situations where parallel bridges exist between two network segments. A simple case of this is illustrated in Figure 3.6. Bridge B is blocking its ports, while bridge C is forwarding frames between the two middle segments. If bridge A was not blocking, it would

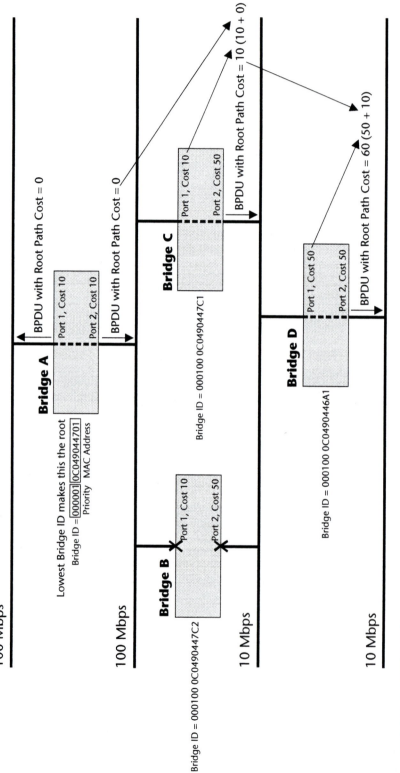

FIGURE 3.6 Bridging with spanning tree operation.

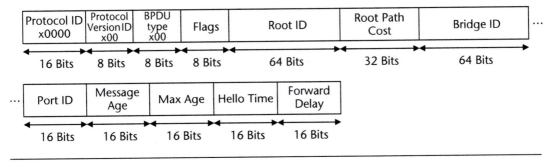

FIGURE 3.7 BPDU packet details.

forward frames from bridge C and C would forward frames from A, causing an infinite loop and saturating the bandwidth of both network segments.

Every two seconds, by default, a designated bridge (the bridge actively forwarding frames) sends out a configuration Bridge Protocol Data Unit (BPDU), as shown in Figure 3.7. The BPDU is sent to the multicast address of hex 0180C2000000 on Ethernet or to the group address of hex 800143000000 on Token Ring (notice that each byte in the address is bit-swapped from Ethernet per our earlier discussion).

Figure 3.8 contains an example of a BPDU as captured and decoded by the Microsoft Network Monitor. By setting your analyzing capture filter on the BPDU protocol or on the destination addresses of hex 0180C2000000 on Ethernet, you can capture and study only the BPDUs. Note that Network Monitor is substituting the characters "IEEE" for the upper three bytes of the destination MAC address.

By capturing for several seconds (or several minutes for a longer term study), then observing the BPDU packets in your capture buffer, you can verify whether or not they are being sent at the proper interval. By setting your timestamp to show delta time or the time from the previous packet, you can see the time span between the BPDUs.

In the example, you can see from the packet detail that the hello timer is set to 2.0 seconds (512 units $\times$ 1/256 seconds/unit = 2.0 seconds). In the packet summary, you see that the bridge (actually a switch port) is deviating slightly from this time due to the load on the switch and other traffic on the segment you are capturing from. This slight deviation is of little concern at this point.

Referring back to Figure 3.6, if bridge B doesn't see the BPDU broadcasts from bridge C after a certain amount of time, it goes into a learning and eventually forwarding state, taking over from bridge C and becoming the designated bridge. Using the previous example, it would take a BPDU delay greater than the maximum age time plus the forward delay time before a

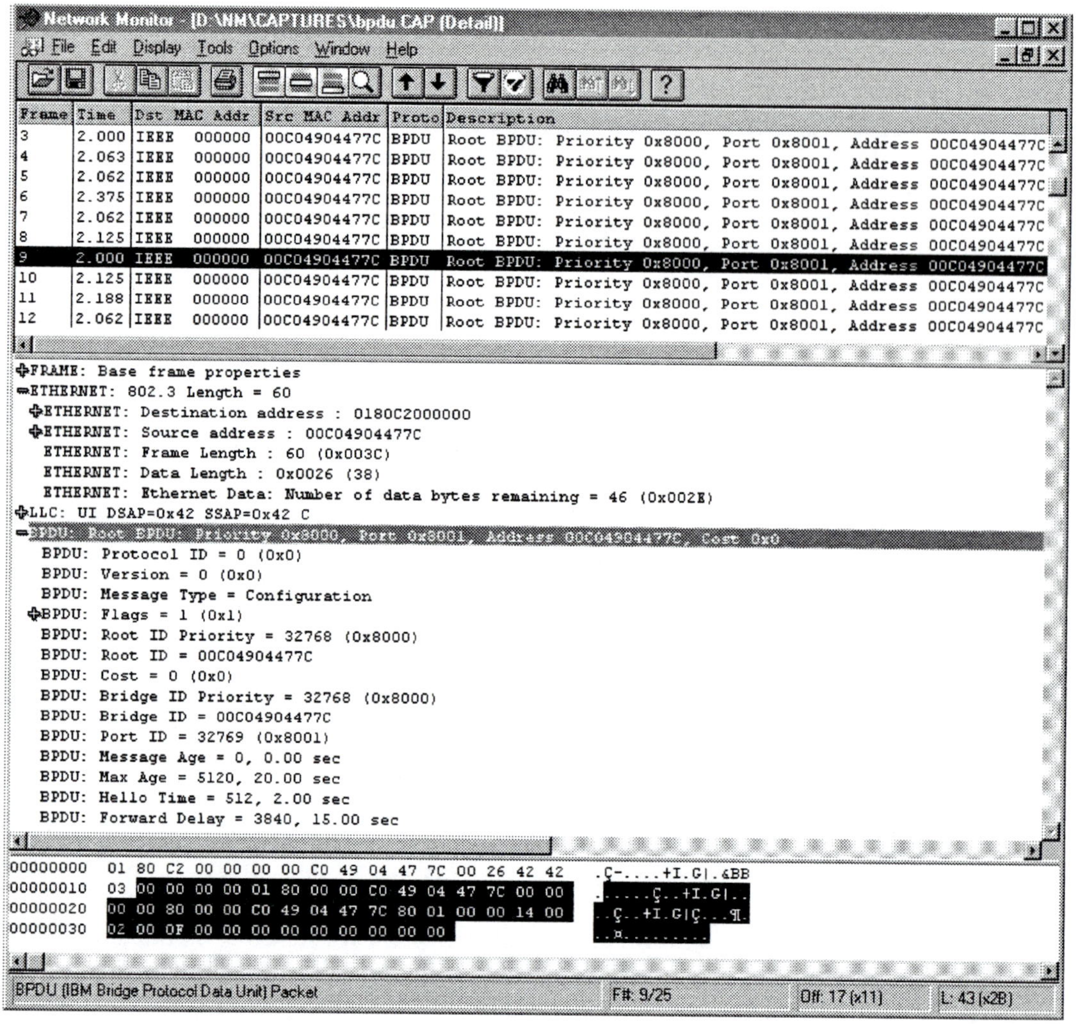

FIGURE 3.8 A configuration BPDU sent by a root bridge.

backup bridge would begin forwarding packets. In the example, this is 20.0 seconds plus 15.0 seconds, or 35.0 seconds.

If there's a change in the root bridge (or root port on a switch) or there's a new designated bridge, a Topology Change Notification BPDU is sent by the new root or designated bridge. When the root sees a Topology Change Notification BPDU from another bridge, it sets a flag in its configuration BPDUs for some period of time to indicate a topology change. This way, all the bridges throughout the network will realize that there's been a change in the active topology and they can flush their forwarding tables.

During the course of normal operation, each configuration BPDU sent contains the bridge ID of a root bridge, the bridge ID of the transmitter of this BPDU, and the cost of the least cost path from the root via this bridge. For example, the root bridge B in Figure 3.6 transmits a BPDU with a cost of 0. The designated bridge C does not forward the BPDU (one of the few exceptions to the rule that all multicast packets are transparently forwarded), but rather sends a new BPDU with a cost of 10 (using the root cost of 0 from the BPDU plus the port 1 cost of 10).

Lower configuration numbers always have higher priority in spanning tree. In the event of a tie in path cost, the NIC address of the bridge or switch port forms the lower portion of a bridge ID. Even though bridge B also has a cost of 10 to the lower segment, it is blocking because bridge C has a lower MAC address and thus a lower bridge ID. To make bridge B the preferred forwarding bridge, you could lower the path cost on port 1 or make its priority "higher" (by lowering the priority value; remember, the lower the priority number, the higher the priority of the bridge).

The costs assigned to bridge ports are arbitrary. It's a good practice to assign lower numbers to faster network segments. In the example in Figure 3.6, a cost of 10 was assigned to a 100 Mbps segment, and a cost of 50 to a 10 Mbps segment. Assigning 100 to a 10 Mbps segment would have kept the cost proportional to the speed of the segment. How you manage your path costs is up to you.

Every BPDU also contains the root ID = priority (16 bits) followed by the root's NIC address. Setting the root priority of a switch port to 1 (the minimum IEEE value) gives that port a high probability of becoming the root. In the event of a tie with another port set to a priority of 1 on this or another switch, the lower NIC address wins out and becomes the root. In the example packet shown in Figure 3.8, the priority is set to 32768, giving this bridge a low priority. This was most likely the default value and was never reconfigured. Note that the analyzer is decoding this packet as a "Root BPDU" because the cost inside the packet is 0, meaning that this packet must have been transmitted by a bridge root port.

In a spanning tree network, being a root port doesn't mean that all packets will pass through that port. There must be one and only one root port as a reference point for calculating relative path costs throughout the bridged network. As was mentioned earlier, a root bridge sends out periodic BPDUs, every two seconds by default. All other bridges "downstream" sending BPDUs are timed off this packet. For example, in Figure 3.6, bridge C sends its BPDU when it sees a BPDU from A, and D sends its BPDU when it sees a BPDU from C. Information about the hello timer, maximum age, and forwarding delay are all set by the root bridge and picked up by the other bridges. Thus, to change the hello timer for instance, you only need to change it at the root bridge, although it's good practice to set the other bridges as well, in case one of them becomes a root.

Usually the root selection is not super-critical unless you have an incredibly complex hierarchy of bridges (the maximum recommended number of bridge "hops" per 802.1D is seven); just don't assign it to a remote bridge over a WAN or a bridge that is highly used because BPDUs may become delayed, making for a potentially unstable topology. If you don't have any bridges in parallel, the issue of which bridge is the root is moot. In fact, you don't even need spanning tree at all—just don't accidentally hook up two switches in parallel!

3.4.3 Troubleshooting in Bridged and Switched Environments

Switches are very popular because they are a low-cost way to break up a large shared media segment into several smaller ones for greater overall bandwidth gain. Devices such as routers, servers, and even end-users often have their own dedicated ports.

Because switches isolate traffic by segment, they pose some interesting protocol analysis challenges. In the old days, you could slap a protocol analyzer on a workgroup or backbone Ethernet segment and see a large percentage of traffic in your network. As you microsegment your network, the amount of traffic you can capture and analyze, as a whole, becomes less and less.

I remember that a columnist a few years back predicted the death of protocol analyzers as switches gained market share. Quite the contrary. In many ways, switches have increased the reliance on protocol analyzers for troubleshooting problems and actually make it easier to troubleshoot problems.

For example, a switch is already doing us a favor by filtering extraneous traffic. If you want to analyze all the broadcast traffic going through a switch, you can simply put an analyzer on a switch port all by itself. If you suspect a server or router problem, a good place to start is by analyzing traffic on the switch port to which the server or router is attached. On the down side, it may not be as easy as simply attaching an analyzer to a hub port because switches can pose some physical barriers to attaching an analyzer.

Figure 3.9 illustrates several methods for tapping into a switch port. Analyzing a half-duplex connection is a no-brainer. You simply tap off an existing hub connected to the switch port or put a temporary "pocket hub" on the port.

Analyzing full-duplex connections is a bit trickier. This requires a special splitter tap for the analyzer, pass-through ports built into the analyzer, or port mirroring capability on the switch. For fiber media, optical splitters are

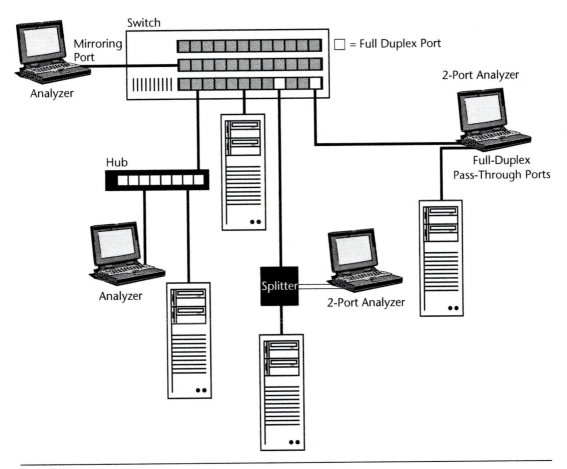

FIGURE 3.9 Tapping into a switched environment.

available from several vendors. Shomiti is a vendor that makes a tap for Category 5 copper connections.

Analyzers such as those from HP, Wavetek Wandel Goltermann, and GN Nettest contain pass-through ports that interface to both sides of a full-duplex connection. Because you are now capturing from two ports, the aforementioned analyzers combine the two traces together to form a unifying view of the capture. Shomiti also makes a full-duplex analyzer that works by combining two PCI NICs for a desktop computer.

If you don't have a full-duplex analyzer, you can always attach two analyzers, one to each side of the splitter. It is more difficult, however, to match and compare command and response packets from both sides of the connection.

Perhaps the easiest way to monitor a switch port is to be able to mirror, or "span," an active port to a monitoring port. Make sure your switch has the capability to truly buffer all packets to and from a given port and forward them to a monitoring port. Be careful if you are using a slower speed port, such as a 10 Mbps port to monitor a 100 Mbps port, because packets may overrun the monitor port. Also be careful if you are using one port to monitor a group of ports, for the same reason.

3.4.4 Case Study: A Switched Network Meltdown

To illustrate what happens when a root bridge becomes busy in a network with thousands of users, here's a real example. The network is a redundant bridged infrastructure conceptually similar to that illustrated in Figure 3.10.

Using a protocol analyzer attached to a segment on the top set of switches, I observed numerous Topology Change Notification BPDUs coming from the secondary bridge. By using another analyzer on a segment attached to a different set of switches, I could see more Topology Change Notification BPDUs occurring at about the same time as the other segment being monitored. This indicated that the problem was more likely to be "upstream", i.e., toward the root rather than specific to a local switch. This preliminary diagnosis was reinforced by the fact that on many occasions, the normal configuration BPDUs that should have been sent every 2 seconds from the designated bridges were sometimes disrupted with intervals like 3.2 seconds, 7.4 seconds, 9.1 seconds, and so forth.

When the interval is too long and the backup switch doesn't see a configuration BPDU, it sends a Topology Change Notification BPDU and goes into the learning state. This means that the secondary switch is about to start forwarding packets.

Depending on the spanning tree timers, a backup switch can begin forwarding frames in as little as 10 seconds, based on the minimal timer values (6 seconds of aging plus a 4-second forwarding delay) recommended by the IEEE 802.1D bridging standard. Coincidentally, the default timer values recommended by IBM for spanning tree operation are the same as the minimal IEEE values. The critical spanning tree timers and recommended settings are summarized in Table 3.1.

TABLE 3.1 IEEE 802.1D Spanning Tree Timer Values

Parameter	Recommended or Default Value (in seconds)	Range
Hello Time (Configuration BPDU interval)	2.0	1.0–10.0
Max Age	20.0	6.0–40.0
Forward Delay	15.0	4.0–30.0

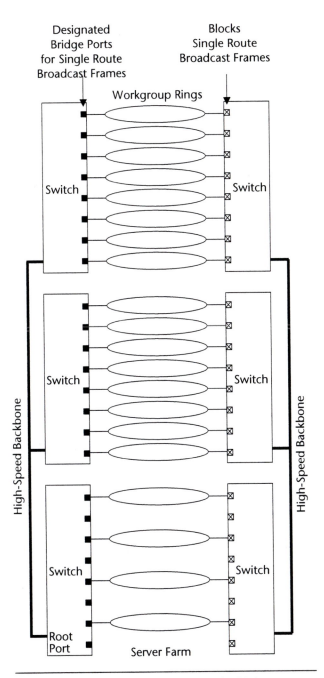

FIGURE 3.10 A redundant layer 2 switched infrastructure.

Having timer values on the low side helps to quickly reestablish connectivity in the event that a designated switch port fails. The problem with low values, however, is that if the designated switch becomes so busy that it can't process BPDUs, a backup switch will eventually begin forwarding packets, leading to a potentially disastrous meltdown with looping of packets and the saturation of the network segment's switches, resulting in even *less* time for a switch to process BPDUs.

Fortunately the dust eventually settles because the switches were configured for source route bridging and subsequently add source route information to each frame as it passes through, with a limit of seven routes or switch hops. Frames that already have seven routes in them are discarded when received by the switch. (More about source routing later in this chapter in the Token Ring discussion.)

You may be wondering at this point why the switches are using the spanning tree algorithm normally associated with transparent bridging, not source route bridging. In a source route–bridged environment, the spanning tree algorithm is actually used to select which bridges will forward a single route broadcast frame such that the originating broadcast frame appears only once on each ring.

Traffic that has already been established between two end-nodes is not affected when parallel switches both start forwarding frames because specific source routing continues between these end-points. The problem starts when a single route broadcast packet, also known as a Spanning Tree Explorer (STE) in IEEE terminology, is sent. The purpose of this packet is to explore the spanning tree by propagating one packet per segment in the tree in order to find an end-node. Unfortunately, with parallel bridging and both sides open, neither side blocks the packet, resulting in an exponential flood of crisscrossing packets.

The root switch in this network turned out to be one of the busier switches. The cause of the BPDU deprivation was traced to the root switch in that, on occasion, it had to process over 1000 single route broadcasts/second. In doing so, it had to add a ring number to the Routing Information Field (RIF) field of each frame as it forwarded it to each of 18 other ports, thus processing over 18,000 outgoing frames/second. This single route broadcast RIF process required the use of the main CPU of the switch, which interfered with its ability to process and/or queue up a BPDU.

A pair of switches with only a few Token Rings between them has less of a problem processing frames because there's less source route broadcast crunching to perform due to less destination ports. Thus switch pairs containing a large number of rings between them were most susceptible to this problem.

When a backup switch port opens up while the designated switch is still forwarding frames and a broadcast frame hits the switch, the impact is catastrophic even though the frame "dies" after looping through seven switches.

I did a whiteboard analysis of the actual number of packets that were generated between two open parallel switches and then programmed a permutation and summation computation into Excel that I verified against the whiteboard findings.

As the number of ports on a switch increases, the number of packets generated that are triggered by one lousy source route broadcast frame is truly astonishing—up to 64 million with 16 ring segments sitting between two forwarding switches.

Obviously there's not enough processing and buffering to handle a load of this magnitude, leading to a large number of dropped packets. The process eventually dies, thanks once again to a maximum source routing of seven hops. Then, in the absence of a fresh supply of another source route broadcast storm, the designated switch recovers and sends out a BPDU advertising a path closer to the root bridge, causing the backup switch port to begin blocking again.

For a short-term solution, I reconfigured the switches with the 802.1D recommended default values for spanning tree, which allows a switch to process a high rate of single route broadcast frames and other frames requiring the CPU for a much longer period of time (50 vs. 10 seconds). Longer term, I focused on source route broadcast reduction and monitoring broadcast rates on a regular basis.

With two nonblocking bridges in parallel between two segments, you end up with infinite looping, especially in an Ethernet with transparent bridging and no "hop limits" to stop the frame, as with source routing in Token Ring. I should note that, in the event of looping in a routed environment, the packet will also eventually die as the Time To Live (TTL) in an IP packet reaches zero, or the hop count in an IPX packet reaches the maximum of 15.

The big risk is when you have many switch ports in parallel between segments.

3.5 IEEE 802.3/Ethernet

3.5.1 Ethernet History in a Nutshell

Ethernet was the brainchild of Bob Metcalfe at Xerox Palo Alto Research Center (PARC) back in 1973. At the time, it was based on a physical coaxial bus topology and ran at 3 Mbps. The transmission rate was raised to 10 Mbps and standardized by DEC, Intel, and XEROX (DIX Ethernet) in 1979, with the infamous Ethernet "blue book" Version 2.0 appearing in 1980.

About that same time, a committee was formed within the IEEE to develop a LAN (read: one, single, uno) standard designated "802." IBM was quick to jump in and criticize Ethernet, saying that it was prone to collisions and didn't have deterministic capabilities. Enter Token Ring. Then, a few industrial vendors wanted a deterministic system for the factory floor. Enter Token Bus based on broadband Radio Frequency (RF) CATV technology.

Ethernet became the responsibility of the 802.3 committee; Token Ring, 802.5; and Token Bus, 802.4. Then the 802 committee decided, with influence from IBM, that there ought to be a common interface to all these networks. Enter Logical Link Control (LLC), 802.2.

Eventually, 802.3 evolved to the point of incorporating 100 Mbps and 1000 Mbps (gigabit) transmission speeds, support for twisted pair and fiber media, and support for full-duplex operation.

3.5.2 Ethernet Access Mechanism

Prior to switching and full-duplex operation, Ethernet was strictly a broadcast bus, shared media network. The bus access mechanism is very straightforward as simplified in Figure 3.11. When a station needs to transmit a

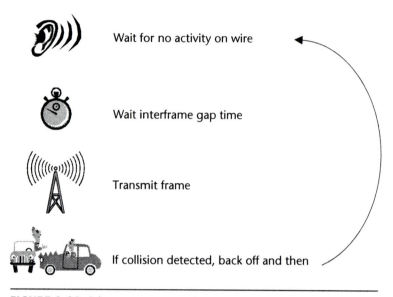

Wait for no activity on wire

Wait interframe gap time

Transmit frame

If collision detected, back off and then

FIGURE 3.11 Ethernet access mechanism.

frame, it simply listens for the presence of a carrier (activity) on the bus. If there is activity, the station waits or defers transmission for a brief amount of time until the bus is "dead," i.e., no activity is sensed.

The station then waits for a quiet time of at least the interframe gap requirement. Why waste more time before sending? The reason is simple: There must be a brief gap between every packet to give stations a chance to contend for transmission. Otherwise, a station could send back-to-back packets, not allowing other stations a chance to transmit. The gap time is 9.6 microseconds at 10 Mbps and 0.96 microseconds at 100 Mbps, or a total of 96 bits of essentially wasted bandwidth.

I've heard of some Sun workstations, Cisco devices, and even Intel PCI NICs that can use a gap of less than 9.6 microseconds in order to have "priority" in transmitting frames. I do not recommend nonstandard practices that can monopolize a shared Ethernet segment and lead to other problems. On a full-duplex connection (where there's no contention with other stations for sending frames), however, a smaller gap time, if implemented properly, could lead to a small improvement in performance.

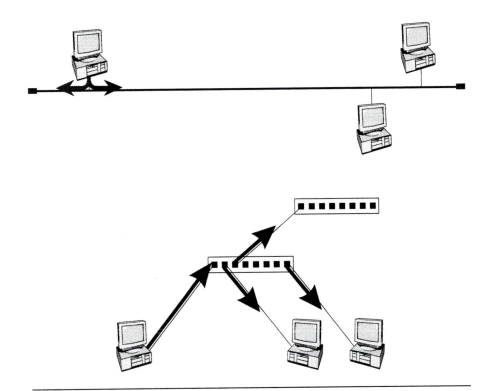

FIGURE 3.12 Packet propagation on Ethernet.

If the bus is still quiet at the end of the gap time, the station begins transmitting a preamble, followed by the frame data and, of course, the CRC. The packet is "broadcast" on the bus in the sense that the signal starts at the station's transmitter and propagates through the network. Figure 3.12 illustrates this broadcasting concept in Ethernet, literally wired physically like a bus (all Ethernets used to be wired like this), and today's Ethernet wired physically like a star.

If another station decides to transmit at exactly the same time, a collision results. Both stations then need to stop their transmissions and retry at a later, randomized time.

If you put this all together, you have the Carrier Sense Multiple Access with Collision Detection protocol, or simply CSMA/CD.

Figure 3.13 shows the Ethernet timing in more detail. After the listen time, the station begins transmitting something known as a preamble. The preamble alternates between binary 1s and 0s, and ends with two 1s, for a total

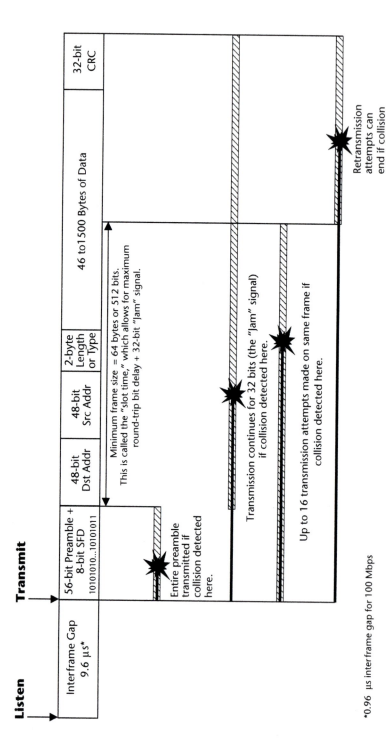

FIGURE 3.13 Ethernet timing details.

of 64 bits. It might seem odd to waste another 64 bits of bandwidth, so why have a preamble?

The answer lies in the way the physical layer transceivers work. The receive side of a station's transceiver clocks off the Manchester signal, which was examined in Chapter 2. It takes a few bits to "lock on" to the signal using Phase Locked Loop (PLL) technology. If you didn't have a preamble, the first few bits of your frame, the destination address, would always be garbled.

The last byte of the preamble, which 802.3 also calls the Start Frame Delimiter, ends in two 1s, which tells the transceiver to begin passing the bits to the DLC layer. Immediately following the preamble is the 48-bit MAC destination address. The DLC layer then checks the destination address to see if it's this station's address, an all stations (all 1s) broadcast, or a multicast address that this station is programmed to receive. If the address passes, the rest of the frame is received into a buffer on the NIC, the CPU is interrupted, and a NIC driver retrieves the packet into main memory and notifies an upper layer protocol stack for further processing.

Some NICs contain bus mastering, in which the NIC places the packet directly into main memory without the CPU's intervention. In some cases, the NIC begins transferring the packet before it is completely received off the Ethernet, a technique that 3Com calls parallel tasking.

If there is a collision detected in the preamble, the remainder of the preamble is sent as a way of "reinforcing" or "jamming" the collision to make sure that the other station that is transmitting recognizes the collision. If the collision is in the frame, the station continues to send for 32 bits as a jam to reinforce the collision.

If the collision is within the first 64 bytes or 512 bits of the frame data, an attempt is made to retransmit the frame. If the collision is beyond the first 512 bits, retransmission is implementation dependent, that is, it depends on the chip set. This is not a big issue because the vast majority of collisions in an Ethernet that's within the wiring and maximum repeater specifications occur in the preamble.

The first 512 bits are also known as the slot time, which allows for the maximum round-trip bit delay in the cable and repeaters plus the extra 32-bit jam. The slot time is used in calculating a retransmission in the event of a collision. After the first collision, the DLC layer generates a random number from 0 to 2 and multiplies this by the slot time of 512 bits or 51.2 microseconds at 10 Mbps and 5.12 microseconds at 100 Mbps. Thus, on average, the first retransmission is 51.2 microseconds plus the 9.6-microsecond gap, or roughly 60 microseconds after the collision. The second workstation that collided must wait longer, until the first workstation's frame has completed transmission.

It is possible for more than two transmissions to collide. It is also possible to have more than one collision in succession. For every successive collision, the DLC layer doubles the amount of time it may have to wait to retransmit the packet. After a second collision, for example, the DLC layer picks a random number between 0 and 4 and multiplies it by the slot time before attempting to resend. After three collisions, the number is between 0 and 8; four collisions, 0 and 16; five collisions, 0 and 32; and so on. The maximum range is between 0 and 1023, which is reached after 10 successive collisions. The DLC layer gives up after 16 attempts and notifies the NIC driver. Users eventually see an error message appear on their screen like "Abort, retry, ignore?", "Error receiving from network", "Network resource is no longer available", or some other useless error message that fails to pinpoint the real problem and its cause. That's where network troubleshooting professionals come in.

> **❶**
>
> I'm frequently asked, "What should my maximum collision rate be?" On average, look for collision rates to be 5 percent or less over a period of a few seconds at most. Even at these rates, you many want to do a quick collision analysis, using the technique described later in this chapter.

3.5.3 Full-Duplex Ethernet

Full-duplex Ethernet operation is described in detail in the 802.3x standard. By using one twisted pair or fiber exclusively for receiving and another for sending, collisions are nonexistent. Theoretically, you can double your server or router's throughput, given the right mix of traffic (balanced equally in both directions, which is, of course, difficult to achieve in reality).

The big question is: Is this really Ethernet? Not really. With full-duplex operation, you essentially have a point-to-point connection that's a network all by itself, connected to other segments via switching or routing. However, even though the CSMA/CD protocol is not required in full-duplex operation, you still have the "standard" Ethernet frame formats.

3.5.4 Ethernet Frame Formats

A NIC driver determines which protocol stack will process the frame, based on information contained in the Ethernet frame header. Over the history of Ethernet and IEEE 802.3, four frame formats have emerged, as depicted in Figure 3.14.

Associated with the DLC layer is a term called Maximum Transmission Unit, or MTU. The MTU is the maximum amount of 8-bit bytes that a frame can

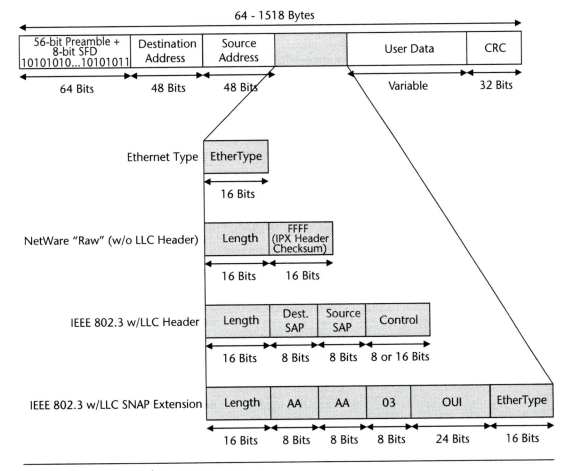

FIGURE 3.14 Ethernet frame types.

contain, usually excluding any preamble bytes but including (per the IEEE standards) the CRC. For Ethernet, the MTU must be at least 64 bytes and the maximum is 1518 bytes.

The original Ethernet frame defines a 16-bit field, the type field, immediately following the source address. This particular Ethernet format is referred to by several names including DIX, Ethertype, or Ethernet II (by NetWare).

The Ethertype identifies the next layer of protocol encapsulated in the frame. Thus the field following the Ethertype is the first field of the next protocol, such as IP. In the case of IP, the Ethernet will be set to hex 0800. For IPX, the value is hex 8137.

When 802.3 was formed, the 16-bit type field was replaced by a 16-bit length field. The length field refers to the number of bytes immediately *following* the length field, but not including the CRC. Because the next protocol is no longer identified, frames with the length field are assumed to contain an LLC header. As seen in Figure 3.14, the LLC header contains an 8-bit Source Service Access Point (SSAP) and Destination Service Access Point (DSAP). Six of the SAP bits serve the same purpose as the Ethernet type field in identifying the next layer of protocol in the packet, although you can only get 64 protocol types with a 6-bit SAP value. The other two of the DSAP bits (look ahead to Figure 3.21 for details) are used to indicate a group or individual SAP and whether the SAP is user-defined (akin to a locally administered SAP). The other two bits of the SSAP are used to indicate a Command or Response LLC frame and whether the SAP is user-defined.

How do you tell the difference between an Ethertype packet and 802.3? The largest DLC payload (the bytes following the Ethernet DLC header, excluding the CRC) is 1500 bytes, or hex 5DC. Thus any value less than or equal to 1500 bytes tells you that there's an LLC header that follows, with one little exception that is discussed in a bit.

Earlier I noted that IBM had a lot of influence on the IEEE 802.2 LLC standard. LLC was originally designed to replace HDLC as a means for carrying SNA traffic over Token Ring. This was an unfortunate development for a couple of reasons.

First, other than for certain SNA exchanges, you would never send to a different destination protocol than the source protocol. Thus the DSAP is somewhat of a waste of 8 bits. It would have been better to combine the two fields into one 16-bit SSAP, so you could map all the Ethertypes to a SSAP.

Second, how do you accommodate all those 16-bit Ethertypes into a 6-bit SSAP in the LLC header? DEC, for instance, couldn't run DECnet on Token Ring because there weren't enough LLC SAPs to be allocated.

Enter Ethernet frame format 3: LLC with Sub-network Access Protocol (SNAP) extension. SNAP is identified by a SSAP of hex AA and includes a 5-byte extension that defines the OUI of the protocol followed by the Ethertype, as shown in Figure 3.14.

The 3-byte OUI of the protocol is somewhat of a waste. The intent was to identify the owner of the Ethertype protocol, and about the only time I've seen this set to anything other than all 0s is for AppleTalk, in which the AppleTalk OUI of hex 080007 is present.

The SNAP format was added because of an "oops" in the standards process. After all, why would IBM need more than six bits to handle all the SNA-related protocols?

On another note, SNAP is required to run IP on Token Ring. Why? If you look carefully at the LLC SAP table in Appendix A, you won't find an equivalent SAP type for Ethertype 0806, ARP, only for Ethertype 0800, IP. To make

IP work, you need to support ARP. What a disaster in prematurely standardizing the LLC format.

To make matters worse, about the time IEEE was working on 802.3 and 802.3 LLC, Novell jumped the gun and came out with its own Ethernet format with the length field in place of the Ethertype field, but with no LLC header to identify the upper layer protocol!

At one time, Novell was on top of the PC networking industry and growing exponentially, so they got away with it. This posed a little extra work for analyzer and router vendors because there had to be a way to differentiate not only Ethertype from 802.3, but now 802.3 from the proprietary Novell format, known as "Novell Raw" or Ethernet_802.3 in NetWare nomenclature.

If the frame is determined to have a length field rather than an Ethertype, the next step is to look at the next two bytes following the length field. If these bytes are hex FFFF, the Novell Raw format is assumed. Why is that?

As you'll see in Chapter 4, these are the first two bytes of the NetWare IPX header, which is the IPX datagram checksum and set to hex FFFF or null (i.e., not used) by default. If the value is anything other than hex FFFF, a standard LLC header is assumed. If you want to enable the IPX checksum, obviously you can no longer use the Novell Raw encapsulation frame format.

The use of multiple encapsulation types causes some problems, especially in NetWare networks where you can bind in up to four different frame types to your server NIC cards. Router vendors have also bowed to user demand and now allow more than one IPX encapsulation to be defined on a given router port. The danger of multiple encapsulation types is illustrated in Figure 3.15. If server B has Novell Raw bound to its NIC card, can a user with 802.3 and LLC encapsulation communicate to server B? Not directly, because the Ethernet frame types are incompatible.

Server A, however, is bound to all possible frame types. Because servers learn about each other via the NetWare Service Advertising Protocol (SAP—not to be confused with IEEE SAP), server A can reach server B via internal routing because all NetWare servers 3.x and higher have an internal or virtual IPX network defined. So what ends up happening is that user A sends its packets to server A via the 802.3 encapsulation type that both understand. Server A, in turn, "routes" the packet through its virtual IPX network and transmits the packet to server B via the Novell Raw encapsulation type, over the same physical Ethernet. This effectively doubles the number of packets (while user A sends and receives data from server B) and chews up bandwidth.

On a protocol analyzer, you would actually see back-to-back packets that look identical, except for the frame type shown by the analyzer's detailed packet display (it wouldn't be in the summary window) and the fact that the IPX hop count is incremented as the packet goes through the "router," i.e., server A.

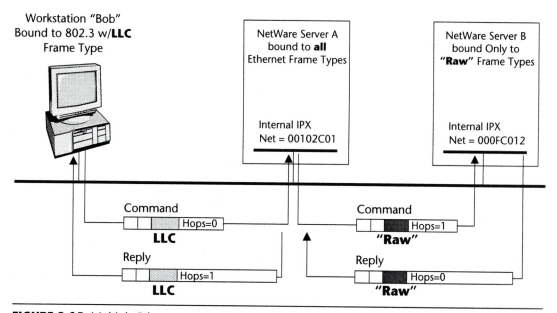

FIGURE 3.15 Multiple Ethernet encapsulation types in a NetWare environment.

Another side effect of multiple IPX encapsulation types is that NetWare SAPs and RIPs are sent for every frame type. Thus server A for example, actually sends four SAP packets every 60 seconds to advertise its name and service type (i.e., a file server), and four RIP packets every 60 seconds to advertise its internal IPX network number.

The solution to these IPX problems is to get down to one encapsulation type. It doesn't matter too much which one because a different encapsulation type for a different protocol such as IP is perfectly acceptable. If you have a bridging between Ethernet and Token Ring or FDDI, pick the IEEE 802.2 or 802.2 with SNAP format so the bridge or switch doesn't have to perform translational bridging to change frame types because the Novell Raw and Ethertype formats are not available on Token Ring or FDDI.

3.5.5 Calculating Network Utilization and Bandwidth Efficiency in Ethernet

The maximum packet rate on Ethernet depends on the packet size. One way to calculate this rate is to start by taking the raw bandwidth of 10,000,000 bits per second and dividing by 8 bits/byte to get 1,250,000 bytes per second. The minimum data frame size is 64 bytes, including the CRC. Because the gap and preamble take away from the available bandwidth, you must also add in 12 bytes for the gap and 8 bytes for the preamble, for a total of 64 + 12 + 8 = 84 bytes per minimum-sized packet.

Then you can divide the 1,250,000 bytes/second of available bandwidth by 84 bytes/packet, for a total of 14,880 packets/second (or 148,800 packets/second at 100 Mbps).

As an exercise, I encourage you to do the same for a maximum-sized Ethernet data frame of 1518 bytes. Don't forget to add in the gap and preamble overhead. You should come up with 880 packets per second.

Obviously the packet rate is much higher with smaller packets, but so is the overhead. So what's the effective bandwidth available for real data bits with a 64-byte packet? Here's the formula: Simply take the packet size of 64 bytes and divide by the 84 bytes computed above for packet size plus overhead. Thus 64/84 = 0.76, or 76 percent, effective utilization. This is how cable testers, monitors, probes, and analyzers measure network utilization.

How do you achieve better network utilization? With longer packets. Take 1518 divided by 1538 and you get 0.986, or 98.6 percent, utilization or efficiency (interesting that 98.6 just happens to be the normal human body temperature!). You may have heard that Ethernet is 98 percent efficient. Well, that's if your average packet size is always equal to the maximum packet size of 1518 bytes and there are no collisions!

> ❗ Is it wise to set an alarm in an RMON probe for Ethernet segments that exceed, say, 60 percent utilization? Emphatically, no! In fact, the higher the utilization the better, at least for a few seconds. If your Ethernet bandwidth never exceeds 60 percent, that tells me there's no device on that segment that can drive the data rate high enough to take advantage of available bandwidth. If the average long-term (minutes) versus short-term (seconds) utilization exceeds 60 percent, then, sure, I'd take a look at it. As a general rule, always design your network infrastructure to accommodate short-term peaks to maintain good user response time but with low long-term utilization.

3.5.6 Case Study: Analyzing Excessive Ethernet Collisions

Chapter 2 discussed at length how collisions are detected and how to keep collisions to a minimum. It was noted that Ethernet collisions often show up as CRC error packets whenever the collision extends beyond the preamble of an Ethernet frame—i.e., into the header of a packet. If your protocol analyzer is capable of capturing and displaying packets with CRC errors, you can do some basic collision analysis.

Recall two important facts about collisions:

1. A station that has its preamble collided with will continue to send the remainder of the preamble.
2. A station will attempt to resend the frame very quickly, usually within 100 microseconds.

The preamble is an alternating series of 1s and 0s ending with two 1s, so it looks like AAAAAAAAAAAA in hex because hex A is 1010 in binary. Normally an analyzer doesn't capture the preamble, *unless two preambles collide and the analyzer starts receiving a packet prematurely.*

Remember that an Ethernet transceiver will go from an idle state to locking on to the alternating bit pattern waiting for the two 1s in a row. If a collision causes the two 1s to appear early, the analyzer will start receiving the packet. Obviously the packet does not have a valid CRC and may be flagged as such. Some analyzers, such as the Domino Mentor and Sniffer Expert, can more accurately recognize this as a collision fragment, not as a "runt" or short packet with a CRC error.

By capturing all the packets on a segment with a high rate of collisions, you can see if any of these preamble collisions make it into the capture buffer. A small percentage usually do, which is adequate for collision analysis purposes.

Because two preambles collided, the fragment in the analyzer's capture buffer may not always be a perfect AAAA... pattern. It may also be a string of hex 5555... because hex 5 is 0101 in binary, or a combination of As and 5s. Regardless, these fragments are very easy to spot. Some analyzers, such as the Sniffer, also have a predefined display filter to show only the error packets. Don't set your capture filter to capture only error packets, however, because valuable information immediately follows a collision.

Recall the second collision fact: A station will attempt to resend the frame very quickly, usually within 100 microseconds of a collision. This means that two or more (if more than two stations' frames collided) packets are guaranteed to appear immediately following the odd looking fragment in the buffer.

By looking at the source address of the next two or three frames following the collision, you can be fairly sure that at least two of the addresses identify stations that were involved in the collision. By analyzing several samples, a pattern may emerge where one station's address appears much more frequently than others. If not, the collisions are probably truly random.

If one address sticks out more than others, you may want to increase the traffic load on that device. If it's a router, do a file transfer using FTP across that router and monitor the collision rates at the same time. If it's a workstation, drag and drop a file from the workstation to a server. If the collision rates go way up, there may be something wrong with that workstation's NIC or how it's wired into the network.

In one such network when collision rates peaked as high as 30 percent, I decided to investigate. By capturing a sample of packets during the high collision period, I was able to capture a fair number of collision fragments. An AG Group EtherPeek analyzer snapshot of these fragments is shown in Figure 3.16. Note the fragment patterns and short frame sizes. The delta time between frames is shown in a seconds followed by microseconds format.

EtherPeek - Olicom Ethernet PCI/II 10/100 Adapter - [Capture]

File Edit Capture Send Options Statistics Special Tools Window Help

Packets received:	700
Packets filtered:	700
Packets processed:	700
Bytes available:	1,509,812
Bytes used:	581,740

Start Capture   Initiate Send

Packet	Size	Time-Stamp	Destination	Source	Protocol
1	1518	00s 000000µ	IP-172.10.10.33	IP-172.10.10.1	TCP NetBIOS
2	1518	00s 001260µ	IP-172.10.10.33	IP-172.10.10.1	TCP NetBIOS
3	16	00s 001106µ	00:C0:AA:AA:A...	AA:AA:AA:AA:AA:AA	ETHER-EC-85
4	1518	00s 000154µ	IP-172.10.10.69	IP-172.10.10.30	SMB WBkR
5	1518	00s 001362µ	IP-172.10.10.69	IP-172.10.10.30	TCP NetBIOS
6	1498	00s 001246µ	IP-172.10.10.69	IP-172.10.10.30	TCP NetBIOS
7	64	00s 001027µ	IP-172.10.10.30	IP-172.10.10.69	TCP NB SessMsg
8	64	00s 000065µ	IP-172.10.10.1	IP-172.10.10.33	TCP NB SessMsg
9	1518	00s 000747µ	IP-172.10.10.33	IP-172.10.10.1	TCP NetBIOS
10	99	00s 001130µ	IP-172.10.10.30	IP-172.10.10.69	SMB WBkR
11	1518	00s 000195µ	IP-172.10.10.33	IP-172.10.10.1	TCP NetBIOS
12	1518	00s 001244µ	IP-172.10.10.69	IP-172.10.10.30	TCP NB SessMsg
13	1518	00s 001251µ	IP-172.10.10.33	IP-172.10.10.1	TCP NetBIOS
14	15	00s 001105µ	00:55:55:55:5...	55:55:55:55:55:35	
15	1518	00s 000165µ	IP-172.10.10.69	IP-172.10.10.30	TCP NetBIOS
16	1518	00s 001292µ	IP-172.10.10.69	IP-172.10.10.30	TCP NetBIOS
17	1518	00s 001283µ	IP-172.10.10.69	IP-172.10.10.30	TCP NetBIOS
18	1518	00s 001284µ	IP-172.10.10.69	IP-172.10.10.30	TCP NetBIOS
19	64	00s 000992µ	IP-172.10.10.30	IP-172.10.10.69	TCP NB SessMsg
20	64	00s 000066µ	IP-172.10.10.30	IP-172.10.10.69	TCP NB SessMsg
21	1518	00s 001228µ	IP-172.10.10.69	IP-172.10.10.30	TCP NetBIOS
22	1518	00s 001257µ	IP-172.10.10.69	IP-172.10.10.30	TCP NetBIOS
23	64	00s 001102µ	IP-172.10.10.30	IP-172.10.10.69	TCP NB SessMsg
24	1518	00s 000237µ	IP-172.10.10.69	IP-172.10.10.30	TCP NB DU Dgram
25	1518	00s 001229µ	IP-172.10.10.33	IP-172.10.10.1	TCP NetBIOS
26	14	00s 001100µ	50:55:55:55:5...	55:55:55:55:EB:17	ETHER-A9-E8
27	1518	00s 000162µ	IP-172.10.10.33	IP-172.10.10.1	TCP NetBIOS
28	16	00s 001129µ	00:80:AA:AA:A...	AA:AA:AA:AA:AA:AA	LSAP-0x50
29	1518	00s 000150µ	IP-172.10.10.69	IP-172.10.10.30	TCP NetBIOS
30	64	00s 001101µ	IP-172.10.10.30	IP-172.10.10.69	TCP NB SessMsg

Show Contents

EtherPeek

FIGURE 3.16 Viewing Ethernet collision fragments.

I then suspected a particular workstation after going through the aforementioned collision analysis, looking at the source DLC addresses that immediately followed a collision. By going to the workstation and transferring a large file from a server, sure enough, the collision rates that were in the 1 to 2 percent range jumped up over 20 percent.

This workstation and its NIC had been installed for several months, so I did not suspect a bad NIC card right off. Instead, I decided to investigate how the workstation was wired, starting with a connection to a nearby 10BASE-T pocket hub. From there, I traced the path to the server and discovered a total of five hubs between the workstation and server, which violates the basic Ethernet wiring rules as noted in Chapter 2.

As a quick test, I temporarily rerouted the workstation wiring to a hub closer to the server and reran the file transfer test. Now the collision counts barely increased with heavy traffic from this workstation. The difference was truly amazing.

I've also heard of excessive collisions when a workstation's NIC card is bad and fails to sense the carrier properly, stepping all over other packets. You can usually tell if this is the case by looking at packets with CRC errors and checking for what looks like a preamble pattern an arbitrary number of bytes into the packet. This is different from preambles always showing up at the very start of a fragment, which indicates more of a wiring-related problem rather than a transceiver-related problem.

> **❗**
>
> Frames containing CRC errors on Ethernet are often due to collision fragments or physical layer problems such as noise or bad transceivers. But don't overlook another possibility—errant hub or switch ports that add extra "jabber-like" bytes to the end of a frame. Always compare the erred frame to a good frame of the same type—a much shorter length is probably a collision fragment, the same length is most likely a bit error caused by noise, and a longer length could be garbage bytes added to the end of the frame.

3.5.7 Case Study: A Slow Server on an Ethernet Segment

This particular infrastructure had several Ethernet segments with NetWare servers placed close to the workgroups they served. The segments were connected via routers, routing the IPX protocol. One particular NetWare server appeared to be very slow because its response times were in the range of several seconds even for small file transfers.

A quick snapshot of packets captured using a protocol analyzer off a hub that the server was attached to revealed that the client was often timing out and resending packets after not getting a response from the server. The server's responses, on the other hand, always seemed to be accepted by the client. Because every user was experiencing slow response time and the time of day didn't seem to make a difference (file transfers were slow even with only one user active after hours), I decided to focus on the server side.

Using the bottom-up approach to troubleshooting, I began by analyzing the server's hub and media. The server was attached to a 10BASE-T hub via a built-in 10BASE-T port on the server's NIC card and a Category 5 cable to the hub. I used a cable tester to check for CRC errors and collisions by attaching the tester to another port on the hub to which the server was attached. There were no CRC errors during a file transfer and very few collisions. For good measure, the cable going to the server was tested and it checked out fine.

Next, I wanted to take a close look at the packet exchanges between the client and server. Because I wanted to be close to the server during my analysis, I decided to place the analyzer where the server was located and attach the analyzer "in line" between the server and the hub. I did this by temporarily installing a mini-hub off the back of the server, so I had a port to plug the analyzer into.

The server now plugged into the mini-hub via a short Category 5 patch cable. The mini-hub had an AUI port with an Ethernet AUI-to-10BASE-T microtransceiver that connected back to the original hub into which the server was plugged. The AUI-attached microtransceiver was required because our mini-hub didn't have a built-in crossover port (required when you go from a port on one hub to a port on another). Normally I'd use a crossover cable to connect the pocket hub back to the original hub, but this would have required a crossover cable and an RJ-45 coupler, which I didn't have handy at the time.

After attaching the analyzer to the mini-hub and capturing packets for a while, the problem mysteriously disappeared and the client had good throughput. Putting the wiring back to its original state, with the server directly connected to the hub via its built-in 10BASE-T port, made the problem come back. Because the server cable had checked out and it worked fine with the mini-hub, I suspected a possible problem with the server's NIC built-in 10BASE-T port.

Recall that in a previous packet capture, there were several packet retransmissions from the client to the server, but never from the server back to the client. For this reason, I suspected a problem with the receive side of the server's 10BASE-T port.

But why did the server work fine with the 10BASE-T port connected to my mini-hub? Recall that when it was connected to the temporary mini-hub, there was only a short 5-foot Category 5 wire between the server and the mini-hub. From there, the mini-hub connected to the original, much longer cable that ran back to the main hub.

As it turned out, the server's NIC card also had an AUI port, just like the mini-hub. So I took the transceiver off the mini-hub and attached it to the back of the server's AUI port and plugged the original cable into the transceiver. The server was then reconfigured to use the AUI port instead of the built-in 10BASE-T port.

The client showed a remarkable improvement in response time, and with my analyzer capturing packets off a port on the main hub, I didn't see any packet retransmissions.

The short-term solution was to leave the micro transceiver on the server's AUI port. Meanwhile, it was discovered that according to the server vendor (a well-known vendor whose name begins with a "C"), the server's NIC card had known problems and needed to be replaced with a newer version. Meanwhile, a check was done to make sure that this NIC card was not being used elsewhere in other servers.

3.6 Token Ring/IEEE 802.5

Token Ring was developed by IBM in the early to mid 1980s. It was based on the Zurich Ring, a prototype LAN developed by 1982 at the IBM Zurich Research Laboratory in Rueschlikon, Switzerland. Many of the characteristics of the Zurich Ring found their way into the Token Ring, including 4 Mbps transmission rate, shielded twisted pair wiring, a star-ring physical wiring topology, token controlled access, and a monitoring function present in one ring adapter to ensure proper ring operation. Logically a Token Ring resembles a ring, but physically it uses a star daisy chain–like wiring system, as depicted in Figure 3.17.

The IBM Cabling System was announced in 1984, followed by the Token Ring in 1985. IBM also worked closely with IEEE to ensure that the Token Ring became an IEEE standard. Like the Ethernet/IEEE 802.3 standard, the Token Ring/IEEE 802.5 standard evolved to a higher data rate (16 Mbps), full-duplex operation, and support for unshielded twisted pair (Category 3) at 4 Mbps and Category 5 for 16 Mbps operation. As of this writing, 100 Mbps Token Ring was being standardized.

Chapter 2 discussed the early "cable" wars between Ethernet and Token Ring. As part of the early Token Ring hype, IBM also pushed the idea of built-in media access control (MAC) management functions and frames to

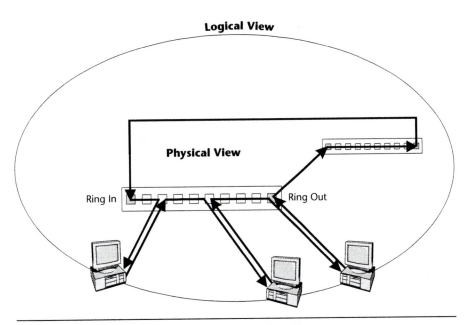

FIGURE 3.17 Logical and physical view of a Token Ring.

support MAC management on a distributed basis, as well as touting the Token Ring as a deterministic system.

By timing the rotation of the token, knowing the number of stations (up to 250, depending on the media type, data rate, use of repeaters, and hub type) on the ring, assuming every station were to send a worst-case sized frame (4,472 bytes for 4 Mbps rings and 17,800 bytes for 16 Mbps rings), and the total cabling distance that formed the ring to compute propagation delay, it was possible to put a guaranteed upper bound on how often you could send a frame.

Despite the more random access nature of Ethernet, it has proven itself time and time again, especially as device populations on Ethernet segments get smaller and get their own switch ports. Therefore, the whole issue of Token Ring having deterministic qualities has diminished.

A more serious problem is that the larger the ring in terms of number of active stations and cable, the more delay there is in passing around the 24-bit token. This is due to propagation delay in the cable as well as bit delay at each active station. The bit delay per attached station is typically 2 bits (but is allowed to be much higher per the 802.5 standard; for precise figures, consult the manufacturer of the Token Ring NIC). If there were 200 active stations, there would be 400 bits of latency just in the adapters alone. (I'll demonstrate later why this is undesirable.)

3.6.1 The Token Passing Process

In accordance with the IEEE 802 standards, I'll be referring to the lower half of the DLC layer as the MAC layer. The MAC layer terminology is something you hear a lot about in Token Ring.

To gain access to the media such that the LLC layer can send a frame, the MAC layer must wait for a free token. By waiting for a token, the MAC layer doesn't have to worry about collisions as Ethernet does. Once a token is acquired, a frame can be transmitted. Because in a Token Ring "what goes around comes around," the station that sends the frame is also responsible for stripping it and generating a new token. This process is summarized in Figure 3.18.

Conceptually, token passing is very simple. It's like a classroom where if you wanted to ask the instructor a question, you'd have to wait for a token such as a paperweight, passed from student to student and eventually to you, before asking a question. The instructor probably does most of the talking (transmitting frames), but the instructor sends the paperweight around the room now and then. This sounds like a bit of overhead and it is. Like the real ring, the instructor has to wait for the paperweight to return before talking again.

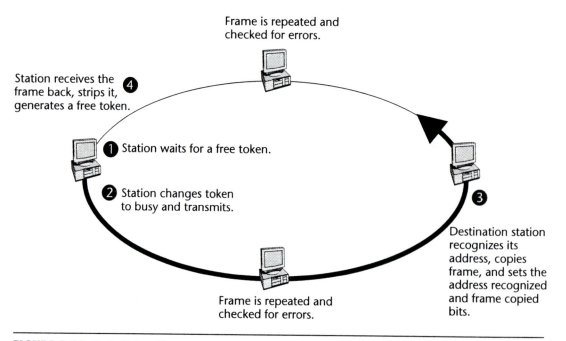

FIGURE 3.18 Basic Token Ring operation.

In contrast, if the classroom operated like Ethernet, the students would jump right in and shout a question at the slightest hesitation in the instructor's voice. And the students would, no doubt, find themselves talking at the same time as someone else, causing one of them to back off and try again later.

One way to cut down on overhead is to allow a station to send multiple frames per token, instead of waiting for 400 bits of delay between each frame for a token (assuming no other stations are talking).

Token Ring allows you to do this. Unfortunately, most vendors of NIC card drivers haven't figured this out and still send only one frame per token. Look how long it took the early NIC drivers to allow sending frames larger than 1518 bytes, a maximum left over from Ethernet.

In Token Ring, a station is allowed to send data for up to 9.1 ms, or 9100 microseconds, before releasing the token. During the time, a station can send one large frame or several small ones. At 4 Mbps, a byte can be transmitted every 1 bit / 500,000 bytes per second, or 2 microseconds per byte. Taking 9100 microseconds and dividing it by 2 microseconds per byte gives us a total of 4550 bytes, very close to the 4472-byte maximum mentioned earlier. (Restricting the size to 4472 allows a source routing bridge to add routing information to a source route broadcast frame, which can grow the frame size.)

For 16 Mbps rings, the token holding time remains the same as 4 Mbps. Thus, the maximum frame size is 4550 bytes $\times$ (16 Mbps $\div$ 4 Mbps) = 18,200 bytes.

3.6.2 Frame and Token Format

The format of the 24-bit or 3-byte token is illustrated in Figure 3.19. The first byte, the J and K symbols (refer back to Chapter 2 for more details), are used to help identify the start of a token.

Because the second byte, the Access Control field, is shared with a frame, the T bit is set to 0 to indicate a token or a 1 to indicate a frame. The priority bits tell the priority of the token or frame, with binary 000 (decimal 0) being the lowest and binary 111 (decimal 7) being the highest. The M, or monitor bit, has a special role that will be discussed later.

The third and final byte, the Ending Delimiter, is another unique 8-bit symbol and bit pattern to denote the end of a token (and frame too.) The seventh bit from the right is the Intermediate bit and is set if this frame is one in a chain of consecutive frames sent by a station, as mentioned earlier. Token and single frame transmissions always have this bit set to 0. The eighth bit, the error bit, is set by any station that senses an error in the token. Incidentally, this usage of the error bit is optional, so not all Token Ring adapters support it. The error bit is, however, required to be set by all NICs that detect a CRC error as the frame passes through the adapter.

Token Format

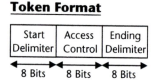

Frame Format

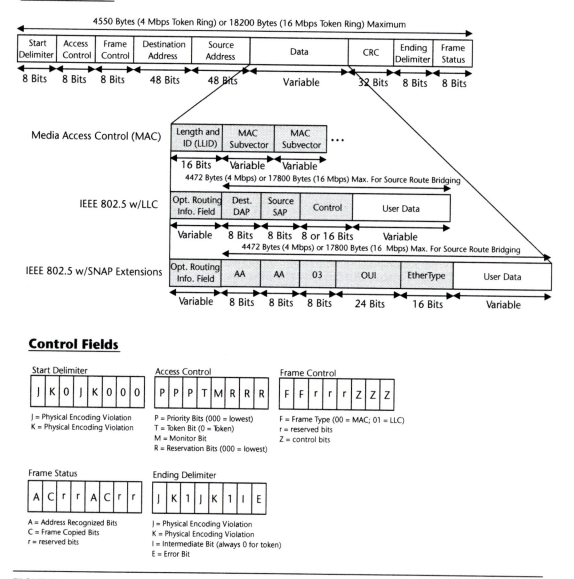

Control Fields

FIGURE 3.19 Token and frame formats for Token Ring.

In Figure 3.19, you'll notice that the first two bytes of the frame are essentially identical to a token. The third frame byte is the Frame Control field that differentiates between MAC frames that manage the ring and LLC frames that send real data between stations. The Z bits are control bits that have a special meaning for certain types of MAC frames.

Frame Control is followed by the now familiar 48-bit IEEE MAC Destination and Source addresses. If any source routing is present, it immediately follows the source address. The format of the source routing information is shown in Figure 3.20.

The presence of a Routing Information Field (RIF) is determined by the first bit of the source address. Because the first bit of the source address is usually 0 (you can't have a broadcast source address, only a destination address), setting this to 1 has the special interpretation "RIF present." This formerly "unused bit" in the source address caused some consternation in the standards community, especially in the Ethernet camp, because it was an IBM feature and no one else was pushing source routing over transparent bridging.

An Ending Delimiter, followed by Frame Status, ends the frame format. The frame status is used to indicate whether or not a destination station recognized its MAC address and if it was able to buffer the frame. Frames sent to a broadcast MAC address have the address recognized (AR) bit set by the first inserted station immediately downstream from the sender.

Even though in a Token Ring "what goes around comes around," the address recognized bit is not used as an acknowledge bit by a sender of an LLC frame. It is used, however, by certain MAC frames such as a station requesting initialization as part of the ring insertion process.

If a station sets the address recognized bit but not the frame copied (FC) bit, it was out of buffers on the NIC card. Also known as receiver congestion, this condition could be caused by such factors as a slow NIC, inadequate receive buffering on the NIC card, slow NIC-to-bus transfer, an inefficient NIC driver, or a slow CPU.

❗

Receiver congestion errors can also be reported in a situation in which a server or workstation hangs, but the adapter is still processing frames that are addressed to that NIC or are broadcast frames. Because the driver removing the frames from the NIC is not functioning, receiver congestion errors are reported. This is not harmful to the rest of the ring because receiver congestion errors are reported every two seconds rather than at the rate of the original broadcasts.

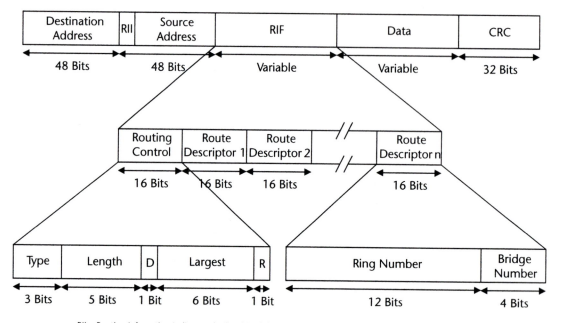

RII = Routing Infomation Indicator, the first bit of the source address. If set to 1, a RIF follows.

Routing Control Field

Type = Broadcast indicators. '0xx' = non-broadcast; '10x' = all-routes broadcast; '11x' = single-route broadcast.

Length = length in bytes of the RIF

D = Direction bit. If set to 0, a bridge interprets the RIF from left to right.

Largest = largest size information field (excluding headers) that can be sent between the two communicating end-stations: '000' = 516 bytes; '001' = 1500 bytes; '010' = 2052 bytes; '011' = 4472 bytes; '100' = 8144 bytes; '101' = 11407 bytes; '110' = 17800 bytes; '111' = used in all-routes broadcast frames.

Route Descriptor

Ring Number = Unique ring number in a multiring network.

Bridge Number = Unique bridge number on a given ring.

FIGURE 3.20 The format of the routing information fields.

3.6.3 Insertion Phases and the Ring Poll Process

If I asked you, "How does a station attach to an Ethernet?" you would quickly answer, "Power it on!" But what if I ask how a station attaches to a Token Ring?

To become a participant in a Token Ring, the "insertion" process is a bit more complicated than Ethernet. There are five basic steps to make this happen:

1. *Lobe test.* The lobe wire is the cable from the point of attachment to the back of a NIC card all the way to the hub or concentrator. When a NIC driver is loaded and the Token Ring adapter is activated, the adapter sends a frame addressed to itself. The frame loops back to the hub because the station is not yet physically inserted into the ring. If the frame is received with no CRC error, the NIC applies a small DC voltage known as the "phantom" signal to activate a relay at the hub port. Upon activation, the station begins to repeat bits and proceeds to step 2.

2. *Monitor check.* An Active Monitor needs to be present on the ring. If the station sees an Active Monitor Present (AMP) or Standby Monitor Present (SMP) frame, it assumes that an Active Monitor is on the ring and proceeds to step 3. If not, it attempts to become the Active Monitor.

3. *Duplicate address check.* From here on, this process can be captured with a protocol analyzer, as shown in Figure 3.21, by setting the capture filter on a specific station's MAC address. Once again, the station sends a frame (actually two frames for good measure; see frames 1 and 2 in the figure and note that this is a locally administered address) to itself. Remember the address recognized bit in the Frame Status byte at the end of the frame? If this bit is set when the frame goes around the ring, the station knows that another station has that MAC address. If the MAC address is not in use, the station proceeds to step 4; otherwise, it deinserts from the ring.

4. *Participate in neighbor notification or ring poll.* This is the Active Monitor/Standby Monitor process that happens every 7 seconds. The station that's the current Active Monitor on the ring initiates the ring poll by sending an Active Monitor Present frame. From there, subsequent stations send out their Standby Monitor Present frames. From this process, a newly inserted station learns its upstream neighbor. This is required to report errors for fault isolation purposes. Note that in Figure 3.21 the station also sends out a frame to the Configuration Report Server (functional address hex C000000010) to indicate that there's been a change in upstream neighbors.

How does a station know when to send out a Standby Monitor Present frame? As soon as it sees an Active Monitor Present frame? At random? As it turns out, the process is very orderly such that when you capture AMP and SMP frames with a protocol analyzer, the frames are in the exact physical order in which the stations are inserted around the ring. A sample ring poll is illustrated in the analyzer trace in Figure 3.22, which shows two ring polls with a total of 12 stations on the ring.

The ring poll process begins with the Active Monitor sending out the AMP frame, as highlighted in Figure 3.22. The AMP frame is sent

```
Network Monitor - [c:\WINDOWS\Desktop\Steve01.cap [Detail]]          _ □ ×
File  Edit  Display  Tools  Options  Window  Help                    _ 8 ×

Frame  Time   Dst MAC Addr                 Src MAC Addr  Protocol  Description
1      0.000  40000045D817                 40000045D817  TMAC      Duplicate Address Test
2      0.000  40000045D817                 40000045D817  TMAC      Duplicate Address Test
3      0.057  *Configuration Report Server 40000045D817  TMAC      Report NAUN Change
4      0.016  *MAC Active Monitor Present   40000045D817  TMAC      Standby Monitor Present
5      0.000  *Ring Parameter Server        40000045D817  TMAC      Request Initialization
6      0.044  40000045D817                 40002122B194  TMAC      Initialize Ring Station
7      0.000  40002122B194                 40000045D817  TMAC      Response

⊕FRAME: Base frame properties
⇒TOKENRING: Length =  26, Priority Normal (No token) MAC Frame
 ⊕TOKENRING: Access control = 16 (0x10) Original, Frame, Priority: Normal (No token)
 ⊕TOKENRING: Frame control = 0 (0x00), MAC Frame, buffer priority = 0
 ⊕TOKENRING: Destination address : 40000045D817
 ⊕TOKENRING: Source address      : 40002122B194
  TOKENRING: Frame length : 26 (0x001A)
  TOKENRING: Tokenring data: Number of data bytes remaining = 12 (0x000C)
⇒TMAC: Initialize Ring Station
  TMAC: Command = Initialize Ring Station
  TMAC: Source Class = Ring Parameter Server
  TMAC: Destination Class = Ring Station
 ⇒TMAC: Subvector: Correlator 0xD
   TMAC: Subvector Command = Correlator
   TMAC: Correlator = 13 (0xD)
 ⇒TMAC: Subvector: Local Ring Number 0x22B
   TMAC: Subvector Command = Local Ring Number
   TMAC: Ring Number = 555 (0x22B)

00000000  10 00 40 00 00 45 D8 17 40 00 21 22 B1 94 00 0C   ..@..E+.@.!";ö..
00000010  05 0D 04 09 00 0D 04 03 02 2B                     ........+

Ring number of the sending ring station.       F#: 6/377        Off: 24 (x18)    L: 2 (x2)
```

FIGURE 3.21 A Token Ring station completing the insertion process.

to the local ring broadcast address of hex C000FFFFFFFF and contains the address of the upstream neighbor. Notice in the figure that the Active Monitor is reporting the address of the last station in the ring poll. All stations receive this broadcast, and the first station downstream from the Active Monitor sets the address recognized and frame copied bits in the Frame Status as the frame is repeated.

Because the address recognized bit was 0 before receiving the frame, the station knows that its neighbor is the Active Monitor. It remembers its neighbor's MAC address and queues up an SMP frame. The other stations do not queue up an SMP frame because the address recognized bit was already set.

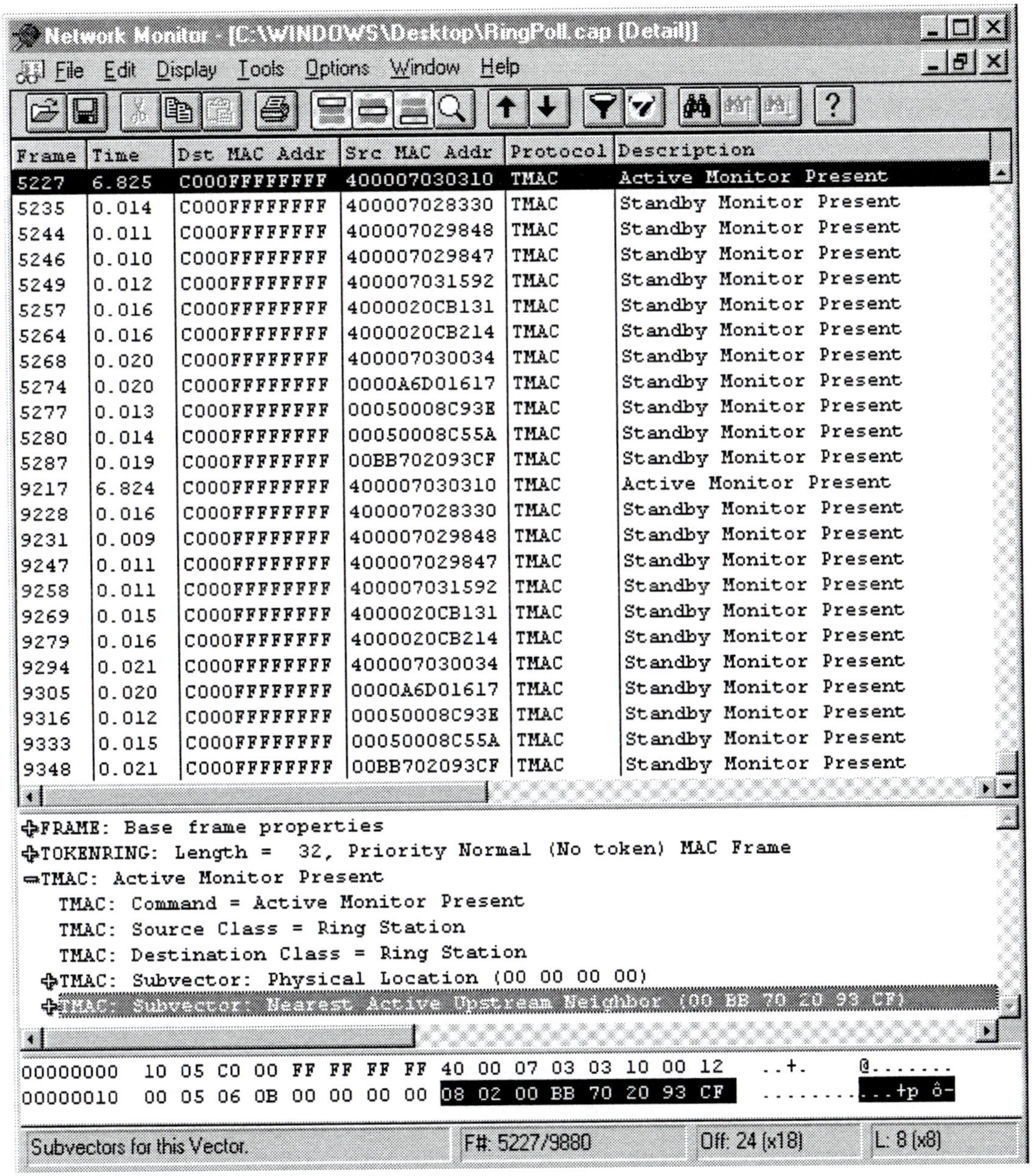

FIGURE 3.22 A ring poll.

The station then sends the SMP frame at the next token opportunity. The station downstream sees the frame, sets the address recognized bit and queues up an SMP frame, and the process continues to

the last station in the ring, just prior to the Active Monitor. The Active
Monitor knows that the process is complete when it sees an SMP
frame without the address recognized bit set.

5. *Request Initialization.* The station sends a "Request Initialization" MAC
   frame to the functional address (hex C00000000002) of a Ring
   Parameter Server (RPS). The MAC frame includes the station's
   Nearest Active Upstream Neighbor (NAUN) and other information
   such as the microcode level of the NIC card or the version of the
   adapter's NIC driver. If an RPS is on the ring, it sends a MAC frame
   back to the station containing one or more of the following pieces of
   information: the ring number the station is on, the soft error report
   timer (the default is 2 seconds), and/or the physical location. In Figure
   3.21, the station responding to the functional address of the Ring
   Parameter Server in frame number 5 is returning the ring number in
   frame number 6.

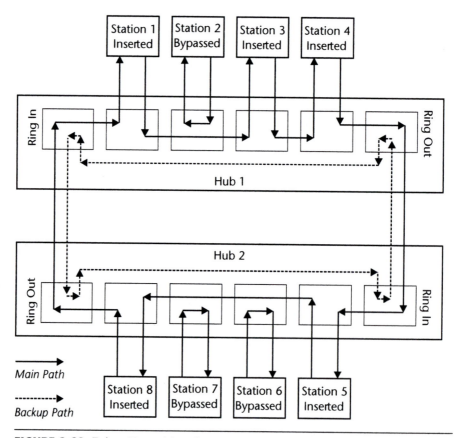

FIGURE 3.23 Token Ring wiring showing inserted and deinserted stations.

Bridges and switches with source routing enabled as well as certain managed Token Ring hubs can act as Ring Parameter Servers. Usually the only information the RPS provides is the ring number.

Getting RPS information is one of those rare Token Ring protocols that actually takes advantage of the AR and FC bits. When a station receives a frame in response from the RPS, the RPS checks the returned AR and FC bits in the frame just sent. If both bits are not set, meaning the station recognized its address and was able to copy the frame, the RPS actually sends the frame again.

Similarly, if a station sees that a station set the AR bit in the original Request Initialization MAC frame sent to the RPS functional address, it expects a reply. If none is received, it retries several times. If no response is received, the station deinserts from the ring. I've seen this happen with some early Token Ring adapters with Windows 95 that were actually recognizing the RPS address but, of course, were not really Ring Parameter Servers. This prevented other stations from inserting into the ring because the RPS process never completed.

If there is an RPS, the station sends a "MAC ack" back to the RPS (frame 7 in Figure 3.21). If there is not an RPS, the station sends one more Request Initialization frame. If there is no response and the AR bit is not set, the station assumes that there is no RPS and stays on the ring.

Whew, insertion complete!

Figure 3.23 shows two Token Ring hubs with inserted as well as deinserted stations.

3.6.4 Roles of the Active Monitor and Standby Monitor

The Active Monitor plays an important role in keeping the ring poll process going, but it needs to perform other important functions as well.

In Token Ring, every station's receiver is clocked off the Active Monitor. All other stations (Standby Monitors) compare the receiver's clock with an internal reference for 4 Mbps or 16 Mbps. I have yet to see a Token Ring NIC that does not agree with the Active Monitor clocking, other than trying to insert at the wrong speed. But for normal operation, variance in the clocking does not seem to be an issue.

There are problems, however, with a phenomenon known as jitter. Jitter occurs when the signaling becomes distorted as bits are repeated around the ring. It is primarily for this reason that Token Rings are limited to 250 nodes. Some of the first Token Ring NICs had jitter problems that prevented more than a few dozen nodes from working on the ring. Some vendors offer stand-alone or hub-based retiming modules. One of the drawbacks to a retiming module is that each one counts as a station in the node budget, taking away from the 250-station maximum.

The Active Monitor must also check for frames that go around the ring more than once. It is the responsibility of the sender of the frame to strip it as well. If the sender should die after it sends a frame but before it strips it from the ring, the frame could circulate forever. Setting the M bit in the Access Control field of a frame as it passes through the Active Monitor allows the Active Monitor to check it next time the frame is received. A frame with the M bit set will be stripped by the Active Monitor. If such is the case, the Active Monitor then sends out a "Ring Purge" MAC frame and releases a new token.

Another responsibility of the Active Monitor is to make sure that there is always a token circulating on the ring. If not, once again the Active Monitor sends out a "Ring Purge" frame and releases a new token.

As noted earlier, a token can have priority bits associated with it. If a token circulates more than once (i.e., it was not used by a station), the M bit will be set. If the M bit is set and the priority bits are nonzero, (you guessed it) the Active Monitor sends out a "Ring Purge" frame and releases a new token.

Both the Active Monitor and Standby Monitors (all of the other stations) are responsible for watching for signal loss. Standby Monitors are also responsible for ensuring that there's always an Active Monitor on the ring.

If the master (the Active Monitor) dies, the slaves (the Standby Monitors) get a chance to become the master. The first slave to detect the loss of an Active Monitor Present frame sends out a Claim Token frame. The name "Claim Token" is very misleading because the slave is not really asking for a token, but rather to become the master. If another station on the ring has a higher MAC address than the source address in the Claim Token frame, that station is allowed to send a Claim Token frame. The slave with the lower address stops sending Claim Token frames. This process continues for a brief amount of time in which a new Active Monitor, the station with the highest MAC address, is "elected."

Does it matter who the Active Monitor is on the ring? Not really, provided that the Active Monitor is highly reliable. A worst-case scenario would be to have an unreliable NIC with a high address. Then, the Active Monitor would be unstable. Remember, a station attempting to insert into the ring must see an Active Monitor or it won't get in. For stations already in, the ring poll process is not necessary for them to continue to send data frames.

3.6.5 Access Priority and Early Token Release

Why is prioritization necessary in Token Ring? Because the protocol is "too fair." Imagine 100 workstations on a ring with frames in their transmit queues. The bridge would only be able to get rid of one frame from its transmit queue for every 100 frames the workstations transmitted, eventually leading to an overflow in the transmit buffer of the bridge as it tries to get frames back to the users. After all, the 100 frames that went out over the bridge had to get some response frames at some point.

In every token and frame, there are priority and reservation bits in the Access Control byte (refer back to Figure 3.19). In the event that a station has a frame to send, it can look at the next Access Control byte that passes through. If it isn't a free token, the station can set the reservation bits to, say, 100, on the fly. Then, the station that strips the frame (the sender) releases a token with the priority bits set to 100, or priority 4 (the recommended priority for a bridge). Then only stations downstream with a priority of 4 or higher can use the token.

Is it possible for another station to use the prioritized token before the station that requested it? Absolutely. In this case, the station that wanted it in the first place must request it again.

> When a high priority token is used in a frame, the frame's priority bits are set. By setting a bit filter in your protocol analyzer to check that the first three bits of the Access Control field are set to a nonzero value, you can see if priority tokens are being used in your ring. If so, the busier the ring, the more priority frames you will see. Not all protocol analyzers have bit filters, but this is a case in which one comes in handy.

One final note regarding prioritization: The station that set the priority bits at another station's request is responsible for bringing the priority back down to its previous level. Thus you can have different priorities on successive passes of the token. Note that if every station on the ring was set to the same higher priority, it's obviously the same as having no priority at all.

Early token release is a way for a station to release a token immediately after sending a frame, to increase the data transmission efficiency when the frame is shorter than the latency in the ring. Early token release was introduced with the 16 Mbps Token Ring.

Recall that several factors, including cable length and number of active stations, can affect latency in a ring. If it takes, say, 480 bits (60 bytes) of transmission before you see your frame header come back and the frame is only 320 bits (40 bytes) long, what do you do for the remaining 160 bits? Send idle bits. Because you're wasting about a third of the bandwidth, you'd be better off releasing the token right away.

Big problem: Early token release interferes with the priority reservation mechanism. If a station sets the reservation bits in a frame and the sender already released the token, too bad! Thus priority reservation works best when you have larger frames on the ring.

My preference is to have a combination of early token release *and* to write the drivers to legally send up to 18,200 bytes worth of frames per token on 16 Mbps rings.

3.6.6 Case Study: High Rate of Packet Retransmissions

In a nutshell, the basic problem was that users located on busier ring segments throughout a large corporate network were experiencing an abnormally high rate of packet retransmissions. The user rings were connected via switches back to a server farm.

By tracing the packets to and from the server, I determined that most of the time, request packets got to the servers, but the responses didn't always make it back to the local user rings. It looked like the workgroup switches that serviced the local user rings were dropping packets whenever there was a burst of packets (such as a NetWare Packet Burst file transfer from a server to a workstation) or the server was sending back several packets to multiple workstations.

To more precisely measure the loss rate, I set up a switch in a lab environment with traffic generators and protocol analyzers. My motivation for conducting such switch lab tests was not to closely simulate the production environment per se, but rather to test the conditions under which a switch would drop packets in order to better understand under what type of conditions the production network might drop packets.

I ran several tests consisting of sending a total of one hundred 1 Kbyte frames at 1 millisecond intervals. This was a short burst of about 100K of traffic (approximately 2/10 of a second on a 4 Mbps ring) that nearly saturated a 4 Mbps ring (over 90 percent utilization) during this brief period of time. I was most interested in knowing the total amount of data in the short burst (100K) rather than the total number of packets transmitted in order to determine approximately how much transmit buffer there was for a given ring port on the switch. These tests reflect similar conditions in which there are brief bursts of packets in the production environment.

By measuring packet loss, I was surprised to discover that the transmit buffer for each port (i.e., the output port to a user ring) was in the neighborhood of only 30K to 40K bytes and concluded that it was a major contributing factor to packet loss.

Short of dedicating a switch port for each user or limiting the node count on a ring to a very small number (say, 10 stations or less), there are several, more practical ways to accommodate the bursty fluctuations in traffic destined for a given segment. Because LANs are bursty in nature, this is a critical issue.

Also, I didn't want to eliminate broadcast traffic that tends to fill switch buffers nor cripple protocols like FTP file transfers or NetWare packet bursts by limiting them to a one-to-one window that would decrease response time. Thus a more desirable solution was to attempt to tune the switches.

One solution was to allocate more buffer space to the transmit queue of a switch port. This memory "tuning" is common practice in switches and routers, either by sharing dynamically allocated memory from a large memory pool or by expanding the physical memory. Unfortunately the port memory on this particular switch from a well-known network vendor was fixed, so I hit a dead end with this option.

Referring back to the IEEE 802.1D bridging standard, the recommended value for the maximum bridge transit delay is 1.0 second. The maximum bridge transit delay is defined as "the maximum time elapsing between reception and transmission by a bridge of forwarded frames, frames that would otherwise exceed this limit being discarded."

The transmit buffer must be able to accommodate a modest queuing of frames during times of brief fluctuations in traffic that lead to momentary congestion (filling of the transmit buffer). In theory, the bridge in this case should have been able to queue up about one second's worth of data, or about 500K bytes at 4 Mbps.

Not having the option to increase or reallocate memory, I looked at implementing token priority reservation, allowing the bridge more frequent access to the ring. In fact, both the IEEE 802.5 standard and the IBM Token Ring Architecture Reference recommend that bridges operate at a priority of binary 100 or 4, as noted earlier in this chapter.

Guess what? The switch did not have the option to implement priority reservation!

That brought me to solution number three: sending multiple frames per token. Having this feature would certainly help empty the transmit buffers faster. Did the switch have this capability? Nope.

So I was caught in a difficult situation and had to pay very close attention to reducing the broadcast traffic going to all rings that would also contribute to filling up the switch port buffers and to the traffic load on each ring, relying on upper layer protocols to recover from dropped packets. In some cases, users could be moved to rings with lower utilization. This would have to do until a longer term solution with more up-to-date switching technology could be deployed. Adding more switches and ports was not an option at the time.

3.6.7 Token Ring Soft and Hard Errors

By definition, soft errors are intermittent glitches that cause data corruption. Hard errors result in a more serious ring disruption that prevents tokens and frames from circulating. This causes a station to send out a series of "beacon" frames. Some beaconing ring states cannot be recovered from automatically; they require the manual removal of the offending component(s). Token Ring errors can be classified into isolating and nonisolating categories.

Isolating Errors

Isolating errors are those that can be isolated to a given fault domain, which includes a station, its upstream neighbor, and the wire between them. For example, if a station detects a CRC error of any frame as it is repeated through that station (yes, every station is a repeater in Token Ring), it sets the E, or error, bit in the Frame Status byte at the end of the frame. Approximately 2 seconds later, a Soft Error Report MAC frame is sent by the station that detected the error to the functional address (hex C00000000008) of the Ring Error Monitor. Usually a bridge or switch maintains error statistics in a proprietary error table or an SNMP Token Ring MIB that is accessible via an SNMP console. Having a protocol analyzer on the ring is, of course, another way to monitor these errors. Figure 3.24 shows a protocol analyzer's detail of a soft error MAC frame, including a breakdown of each error count.

The error report frame contains the MAC address of the reporting station's upstream neighbor. This information forms the "fault domain." The CRC error could have occurred at any location between the upstream neighbor's transmitter and the reporting station's receiver. Thus it could be a bad transmitter, bad lobe cable, bad cable to the hub, bad hub, bad cable from the hub, a bad cross-connect patch cable, a bad receiver, and so on. By bad cable, I mean a cable that doesn't meet the spec for 4 Mbps or 16 Mbps operation, is incorrectly wired (split pair, for instance), is picking up environment noise, and so on. By the way, these CRC errors are also called *line errors* because errors in code violations in the token or frame delimiters can be detected as well. The high line error count reported by the station in Figure 3.24 was attributable to split pair wiring to that station.

> **!**
>
> When Token Ring users began migrating from the IBM Shield Twisted Pair (STP) wiring system to Unshielded Twisted Pair (UTP) wiring such as Category 3 telephone wire or Category 5 cabling, Type 3 media filters had to be used to bridge the impedance mismatch between STP and UTP. Not having a media filter can lead to a high rate of line errors. One user actually replaced a Token Ring NIC card several times before realizing that a media filter was required.

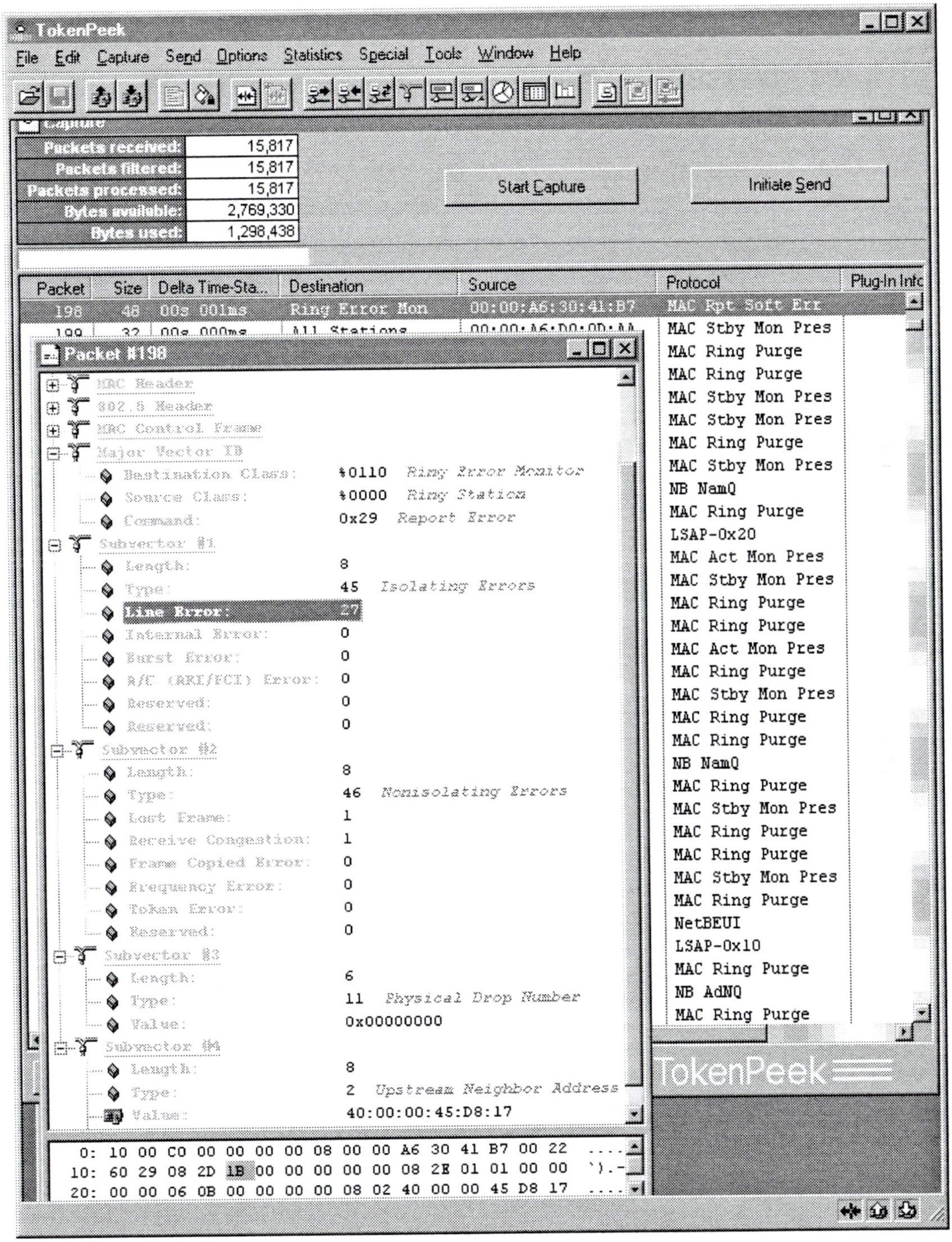

FIGURE 3.24 A soft error report MAC frame.

Another type of isolating error is a *burst error*. Burst errors are a brief absence of a signal (2-1/2 bits) that are usually the result of stations entering and exiting the ring and wrecking a frame in the process. Burst errors are the most commonly seen errors in Token Ring.

Other isolating errors include internal errors, A/C errors, and abort errors. *Internal errors* are when the NIC recognizes a problem internal to itself. Failing NICs can send these error notifications via the Soft Error Report MAC frame. Another cause I've seen is DMA conflicts. Internal errors should be investigated immediately because they impact the end-user or server of that NIC.

A/C errors occur when a station sees consecutive SMP frames with the AR and FC bits set to 0, or an AMP with AR and FC bits set to 0, followed by an SMP frame with the AR and FC bits set to 0. *Abort errors* occur when a station stops a frame transmission before completion. This can occur if a station has a temporary internal error and stays on the ring, if the station detects a permanent internal problem and removes itself from the ring, or if a token is detected in which the third byte is not an ending delimiter.

Nonisolating Errors

The errors defined as nonisolating include lost frame, receiver congestion (discussed earlier), frame copied, frequency error (the master clock deviates from 4 Mbps or 16 Mbps), and token error.

Only the Active Monitor sends out a lost frame or token error Soft Error Report MAC frame. A token error is reported when the Active Monitor had to "purge" the ring by sending a Ring Purge MAC frame, followed by an Active Monitor Present frame to start the ring poll process. A frame copied error is reported when a station detects a frame with its source address, but another station already set the AR bit.

> **!**
>
> Unlike Ethernet where you can monitor CRC errors in real time as they happen, errors on Token Ring are reported 2 seconds later via a Soft Error Report MAC frame. For example, the Active Monitor is the only station that can send Ring Purge MAC frames. Therefore, when you see a Ring Purge frame in the analyzer, be sure to check 2 seconds *later* in the packet buffer for a Soft Error Report MAC frame from the Active Monitor to determine the reason for the Ring Purge.

> ❗ It is also important to realize that stations maintain error counters for each error type that's been mentioned. Therefore, when you see a Soft Error Report MAC frame, look inside to see if there is more than one error type and more than one error for that error type being reported.

3.6.8 Fault Isolation and Recovery

Line errors and burst errors are recoverable. What about a total loss of signal? Figure 3.25 shows three scenarios for signal loss in a Token Ring.

In scenario 1, a broken cable between hubs, station 190 downstream from the break detects a loss of signal within 200 to 250 ms. Station 190 sends out a Ring Purge MAC frame if it's the Active Monitor, or a Claim Token MAC frame to try to initiate a ring poll. Obviously neither frame will make it around the ring. Station 190 then sends a Beacon MAC frame, with station 201 as its upstream neighbor.

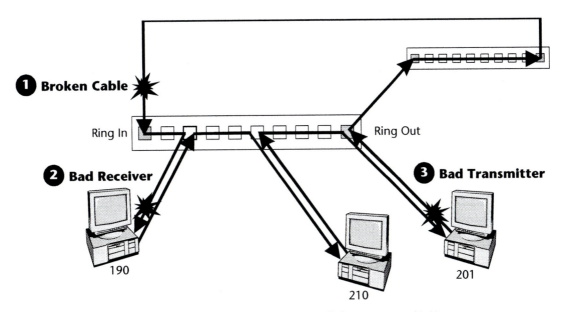

Station 190 is downstream from the signal loss in all three cases and initiates recovery.

FIGURE 3.25 Three Token Ring signal loss scenarios.

When a station sees a Beacon frame with its address as the upstream neighbor, it deinserts from the ring and does a self-test on its adapter and lobe wire. If both pass, it comes back into the ring. In scenario 1, station 201 comes back into the ring, and station 190 continues to beacon for a while. Then station 190 drops off, self-tests okay, and comes back on the ring. After this, station 190 continues to beacon indefinitely (this is also known as a Type 2 beacon) until the cable between the two hubs is fixed or pulled from both hubs, causing the ring-in and ring-out ports to wrap inside the hubs. This causes the main ring path to wrap onto the backup path, as depicted in Figure 3.26.

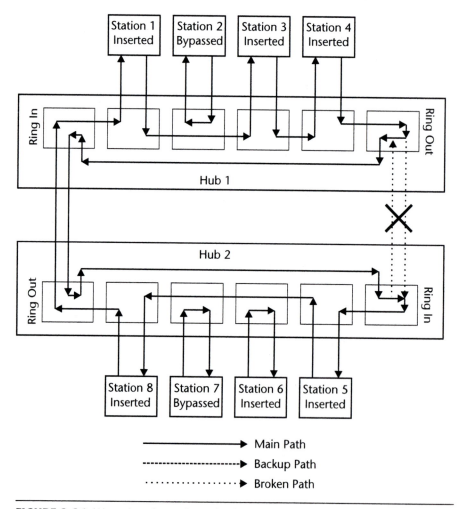

FIGURE 3.26 Wrapping the main path after a cable fault.

This is a real example of what happens when using "dumb" or passive hubs such as the original IBM 8220 hub or equivalent. "Smart" Token Ring hubs are able to automatically wrap the ring-in and ring-out ports between the two hubs with the defective wire. This is done by assigning a MAC layer to each ring-in and ring-out port (thus, a Smart hub has two MAC addresses assigned to it). The hub MAC layers then detect faults just like a station.

In scenario 2, a bad receiver at station 190, the same recovery process is initiated by station 190. This time, however, station 190 won't pass the self-test and it stays off the ring. Note that the instant 190 drops off, the ring completes and recovers.

In scenario 3, a bad transmitter at station 201, station 190 again detects the signal loss and initiates the recovery. This time, station 201 doesn't pass its self-test and it stays off the ring.

So which one of these is the worst case scenario? Obviously it's the broken hub-to-hub cable that requires manual fixing if using a passive hub. What about between scenarios 2 and 3?

In scenario 2, station 190 has to wait several seconds to allow enough time for a downstream station to perform a self-test. Therefore, scenario 3 has the quickest recovery. Station 190 sends Claim Token frames for 1.0 to 1.2 seconds after detecting the signal loss before sending a beacon. Because a signal loss is detected in 200 to 250 milliseconds to begin with, the total recovery time is 250 ms + 1.2 seconds, or about a second and a half.

In scenario 2, station 190 can wait from 15.8 to 26 seconds before self-testing, so a defective receiver takes much longer to recover from than a defective transmitter.

> ❗ Token Ring health checks are simplified when setting your analyzer's capture filter on MAC frames and taking a snapshot of MAC traffic on a "problem" ring for a period of 15 minutes or so. This will capture the critical frames that maintain the ring—soft error reports, Nearest Active Upstream Neighbor (NAUN) change reports as stations enter and leave the ring, and, of course, the ring poll frames that should appear once every 7 seconds as long as no tokens or frames are lost due to burst or line errors. Setting a display filter on the Active Monitor and setting the timestamp to delta time (inter frame time) allows you to verify the 7-second interval.

There are a few other beaconing scenarios that are rare in Token Ring. If a station is stuck sending idle symbols ("fills"), the downstream station detects

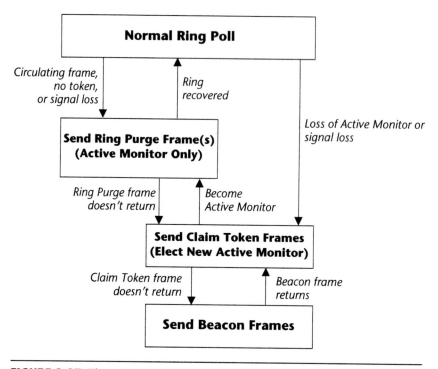

FIGURE 3.27 The various stages of ring recovery.

this and sends out Type 3 beacons. Likewise, if a station is stuck sending claim tokens, again the downstream station detects this and sends out Type 4 beacons. Type 1 beacons are for dual ring operation (which is in the 802.5 standard but not commercially implemented). Thus the most common type of beacon is the aforementioned Type 2 beacon.

Figure 3.27 summarizes the various stages of Token Ring recovery.

3.6.9 Calculating Network Utilization and Bandwidth Efficiency in Token Ring

Like Ethernet, the maximum packet rate on Token Ring depends on the packet size. For a 16 Mbps ring, you can take the 16 million bits per second and divide by 8 bits/byte to get 2 million bytes per second. Unlike Ethernet, no padding is required to meet a minimum frame size of 64 bytes. Token Ring frames can be less than 30 bytes in length for some protocols, such as LLC polling. If you only used 30 byte frames on your 16 Mbps Token Ring, you would have a theoretical frame rate of 2 million bytes/second of available bandwidth by 30 bytes/packet, for a total of 66,666 frames per second.

At the other extreme, using 18,200 byte frames, you would come up with a theoretical maximum of 109 frames per second.

Obviously the packet rate is much higher with smaller packets, but once again so is the overhead. The frame overhead in Token Ring is not as great as in Ethernet, but you can still have frame gaps due to token latency in the ring before you acquire the token and send data. Therefore, the best scenario for maximum Token Ring utilization is to have few stations on a short ring *or* several stations actively sending frames on a larger ring. This is the opposite in the case of Ethernet where less stations can use the bandwidth better. Unlike Token Ring, the probability of collisions in Ethernet increase with the number of stations, but also unlike Token Ring, an Ethernet station doesn't have to wait for a token in order to send data. It experiences just a relatively short interframe gap.

Typically you don't see half-duplex Token Rings with a couple of stations driving the bandwidth higher than about 50 to 75 percent. Like Ethernet, the bigger the frame, the better, in terms of using the maximum bandwidth.

3.6.10 Source Route Bridging

Another contribution IBM made to the LAN community was the concept of source routing at the data link control layer. The idea of source routing flew in the face of the transparent bridge/spanning tree community. After all, isn't routing a layer 3 function?

Recall that IBM's SNA does not have a dynamic routing protocol, relying instead on static defined tables to determine how frames are forwarded in a point-to-point SNA network. Historically SNA was largely a dial-up network from the user's perspective. With the advent of Token Ring and multiple rings bridged together in a LAN setting, it was no longer practical to define and maintain those static "routing" tables in all the bridges. Enter source routing.

Source routing joins the ranks along with Logical Link Control and Local Administered Addresses as yet another contribution IBM made to the networking industry primarily to facilitate support for their own proprietary SNA protocol. Source routing provides a means for a station on the ring to locate another resource on another ring. The originating source node must know the destination's MAC address in order for this to happen. In SNA, for instance, the MAC address of a token-attached 3745 Front End Processor (FEP) is preconfigured at the user's workstation.

In NetWare, a station transmits a Services Advertising Protocol (SAP) packet as a source route broadcast to find the "nearest" server. With IP, source routing is used whenever a station sends an ARP to locate a MAC address for an IP address on its own subnet.

There are two types of source route broadcast packets: single route and all routes. A single route appears only once on each ring when there are parallel bridges between rings. An all routes broadcast appears multiple times in the case of parallel bridges. If there are two or more bridges between every ring, the broadcast frames multiply exponentially.

The advantage of an all routes broadcast is that when the frames reach the destination, the destination has multiple paths to choose from to return the frame to the source. Usually the destination just takes the routing information from the first frame as the route to return on. The theory is that, over time, some frames will make it through before others on somewhat of a random basis, leading to some degree of load balancing with parallel bridges.

So you do have the advantage of load balancing that you don't have with transparent bridging using spanning tree. The load balancing in Token Ring is not that dynamic, however, because once the route is chosen, it doesn't change for the duration of the transactions between, say, a workstation and a server or a workstation and a router.

Figure 3.28 illustrates how each bridge adds the ring and bridge number to a frame as it traverses the network (a source route broadcast frame actually grows in size as it passes through a bridge).

Unlike the example in Figure 3.28, with single route broadcasts, only one bridge per ring is traversed by a source route broadcast frame. The bridge can be manually designated (the old way) as the single route broadcast forwarding bridge or automatically designated (the new way) by using the spanning tree algorithm to select the single route broadcast bridge. Source route bridging is, in fact, now a part of the IEEE 801.1D standard as an annex. In the standard, a single route source route broadcast is known as a Spanning Tree Explorer, or STE, frame.

Figure 3.29 shows a single route broadcast packet (as decoded by Network Instruments Distributed Observer) that has gone through three bridges. The direction bit is set to 0, meaning that the frame originated on ring number hex B0F and ended up (where it was captured) on ring number hex 207. This is an IP RIP packet that was broadcast by a router on the backbone ring B07. Note that you can have the same bridge numbers throughout your source-routed network as long as you don't have two bridges with the same bridge number on the same ring.

During the source route broadcast process, the bridges also adjust the maximum frame length field downward, if necessary, as they forward the frame. In Figure 3.29, you can see that the maximum frame length or Token Ring MTU through all three bridges is 4472 bytes.

If you have parallel bridges but the stations used only single route broadcasts, you wouldn't have any load balancing; the frames would all pass

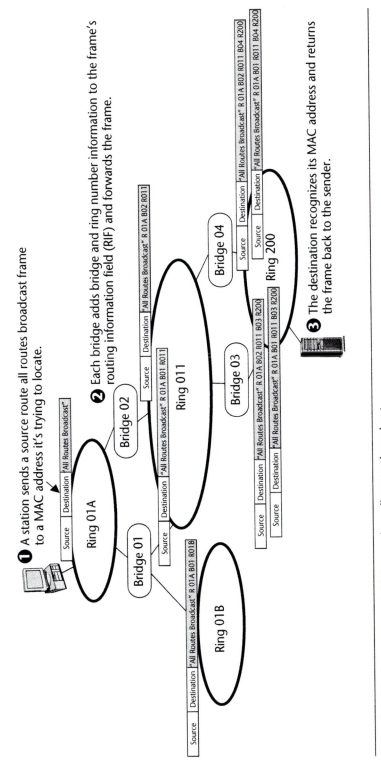

FIGURE 3.28 Source route bridging and an all routes broadcast.

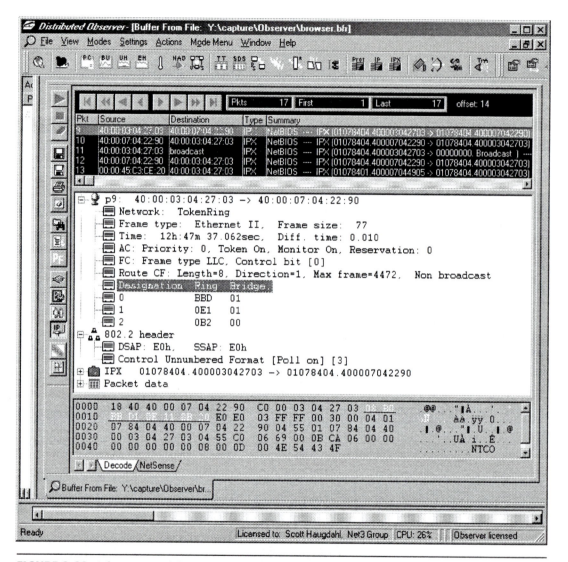

FIGURE 3.29 A frame containing a routing information field (RIF).

through the bridge selected by spanning tree, just like transparent bridging. There is an option for "single route broadcast with all routes return," but it doesn't work the way it sounds. The NIC drivers and protocol stacks are written to pick the first frame and return via the reverse route. So, take your pick: load balancing or extra broadcast traffic!

One thing I do like about source routing is that you can always trace the flow of the packet by looking at the source route information with your protocol analyzer. You always know which segment it came from, the intervening segments (and bridges) it passed through, and the segment it ends up on. Try figuring that out with a transparently bridged packet!

3.6.11 IEEE 802.2/Logical Link Control (LLC)

The IEEE 802.2 LLC standard is another one of those fairly complex standards, so I'll provide you with some of the "need to know" skinny on LLC when it comes to analyzing and troubleshooting.

First and foremost is that there are two types of LLC in widespread use: Type 1 connectionless and Type 2 connection-oriented. A third type defined by the standard, LLC Type 3 (essentially a connectionless protocol with acknowledgments), was never widely deployed.

Second, LLC Type 1 is really nothing more than a "stub" to multiplex or identify the next layer of protocol, as was discussed earlier in this chapter. The LLC Type 1 header is a mere 3 bytes long, with a "3" in the command field to indicate that the frame contains "Unnumbered Information." Figure 3.30 shows an example of a NetWare frame on Ethernet using an LLC Type 1 header.

Third, LLC Type 2 is only used by two major protocols today: SNA and NetBEUI (NetBIOS over LLC). Thus, when it comes to troubleshooting protocols associated with the LLC, you really only need to worry about SNA and NetBEUI.

LLC Type 2 is somewhat complex because it provides transport layer like functions, only at the DLC layer and without an intervening network layer. LLC includes sequence numbers, windowing, and error recovery mechanisms.

As shown in Figure 3.31, the LLC Type 2 header for a data frame (a.k.a. Information, or I, frame) includes send and receive sequence numbers along with a P/F, or poll/final, bit. The poll/final bit is used for two purposes:

1. It is set in an LLC poll that is periodically sent as a keep-alive frame when an LLC connection is not actively transferring data.
2. It is set in a data frame when the sender of an LLC frame wants an immediate acknowledgment from the recipient.

The use of 7 bits for the sequence numbers allows up to 127 LLC frames to be sent before an acknowledgment is required. Acknowledgments are sent back to the sender with the receive sequence number set to the *next* frame that the receiver expects from the sender.

Prior to a station's setting up an LLC connection, the sender notifies the destination of the maximum number of LLC frames it can receive, also known

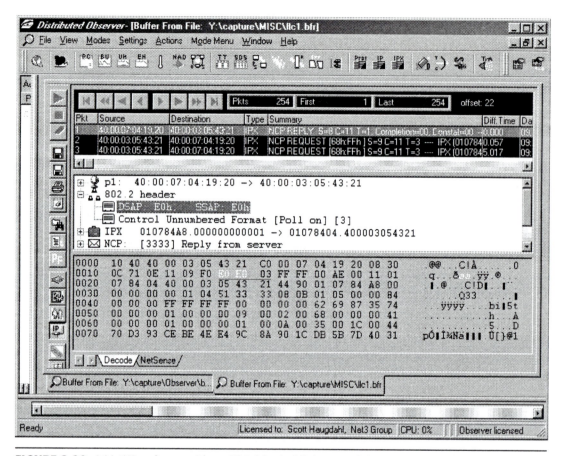

FIGURE 3.30 A NetWare frame with an 802.2 logical link control (LLC) Type 1, 3-byte header.

as the LLC window size, via an Exchange ID, or XID, LLC frame. In return, the window size of the destination is passed back to the sender. Then a "Set Asynchronous Balanced Mode Extended" (SABME) LLC frame is sent to establish the connection.

In early implementations of the OS/2 LAN Support Program, the LLC window size defaulted to 1. Because the OS/2 servers communicated with workstations using the Server Message Block (SMB) protocol over NetBEUI, *every* packet was acked at the LLC layer. On top (literally) of that, NetBIOS was acking every packet. Thus you had a situation of protocol layers not being aware of each other's capabilities, all doing their own acks and causing a rather excessive number of short packets to appear on the LAN.

Fortunately the LLC layer could be tuned to change the window and send an ack, say, every 8 packets instead of every single packet. Another optimization was to set a configuration flag in NetBIOS such that a NetBIOS ack

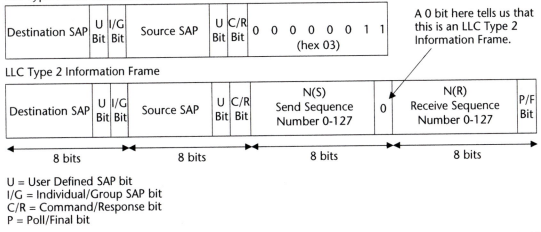

FIGURE 3.31 Logical link control (LLC) headers.

"piggy backs" an LLC ack, all in one packet, eliminating two separate acks. This "two for one" further reduced the number of small packets.

The latest OS/2 Warp drivers do a much better job of optimizing the various layers of protocol. Windows 95/98/NT also does a pretty good job of optimizing the NetBEUI protocols and it dynamically adjusts the LLC window size. In Figure 3.32, you can see that at client startup, the LLC layer uses Type 1 frames for NetBIOS name functions and for broadcasting a NETLOGON request looking for an NT server. A server responds to the NETLOGON request and then the client establishes an LLC Type 2 connection with the server. Initially the LLC acks are one for one with the NT server. Provided that no packets are dropped, the LLC window then opens up.

> ❗ Figure 3.32 shows a neat trick you can do with some protocol analyzers, including Sniffer and Network Monitor. By telling the analyzer to only show the decode in the summary window up to a certain layer, such as LLC, you can follow the transactions for that layer. In the figure, the same trace file was opened twice, showing the LLC layer summary side by side with the highest layer summary.

Both the LLC and IBM implementations of LLC will drop back to a window size of 1 if one or more LLC frames are dropped during an LLC session. Once acks are received again, the window size is eventually opened back up to its

Upper layer protocol view of Windows workstation boot using NetBIOS over LLC.

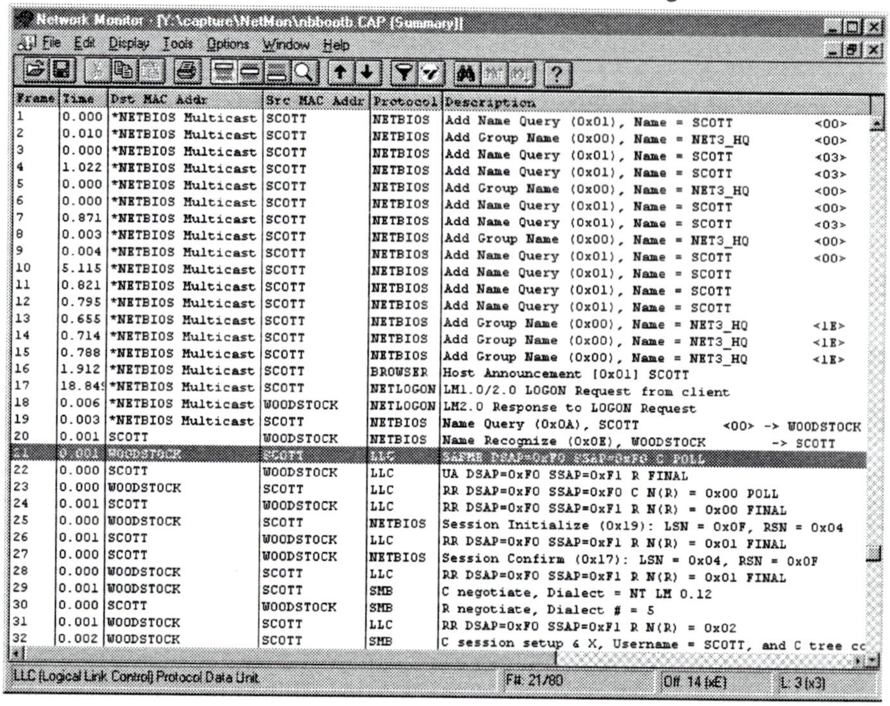
Network Monitor - [Y:\capture\NetMon\nbbootb.CAP (Summary)]
File Edit Display Tools Options Window Help
LLC (Logical Link Control) Protocol Data Unit
F#: 21/80
Off: 14 (xE)
L: 3 (x3)

Frame	Time	Dst MAC Addr	Src MAC Addr	Protocol	Description
1	0.000	*NETBIOS Multicast	SCOTT	NETBIOS	Add Name Query (0x01), Name = SCOTT <00>
2	0.010	*NETBIOS Multicast	SCOTT	NETBIOS	Add Group Name (0x00), Name = NET3_HQ <00>
3	0.000	*NETBIOS Multicast	SCOTT	NETBIOS	Add Name Query (0x01), Name = SCOTT <03>
4	1.022	*NETBIOS Multicast	SCOTT	NETBIOS	Add Name Query (0x01), Name = SCOTT <03>
5	0.000	*NETBIOS Multicast	SCOTT	NETBIOS	Add Group Name (0x00), Name = NET3_HQ <00>
6	0.000	*NETBIOS Multicast	SCOTT	NETBIOS	Add Name Query (0x01), Name = SCOTT <00>
7	0.871	*NETBIOS Multicast	SCOTT	NETBIOS	Add Name Query (0x01), Name = SCOTT <03>
8	0.003	*NETBIOS Multicast	SCOTT	NETBIOS	Add Group Name (0x00), Name = NET3_HQ <00>
9	0.004	*NETBIOS Multicast	SCOTT	NETBIOS	Add Name Query (0x01), Name = SCOTT <00>
10	5.115	*NETBIOS Multicast	SCOTT	NETBIOS	Add Name Query (0x01), Name = SCOTT
11	0.821	*NETBIOS Multicast	SCOTT	NETBIOS	Add Name Query (0x01), Name = SCOTT
12	0.795	*NETBIOS Multicast	SCOTT	NETBIOS	Add Name Query (0x01), Name = SCOTT
13	0.655	*NETBIOS Multicast	SCOTT	NETBIOS	Add Group Name (0x00), Name = NET3_HQ <1E>
14	0.714	*NETBIOS Multicast	SCOTT	NETBIOS	Add Group Name (0x00), Name = NET3_HQ <1E>
15	0.788	*NETBIOS Multicast	SCOTT	NETBIOS	Add Group Name (0x00), Name = NET3_HQ <1E>
16	1.912	*NETBIOS Multicast	SCOTT	BROWSER	Host Announcement [0x01] SCOTT
17	18.84	*NETBIOS Multicast	SCOTT	NETLOGON	LM1.0/2.0 LOGON Request from client
18	0.006	*NETBIOS Multicast	WOODSTOCK	NETLOGON	LM2.0 Response to LOGON Request
19	0.003	*NETBIOS Multicast	SCOTT	NETBIOS	Name Query (0x0A), SCOTT <00> -> WOODSTOCK
20	0.001	SCOTT	WOODSTOCK	NETBIOS	Name Recognize (0x0E), WOODSTOCK -> SCOTT
21	0.001	WOODSTOCK	SCOTT	LLC	SABME DSAP=0xF0 SSAP=0xF0 C POLL
22	0.000	SCOTT	WOODSTOCK	LLC	UA DSAP=0xF0 SSAP=0xF1 R FINAL
23	0.000	WOODSTOCK	SCOTT	LLC	RR DSAP=0xF0 SSAP=0xF0 C N(R) = 0x00 POLL
24	0.001	SCOTT	WOODSTOCK	LLC	RR DSAP=0xF0 SSAP=0xF1 R N(R) = 0x00 FINAL
25	0.000	WOODSTOCK	SCOTT	NETBIOS	Session Initialize (0x19): LSN = 0x0F, RSN = 0x04
26	0.001	SCOTT	WOODSTOCK	LLC	RR DSAP=0xF0 SSAP=0xF1 R N(R) = 0x01 FINAL
27	0.000	SCOTT	WOODSTOCK	NETBIOS	Session Confirm (0x17): LSN = 0x04, RSN = 0x0F
28	0.000	WOODSTOCK	SCOTT	LLC	RR DSAP=0xF0 SSAP=0xF1 R N(R) = 0x01 FINAL
29	0.001	WOODSTOCK	SCOTT	SMB	C negotiate, Dialect = NT LM 0.12
30	0.000	SCOTT	WOODSTOCK	SMB	R negotiate, Dialect # = 5
31	0.001	WOODSTOCK	SCOTT	LLC	RR DSAP=0xF0 SSAP=0xF1 R N(R) = 0x02
32	0.002	WOODSTOCK	SCOTT	SMB	C session setup & X, Username = SCOTT, and C tree cc

Same trace as above, only showing the underlying LLC activity.

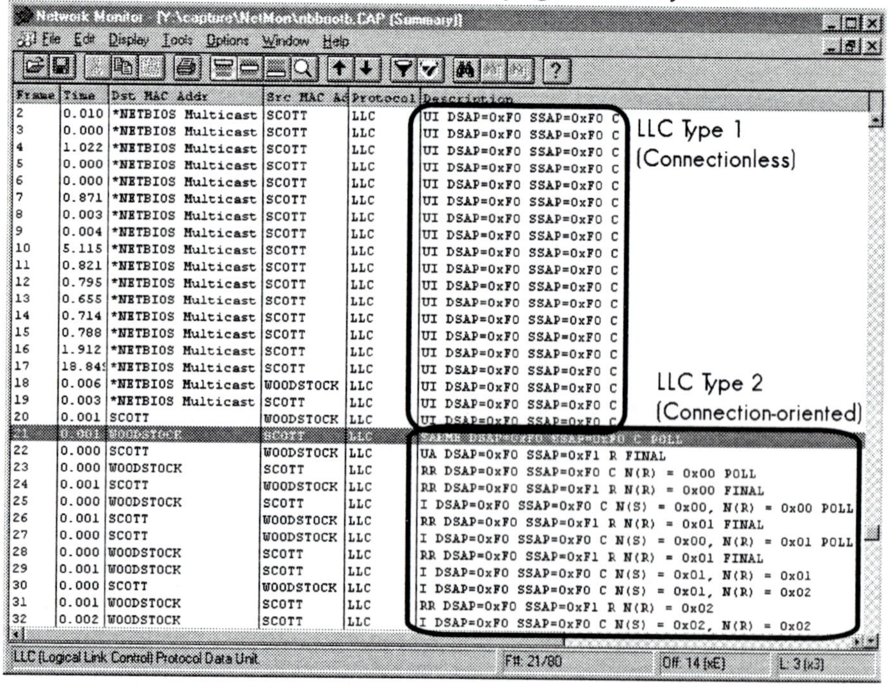
Network Monitor - [Y:\capture\NetMon\nbbootb.CAP (Summary)]
File Edit Display Tools Options Window Help
LLC Type 1
(Connectionless)
LLC Type 2
(Connection-oriented)
LLC (Logical Link Control) Protocol Data Unit
F#: 21/80
Off: 14 (xE)
L: 3 (x3)

Frame	Time	Dst MAC Addr	Src MAC Ad	Protocol	Description
2	0.010	*NETBIOS Multicast	SCOTT	LLC	UI DSAP=0xF0 SSAP=0xF0 C
3	0.000	*NETBIOS Multicast	SCOTT	LLC	UI DSAP=0xF0 SSAP=0xF0 C
4	1.022	*NETBIOS Multicast	SCOTT	LLC	UI DSAP=0xF0 SSAP=0xF0 C
5	0.000	*NETBIOS Multicast	SCOTT	LLC	UI DSAP=0xF0 SSAP=0xF0 C
6	0.000	*NETBIOS Multicast	SCOTT	LLC	UI DSAP=0xF0 SSAP=0xF0 C
7	0.871	*NETBIOS Multicast	SCOTT	LLC	UI DSAP=0xF0 SSAP=0xF0 C
8	0.003	*NETBIOS Multicast	SCOTT	LLC	UI DSAP=0xF0 SSAP=0xF0 C
9	0.004	*NETBIOS Multicast	SCOTT	LLC	UI DSAP=0xF0 SSAP=0xF0 C
10	5.115	*NETBIOS Multicast	SCOTT	LLC	UI DSAP=0xF0 SSAP=0xF0 C
11	0.821	*NETBIOS Multicast	SCOTT	LLC	UI DSAP=0xF0 SSAP=0xF0 C
12	0.795	*NETBIOS Multicast	SCOTT	LLC	UI DSAP=0xF0 SSAP=0xF0 C
13	0.655	*NETBIOS Multicast	SCOTT	LLC	UI DSAP=0xF0 SSAP=0xF0 C
14	0.714	*NETBIOS Multicast	SCOTT	LLC	UI DSAP=0xF0 SSAP=0xF0 C
15	0.788	*NETBIOS Multicast	SCOTT	LLC	UI DSAP=0xF0 SSAP=0xF0 C
16	1.912	*NETBIOS Multicast	SCOTT	LLC	UI DSAP=0xF0 SSAP=0xF0 C
17	18.84	*NETBIOS Multicast	SCOTT	LLC	UI DSAP=0xF0 SSAP=0xF0 C
18	0.006	*NETBIOS Multicast	WOODSTOCK	LLC	UI DSAP=0xF0 SSAP=0xF0 C
19	0.003	*NETBIOS Multicast	SCOTT	LLC	UI DSAP=0xF0 SSAP=0xF0 C
20	0.001	SCOTT	WOODSTOCK	LLC	UI DSAP=0xF0 SSAP=0xF0 C
21	0.001	WOODSTOCK	SCOTT	LLC	SABME DSAP=0xF0 SSAP=0xF0 C POLL
22	0.000	SCOTT	WOODSTOCK	LLC	UA DSAP=0xF0 SSAP=0xF1 R FINAL
23	0.000	WOODSTOCK	SCOTT	LLC	RR DSAP=0xF0 SSAP=0xF0 C N(R) = 0x00 POLL
24	0.001	SCOTT	WOODSTOCK	LLC	RR DSAP=0xF0 SSAP=0xF1 R N(R) = 0x00 FINAL
25	0.000	WOODSTOCK	SCOTT	LLC	I DSAP=0xF0 SSAP=0xF0 C N(S) = 0x00, N(R) = 0x00 POLL
26	0.001	SCOTT	WOODSTOCK	LLC	RR DSAP=0xF0 SSAP=0xF1 R N(R) = 0x01 FINAL
27	0.000	SCOTT	WOODSTOCK	LLC	I DSAP=0xF0 SSAP=0xF0 C N(S) = 0x00, N(R) = 0x01 POLL
28	0.000	WOODSTOCK	SCOTT	LLC	RR DSAP=0xF0 SSAP=0xF1 R N(R) = 0x01 FINAL
29	0.001	WOODSTOCK	SCOTT	LLC	I DSAP=0xF0 SSAP=0xF0 C N(S) = 0x01, N(R) = 0x01
30	0.000	SCOTT	WOODSTOCK	LLC	I DSAP=0xF0 SSAP=0xF0 C N(S) = 0x01, N(R) = 0x02
31	0.001	WOODSTOCK	SCOTT	LLC	RR DSAP=0xF0 SSAP=0xF1 R N(R) = 0x02
32	0.002	WOODSTOCK	SCOTT	LLC	I DSAP=0xF0 SSAP=0xF0 C N(S) = 0x02, N(R) = 0x02

FIGURE 3.32 LLC at startup in a Microsoft Windows environment.

original value. This provides a rudimentary method of flow control in the event of dropped packets or congestion. In the case of congestion, acks are delayed, causing the sending LLC layer to think that a packet has been dropped, and subsequently retreat back to an LLC window size of 1.

Here's one more thing you need to know about LLC Type 2: Some implementations cannot tolerate out of order frames. If a station receives an LLC frame with a sequence number of 196, then one with 198, then 197, it sends an LLC Frame Reject (FRMR) back to the sender. Normally the receiving LLC station should recover from this situation. Unfortunately some LLC implementations will follow the FRMR with an LLC Disconnect (DISC) frame and drop the connection, requiring the user to reestablish the session, such as a terminal session with a mainframe or AS/400.

Obviously, looking for FRMR LLC frames with your protocol analyzer is good practice in SNA and NetBEUI environments. The aforementioned problem is an example of a poorly implemented LLC, but there are several other reasons for an LLC reject frame:

1. The command or response LLC protocol is not defined.
2. A supervisory (such as XID) or unnumbered PDU contains information not permitted.
3. The LLC frame is too long.
4. The window has been exceeded (the sender sent too many packets before the receiver could ack).

For all the nitty-gritty details of the LLC protocol, the reader is referred to the IEEE 802.2 standard. This goes for Ethernet and Token Ring as well. If you have these protocols in your network, you have no excuse not to add these standards publications to your technical library.

Chapter 4

Analyzing and Troubleshooting the Network Layer

4.1 Introduction

The network layer plays a very important role in internetworking by providing the basic datagram packet that must be routed throughout the network to its destination. A datagram is a self-contained packet in that it has all the addressing information necessary to route the packet and for the packet to be recognized by its recipient. The real-world analogy to a datagram is a postal letter. You put an address on an envelope (the packet) to a recipient (the destination), supply a return address (the source), and put a sheet of paper with words on it (the data) inside the envelope.

Because datagram packets have no relationship to previous or future packets, the datagram services provided by the network layer are said to be stateless or connectionless. Datagrams can be sent at any time with no prior agreement or handshaking required with the destination. If there are redundant routes between the source and destination, sending multiple datagrams may cause them to arrive out of order.

In the postal system, if an envelope can't be delivered, it is discarded or returned to the sender, depending on the class of delivery. For example, a first-class letter might be returned with "unknown address" stamped on it. In an IP network, a router can return information about an undeliverable datagram via a protocol known as the Internet Control Message Protocol (ICMP). In an IPX network, an undeliverable datagram is treated as "junk mail" and discarded

A datagram may also contain a checksum, usually a 16-bit word. With IP, the checksum protects the header of the datagram only, not the data itself. In other network layer protocols like IPX and AppleTalk, the checksum protects the datagram header and payload.

As noted in Chapter 1, the end-to-end addressing of the network layer is independent of the DLC layer. Unlike the flat addressing of the DLC layer, a network layer internetwork address consists of network plus host identifiers. The network identifier can be flat like IPX or AppleTalk, broken up into subnets like IP, or hierarchical like DECnet.

4.2 Router Operation

For a sender to transmit a packet containing end-to-end network layer addressing, it must know the immediate DLC address of either the destination station if the destination is on the same network or a router if the destination is on a remote network. The way in which a sender finds this DLC address depends on the network protocol. How this works for IP and IPX is examined a bit later.

Likewise, for a router to forward a packet, it needs to know the DLC address of either the destination station if the destination is on the same network as one of the router ports or another intermediate router if the destination is on a remote network. The way in which a router finds local DLC addresses once again depends on the network protocol.

The way in which routers learn about other routers is via the Routing Information Protocol (RIP) or the Open Shortest Path First (OSPF) protocol, which propagates information about network identifiers to other routers. RIP packets are sent on a periodic basis—every 20 seconds for AppleTalk, every 30 seconds for IP, and every 60 seconds for IPX. With OSPF, small "keep alive" packets are sent periodically, with full routing information packets exchanged only upon router boot and with route table updates when there's a change in topology. Primarily for reasons of efficiency in large networks (with dozens of local and remote routers) or small to medium networks with several slower WAN links, OSPF is the preferred protocol to keep router tables up to date.

The basic operation of a router is illustrated in Figure 4.1. The addressing information is represented in a generic net.node format. The figure shows that the workstation addresses the packet to the DLC address of the router. The router receives the packet, buffers it, looks up the destination network address in a routing table to determine the destination port (port 4, in this case), and retransmits the packet to the DLC address of the server on that

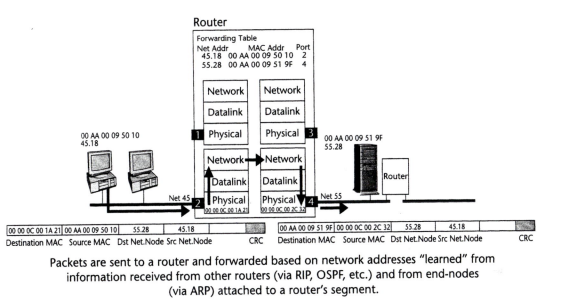

Packets are sent to a router and forwarded based on network addresses "learned" from information received from other routers (via RIP, OSPF, etc.) and from end-nodes (via ARP) attached to a router's segment.

FIGURE 4.1 Basic router operation.

port. If the server's network had been on the far side of the second router in the figure, the router would have addressed the packet to the DLC address of the second router. It is then the second router's responsibility to deliver the packet.

4.3 Network Layer Protocols

4.3.1 AppleTalk

The AppleTalk Phase 2 network layer contains a fixed 24-bit internetwork address consisting of a 16-bit network and 8-bit node component. The AppleTalk network of 0 (zero) can be used to specify the network to which the host is connected.

You can have a single AppleTalk network of 0 with up to 253 nodes. The 8-bit node count is limited to 253 rather than 256 because the node ID of 0 indicates any router on the network specified by the network ID, $FE is reserved on EtherTalk and TokenTalk networks and $FF is a broadcast to all nodes with that network ID. For the 16-bit network ID, the range of $FF00 through $FFFE (65,280 through 65,534) is reserved for the AppleTalk startup process.

At one time, all Macintosh computers and peripherals had built-in LocalTalk ports, a low-speed (230 Kbps) serial network that allowed up to 32 devices to be connected via telephone wire. LocalTalk is known as a "non-extended" AppleTalk network in which each node's 8-bit node ID is unique. Non-extended networks are assigned one network number and one zone name.

Now Macintosh computers and peripherals come with a built-in Ethernet interface. An extended AppleTalk network, required for Ethernet and Token Ring operation, has nodes that are differentiated by a unique network ID and node ID. Extended networks are assigned a range of network numbers and can have multiple zone names.

The way in which network addresses are assigned on an Ethernet or Token Ring is unique to AppleTalk. If a node is booted that has never been on the network, it starts with a "provisional" address with the network ID in the range of $FF00 to $FFFE and a random 8-bit node ID. The node then uses this address to talk to a router, and the Zone Information Protocol (ZIP) sends the router a "GetNetInfo" packet to obtain a range of network numbers as well as the AppleTalk multicast address (Ethernet) or functional address (Token Ring) for that range. If there is no router, the provisional address becomes the node's address.

If the node was previously started on the network, it uses its last network address stored in nonvolatile memory. The node then transmits an Apple-Talk Address Resolution Protocol (AARP) packet to the AppleTalk multicast address for the network range obtained from the router to make sure that no other node has that network and node ID combination.

If there is no reply to the AARP after ten tries (one AARP every 200 ms for a total of 2 seconds), the node can use that ID. If there is a response to the AARP indicating that the node ID is in use, another one is tried. If all the node IDs for a given network number are in use, the node can try another network number within its allowable range.

The core of the AppleTalk protocol for extended networks is the Datagram Delivery Protocol (DDP). The packet format for DDP is illustrated in Figure 4.2.

The first field is the hop count, which is incremented as an AppleTalk datagram is forwarded by a router. The hop count is 4 bits, which limits the total number of routed hops to 15.

The next field, the datagram length, is 10 bits, which theoretically allows you to have datagrams of up to 1024 bytes. AppleTalk, however, limits the maximum data portion of the datagram to 586 bytes.

The next field in the DDP datagram is the checksum. The DDP checksum covers the first byte following the checksum (the first byte of the destination network address) through the last byte in the datagram data. Many AppleTalk implementations, however, choose not to implement the checksum and set its

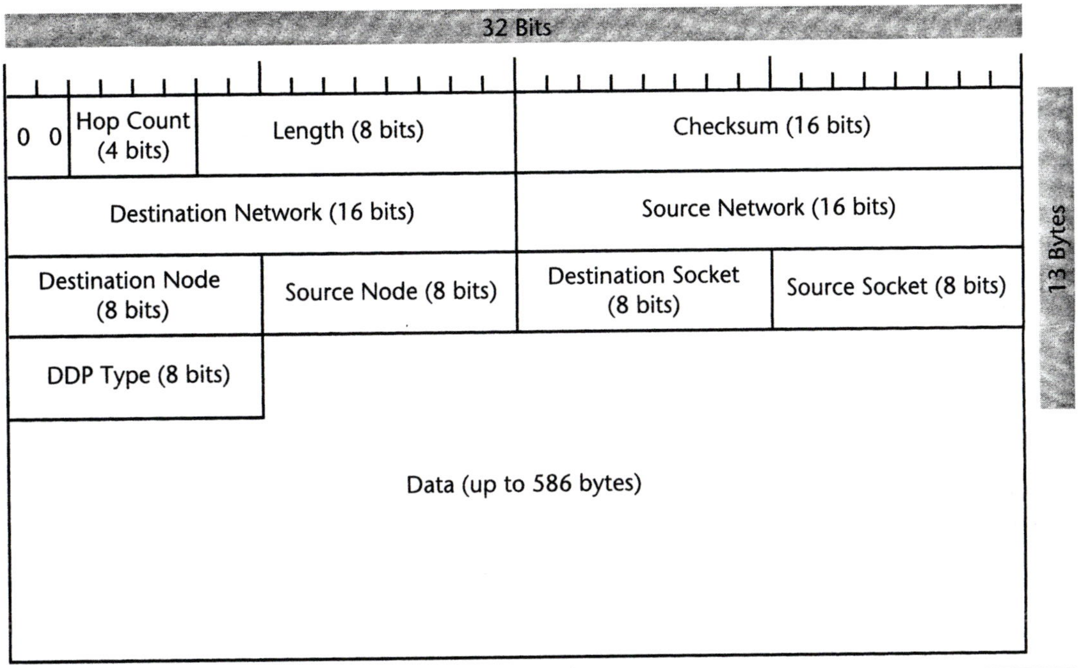

32 Bits			
0 0 Hop Count (4 bits)	Length (8 bits)	Checksum (16 bits)	
Destination Network (16 bits)		Source Network (16 bits)	
Destination Node (8 bits)	Source Node (8 bits)	Destination Socket (8 bits)	Source Socket (8 bits)
DDP Type (8 bits)			
Data (up to 586 bytes)			

13 Bytes

FIGURE 4.2 The AppleTalk Datagram Delivery Protocol (DDP) packet format.

> One of the major drawbacks to AppleTalk is that it can't take advantage of the larger MTU available on virtually every LAN and WAN topology in use today. For example, a 586-byte AppleTalk DDP packet using LLC SNAP encapsulation only uses a total of 608 bytes (including CRC), less than half of an Ethernet's allowable MTU of 1518 bytes. Moving to AppleShare IP, which uses TCP/IP as the transport and datagram delivery protocol, is one way to overcome this drawback.

value to zero, so don't assume that your AppleTalk packets are immune to storing and forwarding corruption inside switches and routers.

Next up is the network address, which is divided into the 16-bit destination and source network numbers and followed by the 8-bit destination and source node IDs.

AppleTalk datagrams are actually sent to sockets within end-nodes as identified by the 8-bit destination and source socket numbers. The protocol that receives the datagram above the network layer is identified by the 8-bit datagram type field. This is usually the layer 4 AppleTalk Transport Protocol (ATP) as identified by a DDP type of hex 03.

4.3.2 Case Study: AppleTalk Users Lose Server Visibility

As discussed earlier, once an AppleTalk node verifies its retained or provisional network address for uniqueness, it broadcasts the GetNetInfo ZIP packet. Any router listening for this packet will reply with the range of valid network numbers and the AppleTalk multicast or functional address for that range.

If a node was using the temporary provisional address, the router sends a reply to the AppleTalk DLC broadcast address because it doesn't know the route back to the startup range of $FF00 through $FFFE.

Upon capturing the packets from the boot-up of a server that the Macintosh users couldn't see in the Chooser, I looked at the trace and noticed that the server had started with a provisional address. Then, the server sent the GetNetInfo packet not once but *three* times, as if it didn't see the reply packets from the router. The reply packets were clearly in the trace buffer, and the analyzer captured the trace from the same network segment as the server. The server then proceeded to use the provisional address, thinking that no router was on the network.

Because the server was on a Token Ring, I suspected that the server wasn't programmed to receive packets sent to an AppleTalk functional address.

Luckily, good servers as well as the non-responding servers were located on the same ring. By sending a short burst of packets with an AppleTalk functional address as the destination address, I noticed that the good servers reported adapter receiver congestion (refer to Chapter 3 for more details), whereas the non-responding servers did not.

This helped to confirm my suspicion that the bad servers were not responding to the AppleTalk functional addresses. Thus the servers in question never obtained a network number from the router and proceeded to use the provisional network ID. Because the users had a different network ID, they could not communicate with the "bad" servers.

The problem was eventually isolated to a particular NIC card and NIC driver that had failed to work properly after upgrading the operating system to a new release. The "good" servers had a NIC card from a different vendor and worked regardless of the operating system release. Thus, by replacing the NIC card with the same type as used in the "good" servers, the problem was solved until the NIC issue could be resolved with the vendor.

4.3.3 DECnet

DECnet refers to a set of products that implement the Digital Network Architecture (DNA). Phase V of DNA, commonly referred to as DECnet Phase V, is the most recent implementation and is based on ISO protocols. Needless to say, ISO protocols never took off in the United States, and the majority of DECnet customers are still operating with Phase IV and migrating upper layer DECnet protocols to TCP/IP.

Along with the Phase IV release of DECnet in the early 1980s, the Local Area Terminal (LAT) protocol was released. LAT is an entirely different protocol separate from DECnet and runs directly encapsulated in the Ethernet frame, i.e., there are no network or transport layers for LAT. LAT is designed for terminal emulation over local Ethernets. To "route" the LAT protocol, Radia Perlman developed the concept of transparent bridging along with the spanning tree algorithm (as discussed in Chapter 3) to avoid loops between parallel bridges.

DECnet Phase IV divides an internetwork into areas. Up to 63 areas are possible with up to 1023 nodes per area. Routers that route within one area are known as level 1 routers, and routers that route to other areas are known as level 2 routers. Level 1 routers take some getting used to because they effectively break an Ethernet into two or more segments (up to 63) yet belong to the same area. This would be like running the same IP subnet on several different network segments, which isn't allowed.

DECnet Phase IV defines the network layer as the "routing layer". There are several different packet formats called "message types" such as the initialization message, level 1 and level 2 routing message, hello message, short and long data packet message, and so on.

The long data packet format as illustrated in Figure 4.3 is used in Ethernet. The first 16 bits constitutes the length field and is present for any DECnet message type. The length field counts from the first byte immediately following the length field to the end of the data.

Following the length field is an optional padding indicator. If the left-most bit of the first byte following the length field is set to 1, the remaining seven bits indicate how many optional pad bytes follow the packet header.

The next 8-bit fields are flags. Reading from left to right, the flags are defined as follows:

Bit 7: Set to 1 if padding follows.

Bit 6: Version (set to 0).

Bit 5: Set to 1 for Intra-Ethernet Packet.

Bit 4: Return to Sender (RTS). Set to 1 if packet is on return trip.

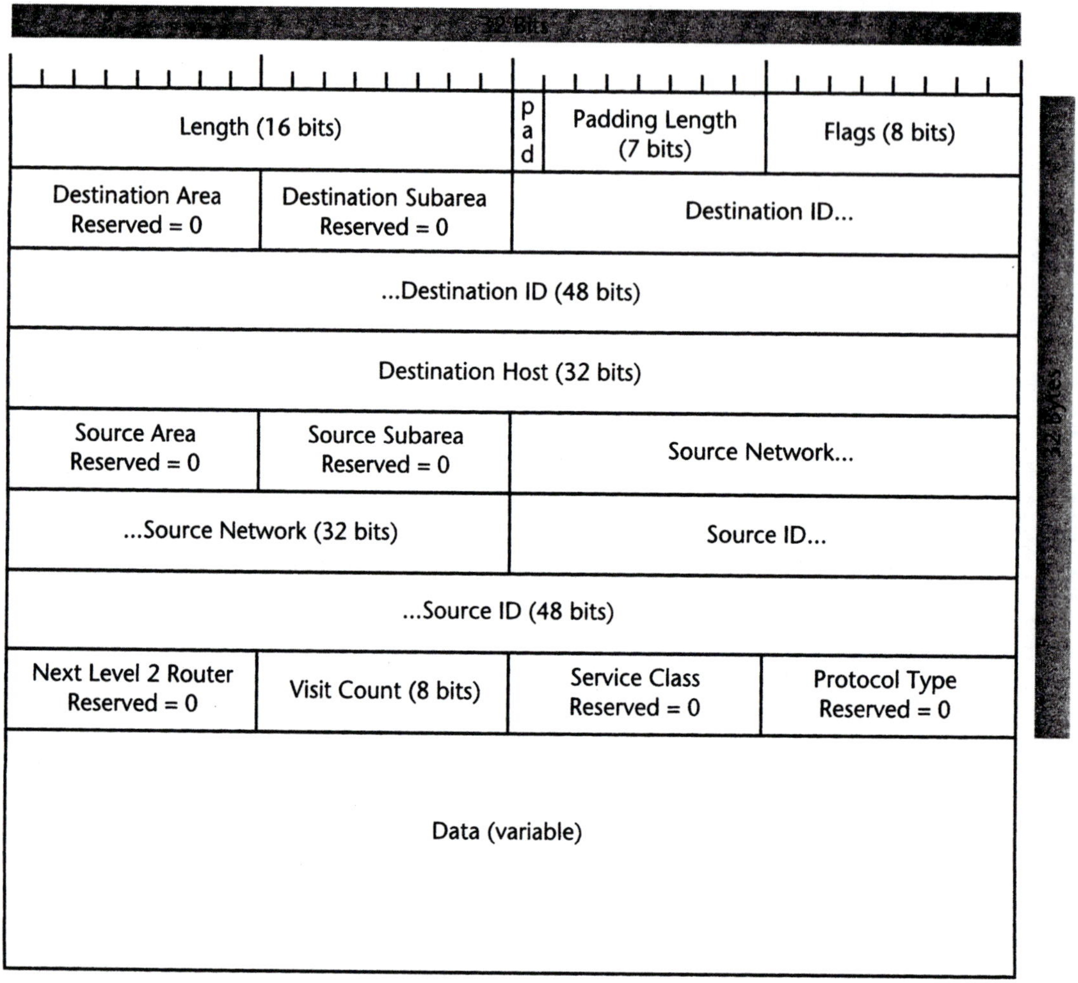

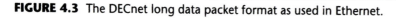

Length (16 bits)		p a d	Padding Length (7 bits)	Flags (8 bits)
Destination Area Reserved = 0	Destination Subarea Reserved = 0		Destination ID...	
...Destination ID (48 bits)				
Destination Host (32 bits)				
Source Area Reserved = 0	Source Subarea Reserved = 0		Source Network...	
...Source Network (32 bits)			Source ID...	
...Source ID (48 bits)				
Next Level 2 Router Reserved = 0	Visit Count (8 bits)		Service Class Reserved = 0	Protocol Type Reserved = 0
Data (variable)				

FIGURE 4.3 The DECnet long data packet format as used in Ethernet.

Bit 3: Return to Sender Request (RQR). Set to 1 to indicate "try to return" packet if destination is unreachable.

Bits 2–0: Message type. Set to binary 110 (6) to indicate a long data packet message.

Following the flags are two 8-bit fields that are reserved, but are defined by DEC as the destination area and destination subareas, respectively. They are always set to 0.

Next is the destination ID, a 6-byte field in the format hex AA000400*xxyy*, where *xx* is the destination area and *yy* is the destination node. This is followed by the source area and subarea that, like the destination area and sub-area, are reserved and set to 0. Following that is the source ID in the same 6-byte format as the destination ID.

The next field, defined as the Next Level 2 Router, is reserved and set to 0. Following that is the 8-bit Visit Count (analogous to a hop count that is incremented as a DECnet packet goes through a router), followed by two reserved bytes called the Service Class and Protocol Type.

Interesting that the protocol type is reserved and always set to 0, isn't it? This is because, unlike other network layer protocols such as IP, the only protocol that sits on top of the DRP network layer is the DECnet Network Services Protocol (NSP). NSP is sort of a cross between a transport and session layer protocol. NSP sets up a "link session" and maintains 16-bit destination and source link identifiers that are analogous to sockets. NSP also contains sequence numbers in the form of Data Segment Numbers and Data Acknowledgment Numbers.

Application layer protocols such as the Data Access Protocol (DAP) and Server Message Block (SMB) protocol sit on top of NSP. DAP is DEC's proprietary data access protocol, whereas SMB is the IBM/Microsoft standard file services protocol.

The DECnet protocol is a bit unconventional in how the area and node numbers are conveyed in a packet. You've seen how it takes 64 address bits just to carry a 6-bit area and 10-bit node address. Part of this overhead is reserved bits and part is the prefix of hex AA000400 for the destination and source address. Why this prefix?

As it turns out, a DECnet Phase IV node (including routers) changes its Ethernet MAC address to hex AA000400xxyy, where xxyy is derived from the area and node ID. This allowed for routerless operation because the MAC address of a destination machine you wanted to communicate with could be derived from its MAC address, eliminating the need for a protocol like the IP Address Resolution Protocol (ARP). Needless to say, this caused major consternation for Token Ring users who are assigned locally administered addresses (see Chapter 3), not DECnet addresses! A few changes had to be made to the DECnet Phase IV specification so Token Ring MAC addresses did not need to be changed to DECnet.

Figure 4.4 is a screen shot of a DECnet packet on Ethernet as decoded by the Network Associates, Inc. Sniffer Pro. Notice how the destination and source MAC addresses are identical to the destination and source DECnet addresses. This tells you that the destination and source nodes are in the same DECnet area, number 7 in this case. If the destination had been in a different area, the destination MAC address would have been that of a router, and you would have seen the Visit Count set to a nonzero value.

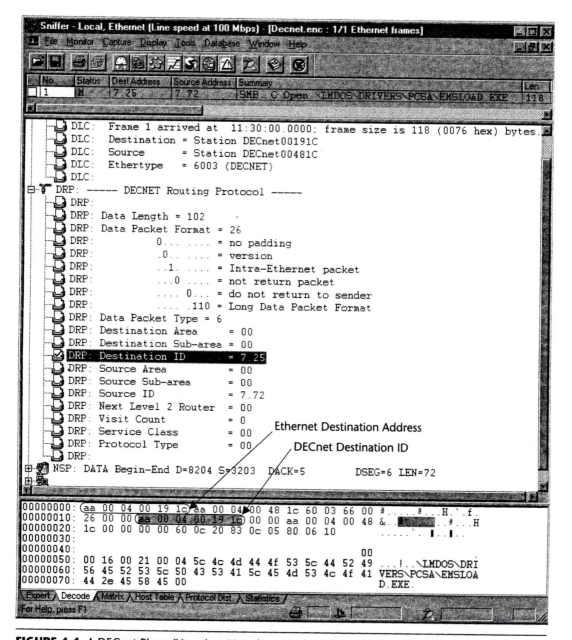

FIGURE 4.4 A DECnet Phase IV packet. Note how the highlighted DECnet Destination ID is encoded the same as the Ethernet destination address.

All routers that have DECnet routing enabled will have their source MAC address in the form of hex AA000400*xxyy*, regardless of the upper layer pro-

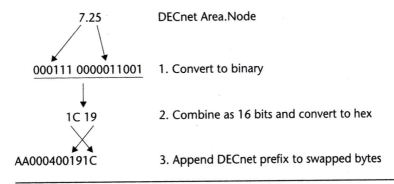

7.25   DECnet Area.Node

000111 0000011001   1. Convert to binary

1C 19   2. Combine as 16 bits and convert to hex

AA000400191C   3. Append DECnet prefix to swapped bytes

FIGURE 4.5 Converting a DECnet address to its hexadecimal representation.

tocol. Because you can no longer identify routers by their OUI, you have to know the DECnet area and node address assigned to that router.

This brings me to my final bit of important information about DECnet. How is an Ethernet MAC address derived from the DECnet address? The first part is easy: a DECnet address always starts with hex AA000400 and so do the first 4 bytes of the Ethernet address. The first 3 bytes, hex AA0004, are often referred to as the DECnet OUI, and many analyzers prefix a DECnet MAC address with the characters "DECnet" in their packet decodes. The lower two bytes of the Ethernet address are a bit trickier.

First, encode the area and node ID into 6 and 10 bits, respectively. Using the destination address of 7.25 in Figure 4.4 as an example, area 7 would be encoded as binary 000111 and node 25 as binary 0000011001. Put these two together and you get 000111000001101, which converted to hex is 1C19. Finally, byte-swap this value to get 191C and append it to the DECnet prefix to get AA000400191C. *Voilà!* Our Ethernet MAC address. This is summarized as a simple process in Figure 4.5.

4.3.4 IP

The Internet Protocol is the core of the TCP/IP protocol suite and is defined by RFC 791, appropriately entitled "Internet Protocol." IP is also sometimes referred to as IP Version 4 or "Classic IP" to differentiate it from IP Next Generation, IPng or IPv6, which has been assigned Version 6.

The IP version number is encoded in the first 4 bits of the IP datagram header, as shown in Figure 4.6. Thus every Classic IP packet starts out with the binary bits 0100, or 4 in decimal. This is followed by a 4-bit field to indicate the length of the IP header in 32-bit (4-byte) words. The standard IP header length without options is 20 bytes. Thus the IP header length field is

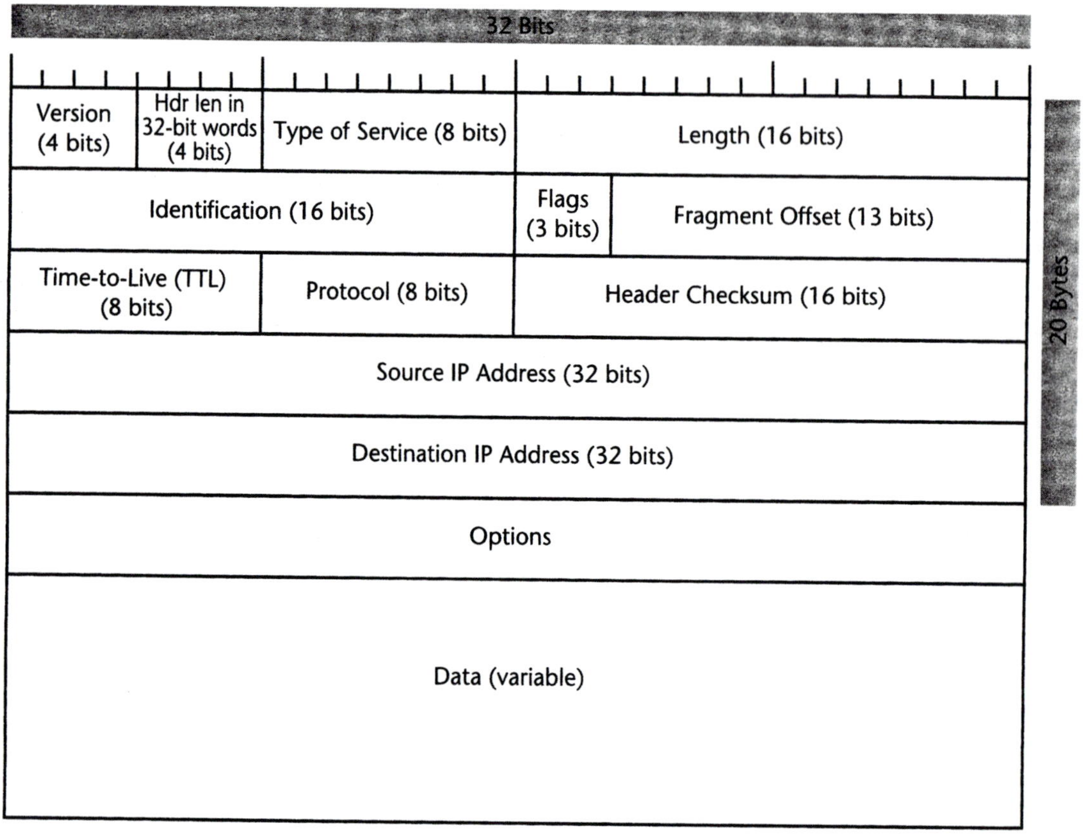

32 Bits				
Version (4 bits)	Hdr len in 32-bit words (4 bits)	Type of Service (8 bits)	Length (16 bits)	
Identification (16 bits)			Flags (3 bits)	Fragment Offset (13 bits)
Time-to-Live (TTL) (8 bits)		Protocol (8 bits)	Header Checksum (16 bits)	
Source IP Address (32 bits)				
Destination IP Address (32 bits)				
Options				
Data (variable)				

20 Bytes

FIGURE 4.6 The IP datagram packet format.

typically set to 5. The maximum allowable header size with options is 15 (the maximum 4-bit number) × 4 bytes, or 60 bytes.

An IP header of 60 bytes may seem adequate, but with some options, it's not. For example, if you use the IP Record route option (available with some PING—Packet InterNet Groper—implementations as a -r option), you cannot record more than a total of nine routes in the header.

The next field in the IP datagram is the 8-bit Type of Service (TOS). The first 3 bits are precedence bits, which are largely ignored in today's IP networks, followed by 4 TOS bits and 1 unused bit. Only one of the 4 TOS bits may be set to 1. The order in which they appear is from left to right: low delay, high throughput, high reliability, low cost. The low-cost bit was added after RFC 791.

TOS bits can often be set by an application, or in the case of Windows 95/98/NT, the default TOS can be set in the registry. RFC 791 notes that "The

> ❗ To discover if any applications on your network are using any IP options such as Timestamp or Record route, use your analyzer to find the offset (which depends on the DLC encapsulation type) of the IP header in a packet and set a pattern match filter to capture packets that don't match the value hex 45 at that offset. For multiple encapsulation types, you'll need to use another pattern match or use the analyzer's "data relative" offset feature, available in some analyzers, to start the offset from the end of the DLC header rather than the beginning of the packet.

type of service is an abstract or generalized set of parameters which characterize the service choices provided in the networks that make up the internet. This type of service indication is to be used by gateways to select the actual transmission parameters for a particular network, the network to be used for the next hop, or the next gateway when routing an internet datagram."

Because the meaning of TOS is abstract, the interpretation of what "minimize delay" means, for example, may vary from router vendor to router vendor. RFC 1349, "Type of Service in the Internet Protocol Suite" does have some clarification on this matter. For example, a router could send an ICMP redirect packet back to the sender if the router can't handle a TOS request in the IP header.

> ❗ If you want to see if the IP Type of Service option makes any difference in your internet, try using the PING command to a remote router or server and compare the pinging over several seconds with and without setting the PING TOS option to a nonzero value. Don't get too excited about changing the default TOS for packets hitting the Internet, however, because it won't make any difference in response time.

Following the TOS is the 16-bit total length field that indicates the total length of the IP datagram in bytes, including the header plus data. Subtracting the header length from the total length yields the length of the data or payload.

The 16-bit identification field identifies each IP datagram sent by a host and is incremented by one for each datagram sent. An exception to this rule is when IP packets are fragmented, in which case the identification field remains the same for an even set of fragments. The flags and fragment offset fields (discussed later) also come into play.

The next field in the IP datagram is the 8-bit Time-to-Live (TTL). The value is decremented every time an IP packet passes through a router, thus limiting the number of hops a packet can traverse. The reason this field wasn't called something like "hops-to-live" is that routers could decrement the field by the number of seconds a packet was held in a buffer. Later this requirement was relaxed such that routers didn't have to trace the time, just decrement the TTL by one as the packet was fowarded.

When a TTL reaches 0, the router discards the packet and sends an ICMP packet back to the sender to indicate that the TTL expired. Although you could set the starting TTL to a low value to limit the "reachability" of the packet, the main purpose of the TTL is to prevent a packet from getting caught in a router loop.

When you examine an IP packet with a protocol analyzer, you never really know how many routers the packet has passed through unless you happen to know the starting TTL of the source. For example, the Windows NT 3.51 and Windows 95 default TTL is 32; for Windows 98 and NT 4.0, it is 128; and for Sun Solaris, 255, the maximum 8-bit value. So, if you see a packet from an IP address of an NT 4.0 Web server and the TTL is 112, chances are pretty good that the packet has traversed through 14 routers, provided that the NT server's default TTL hasn't been changed.

Later on, you'll see how IPX routers *increment* the IPX hop count as the packet passes through. This way, when you examine an IPX packet with your protocol analyzer, you always know how many routers the packet has traversed.

The TTL in IP serves another purpose when a packet arrives at the destination. If the destination doesn't receive all of the fragments of an IP datagram, the TTL eventually expires and the destination sends an ICMP packet back to the sender to indicate that the TTL expired while waiting to reassemble the fragments.

The TTL is followed by the 8-bit protocol ID, which identifies the upper layer protocol embedded in the IP datagram. (In the IP layer detail shown in Figure 4.7, note that the IP packet number has set this field to 17 to indicate a UDP packet.) There are several defined protocol types, although only a handful are commonly used, as indicated in Table 4.1.

TABLE 4.1 Common IP Protocol IDs

Value	Name	Description
1	ICMP	Internet Control Message Protocol
2	IGMP	Internet Group Management Protocol
3	GGP	Gateway-to-Gateway Protocol
6	TCP	Transmission Control Protocol
8	EGP	Exterior Gateway Protocol
17	UDP	User Datagram Protocol

```
Sniffer - Local, Ethernet (Line speed at 100 Mbps) - [nfs_udp.cap : 48/656 Ethernet frames]
 File  Monitor  Capture  Display  Tools  Database  Window  Help
```

No.	Len	Dest Address	Source Address	Summary
47	158	[172.10.10.33]	SCOTT	
48	1514	SCOTT	[172.10.10.33]	NFS: R OK F=A1F4 (8192 bytes)
49	1514	SCOTT	[172.10.10.33]	IP: D=[172.10.10.34] S=[172.10.10.33] LEN=1480 ID=44545
				IP: continuation of ident=44545
50	1514	SCOTT	[172.10.10.33]	IP: D=[172.10.10.34] S=[172.10.10.33] LEN=1480 ID=44545
				IP: continuation of ident=44545
51	1514	SCOTT	[172.10.10.33]	IP: D=[172.10.10.34] S=[172.10.10.33] LEN=1480 ID=44545
				IP: continuation of ident=44545
52	1514	SCOTT	[172.10.10.33]	IP: D=[172.10.10.34] S=[172.10.10.33] LEN=1480 ID=44545
				IP: continuation of ident=44545
53	934	SCOTT	[172.10.10.33]	IP: D=[172.10.10.34] S=[172.10.10.33] LEN=900 ID=44545
				IP: continuation of ident=44545
54	158	[172.10.10.33]	SCOTT	
55	1514	SCOTT	[172.10.10.33]	
56	1514	SCOTT	[172.10.10.33]	IP: D=[172.10.10.34] S=[172.10.10.33] LEN=1480 ID=44801
				IP: continuation of ident=44801

```
 DLC: Ethertype=0800, size=1514 bytes
 IP: ----- IP Header -----
   IP:
   IP: Version = 4, header length = 20 bytes
   IP: Type of service = 00
   IP:        000. ....  = routine
   IP:        ...0 ....  = normal delay
   IP:        .... 0...  = normal throughput
   IP:        .... .0..  = normal reliability
   IP: Total length   = 1500 bytes
   IP: Identification = 44545
   IP: Flags          = 2X
   IP:        .0.. ....  = may fragment
   IP:        ..1. ....  = more fragments
   IP: Fragment offset = 0 bytes
   IP: Time to live   = 128 seconds/hops
   IP: Protocol       = 17 (UDP)
   IP: Header checksum = FAB7 (correct)
   IP: Source address      = [172.10.10.33]
   IP: Destination address = [172.10.10.34], SCOTT
   IP: No options
   IP:
   IP: Multi-Frame IP data. Frames:  48, 49, 50, 51, 52, 53
   IP:
 UDP: D=1021 S=2049  LEN=8300
```

```
 Expert  Decode  Matrix  Host Table  Protocol Dist.  Statistics
For Help, press F1
```

FIGURE 4.7 Detail of the first response packet to an NFS read request for 8 Kbytes of data.

The checksum covers the IP header only. For protection of all of the IP payload, a higher layer protocol such as UDP, TCP, ICMP, or IGMP must be used because they each have their own checksum.

The IP header completes with the 32-bit source internetwork address, the 32-bit destination internetwork address, and options, if any.

The 32-bit IP internetwork address consists of a network ID followed by a host ID. Because there are only 32 bits, the original designers didn't require

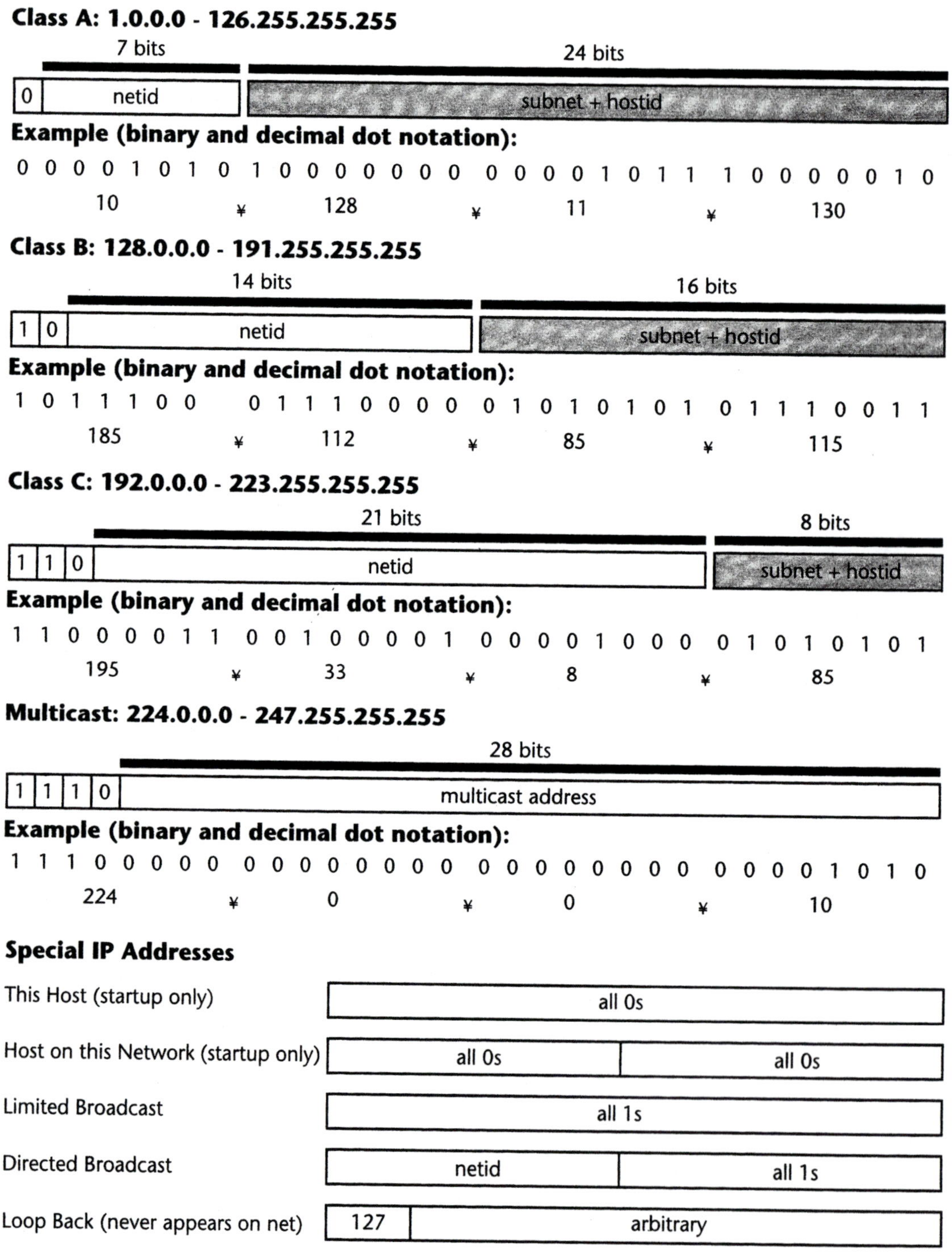

Class A: 1.0.0.0 - 126.255.255.255

7 bits	24 bits

0	netid	subnet + hostid

Example (binary and decimal dot notation):

```
0 0 0 0 1 0 1 0   1 0 0 0 0 0 0 0   0 0 0 0 1 0 1 1   1 0 0 0 0 0 1 0
       10       ¥       128      ¥       11       ¥       130
```

Class B: 128.0.0.0 - 191.255.255.255

14 bits	16 bits

1 0	netid	subnet + hostid

Example (binary and decimal dot notation):

```
1 0 1 1 1 0 0   0 1 1 1 0 0 0 0   0 1 0 1 0 1 0 1   0 1 1 1 0 0 1 1
       185      ¥       112      ¥       85       ¥       115
```

Class C: 192.0.0.0 - 223.255.255.255

21 bits	8 bits

1 1 0	netid	subnet + hostid

Example (binary and decimal dot notation):

```
1 1 0 0 0 0 1 1   0 0 1 0 0 0 0 1   0 0 0 0 1 0 0 0   0 1 0 1 0 1 0 1
       195       ¥       33        ¥       8        ¥       85
```

Multicast: 224.0.0.0 - 247.255.255.255

28 bits

1 1 1 0	multicast address

Example (binary and decimal dot notation):

```
1 1 1 0 0 0 0 0   0 0 0 0 0 0 0 0   0 0 0 0 0 0 0 0   0 0 0 0 1 0 1 0
       224       ¥       0        ¥       0        ¥       10
```

Special IP Addresses

This Host (startup only)	all 0s	
Host on this Network (startup only)	all 0s	all 0s
Limited Broadcast	all 1s	
Directed Broadcast	netid	all 1s
Loop Back (never appears on net)	127	arbitrary

FIGURE 4.8 IP addressing.

a fixed number of bits for the network space and a fixed number of bits for the host space. The number of bits allocated to each depends on the "class" of address. Figure 4.8 illustrates the various classes of IP addresses in use today: Classes A, B, and C, and multicast. The first bit or bits of the address determine the class. An address starting with binary 0 is a class A address, 10 is class B, and 110 is class C. The remaining bits are divided up into the network ID and host ID. The figure also shows specially defined IP addresses, including broadcast addresses and the loop back address.

IP addresses are represented in dotted decimal notation. For example, the address 168.10.115.58 represents a typical class B address. This can be seen if you convert the address to binary and look at the first few bits: 10101000.00001010.01110011.00111010. The first two bits are 10, which indicate that this is a class B address. Because the last 16 bits represent the Host ID, you could say that this is host 115.58 on network 168.10. Because 16 bits are available for the Host ID, you can have up to 16,384 hosts on network 168.10. If you need more hosts or desire more networks, you can simply define another network address, such as 168.11, 168.12, 168.13, and so on.

Doing so works well for a private network, but not for a large network such as the Internet. In the Internet, you want to preserve the network space, which is done in two ways. First, an organization that's lucky enough to get its own class B address only receives one address. To define additional networks within that organization, it will have to "borrow" bits from the host space to define further networks, known as subnets, within the single class B address.

In the sample class B of 168.10.*x.x*, you could borrow 8 bits from the top of the host portion of the address "*x.x*" to define up to 254 additional subnets. Then, you would be left with 8 bits to allocate for hosts, or up to 254 maximum hosts on a given subnet. Your subnet mask in this scenario would be 255.255.255.0. Thus the upper 24 bits represent the network portion (with the lower 8 bits used for subnets) of the address and the lower 8 bits, the node address. Sometimes an address will be represented as 168.10.100.58/24 to show the class B address and the fact that there are 24 subnet mask bits.

Figure 4.9 shows the various subnet masks for different classes of IP addresses. RFC 1878 discusses how to use the subnet of 0 and all 1s to use one or two more subnets in certain situations. Having two more subnets available is especially handy when subnetting a class C address.

Preserving the Internet Address is also achieved by allocating addressees from the large class C address space, which has over 16 million network addresses. Unfortunately the host space is only 8 bits (which leaves little room for subnetting), and the explosion of the Internet is rapidly eating up the class C addresses.

Class A Subnetting

Bits	Subnets*	Hosts	Subnet Mask	Binary
0	n. a.	16, 777, 214	255. 0. 0. 0	11111111. 00000000. 00000000. 00000000
1	0	8, 388, 606	255. 128. 0. 0	11111111. 10000000. 00000000. 00000000
2	2	4, 194, 302	255. 192. 0. 0	11111111. 11000000. 00000000. 00000000
3	6	2, 097, 150	255. 224. 0. 0	11111111. 11100000. 00000000. 00000000
4	14	1, 048, 574	255. 240. 0. 0	11111111. 11110000. 00000000. 00000000
5	30	524, 286	255. 248. 0. 0	11111111. 11111000. 00000000. 00000000
6	62	262, 142	255. 252. 0. 0	11111111. 11111100. 00000000. 00000000
7	126	131, 070	255. 254. 0. 0	11111111. 11111110. 00000000. 00000000
8	254	65, 534	255. 255. 0. 0	11111111. 11111111. 00000000. 00000000
9	510	32, 766	255. 255. 128. 0	11111111. 11111111. 10000000. 00000000
10	1, 022	16, 382	255. 255. 192. 0	11111111. 11111111. 11000000. 00000000
11	2, 046	8, 190	255. 255. 224. 0	11111111. 11111111. 11100000. 00000000
12	4, 094	4, 094	255. 255. 240. 0	11111111. 11111111. 11110000. 00000000
13	8, 190	2, 046	255. 255. 248. 0	11111111. 11111111. 11111000. 00000000
14	16, 382	1, 022	255. 255. 252. 0	11111111. 11111111. 11111100. 00000000
15	32, 766	510	255. 255. 254. 0	11111111. 11111111. 11111110. 00000000
16	65, 534	254	255. 255. 255. 0	11111111. 11111111. 11111111. 00000000
17	131, 070	126	255. 255. 255. 128	11111111. 11111111. 11111111. 10000000
18	262, 142	62	255. 255. 255. 192	11111111. 11111111. 11111111. 11000000
19	524, 286	30	255. 255. 255. 224	11111111. 11111111. 11111111. 11100000
20	1, 048, 574	14	255. 255. 255. 240	11111111. 11111111. 11111111. 11110000
21	2, 097, 150	6	255. 255. 255. 248	11111111. 11111111. 11111111. 11111000
22	4, 194, 302	2	255. 255. 255. 252	11111111. 11111111. 11111111. 11111100

Class B Subnetting

Bits	Subnets*	Hosts	Subnet Mask	Binary
0	n. a.	65, 534	255. 255. 0. 0	11111111. 11111111. 00000000. 00000000
1	0	32, 766	255. 255. 128. 0	11111111. 11111111. 10000000. 00000000
2	2	16, 382	255. 255. 192. 0	11111111. 11111111. 11000000. 00000000
3	6	8, 190	255. 255. 224. 0	11111111. 11111111. 11100000. 00000000
4	14	4, 094	255. 255. 240. 0	11111111. 11111111. 11110000. 00000000
5	30	2, 046	255. 255. 248. 0	11111111. 11111111. 11111000. 00000000
6	62	1, 022	255. 255. 252. 0	11111111. 11111111. 11111100. 00000000
7	126	510	255. 255. 254. 0	11111111. 11111111. 11111110. 00000000
8	254	254	255. 255. 255. 0	11111111. 11111111. 11111111. 00000000
9	510	126	255. 255. 255. 128	11111111. 11111111. 11111111. 10000000
10	1, 022	62	255. 255. 255. 192	11111111. 11111111. 11111111. 11000000
11	2, 046	30	255. 255. 255. 224	11111111. 11111111. 11111111. 11100000
12	4, 094	14	255. 255. 255. 240	11111111. 11111111. 11111111. 11110000
13	8, 190	6	255. 255. 255. 248	11111111. 11111111. 11111111. 11111000
14	16, 382	2	255. 255. 255. 252	11111111. 11111111. 11111111. 11111100

Class C Subnetting

Bits	Subnets*	Hosts	Subnet Mask	Binary
0	n. a.	254	255. 255. 255. 0	11111111. 11111111. 11111111. 00000000
1	0	126	255. 255. 255. 128	11111111. 11111111. 11111111. 10000000
2	2	62	255. 255. 255. 192	11111111. 11111111. 11111111. 11000000
3	6	30	255. 255. 255. 224	11111111. 11111111. 11111111. 11100000
4	14	14	255. 255. 255. 240	11111111. 11111111. 11111111. 11110000
5	30	6	255. 255. 255. 248	11111111. 11111111. 11111111. 11111000
6	62	2	255. 255. 255. 252	11111111. 11111111. 11111111. 11111100

*Add 2 if using all 0s and all 1s as subnets; see RFC 1878 for more details.

FIGURE 4.9 IP subnetting tables.

Fortunately most organizations don't have to worry about address allocation internally. Multiple private IP networks can be defined by allocating as many class A, B, or C addresses as you'd like, without having to subnet at all. Unfortunately most organizations followed the Internet model by choosing one class B address, for example, either privately assigned or publicly assigned as an "official" Internet address by the InterNIC. The organizations then proceeded to use the practice of subnetting the single class B address. This is bad practice for several reasons.

Some organizations requested multiple addresses from the InterNIC, especially multiple class C addresses that only have room for a maximum of 254 hosts *without* subnetting. In many cases, these organizations weren't even connected to the Internet, at least not up until a couple years ago. Needless to say, Internet address allocation is now done much more carefully than it was in the past.

Eventually private organizations realized that it was a good idea to hide from the Internet behind a firewall. And, why not further enhance security by using a proxy server that maps privately allocated IP addresses to Internet addresses for users to access the Internet? Then only the proxy server (and the company's Web and FTP server) would need a "legitimate" IP address for the Internet. For users accessing the Internet, one address is required for each *active* user only. This dramatically reduces the number of Internet addresses required for an organization. There's even an informational RFC for allocating "private" IP addresses: RFC 1597 (Address Allocation for Private Internets). The Internet Assigned Numbers Authority (IANA) has, in fact, reserved the following blocks of the Internet's IP address space for private networks: 10.0.0.0 through 10.255.255.255, 172.16.0.0 through 172.31.255.255, and 192.168.0.0 through 192.168.255.255.

Subnetting practices also led to a mess when switches were introduced for private corporate networks, or "intranets." Layer 2 DLC switches were hyped as a low-cost solution to breaking up user and server segments to provide more bandwidth. After all, breaking up segments this way was less expensive than adding router ports.

4.3.5 IP Fragmentation

Theoretically an IP datagram can be up to 65,535 bytes in length. If an application requests that the IP layer send a datagram larger than what can fit into the MTU of the DLC layer, the IP layer fragments the datagram by sending multiple packets. A classic example of this is Network File System (NFS) implementations that run over UDP. By setting the NFS read and write block size to 8192 bytes on Ethernet, the UDP layer asks the IP layer to send an 8192-byte datagram, which must be fragmented into six packets. This fragmenting is necessary because the maximum IP datagram that can be stuffed into an Ethernet packet is 1492 to 1500 bytes, depending on the DLC encapsulation type. Each datagram fragment packet will have the same 16-bit ID, so that the destination can properly reassemble the packet.

Routers can also fragment IP datagrams if the destination port's MTU is smaller than the current packet. For example, if you send a 4000-byte Token Ring IP packet to a router that needs to forward it to a T1 port with an MTU of 1600 bytes, the router needs to fragment the original packet into three smaller ones.

It is also possible for a sender to set the don't fragment bit as defined in the three 1-bit flags that follow the ID field. The first bit is reserved, the second bit is set to 1 if the sender doesn't want the packet fragmented, and the third bit is the more fragments bit and is set to 1 if this packet is one in a series of fragments. A nonfragmented datagram, the last packet in a series of datagram fragments, has the third bit set to 0.

If the second bit is set to 1, a router is not allowed to fragment a packet and will send an Internet Control Message Protocol (ICMP) packet back to the sender to indicate that the packet was dropped. The sender often uses this protocol to discover the MTU between the sender and receiver. The sender can set the don't fragment bit and try to send a series of larger then smaller packets to a destination until no ICMP can't fragment message is received from a router. In Windows 95/98/NT implementations, MTU discovery is on by default and all outgoing IP packets always have the don't fragment bit set. That way, the IP layer of the sender can automatically adjust the datagram size downward in the event the router returns a can't fragment ICMP packet.

The 13 bits following the fragment flags is the fragment offset within the original datagram. This allows the destination to reassemble the original datagram back in the proper order. Figure 4.7 shows a trace of an NFS Block read request of 8192 bytes (packet number 47). Note how the subsequent packets following the NFS read response are returned as a series of IP fragments. This happens because the host is asking UDP to send 8300 bytes of data (8192 bytes plus some overhead), as you can see in the first reply packet, packet number 48. UDP is asking IP to send a 8300-byte datagram that must be fragmented to fit into multiple Ethernet packets.

Packet 48 is the first fragment for the fragment ID of 44,545, as indicated by the IP fragment offset of 0. All of the subsequent IP fragments associated with the read request are labeled with the same 16-bit ID, namely, 44,545. These fragments are purely IP with no UDP header.

A side effect of fragmentation is that there's no recovery protocol if one fragment is dropped; the entire datagram and all of its fragments must be resent.

> **❗** As you can imagine, fragmenting packets is generally not good practice due to the overhead of fragmentation and reassembly. Routers especially should not be burdened with the task of fragmenting IP packets. In fact, IPv6 recommends that fragmentation be allowed only at the sender.

In Figure 4.7, this means that six packets would have to be resent if one fragment doesn't reach the destination.

Imagine if the block size were 32 Kbytes instead of the 8 Kbytes in this example; then 22 packets would have to be resent! This is one of the reasons that NFS over UDP is a poor choice of protocol to run over the Internet. In this case, running NFS over TCP (which is possible with many NFS implementations) would be preferable. Chapter 8 presents a case study in which dropped IP fragments were impacting the throughput of an NFS file transfer.

4.3.6 IP RIP Operation

To forward packets between IP subnets, a router needs a table to look up the destination IP address. In the table will be the port to send the packet to. How is this table created? One way to create an IP route table is to statically define which ports are to be used for which IP destinations. A more common approach is to create the tables dynamically using the RIP or OSPF (RFC 1278 entitled "OSPF Version 2") protocol.

RIP is the original routing update protocol, which is often called a distance vector protocol because the information supplied by a RIP packet is simply the IP address and hop count.

With OSPF, a router can make a more intelligent decision about the route because it contains more information about each route (such as the line speed). For example, if a T1 has fewer hop counts than a series of ATM links on the way to a given IP destination, an OSPF router may choose the ATM links because of their higher speed.

With RIP, the next hop is determined solely on hop counts, meaning that the T1 will always be chosen—unless, of course, it goes down.

OSPF route updates are only sent when a router boots or when there's a change in the topology. RIP updates are sent every 30 seconds. RIP routers can also send "triggered" updates if a change is determined in the RIP information coming from another router, in order to more quickly propagate the change throughout the network.

Figure 4.10 illustrates a simple IP network and shows how routers learn about IP address destinations from other routers. Another term for RIP is routing by rumor because a router learns about an IP address on one port then turns around and broadcasts the information on its other ports. Routes are not advertised back on the port from which the route was learned, a technique known as split horizon.

RIP packets are broadcast by routers every 30 seconds in a UDP datagram to port 520. Up to 25 routes (IP address and hop count) can be sent per packet. If a router doesn't hear an update for a route for 3 minutes (6 RIP packets), the route is marked for deletion and propagated by the router as an invalid route. The route is then removed from the router table in another 2 RIP cycles, or 60 seconds. Even though the IP datagram header allows up to 255 hops, RIP limits the hop count to 16. An invalid route is advertised with a hop count of 16.

Another drawback to RIP is that it doesn't know about subnet addressing. Routers typically rely on the subnet mask assigned to a particular router port, but this may not be correct if the mask isn't the same for a given IP address throughout the intranet. Protocols like RIP-2, which has extensions to RIP as defined in RFC 1732 (RIP Version 2—Carrying Additional Information), and OSPF have provisions to advertise the subnet mask for each IP route.

4.3.7 Case Study: Locally Routed IP Packets

Before long, managers began collapsing their IP subnets by connecting Ethernet segments and Token Ring segments into a multiport switch. At some point, the switch connected back to a router port, which meant that multiple IP subnets had to be defined for that router port to handle the IP user population. This sounds great until you realize that in order for a user to get to another resource on another subnet connected to the same switch, the packets have to be sent to the router and back again. This defeats one of the reasons for "switching" (pun intended) in the first place: to offload the router!

This "local routing" doubles the number of packets that go through a switch, not to mention that it also consumes buffer and CPU resources in the router. An example of local routing is illustrated in Figure 4.11, with an actual trace from the network shown in Figure 4.12. In this example, I've filtered on traffic to and from the workstation/server pair 158.48.160.41/158.48.11.253. It's easy to see that there are two packets for every read request and every response. Looking at the MAC and IP addresses side by side shows how the first packet goes from the workstation to the router and the second packet from the router to the server. The second packet also has its TTL decremented by 1.

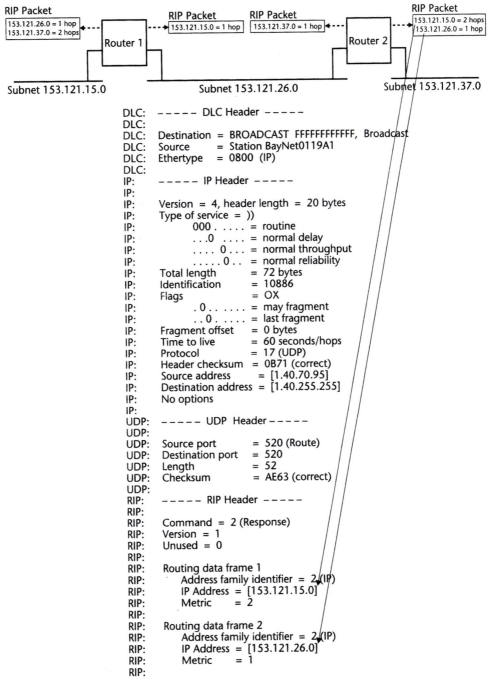

Subnet Mask: 255.255.255.0

RIP Packet
| 153.121.26.0 = 1 hop |
| 153.121.37.0 = 2 hops |

RIP Packet
| 153.121.15.0 = 1 hop |

RIP Packet
| 153.121.37.0 = 1 hop |

RIP Packet
| 153.121.15.0 = 2 hops |
| 153.121.26.0 = 1 hop |

Router 1   Router 2

Subnet 153.121.15.0   Subnet 153.121.26.0   Subnet 153.121.37.0

```
DLC:    - - - - - DLC Header - - - - -
DLC:
DLC:    Destination = BROADCAST FFFFFFFFFFFF, Broadcast
DLC:    Source      = Station BayNet0119A1
DLC:    Ethertype   = 0800 (IP)
DLC:
IP:     - - - - - IP Header - - - - -
IP:
IP:     Version = 4, header length = 20 bytes
IP:     Type of service = ))
IP:          000 . . . . . = routine
IP:          . . .0 . . . . = normal delay
IP:          . . . . 0 . . . = normal throughput
IP:          . . . . . 0 . . = normal reliability
IP:     Total length      = 72 bytes
IP:     Identification    = 10886
IP:     Flags             = OX
IP:          . 0 . . . . . . = may fragment
IP:          . . 0 . . . . . = last fragment
IP:     Fragment offset   = 0 bytes
IP:     Time to live      = 60 seconds/hops
IP:     Protocol          = 17 (UDP)
IP:     Header checksum    = 0B71 (correct)
IP:     Source address     = [1.40.70.95]
IP:     Destination address = [1.40.255.255]
IP:     No options
IP:
UDP:    - - - - - UDP  Header - - - - -
UDP:
UDP:    Source port       = 520 (Route)
UDP:    Destination port  = 520
UDP:    Length            = 52
UDP:    Checksum          = AE63 (correct)
UDP:
RIP:    - - - - - RIP Header - - - - -
RIP:
RIP:    Command = 2 (Response)
RIP:    Version = 1
RIP:    Unused = 0
RIP:
RIP:    Routing data frame 1
RIP:        Address family identifier = 2 (IP)
RIP:        IP Address = [153.121.15.0]
RIP:        Metric    = 2
RIP:
RIP:    Routing data frame 2
RIP:        Address family identifier = 2 (IP)
RIP:        IP Address = [153.121.26.0]
RIP:        Metric    = 1
RIP:
```

FIGURE 4.10 IP RIP propagation and sample RIP packet trace.

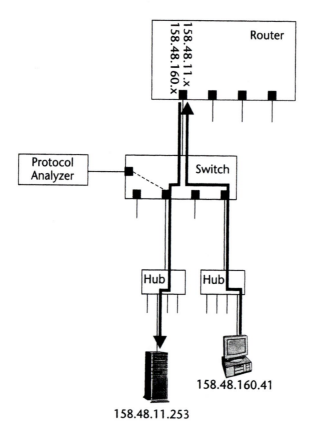

FIGURE 4.11 Locally routed packet flow from 158.48.160.41 to 158.48.11.253.

A general methodology for identifying locally routed IP packets is as follows:

1. Filter on a station pair at the IP layer.
2. If TCP is being used, look for "duplicate" packets for each sequence number.
3. Check the MAC addresses of a duplicate pair.
4. Check the first packet for the destination address of a router.
5. Check the second packet for the source address of a router.
6. Look for a decremented TTL in the second packet.

One solution to the local routing problem is to reallocate the IP addresses to accommodate a larger host space by changing the subnet mask or doing away with subnets altogether and use multiple class B or even class A addresses where multiple IP networks are truly required.

Another solution would be to keep the IP addressing just the way it is, but ask the IP stack vendors (Microsoft are you listening?) to make a small change in the way that IP resources are located in the first place.

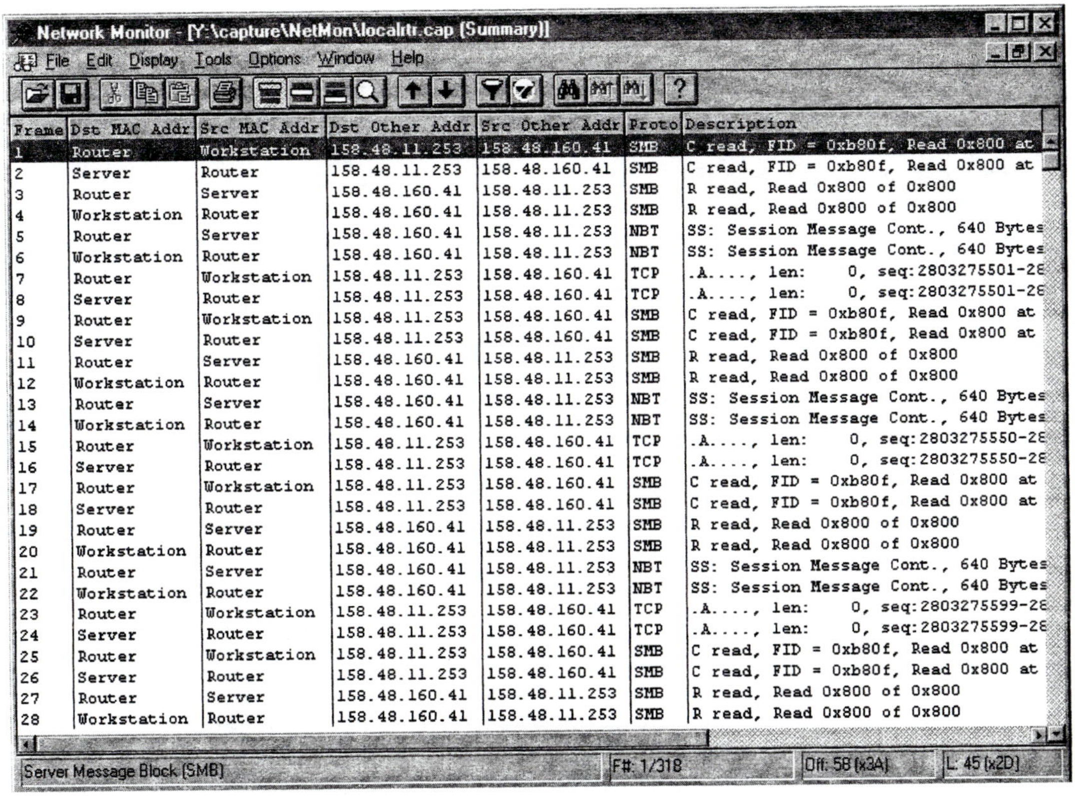

FIGURE 4.12 Locally routed IP packets.

To reach an IP device, the sender must know the IP address of that device. This can be statically defined, as when you set up the IP address of the default gateway, a.k.a. router, in a workstation. IP addresses can also be obtained using Domain Naming Services (DNS), the standard method used by the Internet. Many organizations have their own private DNS servers as well.

Once the IP address is known, the sender also needs to get the proper Ethernet or Token Ring physical MAC address to send the packet to. This is accomplished using the Address Resolution Protocol (ARP). The purpose of ARP is to broadcast out a packet to see if there's a station associated with the IP address as specified inside the ARP packet. If so, the station replies. The problem is that IP stack implementations only ARP if the destination IP address is *determined to be on the same subnet as the sender*, as determined by applying the subnet mask.

```
      10011110 . 00110000 . 10100000 . 00101001      (158.48.160.41, the source IP address)
AND   11111111 . 11111111 . 11111111 . 00000000      (255.255.255.0, subnet mask)
  =   10011110 . 00110000 . 00001011 . 00000000      (158.48.160.0, the source network)

      10011110 . 00110000 . 00001011 . 11111101      (158.48.11.253, the target IP address)
AND   11111111 . 11111111 . 11111111 . 00000000      (255.255.255.0, subnet mask)
  =   10011110 . 00110000 . 00001011 . 00000000      (158.48.11.0, the target network)
```

FIGURE 4.13 Source and target networks are not equal, prompting workstation to send packet to the default router.

If the source and destination are on different subnets, the workstation automatically sends the packet to the MAC address of the default router, as shown in Figure 4.13. Incidentally, the workstation ARPs for the default router as well. Once any addresses are discovered through ARP, the IP address and associated MAC address are stored in an ARP cache.

A simple solution to avoid hitting the router? Have a workstation always ARP first, no matter what the IP address. If there's no reply, *then* send the packet to the default router. As an exercise, consider the case where multiple VLANs are defined in a switch. Because broadcast packets are effectively blocked between VLANs, sending an IP packet to a host on a different VLAN assigned to another port in the switch still requires a router.

The expensive solution to avoid hitting the router? Upgrade the DLC switching to network layer switching, i.e., routing. *Déjà vu,* anyone?

> If you must use subnet masks, always allocate your subnets top down. For example, let's say your class B IP address is 158.10.X.X and your subnet mask is 255.255.255.0 (refer to Figure 4.14). Don't make the mistake of allocating subnets from the lower bits of the mask like 158.10.1.X, 158.10.2.X, 158.10.3.X, and so forth.
>
> Instead, allocate subnets from the *upper* bits. This becomes a bit tricky to compute, so use binary and convert to decimal. For example, 158.10.10000000.X becomes 158.10.**128**.X, 158.10.11000000.X becomes 158.10.**192**.X, 158.10.01000000.X becomes 158.10.**64**.X, and so on. This way you can change the subnet mask later on without having to redefine all the IP addresses. For example, if you need more hosts on a given subnet, just change the mask from 255.255.255.0 to 255.255.254.0. This roughly doubles the number of hosts from 254 to 510 that you can allocate on the existing subnets 128, 192, 64, and so on.

Class B IP Address

158 . 10 . x . x   10011110 . 00001010 . xxxxxxxx . xxxxxxxx

Old Subnet Mask   subnet   host

255 . 255 . 255 . 0   11111111 . 11111111 . (11111111) . (xxxxxxxx)

Allocate subnets from these bits... ⌐⌐⌐...not these bits;

New Subnet Mask   subnet   host

255 . 255 . 254 . 0   11111111 . 11111111 . (1111111)(x . xxxxxxxx)

Then, by changing only the subnet mask, you can double the host space on a subnet without changing any IP addresses.

FIGURE 4.14 Allocating subnet bits from left to right.

The issue of IP addressing and subnetting is more complex than can be addressed here. Many technical and even political factors influence how IP addresses are allocated within an organization. Believe it or not, there's even an entire book dedicated to this subject entitled "TCP/IP Addressing: Designing and Optimizing Your IP Addressing Scheme" written by Buck Graham.

> **❗**
>
> Before making any changes to your IP infrastructure for the sake of the local routing issue, analyze and baseline the amount of traffic that is being doubled up at the router. If several subnets are defined for a router port, but there is rarely any traffic directly between those subnets, the issue of local routing is mute. If more than, say, 20 percent of the traffic is going through the router to get between those subnets, you should probably address this issue.

4.3.8 Internet Control Message Protocol (ICMP) Packet Format and Operation

ICMP (RFC 792) is an integral part of IP used to report an error in datagram processing such as an unreachable network or host. ICMP is also used to send and receive an echo message, a.k.a. to ping.

According to RFC 792, "The purpose of these control messages is to provide feedback about problems in the communication environment, not to make IP reliable. There are still no guarantees that a datagram will be delivered or a control message will be returned. Some datagrams may still be undelivered without any report of their loss. The higher level protocols that use IP must implement their own reliability procedures if reliable communication is required." Further, "To avoid the infinite regress of messages about messages etc., no ICMP messages are sent about ICMP messages. Also ICMP messages are only sent about errors in handling fragment zero of fragmented datagrams."

ICMP messages are also never generated in response to a packet addressed to an IP broadcast address, an IP multicast address, or a packet containing a DLC all stations broadcast (i.e., hex FFFFFFFFFFFF). An ICMP message is carried in an IP datagram (refer back to Figure 4.6). The protocol type of the IP datagram is set to 1 to indicate an ICMP message.

The first four bytes on an ICMP message are always the same. The first byte is the message type, followed by the 1-byte code for that message type, followed by a 16-bit header checksum that protects the integrity of the ICMP message. The remaining fields of the ICMP message depend on the message type. In the case of an error message (i.e., non-Ping), the original IP header is returned along with the first eight bytes of the original datagram.

Figure 4.15 illustrates the ICMP message header for destination unreachable. The various ICMP message types are summarized in Figure 4.16 and discussed in the remainder of this section.

An ICMP message type 8 indicates an echo request message (Ping), and a type 0 indicates an echo reply. The message contains an identifier (in case multiple instances of Ping are running on the same host) and a sequence number. The sequence number is incremented by 1 for each Ping request and

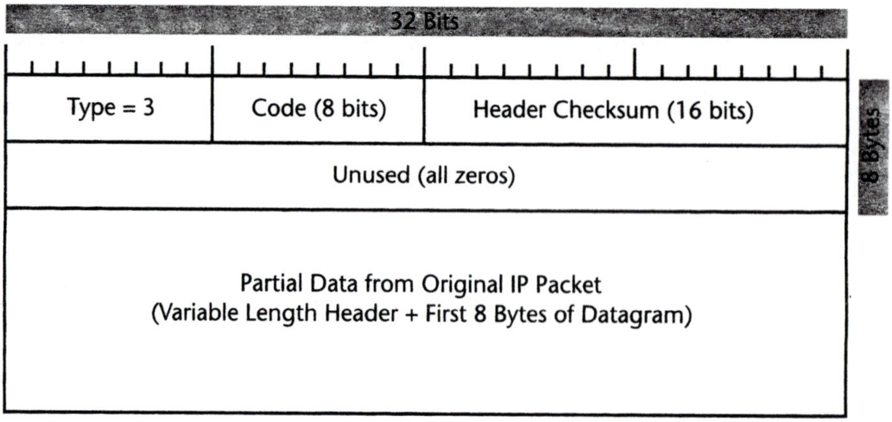

FIGURE 4.15 ICMP message header.

Type	Code	Description
0	0	**echo reply**
3		**destination unreachable**
	0	network unreachable
	1	host unreachable
	2	protocol unreachable
	3	port unreachable
	4	fragmentation needed but don't fragment bit set
	5	source route failed
	6	destination network unknown
	7	destination host unknown
	8	source host isolated (obsolete)
	9	destination network administratively prohibited
	10	destination host administratively prohibited
	11	network unreachable for TOS
	12	host unreachable for TOS
	13	communication administratively prohibited
	14	host precedence violation
	15	precedence cutoff in effect
4	0	**source quench**
5		**redirect**
	0	redirect for network
	1	redirect for host
	2	redirect for TOS and network
	3	redirect for TOS and host
8	0	**echo request**
9	0	**router advertisement**
10	0	**router solicitation**
11		**time exceeded**
	0	time-to-live equals zero during transit
	1	time-to-live equals zero during reassembly
12		**parameter problem**
	0	IP header bad (catchall error)
	1	required option missing
13	0	**timestamp request**
14	0	**timestamp reply**
15	0	**information request**
16	0	**information reply**
17	0	**address mask request**
18	0	**address mask reply**

FIGURE 4.16 ICMP message types.

is used by the sender to identify missing or duplicate packets as echo reply packets are received. Many Ping implementations also allow you to record the route of intermediate routers, up to nine routers maximum, due to a space limitation in the IP options header, as was noted earlier. A better way to map the route of a packet is to use a Traceroute program, especially considering that not all routers support the record route option.

Another Ping option is to record the timestamp for each intermediate router, with up to nine timestamps recorded. Recording timestamps is not all that useful unless you know the exact route of the packet (because there's no router IP address inside the packet to correlate to the timestamp) and the offset of the router's time relative to a reliable time source. Like record route, the timestamp option must also be supported by the router.

Another common ICMP message is type 3, which indicates an unreachable destination. The code byte indicates why the destination couldn't be reached. Explanations for some of the more common type 3 message codes returned by a router are as follows:

- A code of 0 means that the network was unreachable because the router couldn't forward the datagram due to lack of information about the destination network in the routing table.

- A code of 1 means that the host itself was unreachable. The packet was delivered to the router with the physical port for the destination network, but the router was unable to locate the destination host on that network. Before a router delivers a packet to a destination node on an end-network defined on a given port, the router first ARPs for that node. If no response is received, the packet is discarded and an ICMP packet is sent back to the source host.

- Codes of 2 or 3 are returned by the end host to indicate that the host does not understand the protocol or UDP/TCP port, respectively. An example here would be a user trying to FTP to a host that doesn't support FTP.

- A code of 4 is returned by a router when fragmentation is needed but the IP header don't fragment bit is set. This happens when the port to which a packet needs to be forwarded on doesn't have a large enough MTU to handle the packet. Usually the router would fragment the packet, but because the sender doesn't want fragmentation to occur, the router discards the packet and sends back an ICMP message.

An ICMP type 4 message is used for source quench, when a router is running low on buffer space needed to queue the packet for the next network. It can also be used when a destination host is running low on receive buffers for processing IP datagrams. The theory behind a source quench is for the sender to reduce its send rate, then gradually increase the rate until another source quench message is received. This form of congestion control is not real com-

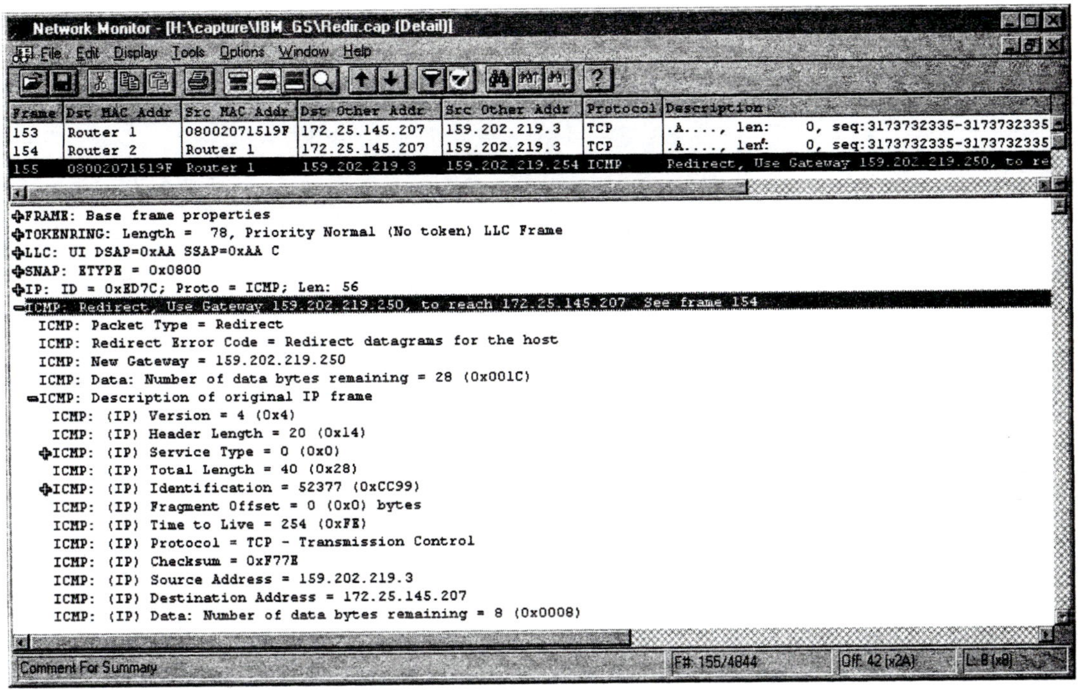

FIGURE 4.17 ICMP redirect packet trace.

mon, and many IP-based networks rely instead on flow control at the TCP layer, using "slow start" and window sizes to regulate end-to-end flow control, a topic covered in more detail in Chapter 5.

An ICMP type 5 message is a redirected message used by a router to inform a host that the packet should have been sent to a different router. This happens when two or more routers are accessible to a workstation, but the workstation is configured to use a particular router as the default, which may not always be the optimal choice.

Figure 4.17 is a packet trace from Network Monitor showing a redirect. In Packet 153, the host with the IP address of 159.202.219.3 is sending a packet to 172.25.145.207. The destination MAC address indicates that the packet is being sent to Router 1 (I've assigned logical names to the router MAC addresses to make them easier to read). The very next packet has the same source and destination IP address and the same TCP sequence number—a tip-off that this packet is being resent. But the MAC addresses indicate that this is not a TCP retransmission, but rather Router 1 sending the packet to Router 2. In packet 155, Router 1 is sending an ICMP redirect back to the host

(159.202.219.3), telling it to use the router with the IP address of 159.202.219.250 when sending packets to 172.25.145.207.

A final type of ICMP message you may encounter is a Type 11, or time exceeded. A Type 11 with code 0 indicates that an IP packet's time-to-live (TTL) expired (decremented to 0) during transit. Either the packet was looping, or, more likely, it simply ran out of hops on the way to a destination, such as when running the Traceroute program. An ICMP message with a Type 11 but a code of 1 indicates that the TTL expired during reassembly of IP fragments by the destination host.

4.3.9 Case Study: Troubleshooting Using Traceroute

Traceroute begins by using an ICMP echo packet (or a UDP datagram depending on the implementation) and setting the TTL in the IP header to 1. Obviously the packet will expire at the first router it hits. That router then returns a "TTL expired ICMP" packet back to the sender. From this, the sender learns the IP address of the first router. Subsequent routers are learned by setting the TTL to 2, then 3, and so on. If Traceroute encounters a "black hole" in which a router doesn't return a response, it increments the TTL and goes to the next router. Eventually the packet is returned by the destination address as a regular Ping reply.

A Traceroute program typically sends three packets for each TTL to get a feel for the average response time. Some implementations also attempt DNS lookup on the source address of the returned ICMP packet. This slows down the traceroute and can be disabled if desired.

Figure 4.18 shows a Traceroute command from Windows 95 and a listing of the corresponding packet capture. Packet 1 is the DNS query to get the IP address associated with www.net3group.com. The host then sends out an ICMP echo (Ping) packet to the destination IP address for www.net3group.com (205.219.138.158) with the TTL set to 1, as highlighted in packet 3. The first router, 208.160.32.56 returns the time exceeded ICMP message back to the host. The host does this three times, then performs a DNS look-up on the router's IP address, in packet 9.

Note that the target IP address for the DNS look-up is decoded backward in the summary line: 208.160.32.56 is shown as 56.32.160.208! This is one reason why you can't take everything the analyzer tells you at face value, and I'm not just picking on the Network Monitor analyzer.

The DNS response in packet 10 returns the name associated with the first router, usimsptc7.usinternet.com, as you can see in the first line of the response to the trace command. The process repeats until echo replies are received from the host, packets 28, 30, and 32.

```
Tracing route to www.net3group.com [205.219.138.158]
over a maximum of 30 hops:

  1   185 ms  2346 ms   169 ms  usimsptc7.usinternet.com [208.160.32.56]
  2   155 ms   160 ms   210 ms  border-GC-minneapolis.usinternet.com [206.152.221.70]
  3   170 ms   209 ms   169 ms  border1-hssi2-0.minneapolis.usinternet.com [206.152.221.91]
  4   196 ms   207 ms   189 ms  www.net3group.com [205.219.138.158]

Trace complete.
```

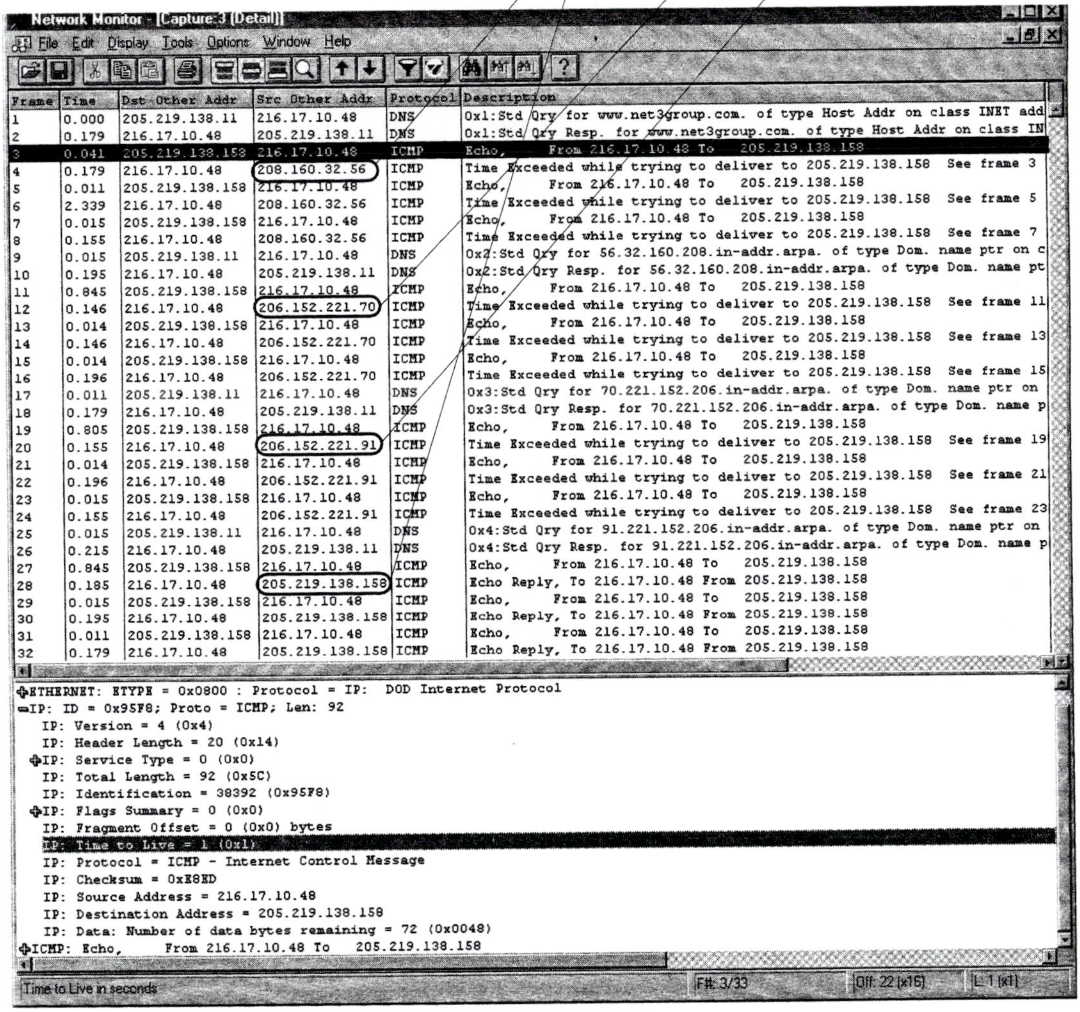

FIGURE 4.18 A traceroute and corresponding packet trace.

If a destination is unreachable, you may want to run traceroute to see how far the packet gets. Another use for traceroute is when response time slows to a crawl and you want to see if the route to your destination has changed.

Obviously you need a baseline traceroute—one that you ran when your network was running smoothly—to compare to.

Figure 4.19 shows a traceroute between AT&T Worldnet and my ISP provider before and after an MCI backbone failure in the Internet. The underlined router in the first traceroute was the problem that was routed around, as seen in the second traceroute. In the workaround, the packets are not only taking six more hops than before, but are traveling a much larger geographical distance. Instead of going from Chicago to Minneapolis, the packets are going from Chicago to LA to Bloomington and then Minneapolis. This was pretty amazing, considering that my ISP was located about 12 miles from me when I dialed into AT&T WorldNet. The last report in both traceroutes, "Destination net unreachable," is due to the behavior (a "security enhancement") of my ISP router in processing Ping requests.

4.3.10 Case Study: Troubleshooting Using PING and ICMP

This is an interesting situation in which an automatic IP MTU discovery ended up masking a fundamental networking problem.

Two campuses in a major metropolitan area were linked by a T1, as shown in Figure 4.20. The basic problem was unreliable packet transfer whenever the MTU on the router ports at both ends of the T1 was set to 1600 bytes. The 1600 bytes was the default MTU and was sufficient to handle maximum-sized Ethernet packets being sent between the campuses.

As an interim fix, the MTU was lowered to accept Ethernet packets up to 1100 bytes (not including the CRC) in length. TCP/IP stacks that have MTU discovery are able to recover when attempting to send packets greater than the allowable MTU over the T1.

For example, in Figure 4.21 I had a packet trace of a Windows 95 workstation on an Ethernet segment located at campus A writing data to an NT server located at campus B. The first file open and file write of 358 bytes worked just fine. The attempt to write 1058 bytes to the second file, however, failed.

The router sends back an "ICMP Net Unreachable" packet to the workstation, noting that fragmentation of the packet is needed but the IP don't fragment bit was set. The IP layer at the workstation notes to the upper layer protocol (TCP, in this case) that the datagram size is too large for the IP packet. TCP lowers the amount of data to send over IP by 64 bytes, and resends the original TCP packet as two packets. Packet 59 is the remaining 64 bytes of NetBIOS that couldn't be sent in packet 57. Note how Sniffer Pro is decoding this as a NetBIOS packet, even though if you were to look at the packet in hex, it would only go up to the TCP layer. Because the TCP destination port is 139, or NetBIOS, Sniffer Pro is merely letting us know that the TCP data belongs to NetBIOS.

Before MCI Backbone Failure

```
Tracing route to www.net3group.com [205.219.138.158]
over a maximum of 30 hops:

  1   208 ms   169 ms   169 ms  199.69.67.23
  2   170 ms   209 ms   179 ms  1.minneapolis-01-02rs.mn.dial-access.att.net [12.75.128.1]
  3   214 ms   329 ms   229 ms  199.69.127.29
  4   184 ms   179 ms   199 ms  br2-a350s7.cgcil.ip.att.net [12.127.11.177]
  5   205 ms   214 ms   199 ms  gr1-a3100s1.cgcil.ip.att.net [192.205.31.121]
  6   198 ms   209 ms   209 ms  192.205.31.102
  7   249 ms   219 ms   229 ms  core2.KansasCity.cw.net [204.70.4.249]
  8   224 ms   469 ms   289 ms  border7-fddi-0.KansasCity.cw.net [204.70.197.51]
  9   us-internet.KansasCity.cw.net [204.70.200.106]  reports: Destination net unreachable.

Trace complete.
```

During Backbone Workaround

```
Tracing route to www.net3group.com [205.219.138.158]
over a maximum of 30 hops:

  1   169 ms   209 ms   180 ms  199.69.67.23
  2   195 ms   169 ms   190 ms  1.minneapolis-01-02rs.mn.dial-access.att.net [12.75.128.1]
  3   209 ms   189 ms   259 ms  199.69.127.29
  4   795 ms   225 ms   219 ms  br2-a350s7.cgcil.ip.att.net [12.127.11.177]
  5   185 ms   209 ms   190 ms  gr1-a350s2.cgcil.ip.att.net [192.205.31.105]
  6   229 ms   215 ms   237 ms  Serial12-1-0.GW1.CHI1.ALTER.NET [157.130.96.9]
  7   239 ms   209 ms   219 ms  105.ATM3-0.XR1.CHI4.ALTER.NET [146.188.208.154]
  8   205 ms   195 ms   190 ms  295.ATM2-0.TR1.CHI4.ALTERNET [146.188.208.218]
  9   501 ms   642 ms   490 ms  106.ATM7-0.TR1.LAX2.ALTERNET [146.188.136.138]
 10   489 ms   449 ms   460 ms  199.ATM7-0.XR1.LAX4.ALTERNET [146.188.248.245]
 11   510 ms   709 ms   459 ms  193.ATM1-0-0.BR1.LAX1.ALTERNET [146.188.248.201]
 12   425 ms     *      400 ms  core9-hssi5-0-0.Bloomington.cw.net [206.157.77.57]
 13   409 ms   409 ms   380 ms  core2.KansasCity.cw.net [204.70.4.249]
 14     *        *      410 ms  border7-fddi-0.KansasCity.cw.net [204.70.197.51]
 15     *        *        *     us-internet.KansasCity.cw.net [204.70.200.106]  reports: Destination net unreachable.

Trace complete
```

FIGURE 4.19 A traceroute showing a backbone workaround.

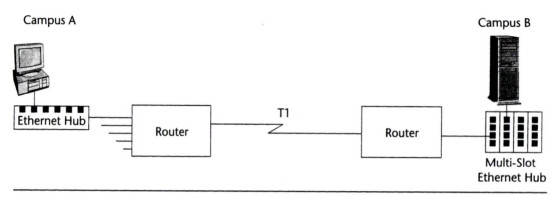

FIGURE 4.20 A simplified view of the connected campuses.

Once the new MTU is tried and works without fragmentation, the Windows 95 TCP/IP implementation is smart enough to remember that to send to station 158.48.227.200, TCP cannot exceed a certain MTU (1046 bytes, in this case) to pass to the IP layer for all subsequent packet transmissions. Other connections to other servers not at the remote site are not affected and can continue to use the larger MTU.

This method of recovering from an MTU mismatch can be disabled in the Windows 95/98/NT registry using the "EnablePMTUDiscover" setting.

FIGURE 4.21 Packet trace of a recovery from an IP MTU mismatch.

Doing so, however, leads to IP fragmentation at the router, an undesirable side effect discussed earlier in this chapter.

Meanwhile, I set out to investigate the original problem with the higher MTU and began by setting the MTU back to 1600 at both ends of the T1. Using a protocol analyzer to capture large PING packets (large packets can be sent via PING by adjusting the default PING packet size upwards) from a workstation on campus A to a server on campus B, I could see that about one in four PINGs were not answered. Obviously a packet loss rate of approximately 25 percent was unacceptable.

The initial packet capture was performed on the Ethernet just prior to the T1 router. By using a WAN analyzer at both ends on the T1, I was able to confirm that the packets were sent and received without error, clearing the T1 of the problem.

At the remote site, protocol analysis of the Ethernet segment on the server to which I was sending the PING revealed that about one in four packets had a CRC error. The hub to which both the analyzer and the server were connected was a multicard, chassis-based hub, with the analyzer and the server plugged into the same hub card. Moving the analyzer to a different card, or "blade," in the same hub didn't show any CRC errors on the PING packets.

The immediate solution was to move the server off the bad hub card to a good one. In doing so, I was able to maintain maximum Ethernet utilization with the large packets, without error. Later, the bad hub card was replaced.

4.3.11 IPX

Internetwork Packet Exchange (IPX) is the primary datagram protocol used by NetWare. In mid 1998, Novell introduced NetWare 5.0 with support for "pure IP," but it will take some time before NetWare sites completely migrate away from IPX. IPX provides datagram delivery services just like IP, but with several subtle differences in the packet format and in the way in which the routers handle the packets.

The packet format for the IPX datagram is illustrated in Figure 4.22. This format is almost identical to the Xerox Internetwork Datagram (IDP) packet used in earlier Xerox Network Systems (XNS) networks.

Unlike IP, the IPX header is a fixed size of 30 bytes—there are no IPX "options." The first field in the header is the 16-bit IPX checksum, which covers the entire IPX datagram. By default, most IPX implementations do not implement the checksum and set the value to all 1s, or hex FFFF. If the checksum is enabled, the NetWare "raw" packet format cannot be used on Ethernet (see Chapter 3 for more details).

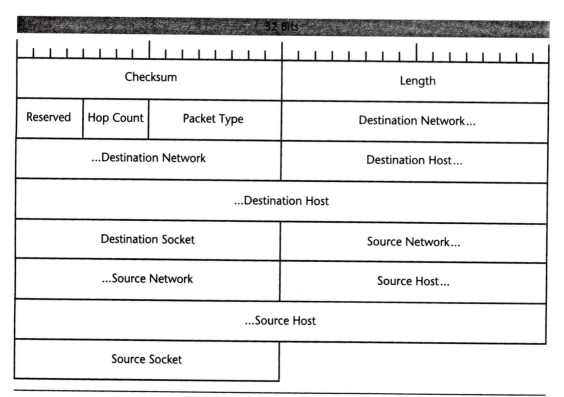

FIGURE 4.22 The IPX datagram packet format.

The next field is the 16-bit length of the datagram, including the header and data. Datagrams of up to 64 Kbytes can be accommodated, but they are much smaller in practice, depending on the MTU of the underlying DLC layer. Unlike IP, IPX datagrams cannot be fragmented by host or routers.

The next 4 bits are reserved, and if you were to look at an XNS IDP packet, these bits are the maximum packet lifetime (MPL), which provides the time, in seconds, that a packet can remain on an XNS internetwork. The MPL is the only field not carried over from the IDP format to IPX.

The next 4 bits are the hop count, which limits an IPX packet to a maximum of 15 routers. If a packet needs to be forwarded by a router that already has a 15 hop count, the packet is discarded. Unlike IP, there is no ICMP protocol to inform the sender that the hop count was exceeded. You must use statistics available from your router to see if IPX packets are being discarded. If you have a NetWare server that is also routing between network segments, you can use the IPXCON utility to check for discarded packets.

> **(!)** Because the IPX hop count starts at zero and is incremented as an IPX datagram passes through a router, you always know how many routers an IPX packet has traversed. Contrast this to IP, where you must know the starting TTL, which can vary from host to host. If you capture IPX packets with your analyzer and filter on one IPX source-destination pair in both directions, you can add the hop counts in both directions to get the total number of routers between the source and destination. This trick works regardless of where your analyzer is placed on a route between the source and destination.

The 4-bit hop count is one of the limitations of IPX. Because the MPL field is not used, Novell could have extended the hop count, which they didn't do until the NetWare Link State Protocol (NLSP) was defined. With routers that implement NLSP, the hop count is allowed to increment as high as 127; otherwise, the maximum hop count remains at 15.

The field following the hop count is the 8-bit packet type. Table 4.2 defines some of the packet types.

The packet type field is followed by the 80-bit destination internetwork address consisting of a 32-bit network address and a 48-bit node address. The destination internetwork address of 0.FFFFFFFFFFFF is a broadcast to all IPX nodes on any IPX network number on the same cable segment as the sender. The destination address of 908.FFFFFFFFFFFF is a broadcast for all nodes on the same cable as the sender that have IPX network 908 assigned to them. Neither of these broadcasts crosses routers. An IPX Type 20, a propagated broadcast packet, is required to broadcast across routers. Propagated broadcast packets are discussed a bit later in this chapter.

TABLE 4.2 IPX Packet Types

Value	Description
0	Unknown or NetWare Link State Protocol (NLSP) Packet
1	Routing Information Protocol (RIP) Packet
4	Services Advertising Protocol (SAP) Packet
5	Sequence Packet Exchange (SPX) or SPX II Packet
17	NetWare Core Protocol (NCP) Packet
20	NetBIOS Propagated Broadcast (IPX Broadcast) Packet
123	Experimentation or Serialization Packet
199	Experimentation or Serialization Packet

If a router receives an IPX packet for which it has no route to the destination, it is discarded. If the IPX segment is defined on a router port (i.e., it is the end IPX segment for which the packet is destined), the router transmits the packet on that port even if there is no node to receive the packet. Note the contrast between this and IP, where the router first verifies that the end DLC node to receive that IP packet actually resides on that segment.

In Figure 4.22, a 16-bit destination socket number follows the node addresses and is not part of the internetwork address, i.e., it plays no part in delivering the datagram to the destination.

The IPX header ends with the 32-bit source network, the 48-bit source node address, and the 16-bit source socket number.

In contrast to IP, the IPX internetwork address is of sufficient size to avoid having to "subnet" the address. Like any network layer protocol, there's no dependency on the DLC layer's address, but because the IPX node address can hold 48 bits, a workstation's 48-bit MAC address is simply replicated at this layer. This, plus the fact that a client learns its 32-bit network ID dynamically, means that you don't have the pain of managing workstation internetwork addresses that you have in IP.

Figure 4.23 shows a trace of a workstation acquiring an IPX network ID. This workstation has been cold booted and does not have a cached IPX network ID, as evidenced by the first packet it sends with an IPX network ID of 0. The first packet sent by the workstation is a Services Advertising Protocol (SAP) packet looking for a file server. The SAP protocol is discussed in more detail in Chapter 6, but all IPX clients start out on the network looking for a file server or NetWare Directory Services (NDS) server.

The SAP response (packet 2) is from a router and contains the logical name of a file server (FS_CORP1) and the virtual IPX network ID (hex 1004201) assigned to that server. The workstation then sends a NetWare RIP packet (packet 3) to find a route to the IPX network hex 1004201. The response (packet 4) contains two important pieces of information: the DLC address that the workstation will send all packets to for network 1004201 and the IPX network number assigned to the NIC card or "cable" of the responding router.

In packet 4, the RIP response, the source and destination IPX network ID is hex 10004200. The workstation then takes on this value as its network ID, as can be seen from the connect request to the server in packet 5.

In a file server, however, the node address is assigned a bit differently. From NetWare 3.x and up, every file server has a unique 32-bit IPX network identifier that is randomly generated or manually configured and assigned to an

The workstation starts out with an IPX network of zero.

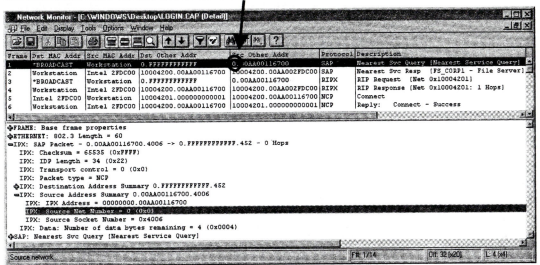

Then it assigns itself IPX network hex "1004200" based on the IPX address in the RIP response (packet 4).

FIGURE 4.23 Packet trace of an IPX client at boot-up.

internal or "virtual" IPX network, as discussed in Chapter 2. Because this virtual IPX network is unique throughout an IPX internetwork, and given there can be multiple NICs in the server each having its own MAC address, the node address portion of the IPX internetwork address of the server is simply set to 1. Thus, when looking at an IPX packet with a protocol analyzer, a packet with a source IPX address such as 10004201.000000000001 in packet 6 in Figure 4.23 can immediately be identified as one that originated from a server.

In Figure 4.23, the "router" is actually a NetWare server connected to the same hub as the workstation. It responds like a router because it is "routing" to its internal IPX network. The server sends out a RIP packet every 60 seconds, just like a router, advertising its internal IPX network ID. Note that in packet 4, the RIP response says the hop count is 1 hop to network hex 10004201. This is because the server, acting as a router, is counting the internal "hop" to its virtual IPX network. If you were to look inside the detail of packet 4, the actual physical IPX hop count is 0.

You may be wondering why a network layer has socket numbers. In IP, socket numbers (or ports as they are called) are at the transport layer in the UDP and TCP protocols. By having well-known socket or port numbers, workstations can connect to applications at a server by specifying a certain destination socket or port. The source socket or port will be dynamically assigned by the workstation such that simultaneous connections can be made to a server over the same protocol. In Figure 4.23, you can see from the detailed decode of packet 6, where the workstation is requesting a connection to a NetWare file server, that the source socket is hex 4003 and the destination socket is hex 451 (NCP). Common socket numbers are listed in Table 4.3.

Recall that the NetWare Core Protocol (NCP) is an application layer file services protocol that runs directly over IPX. Because there is no transport layer to provide port numbers, this function is conveniently provided by socket information carried at the network layer. Thus socket numbers of IPX provide the same functionality as the port numbers of UDP and TCP. This takes some getting used to because socket numbers are not a required function of

TABLE 4.3 Common IPX Socket Numbers

Hex/Decimal	Description
451/1105	NetWare Core Protocol (NCP)
452/1106	Service Advertising Protocol (SAP)
453/1107	Routing Information Protocol (RIP)
455/1109	NetBIOS
456/1110	Diagnostics
457/1111	Serialization

the network layer according to the OSI reference model. Then again, IPX (and IP for that matter) were developed before the OSI model.

> ❗
>
> When analyzing conversations using your protocol analyzer, you can sort specific transactions from an IPX pair that has multiple connections by filtering on socket numbers at the network layer. With IP, you need to filter on UDP or TCP port numbers at the transport layer.

4.3.12 IPX Propagated Broadcast Packets

One of the more unusual IPX packet types is type 20, a propagated broadcast sometimes called an IPX WAN Broadcast. NetBIOS over IPX in Microsoft Windows networks uses an IPX WAN Broadcast to locate resources.

Figure 4.24 shows an IPX type 20 packet as decoded by Sniffer Pro. As the packet passes through a router, the router places the address of the IPX network on which the packet was received in the NetBIOS header. The NetBIOS header contains room for up to 8 IPX networks in sequence, which limits the IPX type 20 broadcast to only 8 router hops. In the example in Figure 4.24, the IPX hop count is 1 and a router has placed the IPX address of 2022 in the NetBIOS header. As the packet is forwarded and IPX networks are added, a router checks the list to ensure that the packet hasn't already traversed this route. This prevents looping when there are parallel routers between segments.

Networks that have redundant routes between end-points can cause a flood of type 20 packets because every router forwards a type 20 packet to every port. For example, if there are two routers between two network segments, both will forward the type 20 packet, causing two broadcast packets on the next segment. If that segment has two routers, the two packets are forwarded by both routers, causing four packets to appear on the next segment, and so on. NetWare servers with IPX routing enabled between NICs and some hardware routers (such as Cisco) allow you to apply additional checking to further limit the forwarding of type 20 packets.

4.3.13 Case Study: The Extra Hop

This was a situation in which traffic levels were higher than expected on certain Ethernet segments. Part of the network I focused on is illustrated in the top half of Figure 4.25. This was a classic situation of a customer who was migrating from NetWare-based routing to stand-alone routers. The routing

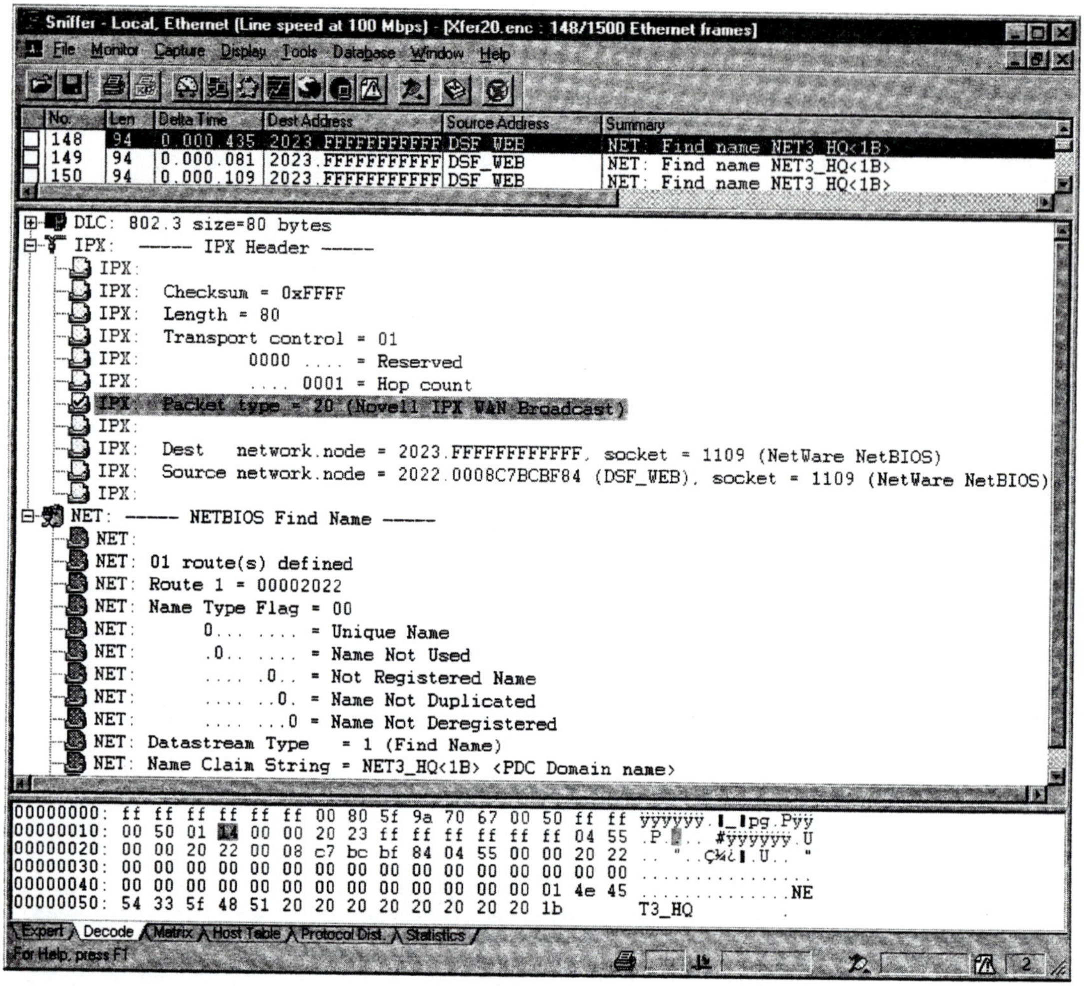

FIGURE 4.24 An IPX type 20 propagated broadcast packet.

function in the file server DAH_001 was disabled after the router was up and running and configured for IPX routing.

Server DAH_001 sends an IPX RIP packet every 60 seconds advertising its internal IPX network number of hex 0000A100 to the top and bottom Ethernet segments in Figure 4.25. Server MCH_001 sends a RIP packet every 60 seconds advertising its internal IPX network of hex 0000A101 to the bottom segment.

Because the router learns about the two IPX networks—0000A100 and 0000A101—from the bottom segment, it propagates information about these

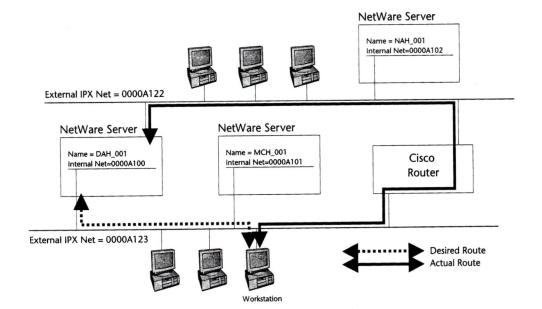

FIGURE 4.25 A NetWare client picks a non-optimal route to the server.

two networks plus network 0000A123 via IPX RIP every 60 seconds to its other ports, or the top Ethernet segment in this case. Likewise, because the router learned about one IPX network—0000A100—from the top Ethernet segment, it propagates that IPX network plus IPX network 0000A122 to the lower segment.

In the packet trace shown in Figure 4.25, packet 281 is the service query from the workstation and packets 282 and 283 are the responses from file servers DAH_001 and MCH_001, respectively. The workstation chooses the first response, file server DAH_001, for its initial connection. Inside packet 282, you can see that file server DAH_001 has an internal IPX network of hex 0000A100. The workstation then sends out a RIP packet to find out who has a route to 0000A100. Because DAH_001 is on the same segment as the workstation, both DAH_001 and the router respond to the RIP query.

Because the workstation once again picks the first response and the router responded before DAH_001, the workstation subsequently sends its packets to the router instead of directly to the server, as you can see in packets 287 and 288. The end result is unnecessary traffic passing through the router and consuming bandwidth on another segment.

If you were looking at a trace during the middle of a file transfer over IPX, you'd never recognize this anomaly unless you were knowledgeable about the topology of your network and noted that all the packets to the server had Cisco destination MAC addresses or that the packets returning from the server had a Cisco source MAC address or an IPX hop count of 1.

How can this be prevented from happening? The NetWare RIP specification notes that if a router hears about an IPX network from more than one port, and each instance has an identical hop and tick count (in Figure 4.25, DAH_001 sends a RIP packet to both the upper and lower segments with a hop count of 1 and a default tick count of 2), the router should not advertise the route at all. In other words, the identical RIP information received on two different ports tells the router that there is a NetWare IPX server in parallel with the router.

Unfortunately not all routers handle this situation in the same way. One way to get around it with Cisco IOS is to use the "ipx maximum-paths" command. For other routers, consult the appropriate documentation.

4.3.14 IPX RIP Operation

IPX RIP works in principle just like IP RIP as discussed earlier. Unlike IP RIP, however, IPX RIP packets can originate from workstations and servers. Like routers, an IPX server RIPs every 60 seconds advertising its internal IPX network identifier. Routers pick up these server RIP packets and propagate the information just like RIP packets from other routers.

> Beware of changing the default IPX RIP interval. If two routers on the same network segment have different timers, the router with the shorter interval may age the IPX entries and advertise the routes as unreachable by sending a RIP packet with the hop count set to 16. Worse, only one unreachable IPX network is sent per RIP packet. Imagine having to broadcast unreachable routes for a table of 2000 IPX network IDs, especially over a slow WAN link.

Workstations use IPX RIP in an unconventional manner in that they don't advertise a route but send out a RIP broadcast to *find* a route to an IPX network. Another subtle difference is that IPX RIP packets also advertise a tick count in addition to the hop count metric for each IPX network. The tick count takes precedence over the hop count when making a routing decision. The hop count is used only as a tie.

The tick count is set to 1 for 10 Mbps Ethernet interfaces. All other line speeds are relative to this. For example, on a 4 Mbps Token Ring, the default tick count is 2. The lower the transmission rate, the higher the tick count. What do you set the tick count to for faster line speeds? Unfortunately, for 16 Mbps Token Ring, 100 Mbps FDDI, 100 Mbps Ethernet, Gigabit Ethernet, and so forth, the tick count remains at 1. Novell proposed a way to use the tick value for higher speed networks, but it never caught on.

RIP packets are broadcast in IPX datagrams with the IPX socket number set to 1107 (hex 0453). Like IP, IPX network entries will time out in 3 minutes (4 minutes in NetWare 4.x and higher servers) if no IPX RIP update is seen for a given IPX network ID.

As was mentioned in Chapter 3, IPX RIP packets are also sent out for each DLC encapsulation type. For example, if you have all four Ethernet encapsulation types bound to a NIC card on a NetWare server, not one but four RIP packets are broadcast every 60 seconds.

By default, up to 50 IPX routes can be advertised in one IPX RIP packet. A large IPX infrastructure that has dozens of IPX network segments and hundreds of IPX devices with internal IPX network IDs can cause routers to generate several RIP packets every 60 seconds. For example, 1000 IPX network IDs will cause a router to send 20 RIP packets every 60 seconds. Some routers also allow multiple IPX encapsulation types, which makes for even more RIP packets.

Microsoft Windows 95/98 clients use IPX RIP whenever auto frame detection is enabled for IPX. On Ethernet, the client sends out a RIP request for the IPX network hex FFFFFFFFFFFF, which means any IPX network, using NetWare "raw" encapsulation, followed by 802.2 LLC encapsulation, followed by Ethertype encapsulation. The client uses the encapsulation type found in the first RIP response packet. The 802.2 LLC SNAP format is not tried because this encapsulation type is not supported by Microsoft on Ethernet, only on Token Ring.

Novell's Client32 also has the auto frame detection capability. Unlike Microsoft, the Novell auto detection detects the frame type by broadcast NetWare Service Advertising Protocol (SAP) packets instead of IPX RIP packets. Client32 also supports the 802.2 LLC SNAP format on both Ethernet and Token Ring.

> **❗**
>
> Avoid using IPX auto frame type detection. For one, more broadcast traffic is generated. For another, if a client picks up a frame type such as Ethertype from a print server that has all encapsulation types enabled, the client will not be able to directly communicate with a server bound to 802.2 LLC.

4.3.15 Case Study: IPX MTU Mismatch

In a previous case study, you saw how IP can recover from an MTU mismatch. This case study examines how this recovery is achieved with IPX. The problem network in question was a nationwide network with a centralized headquarters and links to remote sites over dedicated leased lines. Directory listings to a remote server were quick, but file transfers, even small ones, were slow.

In analyzing a file transfer from the campus to a remote NetWare file server over a 256 Kbps connection, the file transfer took much longer than I expected. Even for files as small as 20 Kbytes, it was taking over a half minute. Doing some quick math, 256 Kbps is about 32 Kbytes per second. It seems that the 20 Kbyte file transfer should have taken only a second or less!

When IPX was initially designed, the maximum IPX MTU in routed networks was 576 bytes. This followed the XNS recommendation that the maximum datagram size be limited to 576 bytes. Not surprising, there are also recommendations in some of the earlier RFCs that the IP datagram size not exceed 576 bytes in routed networks. This ensures that no matter what the underlying network topology, from Ethernet to X.25, a datagram will be able to pass through and, in the case of IP, without fragmentation.

When an IPX client sends data to a server, it would normally restrict the maximum IPX MTU (that is, the maximum size of the IPX portion of the packet as indicated in the IPX header length field) to 576 bytes if it knows that that

SUMMARY	Delta T	Rel Time	Bytes	Destination		Source	Summary
M 1		0.000	60	20002100.1		20003201.MADGE 146C23	NCP C Create Connection
2	0.103	0.103	61	20003201.IBM	128A01	20002100.1	NCP R OK
3	0.001	0.103	63	20002100.1		20003201.MADGE 146C23	NCP C Get file server info
4	0.110	0.213	189	20003201.IBM	128A01	20002100.1	NCP R OK
5	0.001	0.213	63	20002100.1		20003201.MADGE 146C23	NCP C Get big packet max size 4174
6	0.100	0.313	66	20003201.IBM	128A01	20002100.1	NCP R OK, accepted max size 4174

FIGURE 4.26 Negotiating the IPX large internet packet (LIP) size.

server is on the other side of a router, by looking at the hop count in a packet returned from the server. To take advantage of larger MTUs in LANs, Novell added the Large Internet Packet (LIP) protocol. With LIP, the client and server negotiate the maximum MTU.

Figures 4.26 through 4.28 are packet trace summaries from my headquarters workstation on a Token Ring, connecting to a remote server also on a Token Ring. The capture is from the workstation segment.

In Figure 4.26, as part of the server connection sequence, the workstation asks the server if it can handle a LIP packet (decoded as a "Get big packet max size" by Sniffer Pro) of 4174 bytes, which it can.

Later on, the workstation attempts to read a file from the server, as shown in Figure 4.27. Up to this point, small packets containing directory listings and file open commands have worked just fine. However, the file read request for 4110 bytes of data fails. The workstation has timed out waiting for the response and tries again about 2.7 seconds later, as seen in the time difference between the two read requests.

SUMMARY	Delta T	Rel Time	Bytes	Destination		Source	Summary
M 1		0.000	73	20002100.1		2003201.MADGE 146C23	NCP C Open file FILE1.DAT
2	0.103	0.103	97	20003201.IBM	128A01	20002100.1	NCP R OK, Opened F=1A17 0000
3	0.001	0.104	73	20002100.1		20003201.MADGE 146C23	NCP C F=1A17 0000 Read 4110 at 0
4	1.813	1.918	73	20002100.1		20003201.MADGE 146C23	NCP C F-1A17 0000 Read 4110 at 0
5	2.746	4.664	73	20002100.1		20003201.MADGE 146C23	NCP C F=1A17 0000 Read 4110 at 0
6	0.004	7.410	59	0.FFFFFFFFFFFF		20003201.MADGE 146C23	IPX RIP request: find 1 network, 20002100
7	0.001	7.415	63	20003201.IBM	128A01	20003201.Cisco 1976A1	IPX RIP response: 1 network, 20002100 at 6 hops
8	2.746	7.415	73	20002100.1		20003201.MADGE 146C23	NCP C F=1A17 0000 Read 4096 at 0
9	0.004	10.156	73	20002100.1		20003201.MADGE 146C23	NCP C F=1A17 0000 Read 3584 at 0
10	0.001	12.902	73	20002100.1		20003201.MADGE 146C23	NCP C F=1A17 0000 Read 3072 at 0
11	2.741	15.649	73	20002100.1		20003201.MADGE 146C23	NCP C F=1A17 0000 Read 2560 at 0
12	2.746	18.395	73	20002100.1		20003201.MADGE 146C23	NCP C F=1A17 0000 Read 2048 at 0
13	2.746	21.141	73	20002100.1		20003201.MADGE 146C23	NCP C F=1A17 0000 Read 1536 at 0
14	2.746	23.887	73	20002100.1		20003201.MADGE 146C23	NCP C F=1A17 0000 Read 1024 at 0
15	0.183	24.070	1087	20003201.IBM	128A01	20002100.1	NCP R OK, 1024 bytes read
16	0.001	24.071	73	20002100.1		20003201.MADGE 146C23	NCP C F=1A17 0000 Read 1024 at 1024
17	0.185	24.256	1087	20003201.IBM	`128A01	20002100.1	NCP R OK, 1024 bytes read
18	0.001	24.257	73	20002100.1		20003201.MADGE 146C23	NCP C F-1A17 0000 Read 1024 at 2048
19	0.186	24.443	1087	20003201.IBM	128A01	20002100.1	NCP R OK, 1024 bytes read

FIGURE 4.27 Discovering the IPX MTU (NetWare shell).

Having no response after a second attempt, the workstation thinks that maybe the route to the destination has changed and it sends an IPX packet RIP packet, looking for a route to the remote server's internal IPX network ID of hex 20002100. The response to the RIP packet is from the same router as before, and the workstation proceeds.

The next read request is actually for a slightly smaller amount of data, 4096 bytes. Once again, there's no reply. The workstation then decrements the amount of data requested by 512 bytes on successive packets until a reply is received, 1024 bytes.

The problem with this recovery algorithm is twofold:

1. It took approximately 24 seconds from the first read attempt to the first successfully returned packet (packets 1 through 15 in Figure 4.27).
2. 1024 is not necessarily the optimal MTU. Could there be a better MTU between 1024 and 1536 bytes?

The MTU discovery algorithm just described is used in the original NetWare shells known as NETX that run under real-mode DOS. Novell has since improved the algorithm for VLM and Client32 redirectors.

Figure 4.28 shows a packet trace of the same workstation communicating to the same remote server, but this time using a VLM redirector instead of the NETX shell. This time the workstation discovers the maximum MTU by performing a LIP echo test *immediately* after negotiating the LIP size to make sure that an IPX datagram of that size will really make it to the server and back. These LIP echo tests (incorrectly decoded by the Sniffer as NCP Create Connection packets) are packets 7 through 29 and 32 through 43 in the figure.

After the first echo test in packet 7 with a length of 4197 (this is the Token Ring packet length minus the CRC; the actual IPX datagram length in this packet is 4174 bytes) fails, the redirector then tries with a packet size of 599 bytes, which works. The next size tried is 2407 bytes, or a little over half of the first try of 4197 bytes.

This fails, so echo tests of 1511, then 1063 bytes are tried. Because of the latency to the remote server and back, the 1511 byte echo test is a bit delayed, but does eventually return. The redirector then locks on this MTU (which has an IPX datagram length of 1488 bytes) and continues the echo tests for several packets. In essence, the redirector has performed a binary search to find an optimum MTU for the remote server; the local MTU stays at 4 Kbytes. The additional tests in packets 32 through 43 are required to time the round-trip response time from the remote server in order to optimize the packet burst protocol for subsequent file transfers.

SUMMARY		Delta T	Real Time	Bytes	Destination		Source	Summary
	1		−0.398	60	200021000.1		2003201.MADGE 146C23	NCP C Create Connection
	2	0.177	−0.221	61	20003201.IBM	128A01	20002100.1	NCP R OK
	3	0.001	−0.220	63	20002100.1		20003201.MADGE 146C23	NCP C Get file server info
	4	0.109	−0.111	189	20003201.IBM	128A01	20002100.1	NCP R OK
	5	0.002	−0.109	63	20002100.1		20003201.MADGE 146C23	NCP C Get big packet max size 4174
	6	0.100	−0.009	66	20003201.IBM	128A01	20002100.1	NCP R OK, accepted max size 4174
M	7	0.009	0.000	4197	20002100.1		20003201.MADGE 146C23	NCP C Create Connection
	8	2.677	2.677	4197	20002100.1		20003201.MADGE 146C23	NCP C Create Connection
	9	0.005	2.682	4197	20002100.1		20003201.MADGE 146C23	NCP C Create Connection
	10	2.679	5.361	599	20002100.1		20003201.MADGE 146C23	NCP C Create Connection
	11	0.001	5.362	599	20002100.1		20003201.MADGE 146C23	NCP C Create Connection
	12	0.182	5.544	599	20003201.IBM	128A01	20002100.1	NCP C Create Connection
	13	0.002	5.546	615	20002100.1		20003201.MADGE 146C23	NCP C Create Connection
	14	0.001	5.547	615	20002100.1		20003201.MADGE 146C23	NCP C Create Connection
	15	0.017	5.564	599	20003201.IBM	128A01	20002100.1	NCP C Create Connection
	16	0.168	5.732	615	20003201.IBM	128A01	20002100.1	NCP C Create Connection
	17	0.005	5.737	2407	20002100.1		20003201.MADGE 146C23	NCP C Create Connection
	18	0.003	5.740	2407	20002100.1		20003201.MADGE 146C23	NCP C Create Connection
	19	0.020	5.761	615	20003201.IBM	128A01	20002100.1	NCP C Create Connection
	20	0.207	5.967	1511	20002100.1		20003201.MADGE 146C23	NCP C Create Connection
	21	0.002	5.969	1511	20002100.1		20003201.MADGE 146C23	NCP C Create Connection
	22	0.272	6.241	1063	20002100.1		20003201.MADGE 146C23	NCP C Create Connection
	23	0.001	6.242	1063	20002100.1		20003201.MADGE 146C23	NCP C Create Connection
	24	0.049	6.291	1511	20003201.IBM	128A01	20002100.1	NCP C Create Connection
	25	0.004	6.295	1511	20002100.1		20003201.MADGE 146C23	NCP C Create Connection
	26	0.054	6.349	1511	20003201.IBM	128A01	20002100.1	NCP C Create Connection
	27	0.147	6.497	1063	20003201.IBM	128A01	20002100.1	NCP C Create Connection
	28	0.037	6.533	1063	20003201.IBM	128A01	20002100.1	NCP C Create Connection
	29	0.112	6.645	1511	20003201.IBM	128A01	20002100.1	NCP C Create Connection
	30	0.006	6.651	78	20002100.1		20003201.MADGE 146C23	NCP C Burst mode connection
	31	0.102	6.754	69	20003201.IBM	128A01	20002100.1	NCP R OK, Got burst connection id
	32	0.004	6.758	1511	20002100.1		20003201.MADGE 146C23	NCP C Create Connection
	33	0.011	6.768	1511	20002100.1		20003201.MADGE 146C23	NCP C Create Connection
	34	0.315	7.083	1511	20003201.IBM	128A01	20002100.1	NCP C Create Connection
	35	0.055	7.138	1511	20003201.IBM	128A01	20002100.1	NCP C Create Connection
	36	0.004	7.142	1511	20002100.1		20003201.MADGE 146C23	NCP C Create Connection
	37	0.011	7.152	1511	20002100.1		20003201.MADGE 146C23	NCP C Create Connection
	38	0.311	7.463	1511	20003201.IBM	128A01	20002100.1	NCP C Create Connection
	39	0.054	7.517	1511	20003201.IBM	128A01	20002100.1	NCP C Create Connection
	40	0.005	7.521	1511	20002100.1		20003201.MADGE 146C23	NCP C Create Connection
	41	0.011	7.532	1511	20002100.1		20003201.MADGE 146C23	NCP C Create Connection
	42	0.311	7.844	1511	20003201.IBM	128A01	20002100.1	NCP C Create Connection
	43	0.057	7.900	1511	20003201.IBM	128A01	20002100.1	NCP C Create Connection

FIGURE 4.28 Discovering the IPX MTU (NetWare redirector).

Because the MTU has been determined ahead of time, in 6.6 seconds (as seen from the elapsed relative time from packet 7 to packet 29) subsequent file transfers are at near the wire speed of the 256 Kbps link. This time, the 20 Kbyte file read took only about 1 second to complete. Even adding in the additional 6.6 seconds of wait time to discover the MTU, this still beats 24 seconds from the previous "shell based" file read.

This is a classic example of using the default router MTU for a WAN link. The default MTU on a router WAN port is typically set to, say, 1600 bytes to accommodate Ethernet frames with some margin. If the networks are Token Ring or FDDI on either side of leased lines, you may want to increase the router's MTU on the WAN ports, especially for higher speed links.

Chapter 5

Analyzing and Troubleshooting the Transport Layer

5.1 Introduction

As mentioned in Chapter 1, the transport layer provides a reliable data delivery service to the application or session layer by providing end-to-end flow control and error recovery. Some transport layer implementations such as the Transport Control Protocol (TCP) also provide data segmentation and reassembly such that an application can ask it to send large chunks of data without having to worry about the size of the underlying MTUs. The transport layer also provides to an application one or more "virtual" connections or circuits (also called sessions) between two end-points.

A virtual circuit is analogous to a telephone call. The sender initiates a call by dialing a number, which in turn routes that call via a series of telco lines to the recipient. The circuit is virtual in the sense that the call may be routed via any number of possible physical routes to get to its destination. By answering the phone, the recipient has acknowledged the connection.

As discussed in Chapter 4, the network layer provides a "best effort" delivery of datagrams similar in analogy to the postal system. The transport layer provides additional mechanisms to ensure that these letters—the datagrams—are really delivered. In essence, the transport layer is keeping a close watch over the network layer by providing what looks to the application or session layer like a reliable virtual circuit.

Data segmentation is performed by breaking up a chunk of application data into smaller units acceptable by the network layer. The network layer then encapsulates the transport protocol header and application data and passes it to the DLC layer for transmission over a physical medium.

By having a transport protocol add sequence numbers to each piece of data before handing it off to the network layer, the recipient of the data can ensure that all the pieces are received for proper reassembly. For efficiency, the recipient's transport protocol only needs to acknowledge the last valid packet. If there are any gaps in the sequencing, the recipient can only acknowledge the last packet up to the one that's missing, requiring the sending transport protocol to send one or more chunks of data a second time. This sequencing and error recovery forms the basis for TCP.

Flow control at the transport layer is usually accomplished by limiting the number of packets that are sent before an acknowledgment is required. In some cases, this may be only a single packet. Usually, however, a "burst" of packets can be sent at one time.

Without a transport layer, flow control and error recovery must by done by a higher layer, such as the application layer or the application itself. Although transport protocols are not completely immune to errors, they are usually very persistent in moving data across error-prone networks such as the Internet. If the transport protocol fails to deliver the data, the user receives some type of error message either from the application (such as a Web browser) or the operating system itself.

If you look carefully for duplicate sending sequence numbers in a packet trace, you can identify transport retransmissions. Protocol analyzers with expert systems usually flag this as a symptom, telling you that the packets are being dropped or delayed in transit. A transport retransmission could indicate a network or processing delay in that the sending transport protocol is not allowing enough time for a response or acknowledgment and needlessly sends another packet.

5.2 User Datagram Protocol (UDP)

Calling UDP a transport layer protocol is somewhat of a misnomer. UDP is not reliable in that delivery is not guaranteed (see RFC 768, User Datagram Protocol, for more details). Nor are there any sequence numbers for a recipient to check for duplicate or lost packets. UDP is also a connectionless protocol in that two applications using UDP do not need to establish a connection prior to exchanging data.

UDP does, however, provide two valuable services: 16-bit port numbers to identify the sending and receiving processes or applications and a 16-bit checksum that protects the UDP data and part of the IP header. Figure 5.1 illustrates the UDP packet format.

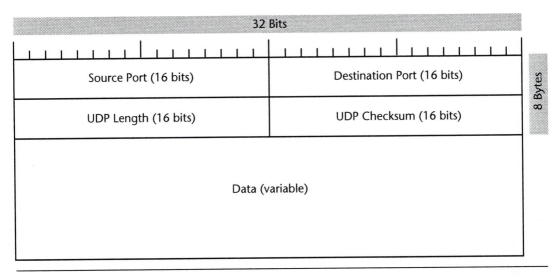

FIGURE 5.1 UDP packet format.

An example of port usage would be an SNMP application doing a get-request operation to an SNMP agent. As illustrated in Figure 5.2, the console application sends the request to the agent's IP address with a UDP header containing the well-known destination port number (161) for SNMP. The source port number in this example is dynamically assigned to port 4000 so that the agent can reply back to that port.

The checksum for UDP as well as TCP includes a 12-byte pseudo-header that is created only by the checksum process. The pseudo-header includes the 32-bit source and destination IP addresses, an 8-bit reserved field set to 0, the 8-bit protocol ID from the IP header, and the 16-bit UDP length field. Figure 5.3 illustrates the creation of the pseudo-header for checksum calculation purposes. Also note that a byte of 0 may be appended at the end of the UDP data to make it an even number of 16-bit words.

Protecting the IP header is somewhat redundant and makes UDP (as well as TCP) inseparable from IP, but it does allow UDP to double check that the IP datagram has arrived at the correct destination. If the checksum is transmitted as a 0, the sending UDP layer did not compute the checksum and the data is not protected.

An application that wants to send datagrams one at a time can use UDP. Examples of popular application layer protocols that use UDP include Boot Protocol (BOOTP), Dynamic Host Configuration Protocol (DHCP, an extension of BOOTP), Domain Name Services (DNS), Network File System (NFS),

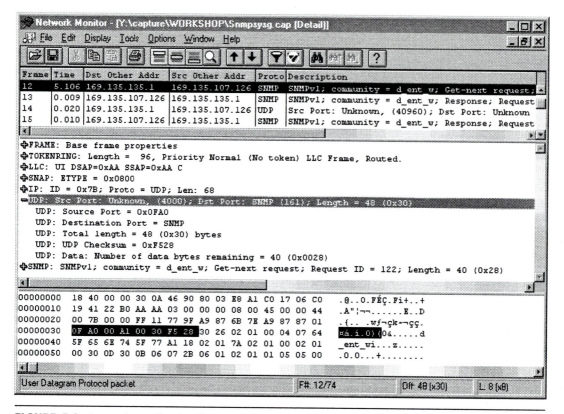

FIGURE 5.2 A sample application (SNMP) using UDP.

Trivial File Transport Protocol (TFTP), and the Simple Network Management Protocol (SNMP).

When using UDP, the application is responsible for error recovery. For example, a DNS query may be sent to a secondary DNS server if no response is heard from the primary DNS server.

The application must also ensure that the total of the 8-byte UDP header, data, and IP header (20 bytes by default) does not exceed the MTU of the underlying DLC layer. Otherwise, IP fragments the UDP data into multiple datagrams.

A good example of this is an NFS implementation that operates over UDP. As discussed in Chapter 4, by setting the NFS read and write block size to 8192 bytes on Ethernet, the UDP layer asks the IP layer to send an 8192-byte datagram. The IP layer in turn must fragment the packet into six smaller packets sent as six Ethernet frames.

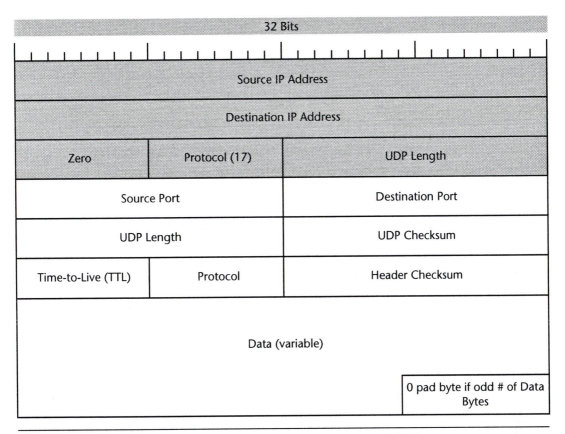

FIGURE 5.3 A pseudo-header (shaded) is added to compute the UDP checksum.

Speaking of error recovery that normally resides in the transport layer, if one of the six aforementioned packets does not reach the destination, the *application* (i.e., NFS) must resend the entire 8192-byte block of data all over again, generating another six packets on the network. Chapter 8 gives an example of this and how it impacts NFS file transfer performance. There are also less widely deployed implementations of NFS that run over TCP.

5.3 Transport Control Protocol (TCP)

TCP is one of the most fascinating protocols to analyze. What makes it so interesting is that every implementation exhibits different characteristics when you analyze it using a protocol analyzer. TCP performance and error

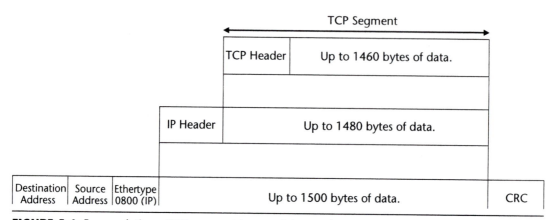

FIGURE 5.4 Encapsulating a TCP segment into an Ethernet frame.

recovery depend on many variables, including the platform it is running on, the network speed and reliability, and the setting of various TCP parameters.

Unlike UDP, TCP is a "real" transport layer protocol in that it has flow control and error recovery. TCP (RFC 783, Transmission Control Protocol) is also connection-oriented; the client must establish a connection with a server before sending TCP data, or "segments," back and forth.

A TCP segment includes the TCP header and payload (or data). The segment size can usually be adjusted in a TCP/IP stack. For example, the default segment size for TCP/IP running over Ethernet using Ethertype encapsulation is 1460 bytes. This allows room for the default TCP header of 20 bytes plus the default IP header of 20 bytes, for a total of 1500 bytes, the maximum payload of an Ethernet frame (see Figure 5.4). If you set the segment size higher than 1460 bytes, TCP will pass segments to the IP layer that are too large for the Ethernet frame, resulting in IP fragmentation (see Chapter 4 for more details regarding IP fragmentation).

5.3.1 TCP Header

The TCP header is shown in Figure 5.5. The first two fields are identical to the first two fields found in UDP: the 16-bit source port and 16-bit destination port. They serve the same function as in UDP, namely, to identify the process or application that is using TCP. The ports are followed by the 32-bit sending sequence number, then the 32-bit acknowledge number. These are both 32-bit unsigned integers that wrap when reaching their maximum value. Each side maintains its own sending sequence numbers. For this reason, TCP is sometimes referred to as a "full-duplex" protocol because send-

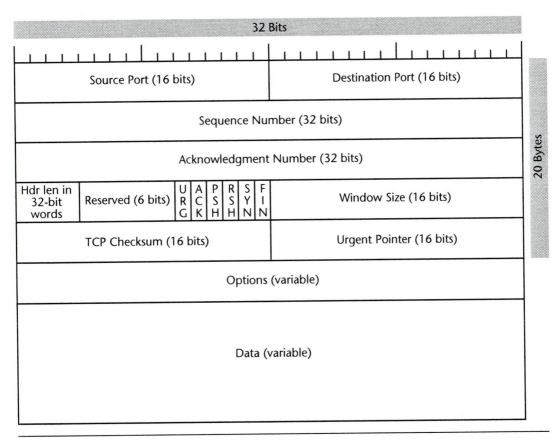

FIGURE 5.5 TCP packet format.

ing a stream of data in one direction is independent of the reverse direction. Examples of applications that operate over TCP include FTP, HTTP, SMTP, and Telnet.

TCP is often called a "byte stream" protocol because the sequence numbers correspond to a sequence of bytes instead of packet counts. Thus, rather than acknowledge the receipt of a single TCP packet, a receiver typically acknowledges the receipt of the amount of TCP data in the packet. For example, if a client sends 900 bytes of TCP data to a server, the TCP process in the server acknowledges (as indicated by the ACK flag in the TCP header) the 900 bytes by returning a sequence number equal to 900 *plus* the sequence number of the original packet containing the 900 bytes.

Suppose you capture a series of TCP packets going back and forth between two IP addresses. If the sequence number of an acknowledgment *equals* the sequence number of a TCP data packet sent just prior to the acknowledgment, the server has *not* yet acknowledged that data. Either the TCP stack is a bit slow in acknowledging the received TCP data or the packets have crossed in transit and the acknowledgment is really for previously sent data.

The next field in the TCP header is the length of the TCP header in 32-bit increments in the same vein as the IP header. Thus the TCP header must be an even increment of 4 bytes. The standard TCP header size is 20 bytes. If there are options such as the maximum segment size (MSS), the header will be longer than 20 bytes.

The first TCP packet sent in a connection sequence is a SYN or synchronize packet as indicated by the SYN flag in the TCP header. The client assigns a dynamic TCP source port and specifies a "well known" TCP port for the server, such as port 23, Telnet. The client can also tell the server the MSS or maximum amount of TCP data the server is allowed to send back to the client.

Likewise, the second packet in the connection sequence is a packet from the server back to the client to acknowledge the connect request, along with the server's MSS to limit the maximum amount of TCP data that the client can send to the server. Note that this is *not* considered to be a buffer size negotiation; rather, each side is telling the other the maximum permissible amount of TCP data (including the TCP header) that can be sent in one packet.

> **!**
>
> When analyzing TCP conversations over TCP, keep in mind that the MSS is announced to the other peer at connection time and defaults to 536 bytes (which is equal to a default IP MTU of 576 bytes minus the 20-byte IP header minus the 20-byte TCP header) if the MSS option is not present. The optimal MSS is usually the MTU of the path between client and server minus protocol overhead up to and including the network layer header. For example, a desirable MSS for Ethernet is 1460 bytes and 1452 bytes for IEEE 802.3 (which allows for an 8-byte LLC SNAP header). Beware that if the segment size is too large for the MTU of any intervening network, undesirable IP fragmentation may result.

> **!**
>
> If you study a trace of TCP packets and question why they are only so large, you will have to go back to the initial TCP SYN connect sequence to determine if the MSS is defaulting to 536 bytes or intentionally set to a small value by the application that opened the connection. If you didn't capture the connect sequence for a given IP address and TCP port, you must restart that application and recapture.

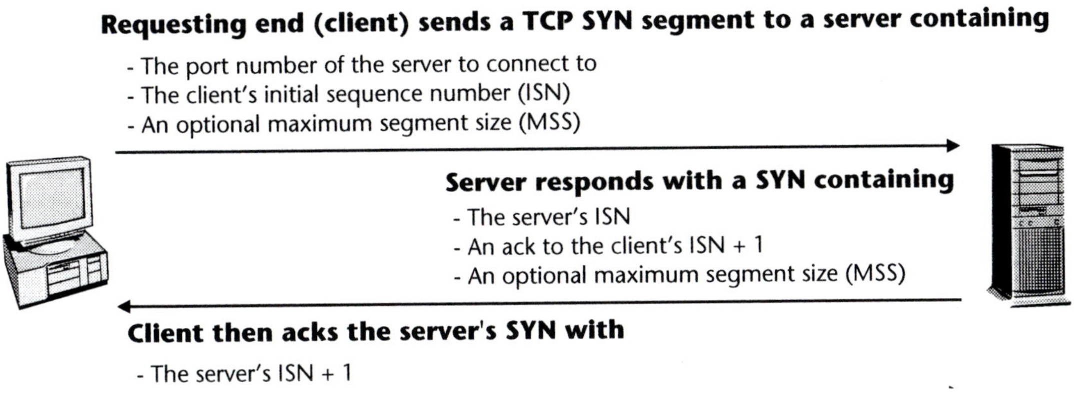

Requesting end (client) sends a TCP SYN segment to a server containing

- The port number of the server to connect to
- The client's initial sequence number (ISN)
- An optional maximum segment size (MSS)

         Server responds with a SYN containing

          - The server's ISN
          - An ack to the client's ISN + 1
          - An optional maximum segment size (MSS)

Client then acks the server's SYN with

- The server's ISN + 1

FIGURE 5.6 The TCP three-way handshake.

The third and final packet in the TCP connection sequence is an acknowledgment of the server's SYN packet. RFC 793 calls this sequence the "three-way handshake," as summarized in Figure 5.6.

Figure 5.7 is a trace showing an actual setup of a TCP connection in preparation for an FTP data transfer. The three-way handshake occurs in frames 47, 48, and 50. (Frames 46 and 49 are FTP control commands sent over a separate TCP connection. FTP commands use the well-known TCP port number 21.)

> ❗ When analyzing an application such as HTTP that operates over TCP, you may want to have your analyzer filter on more than just the client and server IP addresses. Because HTTP sets up several independent TCP connections for every image file, audio file, Java applet, and so on, you may want to capture on a particular client/server IP pair, then set a display filter on a particular TCP port pair such as TCP port 80 (HTTP) and dynamic port 1538. That way, you can more easily follow the TCP sequencing and acknowledgments. This trick also comes in handy when separating FTP commands from data.

As you'll see in Chapter 8, FTP uses one TCP connection for FTP commands and sets up a separate connection for data transfer. Note in Figure 5.7 how the client sends a "STOR oldtips.asp" command to the server and then the *server*, not the client, initiates the TCP connection for data transfer. In the figure, the server is connecting with the client's TCP port number 20, the well-known port number for default FTP data transfer.

Following the 6-bit reserved field in the TCP header are a series of 6-bit flags. The URG flag means that the urgent pointer in the TCP header is valid and

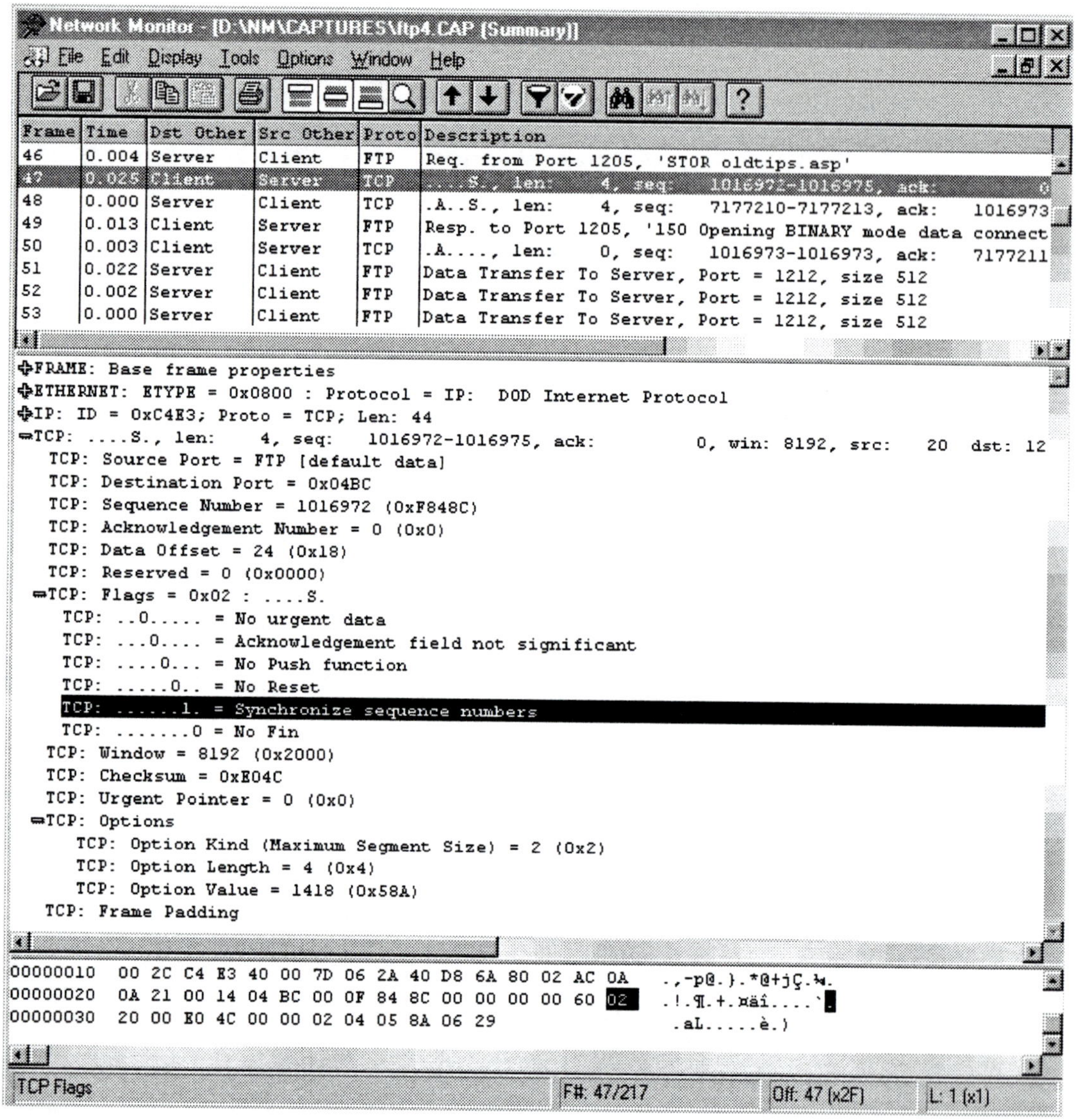

FIGURE 5.7 FTP setting up a TCP connection.

indicates that the packet contains some type of urgent data. The next bit is the ACK bit, as previously discussed.

Following those bits are the PSH, or push, bit, meaning that the receiving TCP stack should immediately inform the application of this data and any other received data not yet sent to the application. Some clients set it when-

> **❗**
> Some protocol analyzers such as Domino, Network Monitor, and Sniffer
> allow you to select which layer of protocol you view on the summary line for
> each packet in the display buffer. Usually only the highest layer of protocol
> decoded or all layers of protocols decoded are summarized. For example, if
> analyzing HTTP transactions between a client and a web server, you may
> want to have the analyzer only show the TCP layer on the summary line so
> you can more easily follow the client and server TCP protocol logic without
> having to dig inside the analyzer's detailed display of every packet.

ever they need to wait for a response from the server. Some TCP clients set
this flag in every packet. Most TCP implementations today simply ignore this
flag when receiving a packet because data is usually never delayed before
passing it up to the application layer. Thus, the PSH bit is really present more
for historical reasons than for usage by modern-day TCP implementations.

Next is the RST, or reset, bit, which is used to reset a connection. This bit is usually set in response to a client that sends a TCP SYN packet to a server for
which there is no process listening on the destination TCP port. Instead of
sending an ICMP (see Chapter 4 for a detailed discussion of ICMP) "port
unreachable" packet back to the sender as UDP would do, TCP instead sends
a reset. Figure 5.8 shows a trace of a user trying to FTP to a server that doesn't
have the FTP application running (at least not on the standard FTP port).

> **❗**
> A user could be trying to reach a service such as FTP that's not implemented
> on the server or trying to Telnet to a nonexistent port. This could very well
> happen in the case of a hacker trying to FTP or Telnet to a nonstandard port
> on your server (you may have moved the well-known FTP or Telnet ports for
> security reasons). Watching for this is simple with a protocol analyzer—just
> set a filter to capture for packets that have the TCP RST bit set to1.

The SYN, or synchronize, bit initiates a connection and synchronizes
sequence numbers. As was previously discussed, the MSS is also disclosed
in a SYN packet.

The FIN bit indicates that the sender is finished sending data. It is used to ter-
minate a TCP connection, provided the other side of the connection sends a
FIN as well. Figure 5.9 shows an example of an application (FTP) closing a
TCP connection.

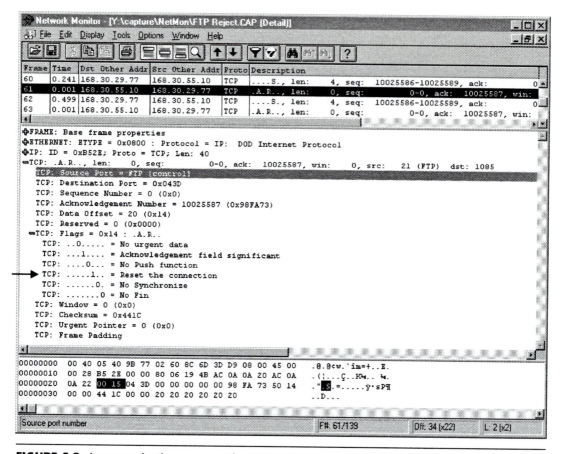

FIGURE 5.8 A server rejecting a request for FTP service on the standard FTP port. Note that the FTP client application tries twice, approximately 1/2 second apart.

If one side of the connection "dies," it is possible to have a "half connection" open, such as when a client kills an FTP application via a task manager or by turning off their workstation. Because there can only be so many open ports on a server, half open connections are undesirable, especially on high-volume Web servers or FTP servers. For this reason, some TCP implementations are configured to send out periodic TCP keep alive packets. In other implementations, if the server hasn't heard any activity for a certain amount of time on an open TCP port, it simply terminates the connection and the user must reestablish the TCP connection.

For HTTP, half open connections on a server are usually not a problem because the TCP connections are active only when HTML text or images are transferred. HTTP terminates the connection immediately upon completion of the transfer.

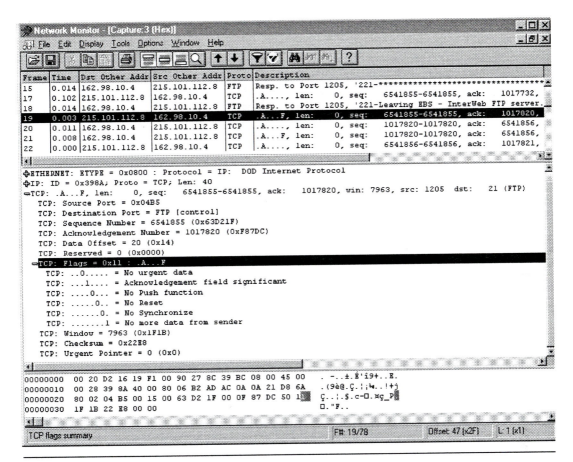

FIGURE 5.9 The TCP close.

For FTP connections, it could be more of a problem because the connection is open as long as the user is connected to the server. That's why servers can handle far more simultaneous browser users than FTP users; the HTTP connections are very short lived, whereas FTP connections are usually longer term.

Following the 6 flag bits is the 16-bit window size, which is the key to flow control in TCP. The window size is sent with every TCP packet to tell the other end how much buffer is available for incoming TCP data. Incoming data includes the TCP header and payload, but not any DLC or IP headers.

Suppose station A is sending FTP data to station B over TCP. Every now and then, station B sends an acknowledgment back to station A that will also contain the amount of available TCP buffer space, or window size, that station B can accommodate.

SUMMARY	Delta T	Bytes	Destination	Source	Summary	
M 349	0.0002	1514	[172.10.10.30]	[172.10.10.69]	TCP D=1049 S=20	ACK=240214726 SEQ=1018790197 LEN=1460 WIN=8760
350	0.0013	1514	[172.10.10.30]	[172.10.10.69]	TCP D=1049 S=20	ACK=240214726 SEQ=1018791657 LEN=1460 WIN=8760
351	0.0013	1514	[172.10.10.30]	[172.10.10.69]	TCP D=1049 S=20	ACK=240214726 SEQ=1018793117 LEN=1460 WIN=8760
352	0.0012	60	[172.10.10.69]	[172.10.10.30]	TCP D=20 S=1049	ACK=1018793117 WIN=2920
353	0.0001	1514	[172.10.10.30]	[172.10.10.69]	TCP D=1049 S=20	ACK=240214726 SEQ=1018794577 LEN=1460 WIN=8760
354	0.0012	60	[172.10.10.69]	[172.10.10.30]	TCP D=20 S=1049	ACK=1018796037 WIN=0
355	0.0026	60	[172.10.10.69]	[172.10.10.30]	TCP D=20 S=1049	ACK=1018796037 WIN=8760
356	0.0018	1514	[172.10.10.30]	[172.10.10.69]	TCP D=1049 S=20	ACK=240214726 SEQ=1018796037 LEN=1460 WIN=8760
357	0.0013	1514	[172.10.10.30]	[172.10.10.69]	TCP D=1049 S=20	ACK=240214726 SEQ=1018797497 LEN=1460 WIN=8760
358	0.0013	1514	[172.10.10.30]	[172.10.10.69]	TCP D=1049 S=20	ACK=240214726 SEQ=1018798957 LEN=1460 WIN=8760
359	0.0011	60	[172.10.10.69]	[172.10.10.30]	TCP D=20 S=1049	ACK=1018798957 WIN=8760

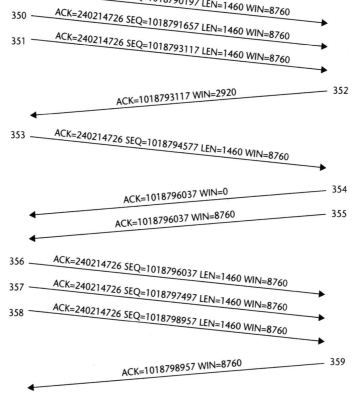

FIGURE 5.10 TCP in action.

Figure 5.10 shows a sample TCP trace along with a diagram to make it easier to follow the TCP behavior. Note that the acknowledgment number of 240214726 from 172.10.10.30 to 172.10.10.69 never changes. This is because 172.10.10.30 is only sending and not receiving any data from 172.10.10.69.

172.10.10.69 is, however, sending acknowledgment packets back to 172.10.10.30 containing the sequence number of the last received byte along with the window size. Packet 352 in the figure contains the acknowledgment of 1018793117 and a window of 2920. Which previously sent data is this packet acknowledging?

To determine this, you have to go back to a previously sent TCP data packet and add the length of the TCP payload to the sending sequence number. In the example, packet 352 is actually acknowledging receipt of all of the data up to and including packet 350. In packet 350, the sending sequence number of 1018791657 plus the TCP payload length of 1460 is equal to 1018793117, the acknowledgment number found in packet 352. Packet 351 is not acknowledged until later.

> **!**
>
> The length of the TCP data is not found in the header. To compute this, you need to take the IP datagram size minus the IP header size minus the TCP header size. Fortunately most analyzers compute this for you and display it on the summary line or inside the packet decode.

Note that, in packet 352, the offered window size is 2920 (also called the *offered* window). Because packet 351 has not yet been acknowledged and contains 1460 bytes of TCP data, 2920 – 1460 = 1460 (also called the *usable* window), meaning that the sender can only transmit one more segment containing 1460 bytes of data before waiting for the receiver's (i.e., 172.10.10.69) window to open back up.

In the example, this doesn't happen right away. Note how 172.10.10.69 in packet 354 is acknowledging all of the TCP data received thus far. The window is zero, meaning that none of the TCP data has been handed off to the application. This happens a short time later in packet 355 when you see that the window has "opened" back up. This took about 0.0026 seconds (2.6 milliseconds), as indicated by the delta time between packets 354 and 355.

> **!**
>
> The window size is used by TCP for flow control. If the window size drops below its maximum, the application is not taking the data off the TCP stack fast enough. If the window stays constant, but the acknowledgments are slow to return, the bottleneck is probably in the network rather than the application. In a dial-up connection, for example, you'll rarely see a drop in window size. On the other hand, you may see it drop on a high-speed LAN.

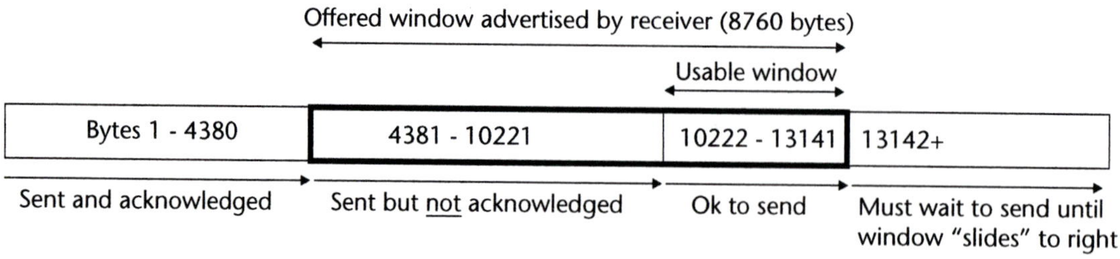

Offered window advertised by receiver (8760 bytes)

Bytes 1 - 4380	4381 - 10221	10222 - 13141	13142+

Usable window

Sent and acknowledged   Sent but <u>not</u> acknowledged   Ok to send   Must wait to send until window "slides" to right

FIGURE 5.11 The TCP sliding window.

The maximum window size can usually be determined by examining what the window sizes are at SYN time. This is not always the case because some TCP implementations can dynamically increase the window size during the course of a TCP connection. In Windows 95/98/NT, the window size is fixed and defaults to 8760 bytes for Ethernet.

Because the receiver's window allows multiple TCP segments to be sent before acknowledging one or more segments, TCP is often called a "sliding window" protocol. As shown in Figure 5.11, 10,221 bytes have been sent and the first 4380 bytes have been acknowledged. The receiver's window includes sent data that has not yet been acknowledged, plus empty buffer space that has yet to be filled. In the figure, the window is "closing down" because 5940 bytes out of a window of 8760 have not yet been acknowledged. Once these bytes are acknowledged, the window "slides" to the right.

> ❗ Using TCP, the maximum achievable throughput = window size divided by round-trip delay or latency in the network. For example, 8760 bytes/.100 seconds = 87,600 bytes/second, or 700,800 bits/second, or about 45 percent of bits outstanding on a full bandwidth T1 before an ack is received. Thus, if this is the only application (such as a nightly backup) using a reliable T1, you may want to increase the receiver's window size so the sender can "burst" more data. Similar situations arise as we reach gigabit speeds in LANs where we can burst out data at a much higher rate.

Changing the TCP window size can sometimes improve performance, especially in situations mentioned in the preceding tip. Do so with caution, however. For example, the Microsoft implementation of TCP/IP found in Windows 95 sends an acknowledgment for every two received TCP data segments. Increasing the receiver's TCP buffer by increasing the window size does not decrease the number of acks, even if a burst of TCP data is received before acknowledging.

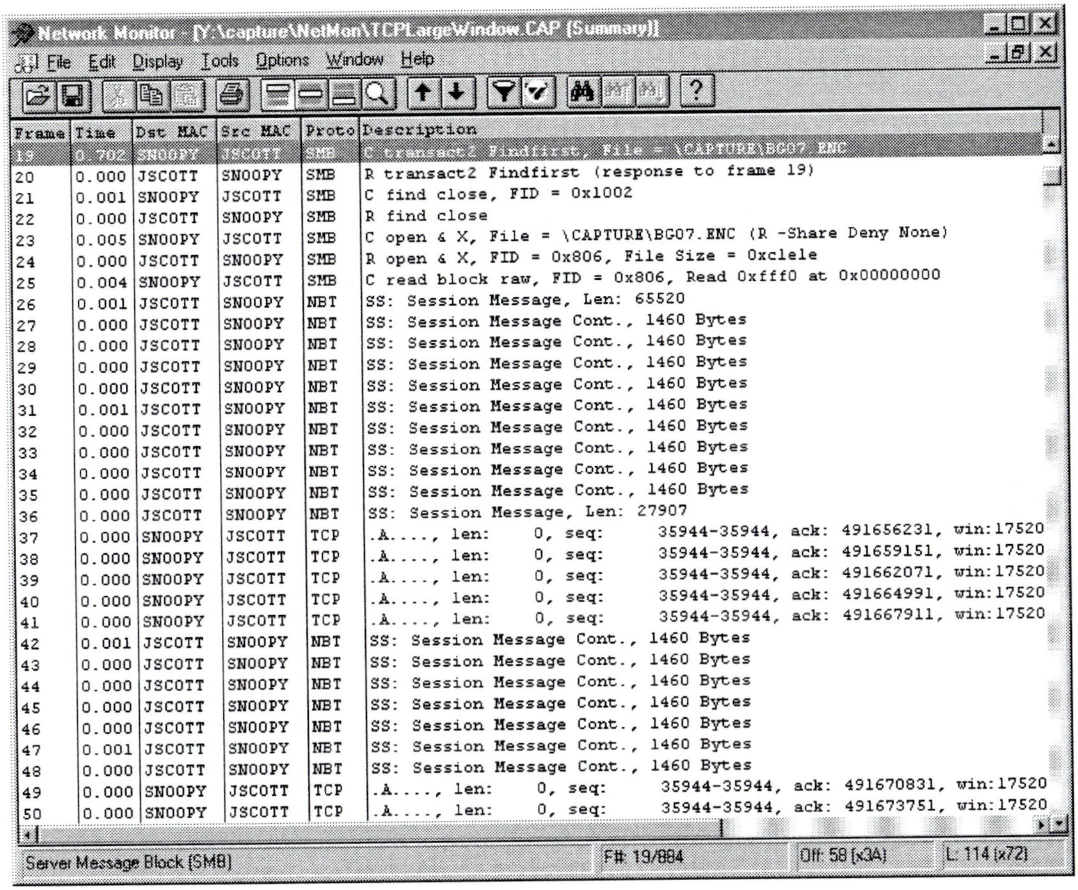

Network Monitor - [Y:\capture\NetMon\TCPLargeWindow.CAP (Summary)]

File Edit Display Tools Options Window Help

Frame	Time	Dst MAC	Src MAC	Proto	Description
19	0.702	SNOOPY	JSCOTT	SMB	C transact2 Findfirst, File = \CAPTURE\BG07.ENC
20	0.000	JSCOTT	SNOOPY	SMB	R transact2 Findfirst (response to frame 19)
21	0.001	SNOOPY	JSCOTT	SMB	C find close, FID = 0x1002
22	0.000	JSCOTT	SNOOPY	SMB	R find close
23	0.005	SNOOPY	JSCOTT	SMB	C open & X, File = \CAPTURE\BG07.ENC (R -Share Deny None)
24	0.000	JSCOTT	SNOOPY	SMB	R open & X, FID = 0x806, File Size = 0xclele
25	0.004	SNOOPY	JSCOTT	SMB	C read block raw, FID = 0x806, Read 0xfff0 at 0x00000000
26	0.001	JSCOTT	SNOOPY	NBT	SS: Session Message, Len: 65520
27	0.000	JSCOTT	SNOOPY	NBT	SS: Session Message Cont., 1460 Bytes
28	0.000	JSCOTT	SNOOPY	NBT	SS: Session Message Cont., 1460 Bytes
29	0.000	JSCOTT	SNOOPY	NBT	SS: Session Message Cont., 1460 Bytes
30	0.000	JSCOTT	SNOOPY	NBT	SS: Session Message Cont., 1460 Bytes
31	0.001	JSCOTT	SNOOPY	NBT	SS: Session Message Cont., 1460 Bytes
32	0.000	JSCOTT	SNOOPY	NBT	SS: Session Message Cont., 1460 Bytes
33	0.000	JSCOTT	SNOOPY	NBT	SS: Session Message Cont., 1460 Bytes
34	0.000	JSCOTT	SNOOPY	NBT	SS: Session Message Cont., 1460 Bytes
35	0.000	JSCOTT	SNOOPY	NBT	SS: Session Message Cont., 1460 Bytes
36	0.000	JSCOTT	SNOOPY	NBT	SS: Session Message, Len: 27907
37	0.000	SNOOPY	JSCOTT	TCP	.A...., len: 0, seq: 35944-35944, ack: 491656231, win:17520
38	0.000	SNOOPY	JSCOTT	TCP	.A...., len: 0, seq: 35944-35944, ack: 491659151, win:17520
39	0.000	SNOOPY	JSCOTT	TCP	.A...., len: 0, seq: 35944-35944, ack: 491662071, win:17520
40	0.000	SNOOPY	JSCOTT	TCP	.A...., len: 0, seq: 35944-35944, ack: 491664991, win:17520
41	0.000	SNOOPY	JSCOTT	TCP	.A...., len: 0, seq: 35944-35944, ack: 491667911, win:17520
42	0.001	JSCOTT	SNOOPY	NBT	SS: Session Message Cont., 1460 Bytes
43	0.000	JSCOTT	SNOOPY	NBT	SS: Session Message Cont., 1460 Bytes
44	0.000	JSCOTT	SNOOPY	NBT	SS: Session Message Cont., 1460 Bytes
45	0.000	JSCOTT	SNOOPY	NBT	SS: Session Message Cont., 1460 Bytes
46	0.000	JSCOTT	SNOOPY	NBT	SS: Session Message Cont., 1460 Bytes
47	0.001	JSCOTT	SNOOPY	NBT	SS: Session Message Cont., 1460 Bytes
48	0.000	JSCOTT	SNOOPY	NBT	SS: Session Message Cont., 1460 Bytes
49	0.000	SNOOPY	JSCOTT	TCP	.A...., len: 0, seq: 35944-35944, ack: 491670831, win:17520
50	0.000	SNOOPY	JSCOTT	TCP	.A...., len: 0, seq: 35944-35944, ack: 491673751, win:17520

Server Message Block (SMB) F#: 19/884 Off: 58 (x3A) L: 114 (x72)

FIGURE 5.12 Doubling the default TCP window size in a Windows 95 client.

Figure 5.12 shows an FTP data transfer over TCP after doubling the default Windows 95 TCP window size from 8760 to 17,520 bytes. The client and server are on the same 10 Mbps Ethernet segment and have most of the bandwidth to themselves during this capture. Instead of sending out one or two acks for a burst of TCP data, Windows 95 now sends a burst of acks, maintaining about a 2:1 data-to-ack ratio. TCP is just stacking up the acks. There's nothing you can change to tune the TCP acknowledgment algorithm.

In Windows 98 and NT, Microsoft has improved this algorithm to avoid the large number of acks seen in the Windows 95 implementation. When a large amount of bandwidth is available with little network delay (so the acknowledgment timers don't time out), the data-to-ack ratio is more like 4:1. Keep in mind, however, that when analyzing a TCP over a low bandwidth or high delay network, you typically see a lower data-to-ack ratio (i.e., more acks) regardless of the TCP stack implementation.

Another issue involving the TCP window size is what happens when a receiver advertises a small window such as 300 bytes. Is the sender allowed to send 300 bytes worth of TCP data? In most modern-day TCP implementations, the answer is no. If the sender was able to keep the window full by sending small TCP packets, you'd have a lot of small data/ack packets passing back and forth, which would dramatically decrease TCP performance not to mention increase the number of packets a switch or router has to handle. This degradation in segment sizing is also known as the "Silly Window Syndrome" or SWS (see RFC 813, Window and Acknowledgment Strategy in TCP, for more details).

SWS can be avoided by not sending the next TCP segment until the window is at least the size of the receiver's initial MSS (such as 1460 bytes on Ethernet) or the window is at least one half the largest window value ever seen. Likewise, the receiver should never advertise segments that are less than one half the receiver's MSS or maximum window size, whichever is smaller (usually the MSS). You should never see a problem with SWS in modern-day TCP implementations with both sides cooperating to minimize it.

The next-to-last field in the standard TCP header is the 16-bit checksum. Like UDP, the checksum includes a 12-byte pseudo-header that is created only when computing the checksum. (See the discussion of UDP for more information.)

The final piece of information in the TCP header is the 16-bit urgent pointer, which is added to the sequence number to obtain the sequence number of the last byte of urgent data. The interpretation of the urgent data is up to the application using TCP. As an example, Telnet will set the urgent flag when the user types the interrupt key.

5.3.2 TCP Retransmissions

TCP starts a data transfer by sending multiple TCP packets up to the receiver's window size, then continuing to send at the rate allowable by acknowledgments and buffer space (window size) as allowed by the receiver. If a TCP segment is dropped by virtue of never seeing an acknowledgment, the sender must send that and any subsequent segments over again. In other words, the sender may have to back up three or four segments and restart from that point. Do not assume that one TCP packet retransmission means that only one packet has to be resent!

Packet retransmissions can occur whenever:

- A sending TCP segment or returning acknowledgment is dropped by a switch or router.
- The packet is corrupted during transmission (the packet has a CRC error).
- The TCP data portion of the packet is corrupted by a switch or a router (there's a TCP checksum error).
- The recipient is unable to buffer the packet.
- A TCP segment gets fragmented and a fragment is dropped or corrupted.
- An acknowledgment is slow to return and the sender retransmits one or more segments.

A TCP retransmission timer is used to retransmit the first data segment following the last segment that was acknowledged. If no acknowledgment is received, the segment is sent again, but at double the wait time of the first resend. The TCP stack dynamically computes the initial timeout value based on the round-trip time of the connection. Each successive retry is delayed at twice the previous attempt. This exponential back-off allows plenty of time for a response, without overloading the network with retries. A TCP stack will try a predetermined number of times before giving up. In Windows 95/98/NT, this is a configurable registry setting that defaults to five retries.

You can identify TCP retransmissions with your protocol analyzer even without the benefit of an expert system by performing the following three steps:

1. Filter on a pair of communicating IP stations in your display buffer.
2. Look for long delays or exponential delays between successively sent packets, starting at approximately one-third of a second and higher.
3. Check the sending sequence number against previous packets. Keep in mind that the original transmission may have been several packets ago.

Figure 5.13 shows the effect of dropped TCP packets on an FTP file transfer. I've isolated the trace to one client/server pair of IP addresses and one application, FTP. In packets 20 through 23, you spot something that looks as though it could be a series of packet retransmissions as indicated by the long delta times and exponential delay between each packet.

Figure 5.14 shows the same trace, but this time the analyzer is set up to show the summary up to the TCP layer. Now, it becomes clear that these are TCP packet retransmissions as evidenced by the same starting sequence number (1059502088) in packets 20 through 23. By looking at the sequence numbers of the previously sent packets from 172.10.10.30 to 172.10.10.69, you can see that packet 14 has the same sequence number. 172.10.10.30 isn't just retransmitting a single packet, but packets 14, 15, 16, 17, and 18 have to be retransmitted, for

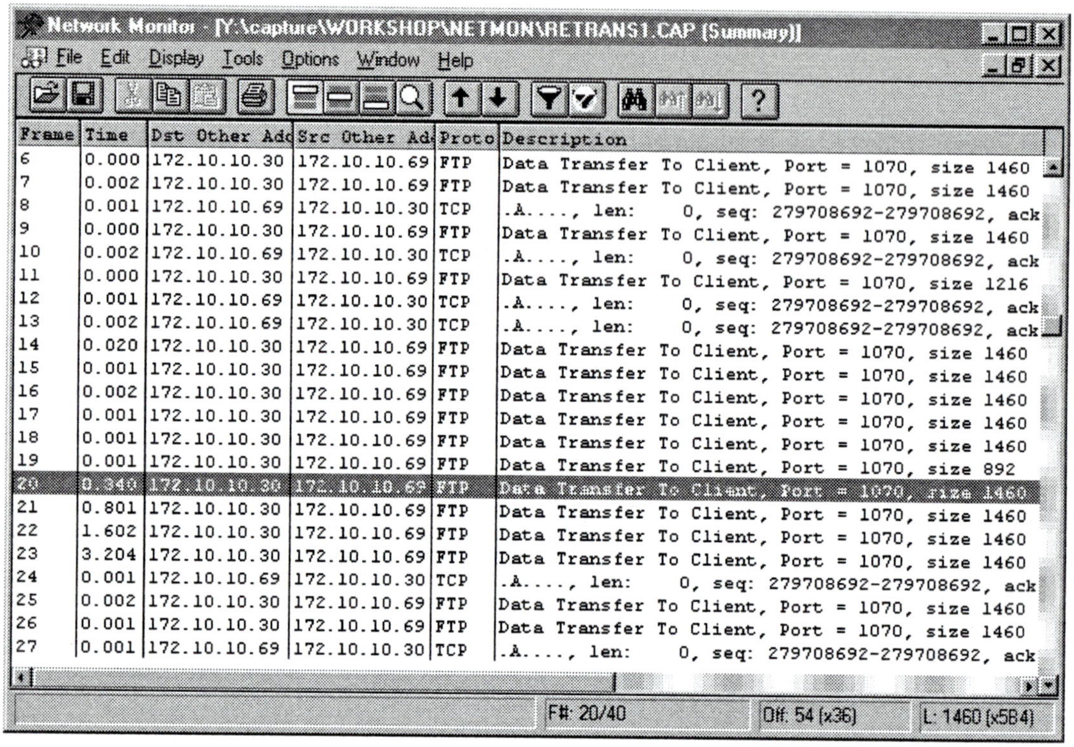

Network Monitor - [Y:\capture\WORKSHOP\NETMON\RETRANS1.CAP (Summary)]

Frame	Time	Dst Other Add	Src Other Ad	Proto	Description
6	0.000	172.10.10.30	172.10.10.69	FTP	Data Transfer To Client, Port = 1070, size 1460
7	0.002	172.10.10.30	172.10.10.69	FTP	Data Transfer To Client, Port = 1070, size 1460
8	0.001	172.10.10.69	172.10.10.30	TCP	.A...., len: 0, seq: 279708692-279708692, ack
9	0.000	172.10.10.30	172.10.10.69	FTP	Data Transfer To Client, Port = 1070, size 1460
10	0.002	172.10.10.69	172.10.10.30	TCP	.A...., len: 0, seq: 279708692-279708692, ack
11	0.000	172.10.10.30	172.10.10.69	FTP	Data Transfer To Client, Port = 1070, size 1216
12	0.001	172.10.10.69	172.10.10.30	TCP	.A...., len: 0, seq: 279708692-279708692, ack
13	0.002	172.10.10.69	172.10.10.30	TCP	.A...., len: 0, seq: 279708692-279708692, ack
14	0.020	172.10.10.30	172.10.10.69	FTP	Data Transfer To Client, Port = 1070, size 1460
15	0.001	172.10.10.30	172.10.10.69	FTP	Data Transfer To Client, Port = 1070, size 1460
16	0.002	172.10.10.30	172.10.10.69	FTP	Data Transfer To Client, Port = 1070, size 1460
17	0.001	172.10.10.30	172.10.10.69	FTP	Data Transfer To Client, Port = 1070, size 1460
18	0.001	172.10.10.30	172.10.10.69	FTP	Data Transfer To Client, Port = 1070, size 1460
19	0.001	172.10.10.30	172.10.10.69	FTP	Data Transfer To Client, Port = 1070, size 892
20	0.340	172.10.10.30	172.10.10.69	FTP	Data Transfer To Client, Port = 1070, size 1460
21	0.801	172.10.10.30	172.10.10.69	FTP	Data Transfer To Client, Port = 1070, size 1460
22	1.602	172.10.10.30	172.10.10.69	FTP	Data Transfer To Client, Port = 1070, size 1460
23	3.204	172.10.10.30	172.10.10.69	FTP	Data Transfer To Client, Port = 1070, size 1460
24	0.001	172.10.10.69	172.10.10.30	TCP	.A...., len: 0, seq: 279708692-279708692, ack
25	0.002	172.10.10.30	172.10.10.69	FTP	Data Transfer To Client, Port = 1070, size 1460
26	0.001	172.10.10.30	172.10.10.69	FTP	Data Transfer To Client, Port = 1070, size 1460
27	0.001	172.10.10.69	172.10.10.30	TCP	.A...., len: 0, seq: 279708692-279708692, ack

F#: 20/40 Off: 54 (x36) L: 1460 (x5B4)

FIGURE 5.13 TCP retransmission example—Upper protocol layer view.

a total of five packets and 7590 bytes (5 packets × 1518 bytes/packet). A dropped TCP data or ack packet now and then shouldn't impact your application a great deal, but several of them in a trace tell you that your application response time is being impacted tremendously.

In Figure 5.15, I ran the trace through an analyzer with an expert system, Sniffer Pro. As you can see, the expert system flags the packet retransmissions, making them much easier to spot. By packet 22, the expert is also saying that there's a nonresponsive station (or it could be a nonresponse network).

I've also turned on relative time and set a marker at packet 14. By the time that packet is retransmitted several times and finally acknowledged by 172.10.10.69 in packet 24, I've lost 5.954 seconds, or nearly 6 seconds. You can also compute the lost time by adding up the delta times from packets 20 through 23 in Figure 5.14.

In some case, there may already be clues in your analyzer's buffer as to why there are retransmissions. Some possibilities include:

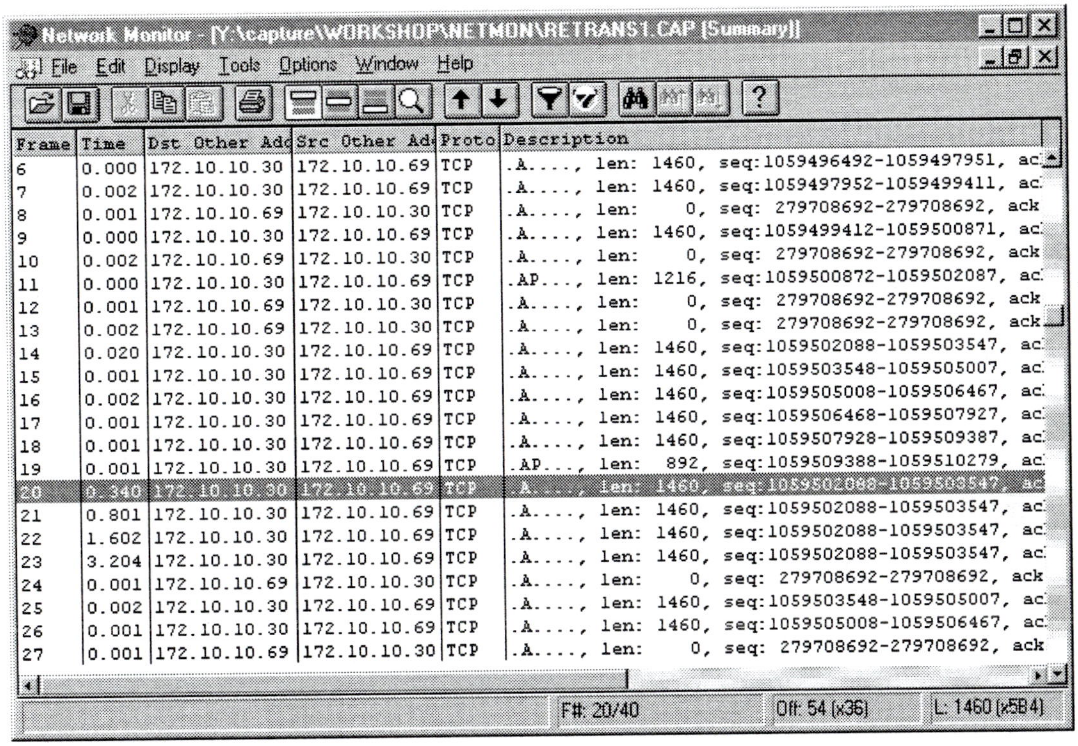

Frame	Time	Dst Other Add	Src Other Ad	Proto	Description
6	0.000	172.10.10.30	172.10.10.69	TCP	.A...., len: 1460, seq:1059496492-1059497951, ac
7	0.002	172.10.10.30	172.10.10.69	TCP	.A...., len: 1460, seq:1059497952-1059499411, ac
8	0.001	172.10.10.69	172.10.10.30	TCP	.A...., len: 0, seq: 279708692-279708692, ack
9	0.000	172.10.10.30	172.10.10.69	TCP	.A...., len: 1460, seq:1059499412-1059500871, ac
10	0.002	172.10.10.69	172.10.10.30	TCP	.A...., len: 0, seq: 279708692-279708692, ack
11	0.000	172.10.10.30	172.10.10.69	TCP	.AP..., len: 1216, seq:1059500872-1059502087, ac
12	0.001	172.10.10.69	172.10.10.30	TCP	.A...., len: 0, seq: 279708692-279708692, ack
13	0.002	172.10.10.69	172.10.10.30	TCP	.A...., len: 0, seq: 279708692-279708692, ack
14	0.020	172.10.10.30	172.10.10.69	TCP	.A...., len: 1460, seq:1059502088-1059503547, ac
15	0.001	172.10.10.30	172.10.10.69	TCP	.A...., len: 1460, seq:1059503548-1059505007, ac
16	0.002	172.10.10.30	172.10.10.69	TCP	.A...., len: 1460, seq:1059505008-1059506467, ac
17	0.001	172.10.10.30	172.10.10.69	TCP	.A...., len: 1460, seq:1059506468-1059507927, ac
18	0.001	172.10.10.30	172.10.10.69	TCP	.A...., len: 1460, seq:1059507928-1059509387, ac
19	0.001	172.10.10.30	172.10.10.69	TCP	.AP..., len: 892, seq:1059509388-1059510279, ac
20	0.340	172.10.10.30	172.10.10.69	TCP	.A...., len: 1460, seq:1059502088-1059503547, ac
21	0.801	172.10.10.30	172.10.10.69	TCP	.A...., len: 1460, seq:1059502088-1059503547, ac
22	1.602	172.10.10.30	172.10.10.69	TCP	.A...., len: 1460, seq:1059502088-1059503547, ac
23	3.204	172.10.10.30	172.10.10.69	TCP	.A...., len: 1460, seq:1059502088-1059503547, ac
24	0.001	172.10.10.69	172.10.10.30	TCP	.A...., len: 0, seq: 279708692-279708692, ack
25	0.002	172.10.10.30	172.10.10.69	TCP	.A...., len: 1460, seq:1059503548-1059505007, ac
26	0.001	172.10.10.30	172.10.10.69	TCP	.A...., len: 1460, seq:1059505008-1059506467, ac
27	0.001	172.10.10.69	172.10.10.30	TCP	.A...., len: 0, seq: 279708692-279708692, ack

FIGURE 5.14 TCP retransmission example—TCP protocol layer view.

- Prior segments or acknowledgments have a CRC error (Ethernet).
- Soft errors are being reported (on Token Ring) by a station approximately 2 seconds later.
- A TCP checksum error in a previous packet indicates possible bridge or router corruption.
- A TCP checksum error in the previous and the currently retransmitted packet indicates a sender problem (that may not be computing the TCP checksum properly, for example).
- There are missing or delayed acknowledgments, in which case you may have to move your analyzer to other segments to pinpoint the problem.

If you suspect a large number of TCP retransmissions at a particular workstation or server, you can use the netstat command. The most common use for the netstat command is to obtain routing information (netstat -r), i.e., the route table for that workstation or server that generates a list of IP addresses and the corresponding router for each address. Netstat can also be used to obtain information protocol statistics by typing "netstat -s." The Windows

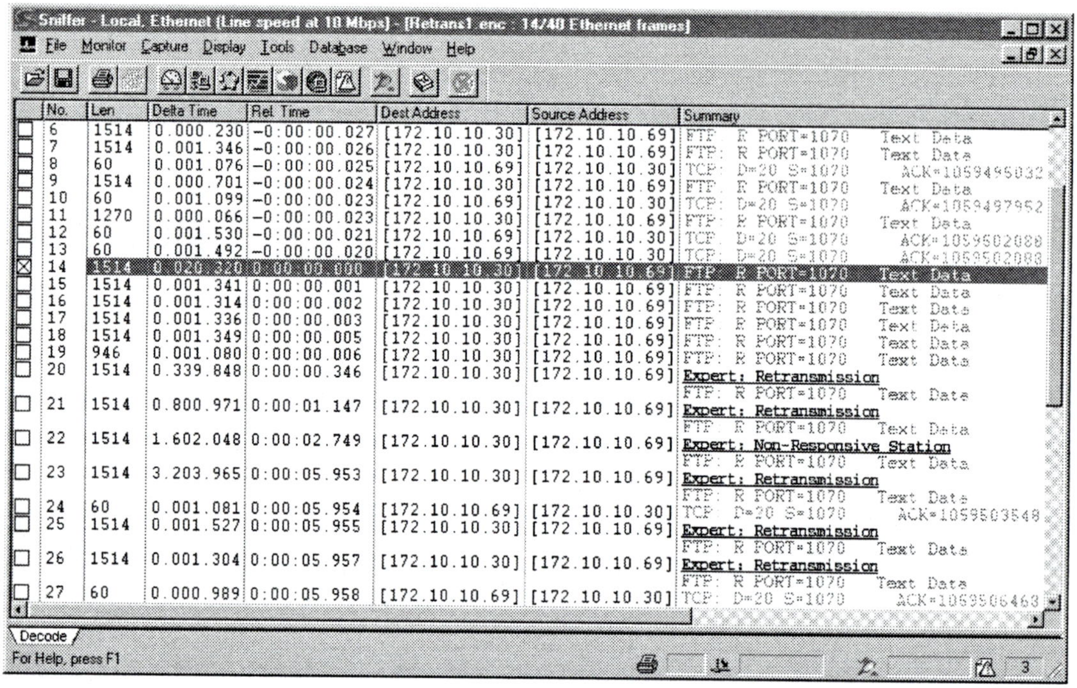

FIGURE 5.15 TCP retransmission example—Expert analyzer view.

95/98/NT version of netstat also allows you to specify a given protocol. For example, typing "netstat -s -p tcp" on one particular NT server yielded the following information:

```
TCP Statistics

    Active Opens                    = 23232
    Passive Opens                   = 7242
    Failed Connection Attempts      = 2123
    Reset Connections               = 1691
    Current Connections             = 9
    Segments Received               = 527604
    Segments Sent                   = 498933
    Segments Retransmitted          = 4396

Active Connections

Proto   Local Address       Foreign Address      State
TCP     snoopy:1026         localhost:1027       ESTABLISHED
TCP     snoopy:1027         localhost:1026       ESTABLISHED
TCP     snoopy:1028         localhost:1030       ESTABLISHED
TCP     snoopy:1030         localhost:1028       ESTABLISHED
TCP     snoopy:1040         localhost:1042       ESTABLISHED
```

```
TCP     snoopy:1042           localhost:1040        ESTABLISHED
TCP     snoopy:1025           WOODSTOCK:nbsession   ESTABLISHED
TCP     snoopy:2601           WOODSTOCK:nbsession   ESTABLISHED
TCP     snoopy:nbsession      ROBERT:1121           ESTABLISHED
```

The active connections show the host and port number for each TCP connection. The host is shown by name, but you can also specify that it be shown by IP address. In addition to the ESTABLISHED state, you can also determine what TCP ports are in a LISTEN state, such as an FTP server or SNMP agent.

In the preceding netstat example, you can see that 498,933 TCP segments were sent by the server and 4,396 of these were retransmitted, less than 1 percent. If the percentage were much higher, the next step would be to put an analyzer on that server's segment and study the TCP traffic.

5.3.3 Case Study: Dropped Terminal Sessions

This was an interesting troubleshooting challenge that I faced at an outpatient client that was part of a large hospital complex. The basic problem was that doctors, nurses, and administrators were losing their terminal sessions when reading or entering data into patient records. They would be put back to a main logon screen and have to start all over again. This was especially annoying to doctors who were entering diagnosis information and were about to submit the record when they were dropped back to the logon screen.

I needed to know two important pieces of information to begin troubleshooting this problem: how the information flowed from the user to the server and the topology of the network. The user application was a terminal emulator that ran under Windows 95 or NT and communicated to a DEC Alpha minicomputer. The user's workstation was attached to an Ethernet hub in a wiring closet. From there, several wiring closets were collapsed into a bridge from the Ethernet to an FDDI backbone. The minicomputer was attached directly to the FDDI backbone.

The terminal emulator communicated via Telnet to a gateway located on the FDDI backbone. The gateway in turn translated the Telnet protocol to the DEC Local Area Transport (LAT) protocol to communicate with the minicomputer. Thus user data would come into the gateway via Telnet over TCP/IP and out the gateway directly to the minicomputer via LAT, a proprietary network layerless protocol (LAT runs directly over the DLC layer, which in this case was FDDI).

I then proceeded to set up a "stake out" inside a nice, cozy wiring closet (which quickly became cramped, hot, and stuffy), watching a particularly busy Ethernet segment with a protocol analyzer and asking users to notify me as soon as they experienced a dropped terminal session. Having done

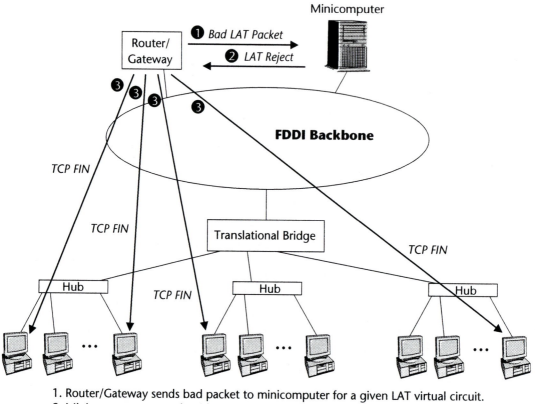

1. Router/Gateway sends bad packet to minicomputer for a given LAT virtual circuit.
2. Minicomputer responds with a LAT reject packet.
3. Router/Gateway terminates TCP sessions for that LAT virtual circuit.

FIGURE 5.16 Dropping terminal sessions.

this, it wasn't too long before a user informed me that a terminal session had dropped. Looking at the trace of captured packets, I could see why the terminal session was dropped. As it turned out, the gateway had sent a TCP FIN packet to the user's terminal emulation software to close the connection. The terminal emulator honored the close request by sending a FIN back to the terminal server, shutting down the application, and reverting back to the logon screen.

During one such drop, two users notified me at about the same time. Looking at the trace, there were actually three or four users who were dropped as the gateway sent TCP FIN packets to multiple users as summarized in Figure 5.16.

Now I had to figure out why the gateway was arbitrarily disconnecting users. One thought that came to mind was that LAT is a protocol that is very sensitive to the slightest delays. It didn't seem that this was a factor because both the gateway and the minicomputer were connected to the same high-speed FDDI backbone. Maybe it was an FDDI problem?

Using an FDDI protocol analyzer showed no errors or bandwidth problems on the backbone, and analysis of LAT packets didn't show any significant delay. Now what?

As a next step, I decided to watch the traffic in and out of the gateway on the backbone. Once again, I asked users to let us know when they lost their connection. Doing so and reanalyzing the TCP/IP traffic in and out of the gateway along with the LAT traffic gave me the answer.

A "virtual circuit" formed by the LAT protocol between a LAT terminal server or a gateway and host can carry multiple terminal sessions simultaneously. If you look inside a LAT packet, you may actually see terminal data from more than one user.

Just prior to a dropped terminal session, there was a LAT reject packet from the minicomputer to the gateway decoded by the analyzer as "Illegal format." The gateway would then proceed to disconnect *every* user on the virtual circuit that the LAT reject packet referred to by sending a series of TCP FIN packets.

Obviously the gateway was sending something to the minicomputer that it didn't like. The gateway was actually a router running LAT translation software from the router vendor. Because the router vendor didn't have an answer to this disconnect "bug/feature" the solution was to migrate users off the gateway by Telnetting directly to the minicomputer. This was accomplished by upgrading the patient record-keeping application on the minicomputer to communicate to end-users via Telnet as well as LAT.

5.3.4 Case Study: Tuning Side Effects

Not all problems will be reported by users as long as the application has reasonable response time to them and doesn't fail altogether. It doesn't mean that your network is in top shape, however. This is one of those problems I happened across one day when analyzing a particular Ethernet segment. As a network analyst, I have found that it often pays to have the occasional luxury of being proactive and preemptive instead of reactive and fighting fires.

A snapshot of what I saw with the analyzer is shown in Figure 5.17. A Windows 95 workstation (172.10.10.34) is opening a file located on an NT server (172.10.10.69). In packet 24, the workstation's Server Message Block (SMB) protocol is requesting a block read of 65,520 bytes, beginning at offset zero. Note that the analyzer has this information backward, saying "Read Block Raw 0 at 65520." Oops.

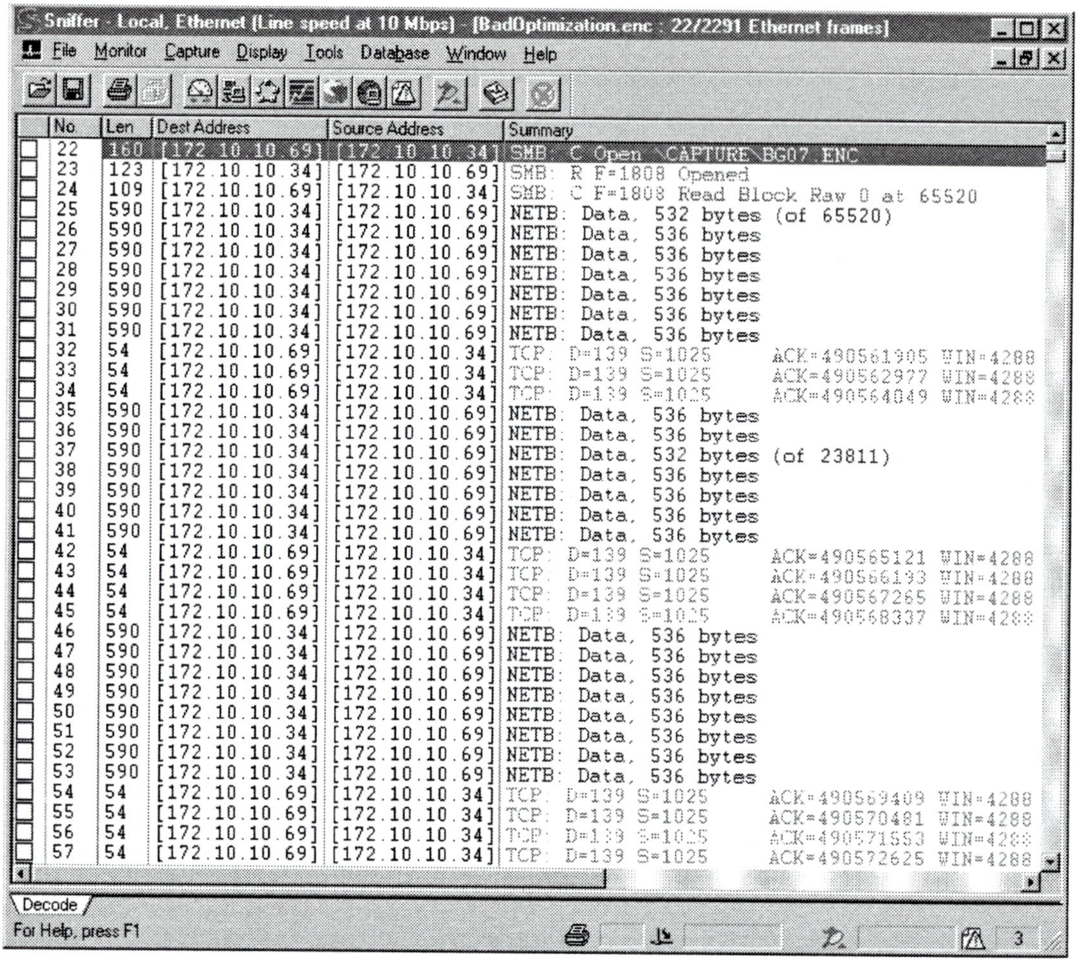

FIGURE 5.17 A suboptimal file transfer over TCP.

The server then proceeds with a series of NetBIOS over TCP data transfers. So far so good, but look at the NetBIOS data packet sizes—they're only 590 bytes in length (actually 594 bytes, including the 4-byte DLC layer CRC which the Sniffer analyzer doesn't include in its length calculator). This is undesirable because the user is not taking advantage of the Ethernet MTU, generating more packets, acknowledgments, and protocol header overhead than necessary. This trace shows about a 2:1 ratio in data to acks, a characteristic of the Windows 95 TCP implementation, as was mentioned earlier.

Figure 5.18 shows the TCP layer details. Notice how the TCP segment size is only 536 bytes. Seem familiar? This is the default MSS when no MSS is given to the server at connect time. This seemed a little unusual because I've never

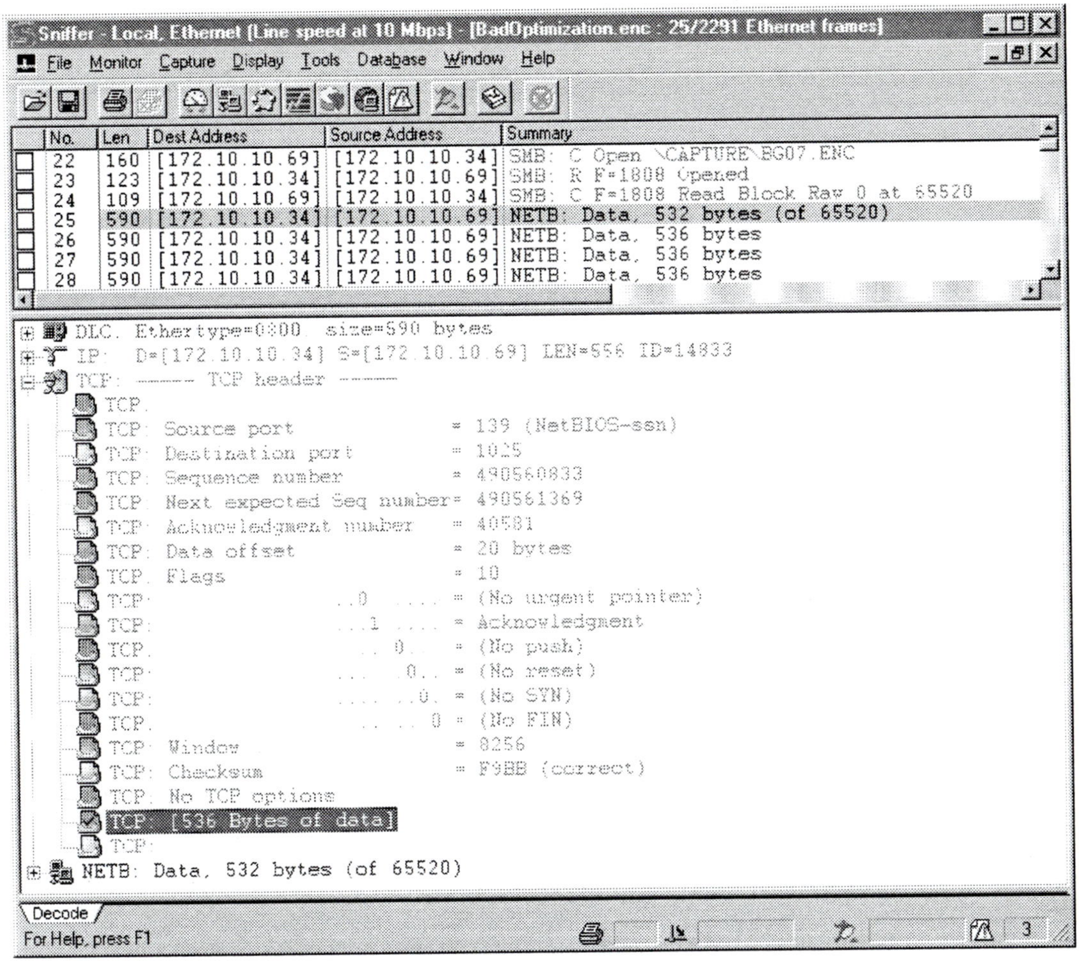

FIGURE 5.18 TCP details of the suboptimal file transfer.

seen a Windows workstation or server not send along the MSS with a TCP SYN packet.

Going back and finding a TCP SYN sequence between this workstation and server allowed me to find out if the MSS was missing. As it turned out this wasn't the case—the MSS was there and set to 536 bytes. This means that the user must have changed the default IP MTU to 576 bytes, allowing for 536 bytes of TCP data (576 bytes minus the 20 byte IP and 20 byte TCP headers).

I went to that user's workstation and checked the registry settings for the IP MTU. Sure enough, it was now set to 576 bytes. As it turned out, this user also had a V.90 modem installed in a workstation and occasionally accessed the Internet via dial-out. The user had downloaded one of those shareware "Internet optimizing" programs that allows you to change the IP MTU and the receive buffer size for TCP.

The user had accidentally changed the profile for the Ethernet adapter, not the dial-up network connection. You can also see in Figure 5.17 that the user's window size is 4288 bytes, less than half of the original default of 8760 bytes. This allows 8 (4288/536) TCP segments to be outstanding at any given time.

> **!**
>
> Any time the TCP MSS is changed, the window size should also be changed to a multiple of the MSS. A multiple of six to eight usually works well. For example, the default Windows 95 IP MTU of 1500 leaves 1460 bytes (1500 minus the 20 byte IP and 20 byte TCP headers) for the TCP MSS. The default receive buffer size (window) is 8760 bytes, or 6 times the MSS. Keeping the window an increment of the MSS increases the percentage of full-sized TCP segments received during file transfer, improving the overall efficiency.

Promoters of these Internet optimizers sometimes note that IP RFC 791 states "All hosts must be prepared to accept datagrams of up to 576 octets (whether they arrive whole or in fragments). It is recommended that hosts only send datagrams larger than 576 octets if they have assurance that the destination is prepared to accept the larger datagrams." Keep in mind, however, that this RFC dates back to 1981, when X.25 was the WAN. Chances are, your Internet traffic won't be crossing an X.25 backbone! The base IP MTU these days is 1500 bytes, based on Ethernet Ethertype encapsulation, not X.25.

There may be some gains by lowering the dial-up MTU in certain situations, but caution must be exercised because setting the registry under the wrong profile could affect your LAN settings.

5.3.5 Transport Layer Components of the NetWare Core Protocol (NCP)

Recall that the NetWare Core Protocol (NCP) over IPX does not have a separate transport layer, requiring NCP to take on some of the duties of a transport layer. NCP determines the IPX MTU using a buffer negotiation protocol when a client connects to a server. Chapter 4 showed how a client negotiated with a server a maximum IPX MTU of 4174 bytes on a Token Ring. The actual maximum packet size will be slightly larger due to Token Ring DLC and 802.2 LLC headers along with optional source routing information.

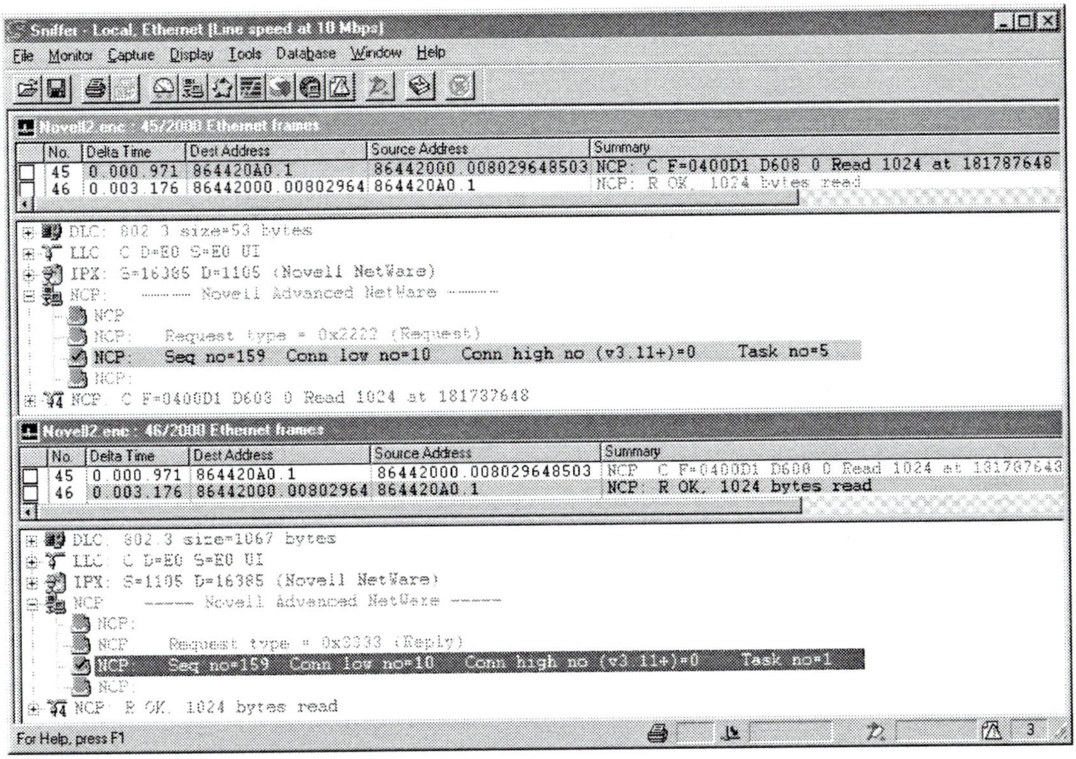

FIGURE 5.19 NCP command and reply packets (45 and 46) showing use of a matching sequence number.

NCP also contains sequence numbers, as illustrated in Figure 5.19. The sequence number is incremented by 1 for each NCP command. The reply to the NCP command will match the sending sequence number.

Flow control and error recovery is simplified with NCP. NCP packets are "implicitly" acknowledged because only one packet can be outstanding at a time. By virtue of a reply, the command is acknowledged. An example would be an NCP "read file" command, followed by a packet containing the file data. If the client never received the data, the client times out and sends another read file command. NCP also maintains its own sequence numbers that are incremented by 1 for each command/reply packet pair.

The NCP retransmission timer was originally based on PC clock ticks that date back to the original 8088-based IBM PCs. The clock timer was set at 18.2 ticks per second, or approximately 55 milliseconds. The default retransmission time was 10 clock ticks or 550 milliseconds, just over a half second. When no reply was seen, another packet would be sent about a half second

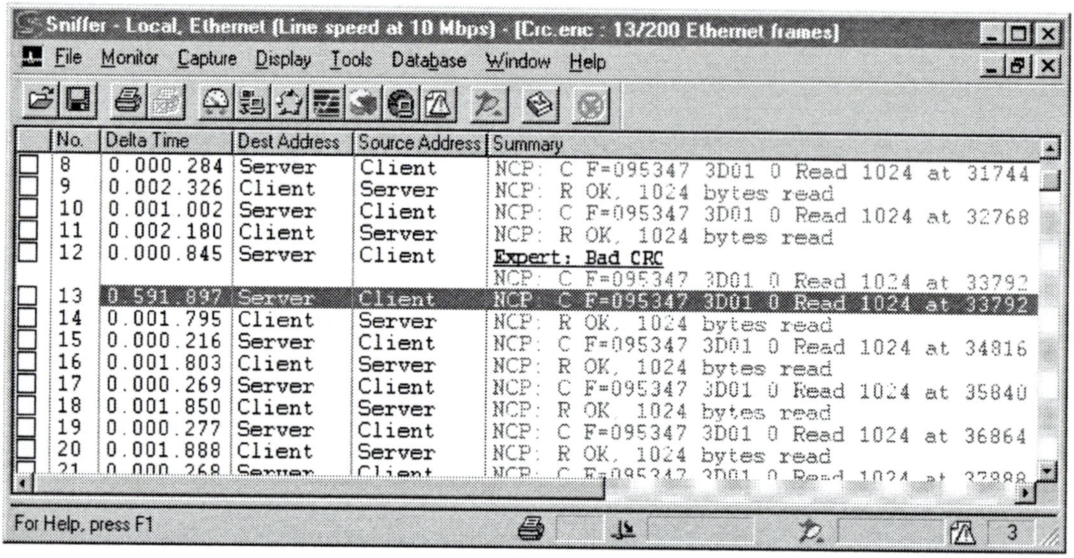

FIGURE 5.20 NCP retransmission example.

later. If still no reply was received, another packet would be sent a half second later, and so on. Eventually after ten retries or so, the user would receive an error message.

Figure 5.20 shows an example of an NCP retransmission based on the fixed timer. The workstation is running an earlier version of Windows (3.1) with a DOS-based NetWare shell. Packet 13 is a retransmission of packet 12, due to a CRC error in packet 12. The delta time between the two packets is 0.591 seconds, or 591 milliseconds, very close to the default retransmission timer value. This value can be shortened, but then you run the risk of transmitting excessive packets if it is set too low because you have to allow for a response in networks that are heavily loaded or have high latency (such as satellite or frame relay networks).

Error-prone networks using NetWare client shells were subject to poor response time and throughput because whenever a packet had a CRC error or was dropped, there was a half second delay to recover. Newer NetWare clients use Virtual Loadable Modules (VLMs) or Client32. The retransmission algorithm has been changed from a fixed retry time-out used by the older shells to a dynamic value. The initial retry value adjusts itself based on response time seen in previous packets. If there is more than one NCP packet retransmission, the back-off time grows exponentially, doubling in value each time, just like TCP.

Using this new algorithm has actually led to an *increase* in NCP packet retransmissions in error-free, low latency networks. The first retry is often immediately following the original packet, sometimes within 1 millisecond. This does not allow enough time for a server to respond. The Sniffer expert system flags these retransmissions as "fast" retransmissions.

You can identify NCP retransmissions with your protocol analyzer by performing the following three steps:

1. Filter on a pair of communicating IPX stations in your display buffer.
2. Look for successive NCP packets because there should always be a command/response pair.
3. Check the NCP command sending sequence number against the previous NCP command packets.

In some cases, your analyzer's buffer may already contain clues as to why there are retransmissions. Some possibilities include:

- Prior segments or acknowledgments have a CRC error (Ethernet).
- Soft errors are being reported (on Token Ring) by a station approximately 2 seconds later.
- There are missing or delayed NCP reply packets, in which case you may have to move your analyzer to other segments to pinpoint the problem.

Chapter 8 discusses NCP in greater detail.

5.4 NetWare Sequenced Packet Exchange (SPX) and SPX II Protocols

SPX is a simple transport layer protocol that provides a reliable connection-oriented data delivery service that is modeled after the Xerox Network Systems (XNS) Sequenced Packet Protocol (SPP). A connection with a peer is established before data is sent, and acknowledgments are required to verify delivery. SPX II provides a number of enhancements to SPX.

SPX is used primarily by NetWare utility software such as RCONSOLE for remote file server console access and third-party software such as tape backup servers and SNA or TCP/IP gateways.

The SPX packet format is illustrated in Figure 5.21. The 8-bit connection control field indicates the type of SPX packet. The control bits are defined in Table 5.1.

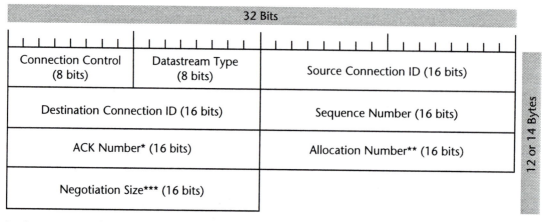

*   Sequence number of next SPX packet from partner
** Number of receive buffers available; starts at 0 for 1 buffer
*** SPX II field only

FIGURE 5.21 SPX/SPX II packet format.

The 8-bit datastream type indicates the type of packet data. Hex FE is a request to terminate the connection. Hex FF acknowledges the connection termination. Hex 80 through FD are reserved for SPX II, and the remaining values, hex 00 through 7F, are application defined.

The 16-bit source connection ID is assigned by the initiator of the SPX connection, whereas the 16-bit destination connection ID is assigned by the receiving partner when responding to an SPX handshake.

The 16-bit sequence number is incremented for each packet sent. This is followed by the 16-bit sequence number of the *next* packet expected from the other side of the connection. For example, if station A sends an SPX packet

TABLE 5.1 Control Bit Definitions

Control Bit	Description
XHD	Used by SPX II to indicate an extended header.
RES1	Reserved.
NEG	Used to negotiate an SPX II request/response.
SPX II	Set to indicate that this is an SPX II packet.
EOM	Set by a client to indicate the end of a message.
ATN	Used by SPX II for attention indication.
ACK	Request an acknowledgment for this packet.

to station B with a sequence number of 487 and the ACK bit set, it expects a packet from station B with an acknowledgment of 488.

The allocation number is the sequence number of the available receiver buffers. To calculate the number of receive buffers, you need to take the acknowledgment number – allocation number + 1. If the allocation number is lower than the acknowledgment number, no SPX buffers are available to receive the next packet and the sender must wait for another ack packet. This is similar to TCP when a window size of zero is sent back to the sender when no more TCP packets can be processed. Unfortunately, for SPX, you can't set a filter to capture packets with a window of zero to check for slow clients or servers. Instead, you have to do some arithmetic on the fields inside the SPX packet, something that no protocol analyzer is currently capable of doing.

The last field is only present with the SPX II extended format header (when the XHD bit is set). This allows SPX II to negotiate the end-to-end packet size while establishing the connection.

There are some critical shortcomings to the original SPX protocol. For starters, because SPX cannot determine the maximum packet size between two end-points, the maximum IPX datagram length to carry SPX information is limited to 576 bytes. Subtracting the 30-byte IPX header and the 12-byte SPX header leaves you with only a maximum of 534 bytes for SPX data.

Second, SPX is very "chatty" in that reliable delivery is accomplished by setting the acknowledgment bit in each and every sent packet because only individual packets are acknowledged.

Figure 5.22 shows an example of an SPX conversation between two nodes, a client and a Lotus Notes server. Packet 703 is the initial connection request from the client to the server. Note how the destination connection ID is set to hex FFFF because it hasn't been assigned yet by the receiver. This happens in packet 704, which is acknowledging packet 703.

Packet 709 contains 9 bytes of SPX data from the Notes server to the client with a sequence number of 1 (as indicated by NS=1 in the summary display) and the ACK bit set. Packet 710 is an acknowledgment from the client with the acknowledgment number set to the next expected packet from the server, packet number 2 (as indicated by NR=2 in the summary display).

Packet 711 is a data packet from the client to the server with a sequence number of 2, whereas packet 712 is from the server acknowledging packet 711.

It seems silly to require a separate ack packet followed immediately by a data packet. Why not just piggyback the acknowledgment with the data and cut the packet exchanges in half when data is bi-directional? For better or worse, this is the way the SPX algorithm was originally designed. To do better, you need to upgrade the client and server to SPX II or move to a different protocol altogether.

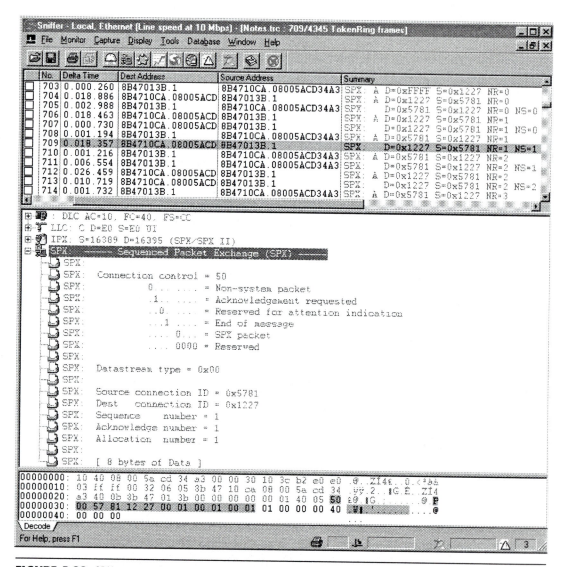

FIGURE 5.22 SPX connection and data exchanges.

5.4.1 SPX II

SPX II overcomes many of the limitations of SPX. Data is no longer limited to an IPX MTU of 576 bytes. For example, an IPX MTU of 1500 bytes on Ethernet gives SPX II the ability to send up to 1466 bytes of data per packet. When an SPX II client requests a connection with an SPX II peer located on Ethernet, the peer replies and includes a negotiation size of 1500 bytes. The client then tests the end-to-end IPX MTU by sending an Ethernet frame with

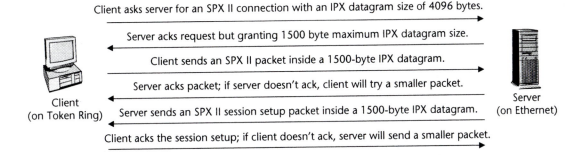

Client asks server for an SPX II connection with an IPX datagram size of 4096 bytes.

Server acks request but granting 1500 byte maximum IPX datagram size.

Client sends an SPX II packet inside a 1500-byte IPX datagram.

Server acks packet; if server doesn't ack, client will try a smaller packet.

Server sends an SPX II session setup packet inside a 1500-byte IPX datagram.

Client
(on Token Ring)

Server
(on Ethernet)

Client acks the session setup; if client doesn't ack, server will send a smaller packet.

FIGURE 5.23 SPX II session setup process.

a 1500-byte IPX datagram to the peer. If the packet makes it to the peer okay, the peer acknowledges it. If not, the client must try a smaller IPX MTU.

Assuming that an IPX MTU of 1500 bytes is okay, the peer then sends a 1500-byte IPX/SPX II session setup packet back to the client. The client acknowledges this packet, and the SPX II setup is complete. This process is summarized in Figure 5.23.

SPX II also incorporates a windowing mechanism allowing multiple packets to be sent before an acknowledgment is required. By default, the SPX II window size is set to 8, allowing up to eight packets to be sent before an ack is required. Like SPX, the sequence number is incremented by 1 on a packet-by-packet basis. The acknowledgment packet contains the next expected packet from the sender. Unlike SPX, SPX II can also send negative acknowledgments to identify missing packets. This is actually better than TCP because you only have to resend the missing packets, not all of the packets from the missing packet on up.

Figure 5.24 is a trace of SPX II packets from a 10 Mbps Ethernet. Note the burst of packets (9 through 14) from IPX station 10.1. As seen by the packet delta times, these packets are nearly back to back on the media because it takes approximately 1.2 milliseconds to send a maximum-sized Ethernet packet. The application (Arcserve) generating this traffic is performing overnight backup of a series of file servers over the network using tape drives.

Which packet is the receiving station, 100.1, acknowledging in packet 15? Recall that the acknowledgment number of 4389 is 1 higher than the last packet received. Therefore, 100.1 is acknowledging receipt of all data up to packet 13, which has a sending sequence number of 4388.

The larger packet sizes combined with windowing allowed the backup server running over SPX II to back up NetWare servers at over one million bytes per second, about 80 percent of the 10 Mbps Ethernet capacity.

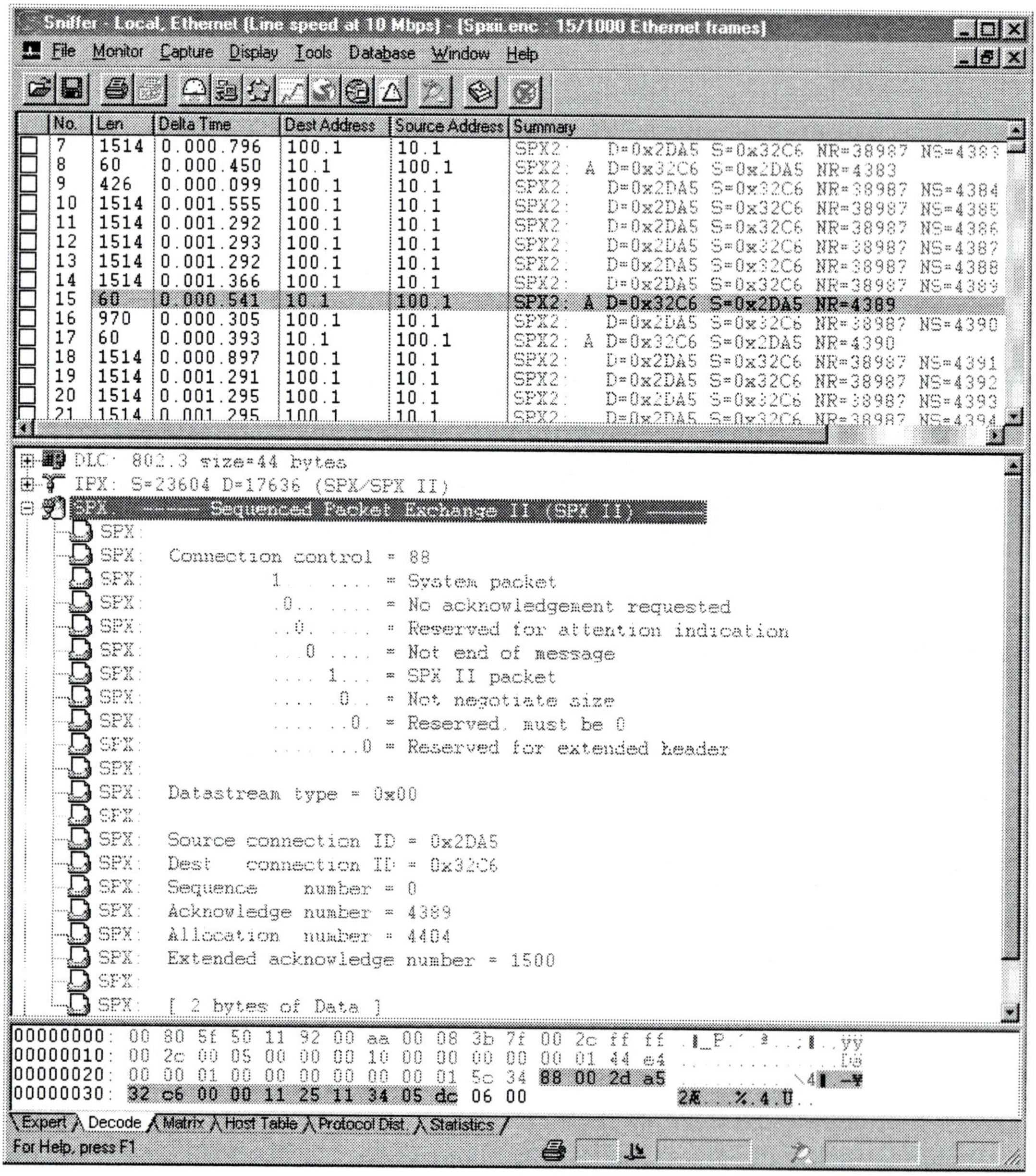

FIGURE 5.24 SPX II example.

5.4.2 SPX Timers

SPX and SPX II make use of several timers, including listen timeout, verify timeout, and abort timeout. The timer values are based on the original PC timer ticks of 18.2 per second, which is 1/18.2 seconds, or approximately 55 milliseconds.

The listen timeout is similar to a keep alive timer. If an SPX connection hasn't seen data for a certain amount of time, it sends a packet and expects an acknowledgment. The default timer is set to 108, which is equal to 108×55 milliseconds, or approximately 6 seconds. Thus, on an idle SPX connection, you will see an SPX keep alive packet exchange every 6 seconds.

The verify timeout controls the transport retransmission timing. Unlike TCP with its exponential retry timing, SPX retries are fixed at a default interval of 54 clock ticks, or roughly 3 seconds. Interestingly, the IPX retry count parameter actually determines how many times SPX (not IPX) will retry and defaults to 20. Thus SPX tries to resend a packet for which the ACK bit was sent, but no ack was received, every 3 seconds for up to 60 seconds.

The abort timeout specifies how long the watchdog process continues with no response, which is 540 clock ticks, or approximately 30 seconds by default. If there is no response after 30 seconds, the SPX connection is dropped.

Chapter **6**

Analyzing and Troubleshooting the Session Layer

6.1 Introduction

The purpose of the session layer is to provide a logical naming service as well as session connection and termination. The naming service allows an application to locate a device by a "friendly" easy-to-remember name rather than a series of numbers that denote the network or MAC address. Once a device is located, a session connection can be attempted with that device.

In the real world, the session layer is not all that separable from the other protocols in the stack. For example, TCP/IP applications use Domain Name System (DNS) to find an IP address associated with a name by sending a query packet to a name server. Once the IP address is found, it is inserted into a routing table or cache and subsequently used by TCP to establish a connection. In this instance, it is really TCP establishing the connection, not the session layer. DNS merely provides the naming service.

Some protocol layering charts depict DNS as an application layer protocol, whereas others see it as a session layer protocol. Because DNS does provide at least some session layer–like functionality, I consider it to be a session layer protocol and discuss it in detail later on in this chapter.

NetBIOS is also considered a session layer protocol. Although NetBIOS provides many session services, including naming services and session establishment, other services are provided such as datagram delivery (packets that don't require a prior connection to be established). Datagram delivery services were included in the original NetBIOS specification because NetBIOS was originally developed for network layerless LANs. Thus the datagram service normally provided by the network layer had to be provided elsewhere.

Of the three major NetBIOS implementations—NetBIOS over LLC (NetBEUI), NetBIOS over IPX, and NetBIOS over TCP/IP—only NetBIOS over TCP/IP is able to register and locate names via NetBIOS naming services, a superset of DNS. The Microsoft implementation of NetBIOS naming services is called Windows Internet Naming Services, or WINS. The other NetBIOS implementations, NetBEUI and IPX, rely on broadcasting to "register" a name (making sure that no other active node is using that name) or to locate a name of an actively listening device.

NetBEUI broadcasts for names using a multicast address for Ethernet and functional address for Token Ring. NetBIOS for IPX uses a broadcasting technique that propagates over routers. NetWare applications that don't use NetBIOS rely on the Services Advertising Protocol (SAP) to find resources by name and their associated IPX address.

Common problems associated with the session layer include not being able to locate a resource, register a resource, nor automatically recover from a dropped session without user intervention. This chapter examines the operation and recovery of DNS, NetBIOS, and SAP.

> **❗**
>
> Troubleshooting problems associated with session layer functionality can be tricky because protocol analyzers don't decode certain NetWare or TCP functions as session layer functions. When troubleshooting a problem, you may need to have the user disconnect and reconnect with the service (or even reboot the user's workstation) to see how the session was established to begin with. Don't just take a protocol trace midstream after a session is already established—collect the whole sample!

6.2 Domain Name System (DNS)

6.2.1 Background

DNS grew out of a real need to a problem as the Internet began to grow. The Internet has its roots in ARPANET, which by the early 1970s connected only a few hundred computers. At that time, a HOSTS.TXT file contained a name-to-address mapping for every host connected to the ARPANET. The file was maintained by SRI's Network Information Center ("the NIC") and distributed from a central site. As the network grew, the file got larger and had to be updated more frequently. File updates were often obsolete by the time they reached remote computers. Obviously this technique to maintain host-to-address translation did not scale well with the Internet.

In 1984, RFCs 882 and 883 were released to describe a new naming architecture, called Domain Name System, or DNS. The latest RFCs describing DNS are 1034 and 1035, supplemented by 1535, 1536, and 1537.

DNS is a distributed database that not only maps host names to IP addresses, but also maintains mail routing information by maintaining a database of mail servers for a particular domain. DNS also defines the protocol and packet format that allow name servers to communicate with other name servers and for clients to communicate with name servers.

The client portion of DNS is known as the resolver. The resolver is responsible for handling a request for host information by turning it into a query to a name server and consequently translating the response. A client can provide a host name and receive an IP address (the most common DNS operation), or it can provide an IP address and receive a host name (often called a "reverse" DNS look-up).

The hierarchical tree structure of the DNS (see Figure 6.1) consists of several domain levels, or zones. Domains at the bottom leaves of the tree usually represent hosts. For example, the host net3group.com consists of the subdomain or zone "net3group," which is a member of the "com" domain. The DNS information about top-level domains such as com, edu, org, net, and so on is maintained by root name servers. Arpa is a special top-level domain used to map all the IP addresses in the Internet for looking up a host name given its IP address.

The net3group domain is registered with the Internet's Network Information Center (InterNIC) and maintained by a root DNS server for com, which contains the IP address of the DNS server for the net3group sub-domain. The DNS server for the net3group domain is known as the authoritative server for that domain and has a database containing the IP address for net3group.

There can be several levels of domains, as in the host names ftp.rs.internic.net or tesseract.pvt.k12.mn.us. If a client asks for the IP address for tesseract.pvt.k12.mn.us and it is not in the user's local DNS server cache, the server sends its query to the root server for "us." The DNS server for "us" passes the request off to the authoritative server for "mn" and so on. Ultimately one of the servers in the tree will respond.

The responding DNS server may not be at the end of the tree because a DNS server may have cached the information from a previous request. For example, the server for the "mn.us" sub-domain or zone may already have the IP address for tesseract.pvt.k12.mn.us. A cached reply is known as a nonauthoritative answer because the information is not permanently configured

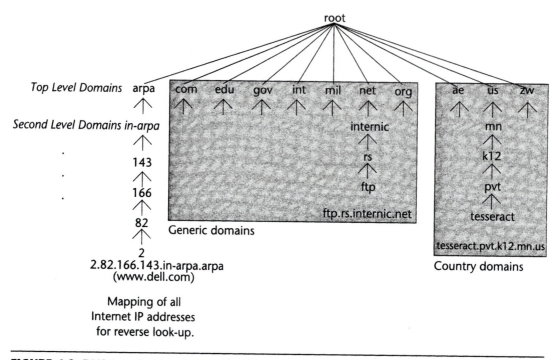

FIGURE 6.1 DNS tree structure (Internet).

and stored on the DNS server's hard disk. Caching is done primarily to reduce the amount of DNS traffic.

Every primary or authoritative server for a sub-domain is configured via a local file and must also have a secondary name server. The secondary name server stores a replica of the DNS information obtained from the primary name server. For increased reliability, the secondary DNS server should not be located in the same room nor on the same power source as the primary DNS server.

As you can imagine, the DNS tree for a public network like the Internet is quite large, with thousands of DNS servers. For a private corporate intranet, however, a primary and a secondary DNS server usually suffices for most internal applications.

Having a few private DNS servers is not always the case, however. One company I worked with had some two dozen DNS servers. Their rationale was to have a primary and secondary DNS server for every IP subnet in their corporation for complete redundancy. A major drawback to this approach is the hardware and software capital investment, not to mention the long-term maintenance and configuration of this large number of DNS servers. In one instance, a DNS server was misconfigured with the wrong authoritative server for a particular domain, causing a looping of a single DNS request back and forth between two DNS servers over a WAN, saturating the WAN link!

If redundancy is a concern, another approach is to have one primary and one secondary server with one caching DNS server for each subnet. This reduces the number of DNS servers and requires only one master database to maintain.

Caching DNS servers are also a good idea for remote locations to minimize DNS look-up traffic over the WAN. You could also turn on DNS caching at critical servers in your intranet so that users can still find the server by DNS name in the event of primary and secondary DNS server failures.

6.2.2 Packet Format

Both DNS queries and replies share a common packet format as illustrated in Figure 6.2. Each DNS packet starts off with a fixed 12-byte header. The 16-bit identification field is set by the client in order to match a reply packet returned from the DNS server. This is followed by a 16-bit flag field that is broken down as shown in Table 6.1.

TABLE 6.1 Flag Field Definitions

Field	Description
OR	A 1-bit field set to 0 for a query or 1 for a response.
OPCODE	A 4-bit field set to 0 for a standard query, 1 for an inverse query, 2 for a server status request, and 3–15 are reserved for future use.
AA	A 1-bit field set to 1 if the response is an authoritative answer.
TC	A 1-bit field set to 1 if the message was truncated (greater than 512 bytes).
RD	A 1-bit field set to 1 if the name server is to pursue the query recursively.
RA	A 1-bit field set or cleared in a response to denote if the name server supports recursion.
Z	A 3-bit reserved field.
RCODE	A 4-bit response code. It is set to 0 for no error, 1 for query format error, 2 for server failure, 3 for name error (only valid for an authoritative response to indicate that the domain does not exist), 4 is not implemented, 5 for a refusal to perform the specified operation for policy reasons, and 6–15 are reserved.

The remaining four fields of the 12-byte header specify the number of record entries. In the simplest case, there will be one question and one answer. See Table 6.2.

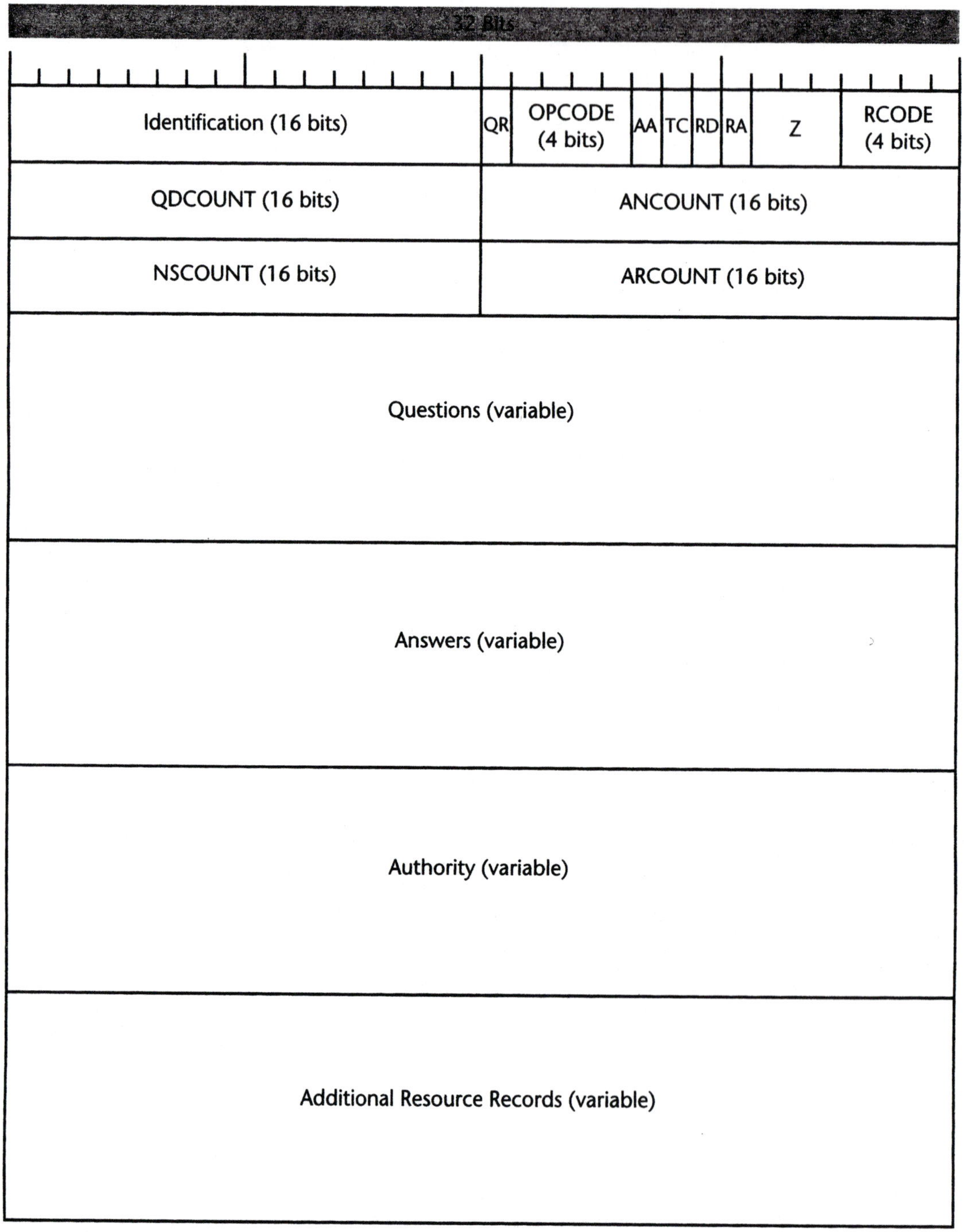

FIGURE 6.2 DNS packet format.

TABLE 6.2 Number of Record Entries Fields

Field	Description
QDCOUNT	A 16-bit unsigned integer specifying the number of entries in the question records section.
ANCOUNT	A16-bit unsigned integer specifying the number of entries in the answer records section.
NSCOUNT	A 16-bit unsigned integer specifying the number of entries in the name server records section.
ARCOUNT	A 16-bit unsigned integer specifying the number of entries in the additional records section.

Every DNS question record has a query type associated with it. When analyzing DNS packets with your protocol analyzer, you will often encounter the record type A, a record containing a query (or answer) for the IP address of a host name. Other record types are noted as follows:

- *PTR.* The reverse of the A record, the PTR record requests a pointer record containing the name associated with an IP address. Figure 6.3 shows an example request packet (number 1) from a browser asking a DNS server for the IP address of www.net3group.com. The response packet (number 2) containing the original question section along with the answer record is shown in detail. Note that following the response packet, the browser immediately proceeds to set up a TCP connection with the web server using the IP address obtained from the DNS response.
- *MX.* The mail exchange record is used to find the mail server or servers for a particular domain.
- *NS.* The name server record provides information about the authoritative DNS server for a particular domain.
- *CNAME.* The canonical name record is a way to associate an alias with another system. For example, an ISP might enter a CNAME record for ftp.joescompany.com associated with ftp.ispprovider.net to make it look as though Joe's Company has its own FTP server.
- *HINFO.* The host info record contains arbitrary information about the CPU and operating system of a host. For security reasons, the host info may not be available or intentionally set to completely inaccurate information.
- *SOA.* The start of authority record lists the contact information for a particular zone. It contains the email address of the zone's technical contact and other information about the entry's unique serial number as well as refresh and expire timers. When a DNS record changes, its serial number must also be changed so that other DNS servers get updated.

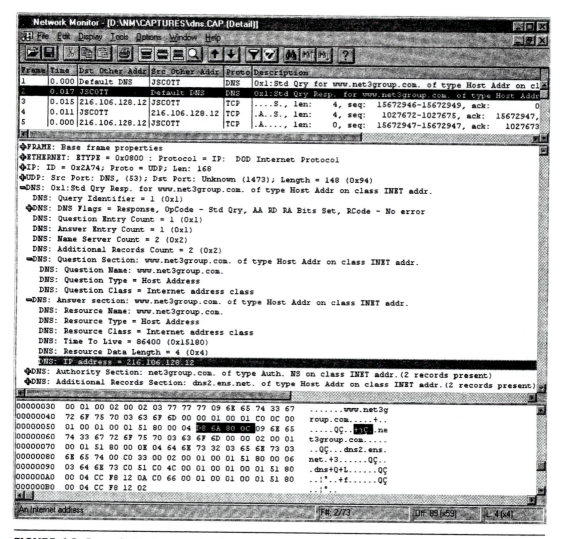

FIGURE 6.3 Example DNS request/reply.

Many DNS problems arise as a result of misconfiguration. For example, if someone has a secondary DNS server listed as their primary DNS server and a change was made at the real primary DNS server, the secondary server won't know about the change unless the serial number in the SOA record of the primary server was changed. This could prevent users from getting to newly defined resources.

Some FTP or download servers on the Internet won't allow an anonymous login if your IP address doesn't have a PTR record associated with it. The download server wants to look up your domain based on your IP address. Microsoft does this if you attempt to download Internet Explorer that uses 128-bit encryption—Microsoft wants to ensure that your IP address is really inside the United States.

6.2.3 Troubleshooting

Most applications that use TCP/IP provide a way to connect to a host either by IP address or name. If there's a problem such as providing the wrong name, the application typically gives the user an error message like "host unknown."

Figure 6.4 shows the packet exchanges where a Windows 95 user typed the wrong name (ftp.ibmm.com) for opening an FTP session. Packet 17 is the original DNS type A address look-up record being sent to the default DNS server. The server replies in packet 18, with an RCODE of 2, or server failure.

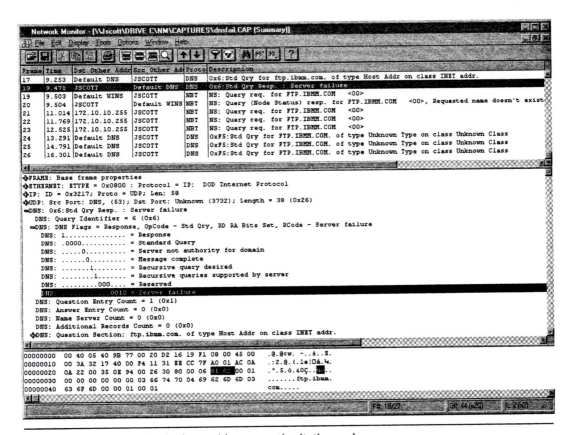

FIGURE 6.4 A failed DNS look-up with a nonauthoritative reply.

This indicates that the server was unable to resolve the name. Because the RCODE was not set to 3, or name error, you know that the default DNS server did not get its answer from an authoritative name server. Either a caching DNS server has the wrong information or the name was simply mistyped. If you thought the name was correct (which, in this case, it wasn't), you'd have to trace the DNS server packets to see where the server is getting its information. You could then check another DNS server's database for the correct answer.

Because this was a Windows client, the FTP application is not quite finished with its name searching. In packet 19, the application is now querying the local WINS server, with a negative response in packet 20; the name does not exist in the WINS server database.

In packets 21–23, the client is now broadcasting the name over an IP subnet broadcast address in hope of a response. As you can see, no one replies.

Finally, in desperation, the client sends a query for ftp.ibmm.com with no specific record type to the default DNS server. The default DNS server does not understand this and turns a deaf ear.

By subtracting the relative time of packet 26 from the start of our DNS query, packet 17, you can determine that the user had to wait approximately 7.1 seconds before the ftp application responded with a "host unknown" message.

Figure 6.5 shows an example of a failed DNS look-up with an authoritative response. This time, the RCODE is set to 3 because the default DNS server probably got the answer from the root server for .net. Looking further into the reply packet you see that there's an additional record returned by the server—an authority record. This record contains the name of the authoritative DNS server that the information came from. In this case, the server is A.ROOT-SERVERS.net maintained by the InterNIC (as evidenced by the email information).

Another tool that can be helpful in troubleshooting DNS problems is nslookup. Nslookup is distributed with Berkeley Internet Name Domain, the most popular DNS server that was developed for Berkeley BSD UNIX and ported to other UNIX (and even NT) systems. It also comes with most flavors of UNIX as well as NT (but not Windows 95/98).

Nslookup is an application that allows you to send commands directly to a DNS server. One big difference is that, unlike a client that uses the default DNS server(s) from a preset list, you can set the name server that sends your DNS queries to any name server you want. So if you wanted to check a sub-domain name like anynet.net, you could directly query A.ROOT-SERVERS.net, just as the default DNS server would.

Nslookup allows you to query any of the record types (A, MX, PTR, etc.) for a particular domain. You can run nslookup from the command line or inter-

```
┌─────────────────────────────────────────────────────────────────────────────────┬───────┐
│ Network Monitor - [\\Jscott\DRIVE C\NM\CAPTURES\dnsfail3.CAP [Detail]]            │ _ □ X │
├─────────────────────────────────────────────────────────────────────────────────┼───────┤
│ File  Edit  Display  Tools  Options  Window  Help                                 │ _ ᵬ X │
├───────────────────────────────────────────────────────────────────────────────────────────┤
│ [toolbar icons]                                                                             │
├───────┬──────┬────────────────┬─────────────────┬──────┬─────────────────────────────────────┤
│ Frame │ Time │ Dst Other Addr │ Src Other Addr  │ Proto│ Description                          │
├───────┼──────┼────────────────┼─────────────────┼──────┼─────────────────────────────────────┤
│ 1     │0.000 │Default DNS     │JSCOTT           │DNS   │0x8:Std Qry for ftp.bobscompany.net. of type Host Addr on │
│ 2     │3.563 │JSCOTT          │Default DNS      │DNS   │0x8:Std Qry Resp. Auth. NS is net. of type SOA on class I │
└───────┴──────┴────────────────┴─────────────────┴──────┴─────────────────────────────────────┘
```

```
⊕FRAME: Base frame properties
⊕ETHERNET: ETYPE = 0x0800 : Protocol = IP:  DOD Internet Protocol
⊕IP: ID = 0xCD3A; Proto = UDP; Len: 139
⊕UDP: Src Port: DNS, (53); Dst Port: Unknown (3798); Length = 119 (0x77)
⊟DNS: 0x8:Std Qry Resp. Auth. NS is net. of type SOA on class INET addr. : Name does not exist
   DNS: Query Identifier = 8 (0x8)
 ⊟DNS: DNS Flags = Response, OpCode - Std Qry, AA RD RA Bits Set, RCode - Name does not exist
   DNS: 1............... = Response
   DNS: .0000.......... = Standard Query
   DNS: .....1......... = Server authority for domain
   DNS: ......0........ = Message complete
   DNS: .......1....... = Recursive query desired
   DNS: ........1...... = Recursive queries supported by server
   DNS: .........000.... = Reserved
   DNS: ............0011 = Name does not exist
   DNS: Question Entry Count = 1 (0x1)
   DNS: Answer Entry Count = 0 (0x0)
   DNS: Name Server Count = 1 (0x1)
   DNS: Additional Records Count = 0 (0x0)
 ⊕DNS: Question Section: ftp.bobscompany.net. of type Host Addr on class INET addr.
 ⊟DNS: Authority Section: net. of type SOA on class INET addr.
   DNS: Resource Name: net.
   DNS: Resource Type = Start of zone of authority
   DNS: Resource Class = Internet address class
   DNS: Time To Live = 86400 (0x15180)
   DNS: Resource Data Length = 59 (0x3B)
   DNS: Primary Name Server: A.ROOT-SERVERS.net.
   DNS: Responsible Authorative Mailbox: hostmaster.INTERNIC.net.
   DNS: Version number = 1999013100 (0x772684EC)
   DNS: Refresh Interval = 1800 (0x708)
   DNS: Retry interval = 900 (0x384)
   DNS: Expiration Limit = 604800 (0x93A80)
   DNS: Minimum TTL = 86400 (0x15180)
```

```
00000020  0A 22 00 35 0E D6 00 77 C0 E4 00 08 85 83 00 01   .".5.+.w+S..àä..
00000030  00 00 00 01 00 00 03 66 74 70 0B 62 6F 62 73 63   .......ftp.bobsc
00000040  6F 6D 70 61 6E 79 03 6E 65 74 00 00 01 00 01 03   ompany.net......
00000050  6E 65 74 00 00 06 00 01 00 01 51 80 00 3B 01 41   net.......QÇ.;.A
00000060  0C 52 4F 4F 54 2D 53 45 52 56 45 52 53 C0 25 0A   .ROOT-SERVERS+%.
00000070  68 6F 73 74 6D 61 73 74 65 72 08 49 4E 54 45 52   hostmaster.INTER
00000080  4E 49 43 C0 25 77 26 84 EC 00 00 07 08 00 00 03   NIC+%w&ä8.......
00000090  84 00 09 3A 80 00 01 51 80                        ä..:Ç..QÇ
```

```
Indicates problems with the response        P#: 2/43        Off: 44 (x2C)    L: 2 (x2)
```

FIGURE 6.5 A failed DNS look-up with an authoritative reply.

actively. Type "nslookup help" to learn all of the various commands you can play with.

One of the more interesting nslookup capabilities is a dump of all the hosts in a zone (sub-domain). The ls command is used to transfer zone information. Because there may be hundreds of hosts in a zone, you can redirect the output to a file. Most servers do not allow you to list out a zone unless you are actually connected to the authoritative name server servicing that domain.

In the following example, I am refused a zone list from the default DNS server when querying a particular newspaper, so I find its name server using a DNS NS query and then go to that name server and reexecute the ls command:

```
C:\>nslookup
Default Server: dns.ens.net
Address: 204.248.18.2

> ls -d startribune.com
[dns.ens.net]
*** Can't list domain startribune.com: Query refused
> set type=ns
> startribune.com
Server: dns.ens.net
Address: 204.248.18.2

Non-authoritative answer:
startribune.com nameserver = NS.MR.NET
startribune.com nameserver = FIREWALL2.startribune.com

NS.MR.NET        internet address = 137.192.240.5
FIREWALL2.startribune.com      internet address = 132.148.80.211
> server ns.mr.net
Default Server: ns.mr.net
Address: 137.192.240.5

> ls -d startribune.com
[ns.mr.net]
 startribune.com             SOA     startribune.com randall.startribune.com.
 (1999012002 10800 3600 86400 7200)
 startribune.com             NS      firewall2.startribune.com
 startribune.com             NS      ns.mr.net
 startribune.com             MX      10    firewall2.startribune.com
 startribune.com             MX      20    service2.startribune.com
 startribune.com             A       132.148.87.5
 ads                         A       132.148.80.3
 www2                        CNAME   webserv0.startribune.com
 stol-dev                    MX      10    firewall2.startribune.com
 stol-dev                    MX      20    service2.startribune.com
 stol-dev                    A       132.148.25.35
 webtest                     A       132.148.5.49
 talk                        MX      10    talk.startribune.com
 talk                        A       132.148.80.3
 listserv                    MX      10    firewall2.startribune.com
 listserv                    MX      20    service2.startribune.com
 listserv                    A       132.148.5.45
 internal3                   A       132.148.85.212
 dataz                       A       132.148.87.9
 starlight                   A       132.148.80.41
 mail                        MX      10    firewall2.startribune.com
 mail                        MX      20    service2.startribune.com
 mail                        A       132.148.71.49
```

6.3 NetBIOS

NetBIOS (Network Basic Input Output System) was at one time literally a network BIOS on a ROM chip, much like a system BIOS for a personal computer. It was developed by IBM and a broadband networking company called Sytek back in 1984 for the IBM PC Network Broadband LAN. Broadband networking back then meant a multichannel RF network that operated over coaxial cable, much like cable TV (CATV). IBM's PC Broadband LAN was a 2 Mbps Ethernet-like system that ran over one 6 MHz CATV channel. Unfortunately the technology was somewhat expensive and complex to engineer for the average business environment due to the intricacies of RF technology.

The concept of broadband LAN technology has died, at least for businesses (it is making a comeback in consumer CATV systems for Internet access), but NetBIOS has survived. One reason that NetBIOS survived is that it was one of the first common APIs for networked applications. It provided a "standard" way for DOS programmers to write peer-to-peer applications via DOS interrupt hex 5C with a pointer to the NetBIOS Control Block (NCB). The NCB contains data required by the various NetBIOS commands and an additional memory pointer to the packet data buffer.

As noted earlier, the functionality of NetBIOS is not a perfect fit for the OSI reference model at the session layer. Session layer services such as locating resources by name and establishing sessions are provided as well as non–session layer services such as sending and receiving datagrams.

Subsequent versions of NetBIOS were developed by IBM to operate over the Logical Link Control (LLC) layer, by Novell to operate over IPX, and by the Internet community for operation over TCP/IP.

The LLC implementation was originally developed to support the IBM DOS-based PC LAN Program over Token Ring. Also known as the NetBIOS Extended User Interface (NetBEUI), NetBEUI was adopted for use in OS/2, LAN Manager (the Microsoft predecessor to NT), and Windows.

Novell developed a proprietary version of NetBIOS for use over IPX. By proprietary, I mean a NetBIOS with the standard hex 5C interface, but having its own packet format embedded inside IPX and a special IPX broadcasting technique for finding resources by name.

The NetBIOS RFCs are RFC 1001 (Protocol Standard for a NetBIOS Service on a TCP/UDP Transport: Concepts and Methods) and RFC 1002 (Protocol Standard for a NetBIOS Service on a TCP/UDP Transport: Detailed Specifications).

Figure 6.6 shows the three major flavors of NetBIOS with respect to the OSI reference model. As you can see, NetBEUI has no network layer and must be switched or bridged to reach other network segments.

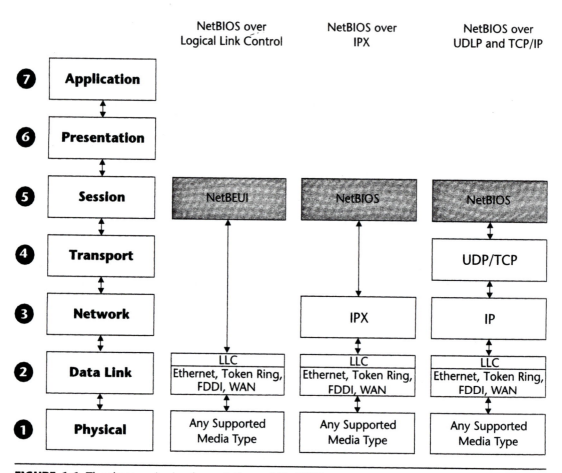

FIGURE 6.6 The three major implementations of NetBIOS.

6.3.1 NetBIOS over LLC

NetBIOS over LLC, or NetBEUI, makes extensive use of both LLC Type 1 and LLC Type 2 packets (refer to Chapter 3 for more details). Figure 6.7 shows a Windows 95 station at startup on an Ethernet. Initially several packets are sent to the NetBIOS DLC multicast address of hex 030000000001. If you bit reverse this address on a byte-by-byte basis, you end up with C00000000080, which is the functional address for NetBIOS broadcasts on Token Ring.

Why are there so many multicasts in Figure 6.7? The workstation is "registering" different names that have different meanings. On top of that, it sends each name three times by default.

Suffix character identifies
NetBIOS name function.

```
 Network Monitor - [Y:\capture\NetMon\nbboot.CAP [Detail]]              _ □ ×
 File  Edit  Display  Tools  Options  Window  Help                        _ ₽ ×

Frame Time   Dst MAC Addr       Src MAC Protocol Description
81    26.170 *NETBIOS Multicast Client  NETBIOS  Add Name Query (0x01), Name = SCOTT      <00>
82    0.010  *NETBIOS Multicast Client  NETBIOS  Add Group Name (0x00), Name = NET3_HQ    <00>
83    0.000  *NETBIOS Multicast Client  NETBIOS  Add Name Query (0x01), Name = SCOTT      <03>
87    1.022  *NETBIOS Multicast Client  NETBIOS  Add Name Query (0x01), Name = SCOTT      <03>
88    0.000  *NETBIOS Multicast Client  NETBIOS  Add Group Name (0x00), Name = NET3_HQ    <00>
89    0.000  *NETBIOS Multicast Client  NETBIOS  Add Name Query (0x01), Name = SCOTT      <00>
90    0.871  *NETBIOS Multicast Client  NETBIOS  Add Name Query (0x01), Name = SCOTT      <03>
91    0.003  *NETBIOS Multicast Client  NETBIOS  Add Group Name (0x00), Name = NET3_HQ    <00>
92    0.004  *NETBIOS Multicast Client  NETBIOS  Add Name Query (0x01), Name = SCOTT      <00>
116   5.115  *NETBIOS Multicast Client  NETBIOS  Add Name Query (0x01), Name = SCOTT
117   0.821  *NETBIOS Multicast Client  NETBIOS  Add Name Query (0x01), Name = SCOTT
145   0.795  *NETBIOS Multicast Client  NETBIOS  Add Name Query (0x01), Name = SCOTT
157   0.655  *NETBIOS Multicast Client  NETBIOS  Add Group Name (0x00), Name = NET3_HQ    <1E>
173   0.714  *NETBIOS Multicast Client  NETBIOS  Add Group Name (0x00), Name = NET3_HQ    <1E>
184   0.788  *NETBIOS Multicast Client  NETBIOS  Add Group Name (0x00), Name = NET3_HQ    <1E>
350   1.912  *NETBIOS Multicast Client  BROWSER  Host Announcement [0x01] SCOTT
367   18.849 *NETBIOS Multicast Client  NETLOGON LM1.0/2.0 LOGON Request from client
369   0.009  *NETBIOS Multicast Client  NETBIOS  Name Query (0x0A), SCOTT        <00> -> WOODSTOCK
370   0.001  Client             Server   NETBIOS  Name Recognize (0x0E), WOODSTOCK    -> SCOTT
371   0.001  Server             Client   LLC      SABME DSAP=0xF0 SSAP=0xF0 C POLL
372   0.000  Client             Server   LLC      UA DSAP=0xF0 SSAP=0xF1 R FINAL
373   0.000  Server             Client   LLC      RR DSAP=0xF0 SSAP=0xF0 C N(R) = 0x00 POLL
374   0.001  Client             Server   LLC      RR DSAP=0xF0 SSAP=0xF1 R N(R) = 0x00 FINAL
375   0.000  Server             Client   NETBIOS  Session Initialize (0x19): LSN = 0x0F, RSN = 0x04
376   0.001  Client             Server   LLC      RR DSAP=0xF0 SSAP=0xF1 R N(R) = 0x01 FINAL
377   0.000  Client             Server   NETBIOS  Session Confirm (0x17): LSN = 0x04, RSN = 0x0F

⊕FRAME: Base frame properties
⊕ETHERNET: 802.3 Length = 61
⊕LLC: UI DSAP=0xF0 SSAP=0xF0 C
⊟NETBIOS: Add Name Query (0x01), Name = SCOTT
   NETBIOS: Length = 44 (0x002C)
   NETBIOS: Signature = 0xEFFF
   NETBIOS: Command = Add Name Query (0x01)
   NETBIOS: Response Correlator = 0x0009
  ⊟NETBIOS: Source Name = SCOTT
    NETBIOS: SMB Name Type = Server (20)

00000000  03 00 00 00 00 01 08 00 5A 38 A3 09 00 2F F0 F0   ........Z8ú../==
00000010  03 2C 00 FF EF 01 00 00 00 00 00 09 00 00 00 00   .,. n...........
00000020  00 00 00 00 00 00 00 00 00 00 00 00 00 53 43 4F   .............SCO
00000030  54 54 20 20 20 20 20 20 20 20 20 20 20 20 20 20   TT

NetBIOS SMB name terminator              F#: 116/754        Off: 60 (x3C)    L: 1 (x1)
```

FIGURE 6.7 NetBIOS over LLC at startup

If you look carefully at Figure 6.7, you'll notice that each NetBIOS name has a sixteenth-character suffix that has a special meaning. Packet 81, an add name query, contains the name "SCOTT" (all NetBIOS names are converted to uppercase) with the suffix character of hex 00, or <00> as decoded by the analyzer. Looking at Figure 6.8, a table of NetBIOS name suffixes, you'll see that <00> denotes the workstation service name, which is also known as the

Unique Names

<00>	Workstation service name; also known as the "NetBIOS Computer Name" or "Redirector Name."
<03>	Messenger service name used when receiving and sending messages.
<1B>	Identifies the primary domain controller and indicates which clients and other browsers to use to contact the domain master browser.
<06>	RAS server service.
<1F>	NetDDE service.
<20>	Server service name used to provide file sharing.
<21>	RAS client service.
<22>	Microsoft Exchange Interchange (MSMail Connector).
<23>	Microsoft Exchange Store.
<24>	Microsoft Exchange Directory.
<2B>	Lotus Notes Server Service.
<30>	Modem Sharing Server Service.
<31>	Modem Sharing Client Service.
<43>	SMS Clients Remote Control.
<44>	SMS Administrators Remote Control Tool.
<45>	SMS Clients Remote Chat.
<46>	SMS Clients Remote Transfer.
<4C>	DEC Pathworks TCP/IP Service on Windows NT.
<52>	DEC Pathworks TCP/IP Service on Windows NT.
<6A>	Microsoft Exchange IMC.
<87>	Microsoft Exchange MTA.
<BE>	Network Monitor Agent.
<BF>	Network Monitor Analyzer.
Forte_$ND800ZA<20>	DCA IrmaLAN Gateway Server Service.
Inet~Services<1C>	Microsoft IIS.

Group Names

<00>	Domain name.
<1C>	A domain group name registered by a domain controller.
<1D>	Used by clients to access the master browser.
<1E>	Browsers broadcast to this name and listen on it to elect a master browser. For IP, these broadcasts are for the local subnet only.
<20>	Internet group name registered with WINS servers to identify groups of computers for administrative purposes.
IS~computer name<00>	Microsoft IIS.
MSBROWSE<01>	Appended to a domain name and broadcast to announce the domain to other master browsers.
IRISMULTICAST<2F>	Lotus Notes.
IRISMULTICAST<33>	Lotus Notes.

FIGURE 6.8 NetBIOS name suffixes (16th character).

NetBIOS computer name or the redirector name. Thus the name "SCOTT" is the unique name for this computer and cannot appear anywhere else on the network, which is why the computer sends out three multicast packets (81, 89, and 92) just to make sure that the name is unique. (The original DOS NetBIOS and earlier OS/2 implementations of NetBIOS actually sent out multicasts ten times for each name.) If there had been another computer with the name "Scott," it would have responded, preventing the second Scott from becoming active on the network.

Packet 82 is a different type of NetBIOS name, a group name of "NET_HQ". Looking again at the NetBIOS name table in Figure 6.8, you can see that a group name of <00> refers to the domain name.

Packet 83 is an add name for "SCOTT" but with a suffix of <03>. This is the messenger service name used to send and receive messages.

Packet 116 looks a bit odd in that you don't see a NetBIOS suffix character in the summary. Looking inside the packet detail, however, you see that the suffix is there; it just wasn't displayed on the summary line. This is another add name of "SCOTT" but with a suffix of <20>. It is the server service name used to provide file sharing. This means that user "SCOTT" has enabled peer-to-peer file sharing under Windows 95. If you have a policy of not having sharing enabled on users' workstations, this is one way to discover who has it enabled!

There's one more NetBIOS name multicast, as seen in packets 157, 173, and 184. This is the name NET3_HQ with a suffix of <1E>. It is used to indicate that the computer is capable of becoming a master browser. Browsers (not to be confused with Internet browsers) are important in Microsoft Windows networks to maintain a list of resources visible in the Network Neighborhood. The MS Browse protocol is discussed in greater detail in Chapter 8.

In packet 367, the workstation is sending out a NETLOGIN NetBIOS multicast packet to request the name of an NT server to log on to. Packet 368 (not shown in the figure) contains a response packet from an NT Primary Domain Controller (PDC) containing the name of the server, which is WOODSTOCK. The workstation then sends a name query packet (369) for the name "WOODSTOCK". The response to this query is packet 370.

Now the workstation asks to establish a NetBIOS session with the server as shown in packet 375 with an acknowledgment from the server in packet 377. Prior to establishing a NetBIOS session, the workstation sets up an LLC Type 2 connection with the server (see Chapter 3 for more details). After the NetBIOS session is established, the workstation initiates an SMB connection with the server and proceeds to log on to the domain.

Figure 6.9 shows a NetBIOS data packet over LLC. A Windows 95 workstation is transferring data from an NT server. The NetBIOS session is identified

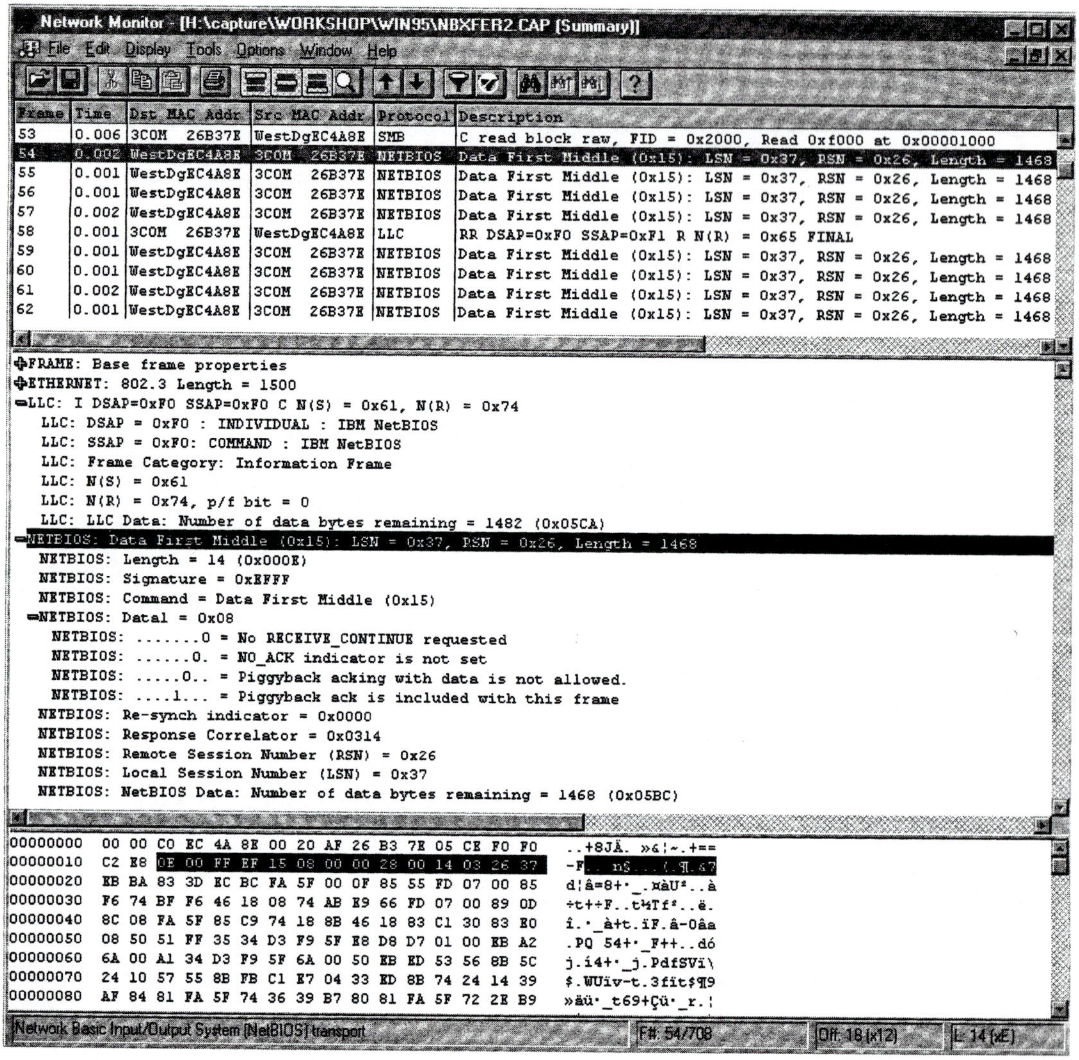

FIGURE 6.9 NetBIOS data over LLC.

by the Local Session Number (LSN) and Remote Session Number (RSN). Because the NetBIOS data transfer is running over LLC Type 2, all sequence numbers are handled by the LLC layer. Note how, in packet 54, a flag is set in the Data1 byte to indicate that a piggyback ack is included with this frame. This minimizes the number of LLC acknowledgments that have to be sent outside the NetBIOS packets like the LLC ack in packet 58. Because of the way in which the LLC Type 2 protocol works, it's impossible to eliminate LLC acks altogether.

6.3.2 NetBIOS over IPX

In Windows for Workgroups and in Windows 95/98/NT networks that have NetBIOS over IPX enabled, the NetBIOS protocol is used primarily for naming services. The IPX flavor of NetBIOS differs from NetBEUI in several key areas:

- Broadcasts are sent using the all stations DLC broadcast address (hex FFFFFFFFFFFF).
- Broadcasts are sent in a special IPX WAN broadcast packet at the IPX layer.
- The protocol is routable.
- Windows SMB data is sent directly over IPX.

Microsoft has also defined an extension to the NetBIOS name service for IPX called the Microsoft Name Management Protocol over IPX (NMPI).

NetBIOS over IPX uses an IPX Type 20 (hex 14) WAN broadcast to locate resources. Recall from Chapter 4 that the Type 20 WAN header contains room for up to eight 32-bit IPX networks that are filled in by routers, one per hop.

Figure 6.10 shows an example of a NetBIOS/NMPI broadcast packet sent to the IPX destination socket of hex 0551, NMPI Name Claim as decoded by the Network Monitor. The source socket is hex 0550, NMPI Server Announce. The Windows 95 workstation is advertising that file sharing is enabled. This is equivalent to the NetBEUI add name query packet with a name suffix of <20>. Note how this packet is being broadcast using the IPX Type 20 WAN broadcast, allowing the packet to be forwarded by up to eight routers.

There are some other subtle differences between NetBIOS over IPX and NetBEUI when booting. With IPX, no individual or group names are broadcast at boot time; only a server announcement is broadcast if the workstation is sharing resources. The NETLOGIN request to find the name of an NT logon server is sent over an IPX Type 20 WAN broadcast packet. The NMPI to locate the server returned by NETLOGIN is *not* sent over a Type 20, but rather a standard IPX Type 4 packet. This means that the logon server *must not* be located on the other side of a router or the workstation won't be able to log on to the domain.

NT domain controllers behave slightly different depending on the underlying network protocol. Chapter 8 looks at some of these issues in more detail and examines the MS browse protocol.

6.3.3 NetBIOS over TCP/IP

NetBIOS over TCP/IP includes services that run over both TCP and UDP. NetBIOS uses UDP for connectionless services, including sending and receiving datagrams, and for name resolution broadcasts when there is no WINS.

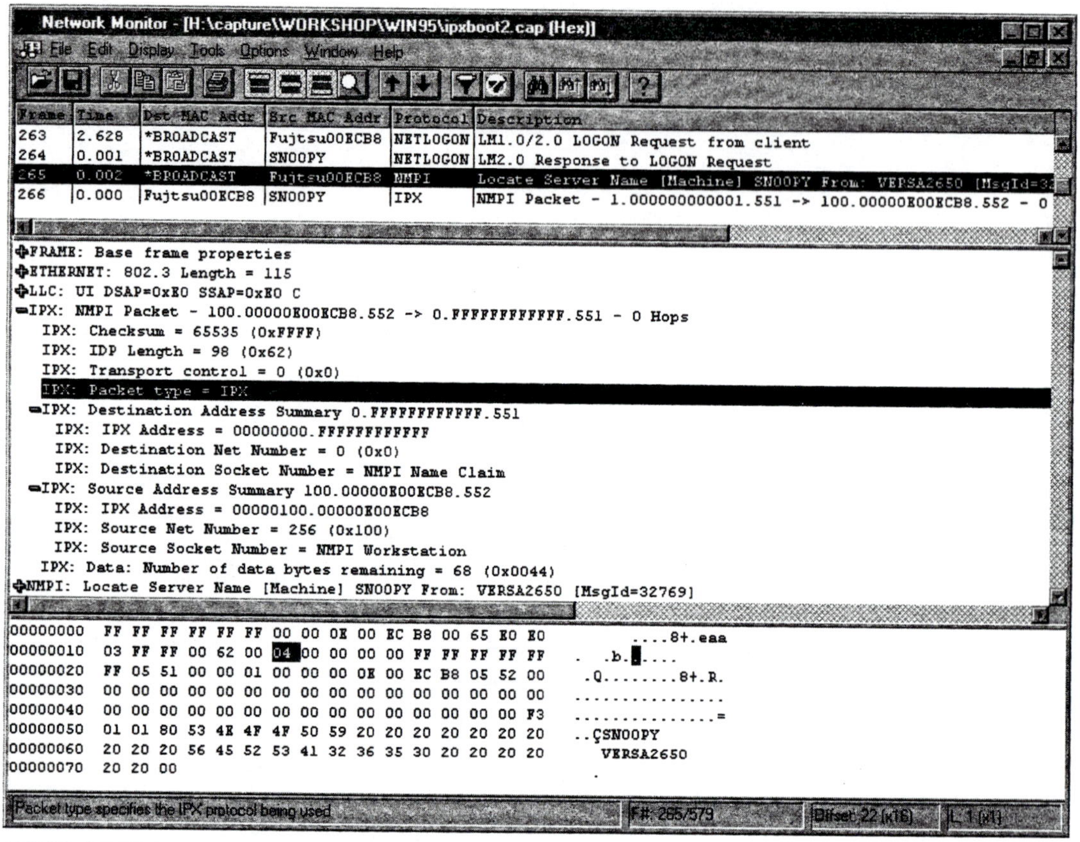

FIGURE 6.10 NMPI over IPX to locate NETLOGON server.

NetBIOS uses TCP for connection-oriented services, including name registration and resolution via a NetBIOS name server (such as WINs), session setup, and reliable sequenced data flow over the standard TCP protocol.

RFC 1001 describes three different ways in which a NetBIOS name query can be performed, depending on the node type. The three node types are broadcast (B-node), point-to-point (P-node), and mixed node (M-node). Microsoft Windows adds a fourth node type, the host (H-node).

A B-node will always broadcast a name query using UDP. Communication is limited to other B-nodes that are listening for NetBIOS UDP broadcasts within a bridged/switched broadcast area. The packet is addressed to the MAC address of hex FFFFFFFFFFFF and the IP broadcast address for that node's subnet. In Figure 6.11, the node has a class B IP address of 172.10.10.33 with a subnet mask of 255.255.255.0 and is broadcasting the name query to

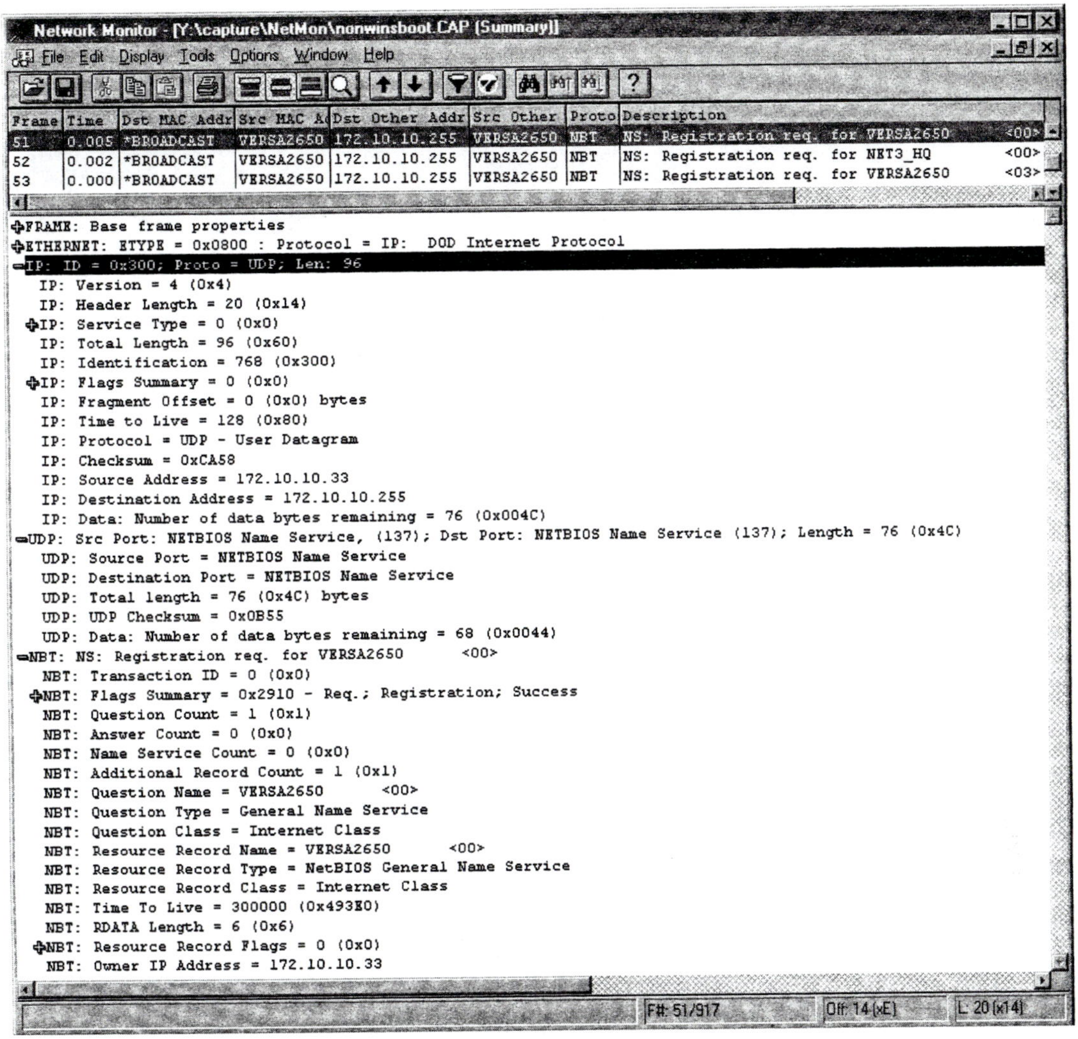

FIGURE 6.11 NetBIOS name resolution over UDP.

the IP subnet broadcast address of 172.10.10.255. The broadcast is using the well-known UDP port number of 137 to indicate a NetBIOS name service. Other important port numbers used for NetBIOS include 138 for datagrams (over UDP) and 139 for sessions (over TCP).

The NetBIOS sixteenth-character suffix naming convention is the same as NetBEUI. Figure 6.11 shows the node sending three name query or name registration packets: the unique computer name, the domain name, and the

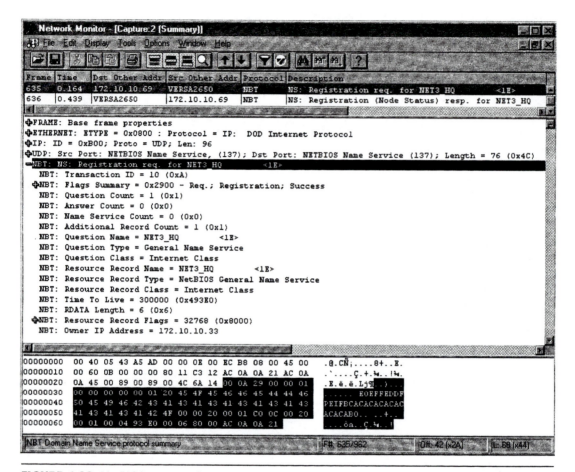

FIGURE 6.12 NetBIOS name registration using WINs.

messenger service name. Not shown in the figure are a total of three broad-casts for each name type, just like NetBEUI.

P-nodes do not broadcast nor listen for NetBIOS UDP name queries. A P-node depends on a NetBIOS Name Server such as WINS for name registra-tion, look-up, and broadcasting.

M-nodes are P-nodes with certain B-node characteristics. M-nodes broadcast name queries before using a NetBIOS name server, the assumption being that most resources reside on the local broadcast medium.

H-nodes are basically the reverse of M-nodes. The H-node registers its name with a WINs server and attempts to use the WINs server for name resolution. If the WINs server doesn't resolve a name, the H-node broadcasts for it.

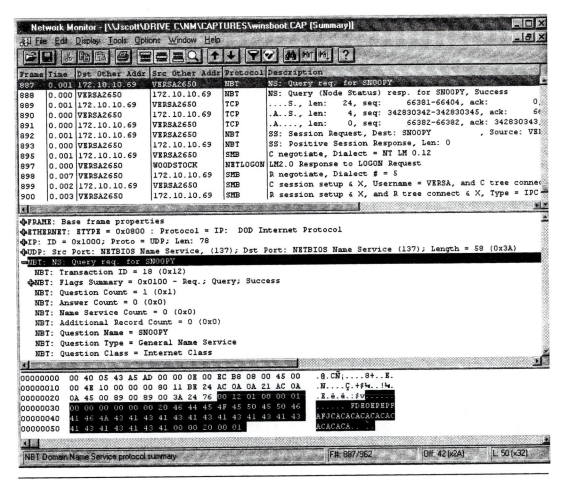

FIGURE 6.13 Setting up a NetBIOS session over TCP.

If WINs is enabled in a Windows 95/98/NT workstation, the default mode of operation is the H-node. If WINs is not enabled, the default is the B-node. Figure 6.12 shows the same node from Figure 6.11, but with WINs enabled. In packet 635, the node is registering its master browse name with an acknowledgment from the WINs server in packet 636.

In Figure 6.13, the node is querying the WINs server for the name "SNOOPY" in packets 887–888, setting up a TCP connection with SNOOPY in packets 889–891, setting up a NetBIOS session in packets 892–893, and finally establishing an SMB connection in packets 895–900. This is a good

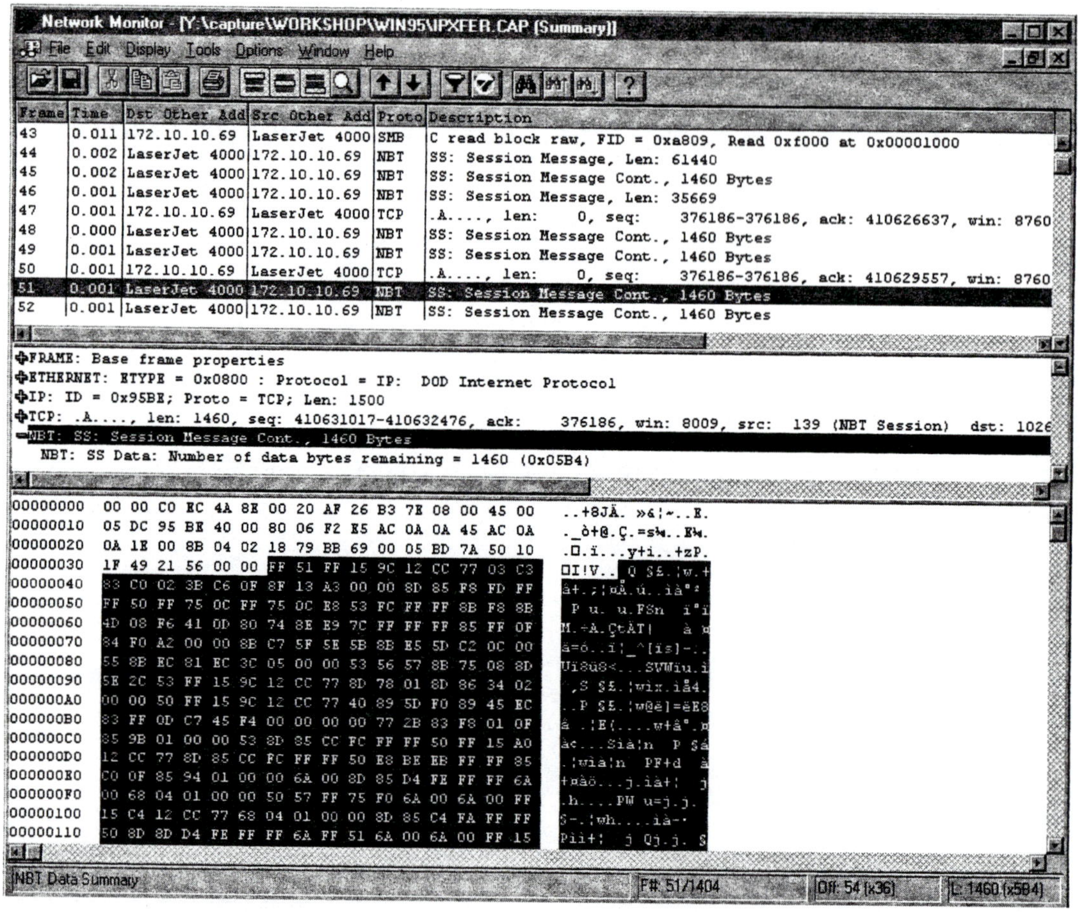

FIGURE 6.14 NetBIOS data transfer.

example of how sessions for different layers of protocol (4, 5, and 7) are built on top of each other.

Once a NetBIOS session is established, there is very little NetBIOS protocol overhead. Figure 6.14 shows a part of a file transfer between a workstation and server. Packet 51 is being decoded as a NetBIOS over TCP packet, but in reality it's just a pure TCP packet. Looking at the detail, you can see that the TCP port number is 139, a NetBIOS session packet. The TCP data is 1460 bytes of pure file data.

If you were to look at the packet detail for the SMB read block raw request in packet 43, you'd see that there's only a 4-byte NetBIOS header. Thus the NetBIOS overhead is really quite low during the course of transferring data.

6.4 NetWare Service Advertising Protocol (SAP)

The NetWare Core Protocol (NCP) over IPX does not have a separate session layer per se, except to locate a resource using SAP. After that, the actual session is established by sending a RIP packet to find the next "hop" to the resource, followed by an exchange of NCP packets with that resource.

Chapter 4 showed how a NetWare client that is booting up first sends a SAP packet looking for a file server. The SAP packet is either a "Find nearest file server" or "Find Nearest NetWare Directory Server (NDS)" and is sent to the MAC all stations broadcast address of hex FFFFFFFFFFFF and the IPX address of hex 0.FFFFFFFFFFFF. The SAP is embedded in an IPX Type 0 packet and does not cross routers.

The SAP response packet (see Figure 6.15) is from a router (or a NetWare server; as discussed in Chapter 4, all NetWare servers are routers) and contains the logical name of a file server and the internal IPX network number assigned to that server. The workstation then sends a NetWare RIP packet to find a route to that internal network number.

The fields in a SAP response packet are described in Table 6.3.

TABLE 6.3 SAP Response Packet Definitions

Field	Description
Operation	A 2-byte field to indicate the packet type. Only four SAP packet types are defined: 1 = general service request; 2 = general service response; 3 = nearest service request; 4 = nearest service response.
Service Type	A 2-byte field that specifies the type of service. For example, hex 04 is for a file server and hex 07 is for a print server.
Service Name	A 48-byte field containing the logical name of the server.
Network Address	The 32-bit network portion of the IPX address.
Node Address	The 48-bit node portion of the IPX address.
Socket Number	The socket that the service is listening on.
Hops to Server	The number of router hops to the server. This includes the "hop" to the internal network of the server; thus the Hops to Server will always be at least 1.

In a SAP request packet, only the first two fields, Operation and Service Type, are present.

Figure 6.16 contains an example of a workstation sending a SAP service request packet for a NetWare Directory Server (NDS) with several servers responding. In this case, the responding servers were attached to several

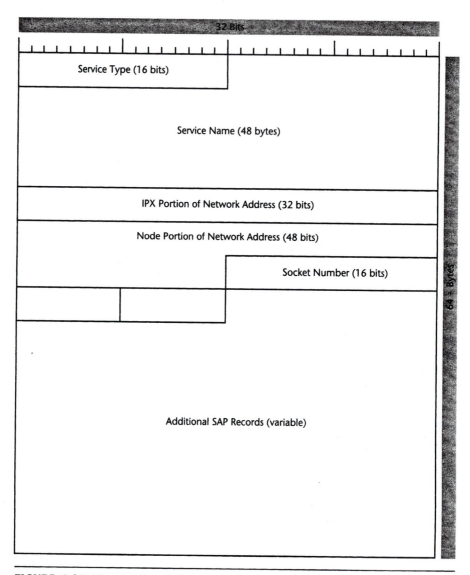

FIGURE 6.15 The NetWare SAP reply packet format.

Token Rings throughout a source-routed network. You would have seen the same type of response in an Ethernet switched/bridged environment.

If all of the NDS servers were on the other side of a router from the user, you would see only one SAP packet from the router. Routers maintain a SAP table just like a RIP table. The SAP update protocol works identically to NetWare RIP. Every 60 seconds, by default, any device that provides a

```
Sniffer - Local, Ethernet (Line speed at 10 Mbps) - [Melisa.trc : 32/8845 TokenRing frames]    _ □ ×
  File  Monitor  Capture  Display  Tools  Database  Window  Help                              _ ଅ ×
```

No.	Len	Delta Time	Dest Address	Source Address	Summary
32	59	0.694.802	Broadcast	400003043911	NSAP: C Find nearest NetWare directory server
33	115	0.000.358	400003043911	400007050905	NSAP: R AEFA-NDS_____ANP.J@@@@@D.RJ
34	115	0.000.301	400003043911	400007050904	NSAP: R AEFA-NDS_____ANP.B@@@@@D.RJ
35	115	0.000.231	400003043911	400007041881	NSAP: R AEFA-NDS_____ANP.J@@@@@D.RJ
36	115	0.000.267	400003043911	400007031600	NSAP: R AEFA-NDS_____ANP.B@@@@@D.RJ
37	115	0.000.018	400003043911	400007042114	NSAP: R AEFA-NDS_____ANP.I@@@@@D.RJ
38	115	0.000.015	400003043911	400007041920	NSAP: R AEFA-NDS_____ANP.J@@@@@D.RJ

```
⊞▒ : DLC AC=10, FC=40, FS=00
⊞▒ RI: Limited Broadcast Fwrd (070)-1-(0E1)-1-(0C7)
⊞▒ LLC: C D=E0 S=E0 UI
⊟▒ IPX: ----- IPX Header -----
   ▒ IPX:
   ▒ IPX: Checksum = 0xFFFF
   ▒ IPX: Length = 34
   ▒ IPX: Transport control = 00
   ▒ IPX:        0000 .... = Reserved
   ▒ IPX:        .... 0000 = Hop count
   ▒ IPX: Packet type = 0 (Novell)
   ▒ IPX:
   ▒ IPX: Dest    network.node = 0.FFFFFFFFFFFF, socket = 1106 (NetWare Service Advertising)
   ▒ IPX: Source network.node = 1078404.400003043911 (MSP-FA-W43911), socket = 16384 (Unknown)
   ▒ IPX:
⊟▒ NSAP: ----- NetWare Nearest Service Query -----
   ▒ NSAP:
   ▒ NSAP: Service type = 0278 (NetWare directory server)
```

```
00000000: 10 40 ff ff ff ff ff ff c0 00 03 04 39 11 c8 30  .@ÿÿÿÿÿÿÀ...9.È0
00000010: 07 01 0e 11 0c 70 e0 e0 03 ff ff 00 22 00 00 00  .....pàà.ÿÿ."...
00000020: 00 00 00 ff ff ff ff ff ff 04 52 01 07 84 04 40  ...ÿÿÿÿÿÿ.R...@
00000030: 00 03 04 39 11 40 00 00 03 02 78              ...9.@...x
```

```
 Expert ╱ Decode ╱ Matrix ╱ Host Table ╱ Protocol Dist. ╱ Statistics ╱
For Help, press F1
```

FIGURE 6.16 A find nearest NetWare Directory Server SAP packet.

NetWare service (file server, print server, gateway, tape back up server, etc.) sends out one SAP broadcast packet containing the name of the service, the type of service, and the internal IPX network number of that service. Up to seven services may be advertised per SAP packet; a file server running RCONSOLE, for example, will send a SAP packet about itself (the file service) and the RCONSOLE service. Routers learn about the services on a particular router port/segment by listening to these SAP broadcasts.

The routers turn around and broadcast a SAP table dump to the other ports. Other routers in turn pick up these broadcasts, update their SAP tables, forward the SAP information, and so on. Soon every router has a SAP table representing all of the NetWare services in the network.

There are a couple of problems with the SAP protocol that apply to medium and large networks (with hundreds of NetWare services). There are usually far more SAP broadcasts than RIPs in a NetWare intranet. Unlike RIP where one can advertise up to 50 NetWare networks per packet, there can only be seven SAP names per broadcast packet. This is because each SAP entry requires 64 bytes (48 bytes for the SAP name alone) coupled with the self-imposed IPX MTU limitation of 576 bytes to ensure that a SAP packet will propagate across any network.

Thus SAP packets usually chew up WAN bandwidth long before RIPs become a problem. In a network with a few hundred file and print servers, there might be 1000 or so SAP names. Every 60 seconds, all routers must send out 1000 / 7, or 143 SAP broadcasts. At a maximum IPX MTU of 576 bytes, these packets take roughly 12 seconds to send on a 56 Kbps link. For this reason, some routers have various SAP filters that can be applied.

Another problem is that a router responding to a "Find Nearest Server" query usually returns the first SAP entry in the router table by default. If that server happens to be ten hops away over several WAN links, so be it! The workstation's first attempt to log on will be to the remote server, even if the workstation has a preferred server statement in the login script. The preferred server connection comes *later*, after a "hand-off" from the first server the user connected to.

Let's say for the sake of argument that the first server in the router table is somewhere within the user's LAN infrastructure. This could still be a problem. Why? I've seen a case where the first server happened to be a CD ROM server with a five-user NetWare runtime license. Even though the user was quickly transferred to a "real file server" by the CD ROM server, when thousands of users logged in every morning they had to wait to first get a connection to the CD ROM server!

> **❗**
>
> Some session layer protocols do not have built-in recovery mechanisms in the event of a lost connection, requiring the user to log on again to that resource or even completely reboot their workstation. With NetWare, for example, only the NetWare Client32 driver has auto-reconnect in the event of a lost connection with a NetWare server. On the other hand, most IP applications that use TCP will recover, provided that neither the end-resource nor the path to the end-resource is down. Recall that TCP recovery can be quite long, due to the exponential back-off timing of TCP packet retransmissions.

Chapter 7

Analyzing and Troubleshooting the Presentation Layer

7.1 Introduction

The responsibility of the presentation layer (layer 6) is to manage abstract data structures. Abstract data structures define data without regard to machine-oriented structures. In theory, the idea is to have a common way of representing and interpreting data on a network-wide basis, regardless of computing platform. This way, the application layer (layer 7) can use data structures that are native to a particular application and not worry about conversion.

In many instances, the representation of data is tied to a particular machine or platform architecture. For example, numerical representation of data on an Intel platform is byte-reversed from that on Sun. As another example, the character set on an IBM mainframe is represented by EBCDIC, whereas a PC is typically ASCII (8-bit) or extended ASCII (16-bit).

In reality, the presentation layer is usually missing from protocol stacks. Unlike standardizing on IP for the network layer or TCP for the transport layer, the presentation layer tends to be tied to a specific application rather than being universally applied. Examples of presentation protocols or formats that are tied to specific applications include the X Window System, a hierarchy of resizable windows that supports device-independent graphics, and PostScript, chosen by Apple as *the* printing language for AppleTalk networks.

Other applications rely on data conversion within the application itself. Examples include 3270 or AS/400 terminal emulation software and SNMP agent and console software. Even though SNMP uses a standard presentation syntax, Abstract Syntax Notation 1 (ASN.1; see X.409, "ISO Abstract Syntax Notation" for more details), the interpretation of ASN.1 data is usually embedded inside the SNMP application rather than requiring a separate presentation layer.

Another standard for common description and encoding of data is found in RFC 1014, "XDR: External Data Representation Standard," developed by Sun Microsystems. XDR is similar in nature to ASN.1, except that XDR uses implicit typing of data, whereas X.409 uses explicit typing of data. NFS is an example of an application layer protocol that uses XDR.

ISO offers a real presentation layer standard (ISO Presentation Protocol, or ISO PP for short), so why not simply adopt *it* for network-wide usage? The answer lies in the amount of overhead that would be required if you forced every platform on the network to conform to a particular standard. Imagine having to convert all characters from ASCII-to-EBCDIC-to-ASCII if EBCIDIC was the character standard or having to convert all data to and from the ASN.1 syntax.

With a "real" presentation layer, you'd be converting data for *all* applications, even if the end-nodes were on the same platforms. The amount of processing required for data conversion would be tremendous, even with the rapid advancement in PC and workstation processing capability. For this reason, most applications will continue to convert data as needed.

7.2 Abstract Syntax Notation 1 (ASN.1)

Because SNMP is such a widespread management protocol that uses ASN.1 as the common presentation syntax, a brief introduction to ASN.1 is presented here.

ASN.1 uses abstract syntax to describe both the data structures and the SNMP management information. To reduce complexity, the SNMP management framework uses only a subset of ASN.1 that doesn't have many "bells and whistles."

ASN.1 defines three kinds of objects: types, values, and macros. *Types* define new data structures, *values* are instances of a type, and *macros* are used to change the grammar of the ASN.1 language. Each of the three objects is named with an ASN.1 word. If the object is a type, the word starts with an uppercase letter, such as the word "Gauge." If the object is a value, it starts with a lowercase letter, such as the word "system." For macros, the word is in all uppercase letters, such as "OBJECT-TYPE."

SNMP uses a subset of ASN.1 simple types:

- *Integer:* A data type with a cardinal number as its value.
- *Bit string:* A data type with zero or more named bits.
- *Octet string:* A data type with zero or more octets (an 8-bit byte).
- *Object identifier:* A data type referring to an authoritative designation with complex semantics, and consisting of a sequence of non-negative integer values that traverse a tree.

Data types such as boolean, real, enumerated, and set are missing but not required. For example, a boolean can be represented by an integer with a "0" for false and "1" for true.

SNMP ASN.1 objects are always prefixed by 1.3.6.1.2. As illustrated in Figure 7.1, this designates the traversal of a tree that says "ISO.identified-organization.DOD.internet.management".

SNMP nodes are managed by querying information from the Management Information Base (MIB). There are three types of MIBs: the standards-based MIBs developed by the Internet Engineering Task Force (IETF) and documented in several RFCs, experimental MIBs under development by the IETF, and enterprise-specific MIBs developed by vendors and specific to their equipment. Standards-based MIBs include the core MIB known as MIB-II as well as MIBs for Ethernet, Token Ring, frame relay, RIP, OSPF, RMON, and so on.

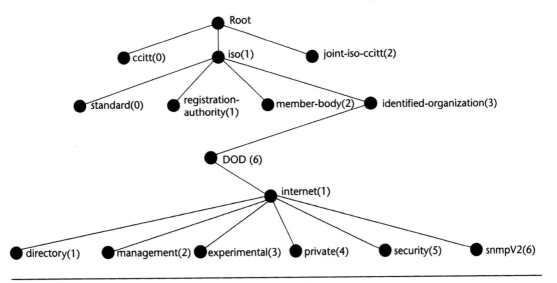

FIGURE 7.1 Object identifier naming tree.

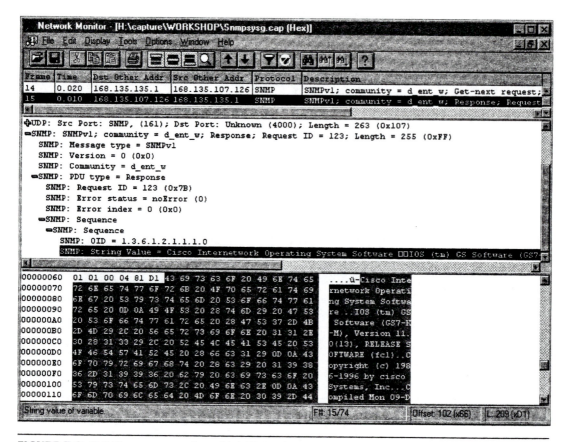

FIGURE 7.2 SNMP response packet with MIB-II information.

An example of a full SNMP object ID is 1.3.6.1.2.1.1.1.0, which is an octet string in a MIB-II system group that describes the node being managed. Figure 7.2 is an example of an SNMP response packet containing information related to this object ID.

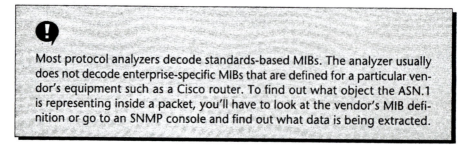

Most protocol analyzers decode standards-based MIBs. The analyzer usually does not decode enterprise-specific MIBs that are defined for a particular vendor's equipment such as a Cisco router. To find out what object the ASN.1 is representing inside a packet, you'll have to look at the vendor's MIB definition or go to an SNMP console and find out what data is being extracted.

MIB-II contains the following object groups: system (as in the preceding example), interfaces (the network attachments), at (IP address translation), ip (Internet Protocol), icmp (Internet Control Message Protocol), tcp (Transmission Control Protocol), udp (User Datagram Protocol), egp (Exterior Gateway Protocol), transmission (media-specific MIBs), and snmp (SNMPv1).

Even though SNMPv2 split MIB-II into several MIB modules, such as the SNMPv2-MIB, IP-MIB, TCP-MIB, and UDP-MIB, the MIB-II grouping is still in widespread use.

7.2.1 X Windows

The X Window System (or X) provides device-independent graphics for a variety of platforms. When analyzing this protocol over the network, you'll first have to get used to the terms "client" and "server."

In X, a *client* is a program displaying on the screen and taking input from that keyboard and mouse. The *server* is the software that manages one display, keyboard, and mouse. The server and client may be running on the same machine or on different machines across the network. Think of the client as being a virtual machine that presents itself to the user in a graphical display.

This is a bit different than what you're used to when you talk about client/server computing. The client in this context is the user's desktop, and the server is another machine executing an application (such as a database server) or file services.

In X, the server is at a user's desktop and sends user input such as keystrokes, mouse movements, and mouse clicks to the client. If the user has several windows open, different clients are receiving input from the user, depending on which window is active (the one with the mouse hovering over it).

The X protocol communicates over a single asynchronous bi-directional stream of 8-bit bytes such as TCP. If the client and server are on the same machine (which requires multitasking), however, shared memory, interprocess communications channels, or UNIX domain sockets are used. Regardless, the bytes that pass back and forth between the server and client are identical in all environments.

The server sends events asynchronously, which can help improve performance. For example, several X events from a server can be sent in a single TCP packet without waiting for responses from the client. An example of this is shown in Figure 7.3.

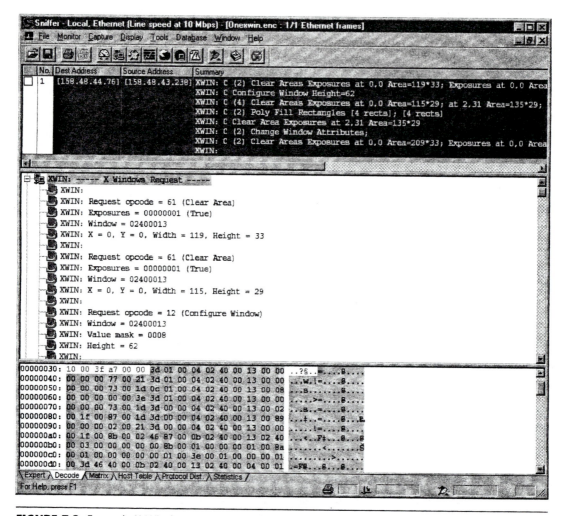

FIGURE 7.3 Example X Windows events sent in a single packet.

Although this seems like a blessing, it can also be a curse because multiple event notifications don't work for every X operation. If you have a lot of "X Windowing" on your network, you could have a lot of "useless" traffic. The following example illustrates this.

> One time I was troubleshooting a problem with poor response time with a particular application. A technique I sometimes employ is to position myself and the protocol analyzer right next to a user who is running the application, so I can see exactly what the user is doing, gauge the response time, and later analyze captured packets for a more detailed and exact response time analysis.

No.	Rel. Time	Dest Address	Source Address	Summary
6	0:00:00.000	[158.48.227.200]	[158.48.227.4]	XWIN: R Query Pointer at 88,35
7	0:00:00.020	[158.48.227.200]	[158.48.227.4]	XWIN: E Motion Notify at 108,36
8	0:00:00.020	[158.48.227.4]	[158.48.227.200]	XWIN: C Query Pointer
9	0:00:00.022	[158.48.227.200]	[158.48.227.4]	TCP: D=1428 S=6000 ACK=1164319334 WIN=4088
10	0:00:00.024	[158.48.227.200]	[158.48.227.4]	TCP: D=1428 S=6000 ACK=1164319334 WIN=4096
11	0:00:00.025	[158.48.227.200]	[158.48.227.4]	XWIN: R Query Pointer at 108,36
12	0:00:00.044	[158.48.227.200]	[158.48.227.4]	XWIN: E Motion Notify at 110,36
13	0:00:00.044	[158.48.227.4]	[158.48.227.200]	XWIN: C Query Pointer
14	0:00:00.046	[158.48.227.200]	[158.48.227.4]	TCP: D=1428 S=6000 ACK=1164319342 WIN=4088
15	0:00:00.048	[158.48.227.200]	[158.48.227.4]	TCP: D=1428 S=6000 ACK=1164319342 WIN=4096
16	0:00:00.049	[158.48.227.200]	[158.48.227.4]	XWIN: R Query Pointer at 110,36
17	0:00:00.094	[158.48.227.200]	[158.48.227.4]	XWIN: E Motion Notify at 111,38
18	0:00:00.094	[158.48.227.4]	[158.48.227.200]	XWIN: C Query Pointer
19	0:00:00.096	[158.48.227.200]	[158.48.227.4]	TCP: D=1428 S=6000 ACK=1164319350 WIN=4088
20	0:00:00.098	[158.48.227.200]	[158.48.227.4]	TCP: D=1428 S=6000 ACK=1164319350 WIN=4096
21	0:00:00.099	[158.48.227.200]	[158.48.227.4]	XWIN: R Query Pointer at 111,38
22	0:00:00.119	[158.48.227.200]	[158.48.227.4]	XWIN: E Motion Notify at 111,48
23	0:00:00.120	[158.48.227.4]	[158.48.227.200]	XWIN: C Query Pointer
24	0:00:00.122	[158.48.227.200]	[158.48.227.4]	TCP: D=1428 S=6000 ACK=1164319358 WIN=4088
25	0:00:00.124	[158.48.227.200]	[158.48.227.4]	TCP: D=1428 S=6000 ACK=1164319358 WIN=4096
26	0:00:00.124	[158.48.227.200]	[158.48.227.4]	XWIN: R Query Pointer at 111,48
27	0:00:00.143	[158.48.227.200]	[158.48.227.4]	XWIN: E Motion Notify at 109,50
28	0:00:00.144	[158.48.227.4]	[158.48.227.200]	XWIN: C Query Pointer
29	0:00:00.146	[158.48.227.200]	[158.48.227.4]	TCP: D=1428 S=6000 ACK=1164319366 WIN=4088
30	0:00:00.148	[158.48.227.200]	[158.48.227.4]	TCP: D=1428 S=6000 ACK=1164319366 WIN=4096
31	0:00:00.149	[158.48.227.200]	[158.48.227.4]	XWIN: R Query Pointer at 109,50
32	0:00:00.168	[158.48.227.200]	[158.48.227.4]	XWIN: E Motion Notify at 99,51
33	0:00:00.168	[158.48.227.4]	[158.48.227.200]	XWIN: C Query Pointer
34	0:00:00.170	[158.48.227.200]	[158.48.227.4]	TCP: D=1428 S=6000 ACK=1164319374 WIN=4088
35	0:00:00.173	[158.48.227.200]	[158.48.227.4]	TCP: D=1428 S=6000 ACK=1164319374 WIN=4096
36	0:00:00.173	[158.48.227.200]	[158.48.227.4]	XWIN: R Query Pointer at 99,51
37	0:00:00.192	[158.48.227.200]	[158.48.227.4]	XWIN: E Motion Notify at 98,51
38	0:00:00.193	[158.48.227.4]	[158.48.227.200]	XWIN: C Query Pointer
39	0:00:00.195	[158.48.227.200]	[158.48.227.4]	TCP: D=1428 S=6000 ACK=1164319382 WIN=4088
40	0:00:00.197	[158.48.227.200]	[158.48.227.4]	TCP: D=1428 S=6000 ACK=1164319382 WIN=4096
41	0:00:00.198	[158.48.227.200]	[158.48.227.4]	XWIN: R Query Pointer at 98,51
42	0:00:00.218	[158.48.227.200]	[158.48.227.4]	XWIN: E Motion Notify at 98,50

FIGURE 7.4 Packet generation caused by a user's mouse movements in X Windows.

This particular user was interrupted by a phone call, and while she was talking to the other party, there was a sustained burst of activity from her workstation (I had set up a capture filter on her IP address). After analyzing the packets, I realized what was happening: the user had a nervous habit of twirling her mouse around on the mouse pad while talking to someone. Whenever the mouse hit an X Window on her PC, a burst of X server events were sent over the network to the client! Figure 7.4 shows pointer updates from the user—42 packets in just a quarter of a second, or about 160 packets per second—just from moving the mouse around.

This isn't all that bad unless hundreds of X Windows users out of thousands are doing something similar, hitting the poor client (that was running on an HP minicomputer) with thousands of mouse position updates per second!

This X Windows behavior was not a problem in this particular network, however, and it wasn't related to another problem that I was working on at the time, but it sure was interesting to observe.

Chapter 8

Analyzing and Troubleshooting the Application Layer

8.1 Introduction and Common Problems at the Application Layer

Layer 7, the application layer, shields the client application from a server. The idea is to have applications behave as if the data exists locally on the user's platform. That's not to say that a programmer couldn't choose to call APIs that are specific to a particular file server.

Part of the application layer software is called a shell, or redirector. The redirector receives requests from the local operating system that are for remote resources. The requests are converted to a language that the remote server can understand such as NetWare Core Protocol (NCP), Server Message Block (SMB), or Network File System (NFS).

A shell is similar to a redirector, except that it intercepts operating system calls for inspection prior to the operating system receiving them. To a remote server, a call from a shell or redirector are one and the same.

When it comes to troubleshooting and optimization, the application layer is often the last layer to receive attention. Part of the reason has to do with complexity. The further up the OSI stack you move, the more complex the protocol. Protocol analyzers have also been slow to embrace application layer protocols. Look how long it took to get Sybase, Oracle, and Microsoft SQL database decodes. Decodes for Lotus Notes? Forget it. Proprietary in-house applications? Good luck!

Lower layer technology like IP and Ethernet have been around for much longer than some of the upper layer stuff. People have a very good understanding of the lower layers due to simplicity and experience with the technology. There's still a lot to learn about the application layer.

When analyzing and optimizing networked applications, you can look for several common characteristics. Let's begin with a problem known as request looping. Request looping happens when an application sends a command, receives a reply, and then repeats the same identical command again and again. Figure 8.1 shows an example from an analyzer.

Looping differs from the transport retransmissions examined in Chapter 5 when the application does not receive a reply or acknowledgment. Differ-

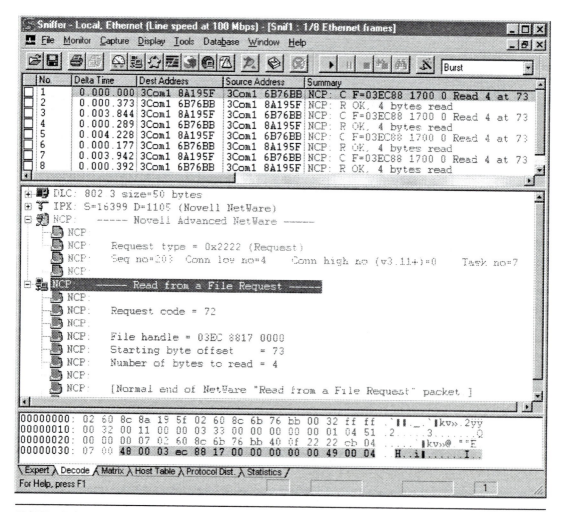

FIGURE 8.1 Example of application request looping.

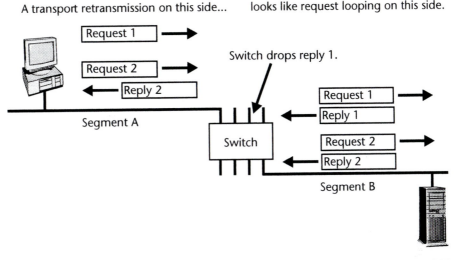

FIGURE 8.2 Application request looping vs. transport retransmission.

entiating between request looping and transport retransmissions can sometimes be a bit tricky, depending on where the analyzer is located. In Figure
8.2, if the analyzer is on segment B, it looks like a request loop because you
can see both the command and reply packet. If the analyzer is on segment A,
you find out the real reason for the repeated request: the reply packet never
made it back to the client. Thus, this is really a transport retransmission
rather than a loop on a request.

If the analyzer on segment B has an expert system, it would probably tell you
that the application is looping on a request. The same analyzer on segment
A would call it a transport retransmission. This is why you often have to perform protocol analysis on more than one segment before drawing conclu-
sions and recommending solutions. If an application is truly looping, either
the application has a problem or the data gets to the client segment but not
all the way up the stack to the application. It could be an issue of a poorly
written adapter driver, inadequate memory allocation on the adapter, poor
bus performance, and so on. More often than not, it's simply a poorly written application.

Another common problem, especially in NetWare environments, is excessive
file searching, as shown in Figure 8.3. One cause of this is when a batch file or
an end-user executes a DOS command that is not on the default drive that is
currently mapped into the command prompt. DOS will then look at the search
path. In many NetWare environments, search paths are set up such that commonly accessed programs and utilities are at the *end* of the search order, caus-

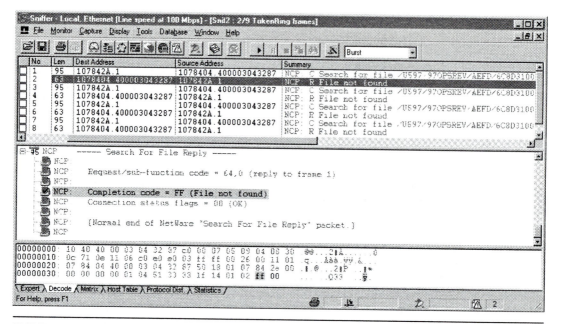

FIGURE 8.3 Excessive file searching.

ing *every* mapped network drive to be hit before the file is found. The solution is to move common files to the first path in the search order or to specify the complete path to the application such as z:\utilities\setlock.com instead of set-lock.com with a search path to z:\utilities.

This doesn't happen too often in the NT server environment simply because of the migration from DOS to Windows applications along with the migration of NetWare to NT. Windows 95/98/NT clients do not automatically set search paths to drives that are automatically remapped at logon time.

Yet another common problem deals with the payload efficiency. If you were to only send 1 byte in an Ethernet packet, the bandwidth overhead would be tremendous. Recalling the discussion of Ethernet frames from Chapter 2, there are 20 bytes wasted in the gap + preamble before each packet plus 64 bytes in a minimum-sized Ethernet packet, including the 4-byte CRC. Thus it takes a total of 83 overhead bytes to send one Telnet character (see Figure 8.4) for an overhead of 830 percent. Compare this to an FTP data transfer with a full TCP payload of 1460 bytes. In this case, the overhead is 83/1460, or about 5 percent.

Using protocol analysis, inefficient applications that talk to NetWare using NCP are much easier to spot than those that talk to NT servers using SMB. Applications that perform small incremental file reads such as shown in

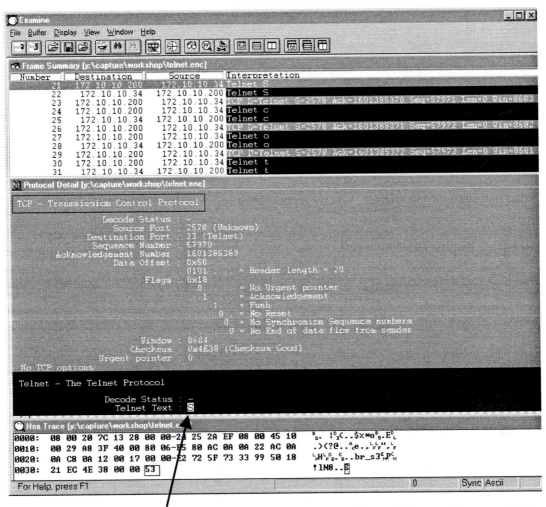

Including the Ethernet frame gap, preamble, and 64-byte minimum packet size (including the CRC), it takes 83 bytes to send this one character.

FIGURE 8.4 Telnet overhead.

Figure 8.5 will show up in NCP packets over the network. *SMB, on the other hand, reads a block of data from the file server to the local workstation's cache for subsequent reading, even if the application only reads a file one byte at a time.* This also holds for applications that overlap their read or write commands. In the first packet, an application asks to read 1024 bytes at file offset 287,000 and receives a reply. The next read request is for 1024 bytes at offset 287,200. The application got all but 200 bytes in the previous read request, so why not use it?

> ❗
>
> When analyzing an application, you should ask yourself whether or not the amount of data makes sense for the application you're analyzing. In the case of Telnet, one character leading to 830 percent overhead in an Ethernet packet is probably okay because most users can't type more than 10 packets (i.e., keystrokes) per second! On the other hand, if you see an application reading a file sequentially in small blocks as indicated by the increments in the file offsets (see Figure 8.5), you have a potential problem to look at.

In some cases, the overlapping is 100 percent, as shown in Figure 8.6. In this trace from the client's network segment, the application repetitively read the same block of data over and over (flagged as a file retransmission by the analyzer) before moving to the next block of 256 bytes. This is an example of a poorly written application that executes file read requests for data that it just read when accessing very small amounts of data. The data being accessed was read-only data, so there was no excuse for writing an application this

SUMMARY	Delta T	Bytes	Destination	Source	Summary
M 1617	0.003	127	Server	WTCNTW150324	NCP C Open/Create file(s): MATTHEW.DAT
1618	0.010	143	WTCNTW150324	Server	NCP R OK, Opened
1619	0.000	67	Server	WTCNTW150324	NCP C Get current size of file F=8C13 1500
1620	0.009	65	WTCNTW150324	Server	NCP R OK, File size is 6145
1621	0.003	73	Server	WTCNTW150324	NCP C F=8C13 1500 Read 256 at 0
1622	0.010	319	WTCNTW150324	Server	NCP R OK, 256 bytes read
1623	0.000	73	Server	WTCNTW150324	NCP C F=8C13 1500 Read 256 at 3072
1624	0.007	319	WTCNTW150324	Server	NCP R OK, 256 bytes read
1625	0.003	73	Server	WTCNTW150324	NCP C F=8C13 1500 Read 256 at 3328
1626	0.011	319	WTCNTW150324	Server	NCP R OK, 256 bytes read
1627	0.000	73	Server	WTCNTW150324	NCP C F=8C13 1500 Read 256 at 3584
1628	0.007	319	WTCNTW150324	Server	NCP R OK, 256 bytes read
1629	0.003	73	Server	WTCNTW150324	NCP C F=8C13 1500 Read 256 at 3840
1630	0.010	319	WTCNTW150324	Server	NCP R OK, 256 bytes read
1631	0.004	73	Server	WTCNTW150324	NCP C F=8C13 1500 Read 256 at 5120
1632	0.009	319	WTCNTW150324	Server	NCP R OK, 256 bytes read
1633	0.000	73	Server	WTCNTW150324	NCP C F=8C13 1500 Read 256 at 5376
1634	0.010	319	WTCNTW150324	Server	NCP R OK, 256 bytes read
1635	0.003	73	Server	WTCNTW150324	NCP C F=8C13 1500 Read 256 at 5632
1636	0.015	319	WTCNTW150324	Server	NCP R OK, 256 bytes read
1637	0.003	73	Server	WTCNTW150324	NCP C F=8C13 1500 Read 256 at 5888
1638	0.010	319	WTCNTW150324	Server	NCP R OK, 256 bytes read

•
•
•

FIGURE 8.5 Inefficient file reading.

SUMMARY	Delta T	Bytes	Destination	Source	Summary
M 3042	0.000	124	Server	WTCNTW150324	NCP C Open/Create file(s): DANIEL.DAT
3043	0.018	143	WTCNTW150324	Server	NCP R OK, Opened
3044	0.000	67	Server	WTCNTW150324	NCP C Get current size of file F=C451 0700
3045	0.007	65	WTCNTW150324	Server	NCP R OK, File size is 2304
3046	0.000	73	Server	WTCNTW150324	NCP C F=C451 0700 Read 256 at 0
3047	0.010	319	WTCNTW150324	Server	NCP R OK, 256 bytes read
3048	0.001	73	Server	WTCNTW150324	NCP C F=C451 0700 Read 256 at 1024
3049	0.010	319	WTCNTW150324	Server	NCP R OK, 256 bytes read
3050	0.003	73	Server	WTCNTW150324	File retransmission NCP C F=C451 0700 Read 256 at 1024
3051	0.011	319	WTCNTW150324	Server	NCP R OK, 256 bytes read
3052	0.000	73	Server	WTCNTW150324	File retransmission NCP C F=C451 0700 Read 256 at 1024
3053	0.008	319	WTCNTW150324	Server	NCP R OK, 256 bytes read
3054	0.003	73	Server	WTCNTW150324	File retransmission NCP C F=C451 0700 Read 256 at 1024
3055	0.017	319	WTCNTW150324	Server	NCP R OK, 256 bytes read
3056	0.001	73	Server	WTCNTW150324	File retransmission NCP C F=C451 0700 Read 256 at 1024
3057	0.008	319	WTCNTW150324	Server	NCP R OK, 256 bytes read
3058	0.003	73	Server	WTCNTW150324	File retransmission NCP C F=C451 0700 Read 256 at 1024
3059	0.009	319	WTCNTW150324	Server	NCP R OK, 256 bytes read
3060	0.000	73	Server	WTCNTW150324	File retransmission NCP C F=C451 0700 Read 256 at 1024
3061	0.030	319	WTCNTW150324	Server	NCP R OK, 256 bytes read
3062	0.003	73	Server	WTCNTW150324	File retransmission NCP C F=C451 0700 Read 256 at 1024
3063	0.016	319	WTCNTW150324	Server	NCP R OK, 256 bytes read
3064	0.000	73	Server	WTCNTW150324	File retransmission NCP C F=C451 0700 Read 256 at 1024
3065	0.010	319	WTCNTW150324	Server	NCP R OK, 256 bytes read
3066	0.003	73	Server	WTCNTW150324	File retransmission NCP C F=C451 0700 Read 256 at 1024
3067	0.011	319	WTCNTW150324	Server	NCP R OK, 256 bytes read
3068	0.000	73	Server	WTCNTW150324	NCP C F=C451 0700 Read 256 at 1280
3069	0.005	319	WTCNTW150324	Server	NCP R OK, 256 bytes read
3070	0.003	73	Server	WTCNTW150324	Read/write overlap NCP C F=C451 0700 Read 256 at 1280
3071	0.012	319	WTCNTW150324	Server	NCP R OK, 256 bytes read
3072	0.000	73	Server	WTCNTW150324	File retransmission NCP C F=C451 0700 Read 256 at 1280
3073	0.008	319	WTCNTW150324	Server	NCP R OK, 256 bytes read
3074	0.003	73	Server	WTCNTW150324	File retransmission NCP C F=C451 0700 Read 256 at 1280
3075	0.018	319	WTCNTW150324	Server	NCP R OK, 256 bytes read
3076	0.000	73	Server	WTCNTW150324	File retransmission NCP C F=C451 0700 Read 256 at 1280
3077	0.004	319	WTCNTW150324	Server	NCP R OK, 256 bytes read
3078	0.003	73	Server	WTCNTW150324	File retransmission NCP C F=C451 0700 Read 256 at 1280
3079	0.019	319	WTCNTW150324	Server	NCP R OK, 256 bytes read
3080	0.000	73	Server	WTCNTW150324	File retransmission NCP C F=C451 0700 Read 256 at 1280
3081	0.009	319	WTCNTW150324	Server	NCP R OK, 256 bytes read
3082	0.000	73	Server	WTCNTW150324	File retransmission NCP C F=C451 0700 Read 256 at 1280
3083	0.020	319	WTCNTW150324	Server	NCP R OK, 256 bytes read
3084	0.003	73	Server	WTCNTW150324	File retransmission NCP C F=C451 0700 Read 256 at 1280
3085	0.015	319	WTCNTW150324	Server	NCP R OK, 256 bytes read

•
•
•

FIGURE 8.6 100 percent overlapping file read requests.

way. This application will run slightly faster with the data on an NT server because of the local SMB data caching as mentioned earlier. In this case, there's still overhead in the file calls, but the calls stay local and you would not be able to see them with a protocol analyzer.

Some client/server applications are really tough to analyze because you might see random I/O in which small chunks of data are read at random locations from one or more files. In this case, you will need to work with the programmer to see if the amount of small packet transactions can be reduced. This can sometimes be accomplished by performing "atomic" operations on a database, where several SQL operations are executed from one request packet, instead of generating several smaller packets with individual SQL statements. I know of one programmer that had to write around a Visual Basic middleware database package to accomplish this. It took a lot of work, but it dramatically improved the performance of the application and was much "kinder" to the network.

Measuring and baselining application throughput and network latency is such an important topic that Chapter 9 is dedicated to the subject. We'll devote the remainder of the current chapter to analysis of specific application layer protocols.

8.2 TCP/IP Related Protocols

This section takes a closer look at a handful of popular TCP/IP application protocols, including Dynamic Host Control Protocol (DHCP), File Transfer Protocol (FTP), Telnet, Sun Network File System (NFS), and the Hypertext Transfer Protocol (HTTP).

8.2.1 Dynamic Host Control Protocol (DHCP)

Before an IP node can send and receive packets, it needs to have an IP address and subnet mask. An IP address can be statically defined at the node or obtained dynamically when the node is booting. If the node also needs to communicate to another node on a different IP subnet, it will also need the address of at least one IP router. Finally, if the node needs to map domain names to IP addresses, these addresses need to be statically defined at the host or the host needs the address of a domain name server (DNS). To understand why DHCP was developed (RFC 2131, Dynamic Host Configuration Protocol) you need to take a look at the protocols that preceded it.

In the early days of IP, diskless workstations would obtain their IP address by using the Reverse Address Resolution Protocol (RARP). One of the limitations of RARP (as well as ARP) is that the packets are sent only to a DLC layer broadcast address and are not forwarded by routers. Using only RARP to assign IP addresses would require an RARP server on every network segment. Further, only an IP address can be obtained via RARP. It would be nice to also obtain the IP subnet mask as well as the IP address for the default router, name server, and possibly other information.

To overcome the limitations of RARP, Bootstrap Protocol (BOOTP) was developed. BOOTP also allows a diskless workstation to load a memory image (using the Trivial File Transfer Protocol, TFTP) in order to boot up to an operating system. The RFC for BOOTP is 951 (Bootstrap Protocol) with additional information provided by RFC 1542 (DHCP Options and BOOTP Vendor Extensions).

The BOOTP packet format is shown in Figure 8.7 and is sent over UDP with a port of 67 for the DHCP server and 68 for the client. The first byte of the BOOTP packet simply indicates if the packet is a request (set to 1) or a reply (set to 2). The HTYPE specifies the type of DLC hardware and the length (HLEN) in bytes of the DLC address. For example, Ethernet will have an HTYPE of 1 and an HLEN of 6. Because BOOTP does allow routers to "relay" BOOTP requests, there is a HOP field that is incremented by the router as the packet is forwarded.

The Transaction ID is a random 32-bit integer set by the client in order to match requests with replies. The seconds field is set by the client to indicate the time since it started the bootstrap process. One use for this field is to have a secondary BOOTP server that won't respond unless a client sends out a BOOTP packet with its Seconds value exceeding a certain value, meaning that in all likelihood, the primary server hasn't responded.

If the client is trying to boot with a previously assigned IP address, the IP Address field may be filled; otherwise, it is set to all zeros (the "unknown" boot IP address of 0.0.0.0). In a BOOTP packet from a server, the assigned IP address (the Your IP Address field) will be filled in. The server IP address field can be filled in by the client if it wants to request a specific DHCP server; otherwise, it is set to all zeros. In the case where the request packet is relayed by a router, then the router will fill in its IP address in the Gateway (a.k.a. Router) IP Address field.

The client will place its DLC address in the client hardware address field. The Server Hostname is a null terminated string that can be filled in by the BOOTP server. If a memory image is required in the case of a diskless workstation, the boot filename field will be filled in by the BOOTP server for subsequent loading by the workstation via TFTP.

The client's assigned IP address is the only configuration parameter the client receives from a server. The rest of the configuration parameters are received

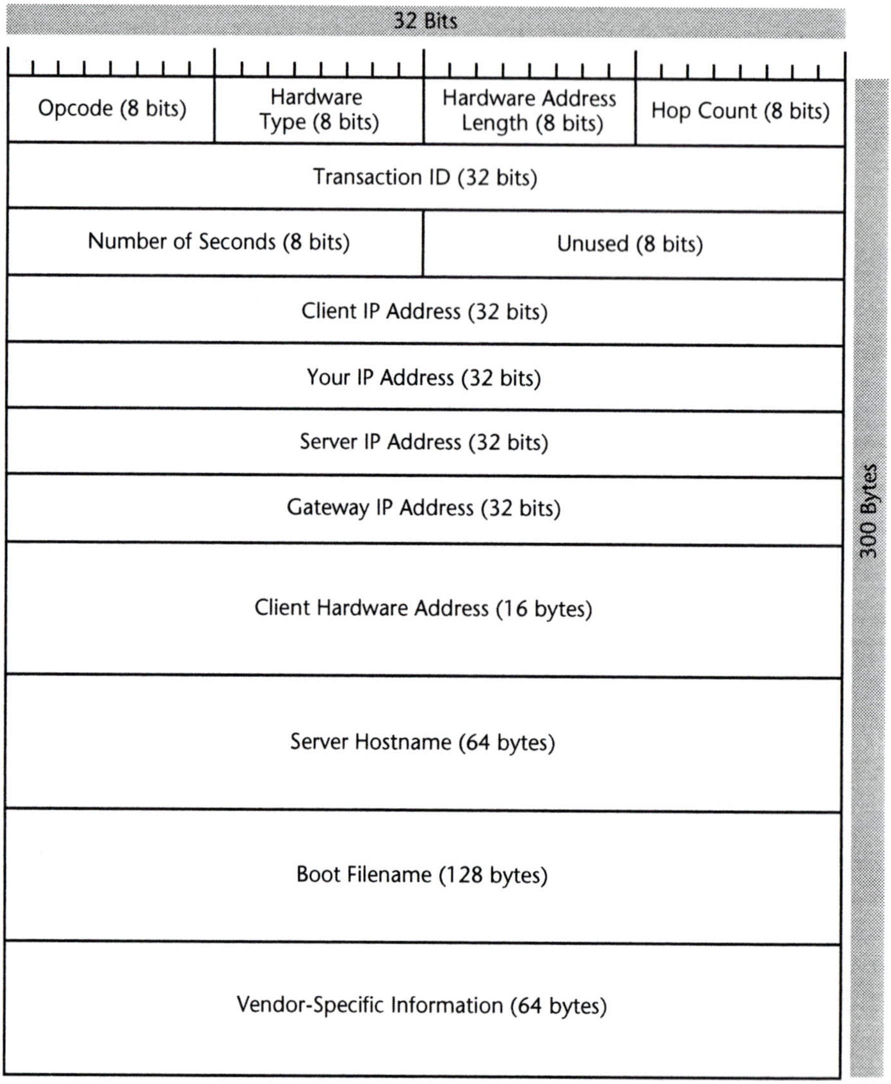

FIGURE 8.7 The BOOTP packet format.

in the vendor-specific area. This includes the subnet mask and the IP addresses of the name server(s) and router(s).

BOOTP seems to address the basic IP bootstrapping requirements, but it does have some serious limitations. For one, it assumes a fairly static environment where a given DLC address will always be assigned a given IP address. This makes it difficult to accommodate wireless nodes, portable laptops, and moving computers to a different location. Another limitation of BOOTP is that the vendor options area is fixed at only 64 bytes, limiting the number of available options. Enter DHCP.

DHCP is a client/server protocol that allocates IP addresses dynamically and has a much larger vendor option area (up to 312 bytes), allowing a client to obtain all the configuration information it needs in one packet.

To allow dynamic address assignment, an administrator of a DHCP server assigns a range of IP addresses that can be allocated. Some IP addresses may never be allocated (because some nodes may have permanent addresses such as a router) and some may be reserved for allocating to certain nodes (as identified by the DLC address in the BOOTP header) in a static fashion just like BOOTP.

Dynamic address assignment is temporary to avoid situations where you could run out of address allocation over an extended period of time. Addresses are "leased" to the client by the DHCP server. If the client has not renewed its lease by the end of the lease period, the address may be allocated to another client.

Typically a client attempts to renew its lease when it is booted, or at half the lease interval if the client is always up and running. For example, if the lease interval is three days, the renewal time is 1 and a half days, or 36 hours from the time the address was obtained. If clients are turned off for more than three days, such as over an extended holiday, some of those clients could obtain a different IP address next time they boot. If no new nodes have been added to that segment, however, chances are fairly good that all of the clients will get their old addresses back, since they will still ask the DHCP server for their previous IP address when booting.

The DHCP packet format is shown in Figure 8.8 and is virtually identical to BOOTP. The major differences are the flags field and the larger options area. The only bit defined in the flags field is the left-most bit. If this bit is set to 1, the DHCP server responds with a broadcast packet rather than a packet sent directly to the client. Why would the client request a broadcast response?

If an IP datagram returns to the client's DLC address, the IP stack may discard the packet because the client may not yet have a valid IP address. On the other hand, IP is required to accept any IP datagram sent to the IP broadcast address of 255.255.255.255. By setting the broadcast response request bit, the client is ensuring that the DHCP server will send a packet to the IP broadcast address, which also sets the DLC address to a broadcast address. (Windows NT DHCP servers actually return a broadcast no matter what the state of the broadcast response bit.) All IP clients on that subnet receive the broadcast and discard it, except for the station awaiting a reply from the DHCP server.

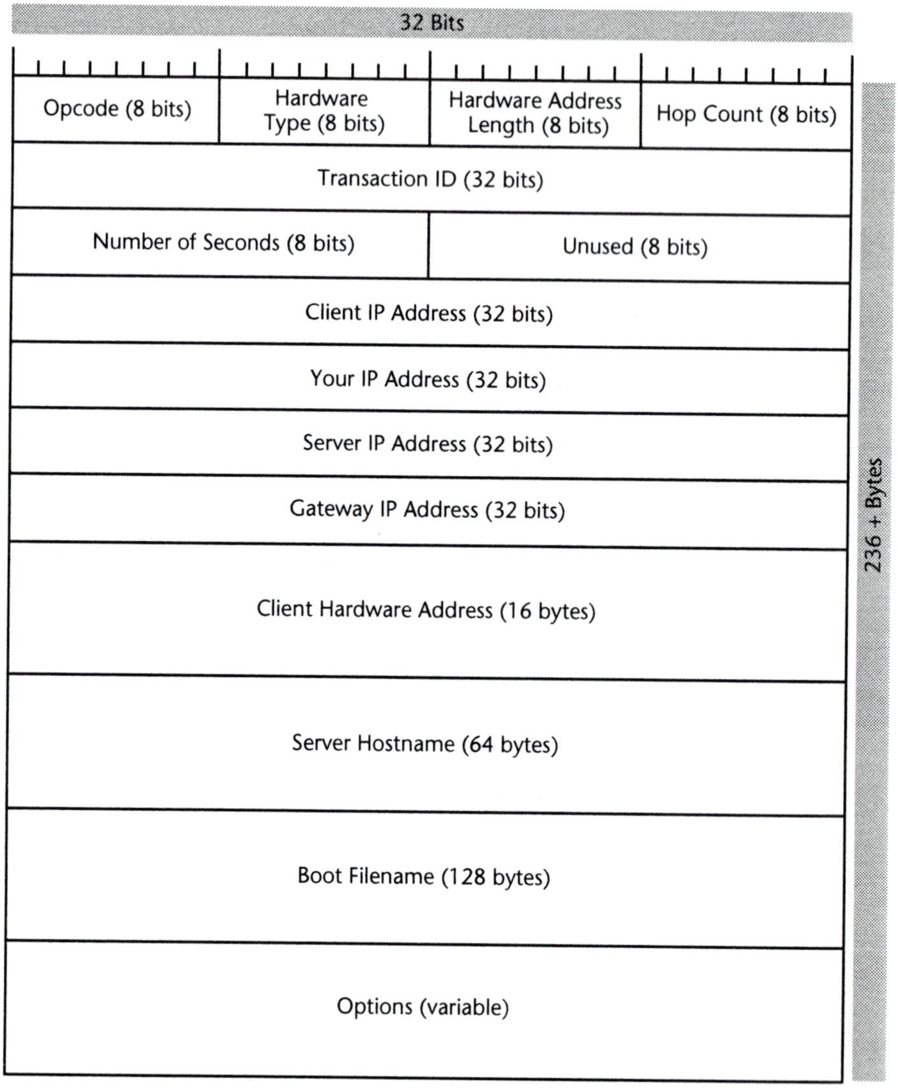

FIGURE 8.8 The DHCP packet format.

The packet exchanges for a client obtaining a new IP address are illustrated in Figure 8.9. The first packet is a "discover" DHCP broadcast packet from the client looking for a DHCP server. The next packet is a broadcast response or DHCP "offer" packet from the server as detailed in the figure. The third packet is a request from the client informing the DHCP server that it is accepting the offer. Note that in this packet, the client still has an IP address of 0.0.0.0. For this reason, the packet is still sent to the DLC broadcast address

```
Network Monitor - [Y:\capture\WORKSHOP\WIN95\dhcpnew2.CAP [Detail]]      _ □ ×
File  Edit  Display  Tools  Options  Window  Help                         _ □ ×
```

Frame	Time	Dst MAC Addr	Dst Other Addr	Src MAC Addr	Src Other Addr	Protocol	Description
1	0.000	*BROADCAST	255.255.255.25	FUJITS00ECB8	0.0.0.0	DHCP	Discover
2	0.053	*BROADCAST	255.255.255.25	00400543A5AD	172.10.10.69	DHCP	Offer
3	0.001	*BROADCAST	255.255.255.25	FUJITS00ECB8	0.0.0.0	DHCP	Request
4	0.046	*BROADCAST	255.255.255.25	00400543A5AD	172.10.10.69	DHCP	ACK

```
⊞IP: ID = 0x1D45; Proto = UDP; Len: 328
⊞UDP: IP Multicast:  Src Port: BOOTP Server, (67); Dst Port: BOOTP Client (68); Length = 308
⊟DHCP: Offer               (xid=E3E8DF93)
  DHCP: Op Code            (op)      = 2 (0x2)
  DHCP: Hardware Type      (htype)   = 1 (0x1) 10Mb Ethernet
  DHCP: Hardware Address Length (hlen) = 6 (0x6)
  DHCP: Hops               (hops)    = 0 (0x0)
  DHCP: Transaction ID     (xid)     = 3823689619 (0xE3E8DF93)
  DHCP: Seconds            (secs)    = 0 (0x0)
 ⊞DHCP: Flags              (flags)   = 0 (0x0)
  DHCP: Client IP Address  (ciaddr)  = 0.0.0.0
  DHCP: Your   IP Address  (yiaddr)  = 172.10.10.33
  DHCP: Server IP Address  (siaddr)  = 0.0.0.0
  DHCP: Relay  IP Address  (giaddr)  = 0.0.0.0
  DHCP: Client Ethernet Address (chaddr) = 00000E00ECB8
  DHCP: Server Host Name   (sname)   = <Blank>
  DHCP: Boot File Name     (file)    = <Blank>
  DHCP: Magic Cookie = [OK]
 ⊟DHCP: Option Field       (options)
  DHCP: DHCP Message Type     = DHCP Offer
  DHCP: Subnet Mask           = 255.255.255.0
  DHCP: Renewal Time Value (T1) = 1 Days, 12:00:00
  DHCP: Rebinding Time Value (T2) = 2 Days, 15:00:00
  DHCP: IP Address Lease Time = 3 Days,  0:00:00
  DHCP: Server Identifier     = 172.10.10.69
  DHCP: Router                = 172.10.10.254
  DHCP: End of this option field
```

```
000000F0  00 00 00 00 00 00 00 00 00 00 00 00 00 00 00 00  ................
00000100  00 00 00 00 00 00 00 00 00 00 00 00 00 00 00 00  ................
00000110  00 00 00 00 00 00 63 82 53 63 35 01 02 01 04 FF  ......céSc5....
00000120  FF FF 00 3A 04 00 01 FA 40 3B 04 00 03 75 F0 33  ...:...·@;...u=3
00000130  04 00 03 F4 80 36 04 AC 0A 0A 45 03 04 AC 0A 0A  ...(Ç6.¼..E.¼.
00000140  FE FF 00 00 00 00 00 00 00 00 00 00 00 00 00 00  þ.............
00000150  00 00 00 00 00 00                                ......
```

```
DHCP Message Option Field            F#: 2/4        Off: 282 (x11A)   L: 60 (x3C)
```

FIGURE 8.9 Obtaining a new IP address via DHCP.

and IP broadcast address because the source IP address is not yet valid. Finally, in the fourth packet, the server is acknowledging the workstation's acceptance of the IP address. The workstation can now use that IP address.

Requesting a specific address at boot time or renewing an address at half the lease time skips the first two steps. In the case of a boot, the source IP address in the IP header and the Client IP Address field in the DHCP header will be set to 0.0.0.0, the destination IP address is set to IP broadcast, and the client will request its old IP address in the DHCP options area.

If the client is renewing, its current IP address will be in the IP header as well as in the Client IP Address field of the DHCP header and the packet will be sent to the destination IP address of the DHCP server.

What happens if the client's DHCP server dies and can't renew a lease? The client will then go into a "rebind" state at 87.5 percent of the lease time. It will then broadcast a DHCP packet as if it were booting, looking for any DHCP server to renew its IP address. If it is not successful, the client is required to stop using the IP address.

Problems with DHCP occur when using a mixture of static and dynamically allocated IP addresses. For starters, you have to ensure that any static addresses used by routers, switches, servers, and so on are not inadvertently allocated by your DHCP server. This is usually accomplished by defining a range or "scope" of IP addresses that the DHCP server is allowed to allocate.

Another problem occurs when using a DHCP server to manage static IP addresses, as we'll see in the following case study.

8.2.2 Case Study: A User Is Unable to Obtain an IP Address

Ideally DHCP allows you to move nodes around to different subnets and to obtain a new IP address for that subnet when the device is rebooted or the user performs a "release and renew" operation. I encountered a situation where it wasn't that easy.

A particular workstation that had been working just fine on one subnet was moved to another subnet and rebooted, and then was unable to obtain an IP address despite being configured to use DHCP. Other workstations on the subnet in question could boot just fine using DHCP, so the problem appeared to be specific to this workstation.

I wanted to see if the DHCP packets were getting to the DHCP server, so I placed a protocol analyzer on the same subnet as the DHCP server. After the workstation booted and failed to get an IP address, I stopped the capture and applied a DHCP protocol filter to the display buffer to focus on what happened during the DHCP process. The DHCP packets of interest are shown in Figure 8.10.

What starts out as a normal exchange of DHCP packets to discover the DHCP server and obtain an IP address ends with a negative acknowledgment packet, as seen in packet 4 in the figure, DHCP NAK. All of the IP

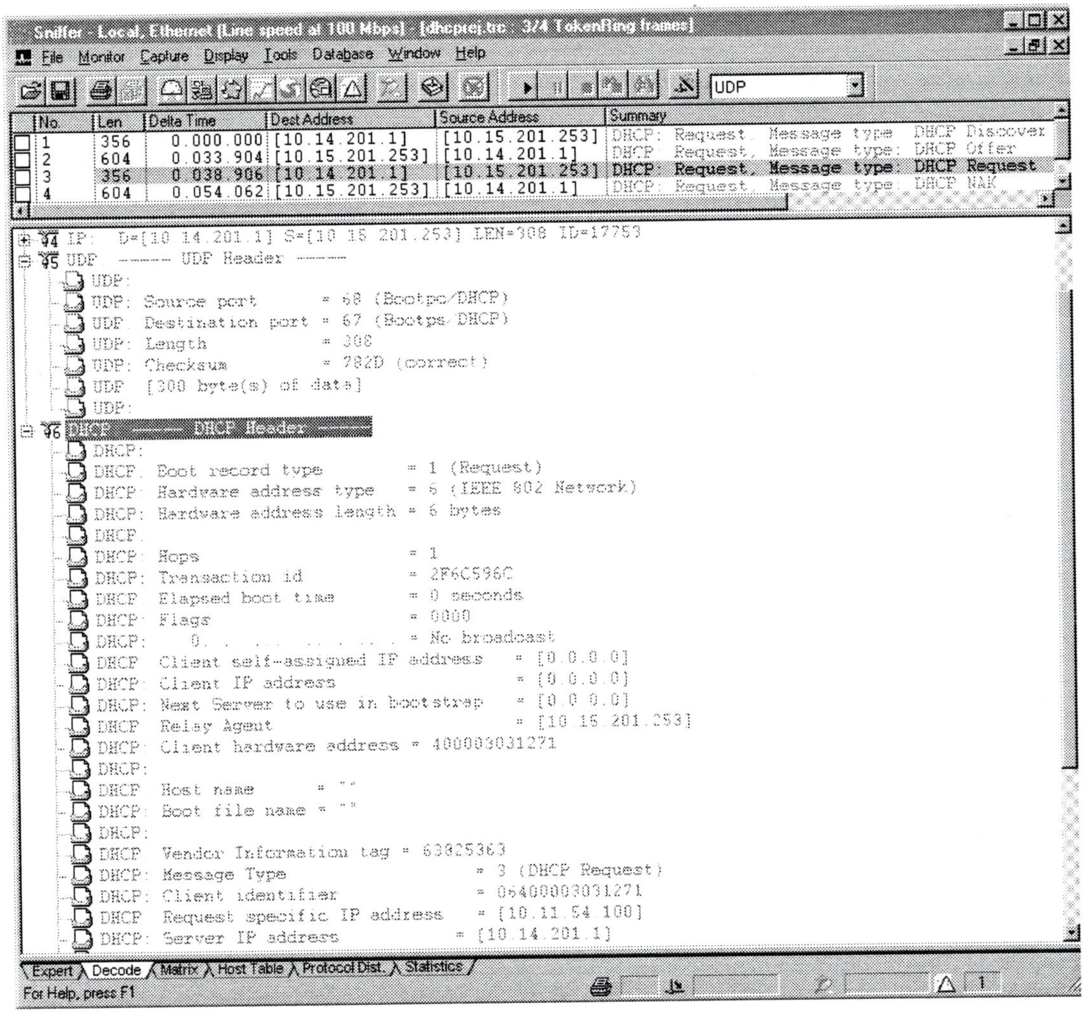

FIGURE 8.10 DHCP reject.

addresses shown are class A, with a subnet mask of 255.255.0.0. The detail of packet 3 gives several important clues:

1. The client did not start out with a previous IP address (the client self-assigned IP address is 0.0.0.0).

2. The client is requesting address 10.11.54.100, which means that the DHCP server must have offered that address in packet 2 (which it did).

3. The packet is going through a DHCP BOOTP relay agent in a router that was relayed from a port with the address 10.15.201.253 (you can see this in the address of the relay agent in the DHCP packet decode or from the source IP address at the IP layer).

4. The router is sending the packet to the DHCP server address of 10.14.201.1.

Putting it all together, you've learned that the originating BOOTP relay IP address is on subnet 15 and therefore the client is also on subnet 15, the DHCP server is on subnet 14, and the client obtained an IP address for subnet 11 from the DHCP server. When the client asks to use the address in packet 3, the response is a DHCP NAK since the DHCP server knows that the client is located on subnet 15, not 11.

Why did the DHCP server offer the "bad" IP address in the first place?

As an alternative to configuring a device with a particular static IP address, you can use the DHCP server to hard wire an IP address to a given DLC address. Recall that a station's DLC address is always passed through in a DHCP packet even if the packet is routed through a BOOTP relay router. The layer 2 DLC address of the packet will change to that of the BOOTP router, while the upper layer DHCP information still retains the originating station's DLC address.

In this case, the DHCP router was told to allocate the class A IP address of 10.11.54.100 to the workstation with the DLC address of 400003031271. When the workstation was moved from subnet 11 to subnet 15, no one bothered to reconfigure the DHCP router to give this node a new IP address, causing the DHCP process to fail. The solution was to simply reconfigure the DHCP address to allocate a valid IP address on subnet 15 for station 400003031271.

> Be careful when applying a station address filter when analyzing problems specific to a given workstation—sometimes a filter can be too selective. In the case of DHCP, if the DHCP packet was broadcast and the analyzer was on the workstation's segment or elsewhere in a layer 2 switched network, you would see the request packet but no response packet! Recall that if a DHCP server doesn't receive a packet via a BOOTP agent, it returns the packet via a broadcast, not to the workstation's unique DLC address. If you suspect a DHCP problem and want to capture only DHCP packets, you need to create a DHCP capture filter by using the offsets for UDP source and destination ports 67 and 68. With an Ethertype frame type, for example, the filter (in hex) would be ((0044 at offset 22) and (0043 at offset 24)) or ((0043 at offset 22) and 0044 at offset 24)). The first pattern match is for client to server DHCP packets, whereas the second is for DHCP replies.

8.2.3 File Transfer Protocol (FTP)

FTP (RFC 959, File Transfer Protocol) is the workhorse for bulk file transfer over the Internet. Unlike the random file access protocols such as Sun's Network File System (NFS) or NT's Server Message Block (SMB), FTP is used when a user or application needs access to the entire file on their local system. FTP is a true client/server protocol in that the user interacts with an FTP server via FTP client software. Rather than transferring bits and pieces of a file, an entire file is transferred in either direction. There are also commands for the user to change to a different directory, list a directory's contents, make a directory, delete files, rename files, and so on.

An FTP server authenticates the user via a simple user name and plain text password (FTP passwords can be easily captured by a protocol analyzer). Some FTP servers also allow anonymous logins without passwords. There is an RFC for security enhancements to FTP (RFC 2228, FTP Security Extensions) that is not widely deployed.

Because FTP relies on TCP when transferring data, error recovery and flow control is built in. Another, much simpler file transfer protocol known as the Trivial File Transfer Protocol (TFTP) runs over UDP and uses fixed packet sizes (512-byte data blocks). TFTP does not make a good file transfer protocol over a large, unreliable network like the Internet, but it is still used in some LAN situations, especially in support of diskless devices.

The FTP protocol can handle text files with ASCII or EBCDIC characters (if the client and server support it) and image or binary files. Data can be transferred in a stream mode (a series of bytes) or block mode. Compression is a rarely used option because FTP does not provide a very efficient algorithm in terms of space reduction.

Any problems at the FTP layer are typically the inability to log in to a server due to a bad user name and/or password, not being allowed to list the contents of a directory, not being allowed to write to a directory, rejecting the connection attempt because the host does not support FTP, and so on.

FTP commands are easy to interpret in a protocol analyzer because they are just as the user enters them (either via a command-based FTP application or a GUI-based FTP program emulating user commands as buttons are pressed), as seen in Figure 8.11. Once a file transfer is underway, it's pure TCP until completion. Therefore, understanding how to analyze TCP flow control and error recovery (see Chapter 5) is extremely valuable when analyzing FTP file transfers.

Another tidbit to keep in mind when analyzing FTP is that two TCP connections are actually created: one for the user commands and a second for the file transfer or in response to a command like LIST a directory. The destination (server) TCP port for commands is 21, and the destination (server) port for data transfer is port 20.

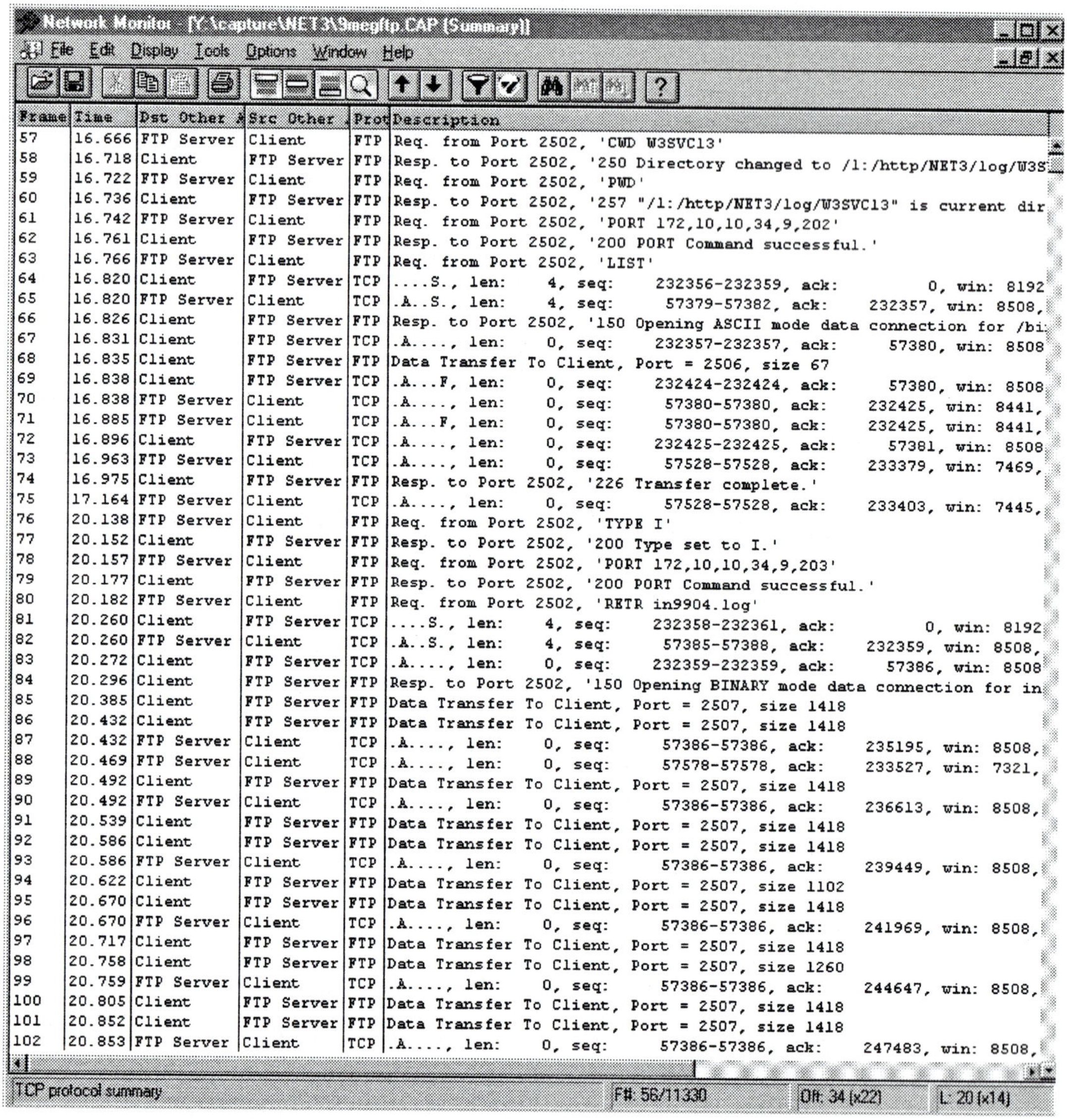

Frame	Time	Dst Other	Src Other	Prot	Description
57	16.666	FTP Server	Client	FTP	Req. from Port 2502, 'CWD W3SVC13'
58	16.718	Client	FTP Server	FTP	Resp. to Port 2502, '250 Directory changed to /1:/http/NET3/log/W3S
59	16.722	FTP Server	Client	FTP	Req. from Port 2502, 'PWD'
60	16.736	Client	FTP Server	FTP	Resp. to Port 2502, '257 "/1:/http/NET3/log/W3SVC13" is current dir
61	16.742	FTP Server	Client	FTP	Req. from Port 2502, 'PORT 172,10,10,34,9,202'
62	16.761	Client	FTP Server	FTP	Resp. to Port 2502, '200 PORT Command successful.'
63	16.766	FTP Server	Client	FTP	Req. from Port 2502, 'LIST'
64	16.820	Client	FTP Server	TCP	....S., len: 4, seq: 232356-232359, ack: 0, win: 8192
65	16.820	FTP Server	Client	TCP	.A..S., len: 4, seq: 57379-57382, ack: 232357, win: 8508,
66	16.826	Client	FTP Server	FTP	Resp. to Port 2502, '150 Opening ASCII mode data connection for /bi
67	16.831	Client	FTP Server	TCP	.A...., len: 0, seq: 232357-232357, ack: 57380, win: 8508
68	16.835	Client	FTP Server	FTP	Data Transfer To Client, Port = 2506, size 67
69	16.838	Client	FTP Server	TCP	.A...F, len: 0, seq: 232424-232424, ack: 57380, win: 8508
70	16.838	FTP Server	Client	TCP	.A...., len: 0, seq: 57380-57380, ack: 232425, win: 8441,
71	16.885	FTP Server	Client	TCP	.A...F, len: 0, seq: 57380-57380, ack: 232425, win: 8441,
72	16.896	Client	FTP Server	TCP	.A...., len: 0, seq: 232425-232425, ack: 57381, win: 8508
73	16.963	FTP Server	Client	TCP	.A...., len: 0, seq: 57528-57528, ack: 233379, win: 7469,
74	16.975	Client	FTP Server	FTP	Resp. to Port 2502, '226 Transfer complete.'
75	17.164	FTP Server	Client	TCP	.A...., len: 0, seq: 57528-57528, ack: 233403, win: 7445,
76	20.138	FTP Server	Client	FTP	Req. from Port 2502, 'TYPE I'
77	20.152	Client	FTP Server	FTP	Resp. to Port 2502, '200 Type set to I.'
78	20.157	FTP Server	Client	FTP	Req. from Port 2502, 'PORT 172,10,10,34,9,203'
79	20.177	Client	FTP Server	FTP	Resp. to Port 2502, '200 PORT Command successful.'
80	20.182	FTP Server	Client	FTP	Req. from Port 2502, 'RETR in9904.log'
81	20.260	Client	FTP Server	TCP	....S., len: 4, seq: 232358-232361, ack: 0, win: 8192
82	20.260	FTP Server	Client	TCP	.A..S., len: 4, seq: 57385-57388, ack: 232359, win: 8508,
83	20.272	Client	FTP Server	TCP	.A...., len: 0, seq: 232359-232359, ack: 57386, win: 8508
84	20.296	Client	FTP Server	FTP	Resp. to Port 2502, '150 Opening BINARY mode data connection for in
85	20.385	Client	FTP Server	FTP	Data Transfer To Client, Port = 2507, size 1418
86	20.432	Client	FTP Server	FTP	Data Transfer To Client, Port = 2507, size 1418
87	20.432	FTP Server	Client	TCP	.A...., len: 0, seq: 57386-57386, ack: 235195, win: 8508,
88	20.469	FTP Server	Client	TCP	.A...., len: 0, seq: 57578-57578, ack: 233527, win: 7321,
89	20.492	Client	FTP Server	FTP	Data Transfer To Client, Port = 2507, size 1418
90	20.492	FTP Server	Client	TCP	.A...., len: 0, seq: 57386-57386, ack: 236613, win: 8508,
91	20.539	Client	FTP Server	FTP	Data Transfer To Client, Port = 2507, size 1418
92	20.586	Client	FTP Server	FTP	Data Transfer To Client, Port = 2507, size 1418
93	20.586	FTP Server	Client	TCP	.A...., len: 0, seq: 57386-57386, ack: 239449, win: 8508,
94	20.622	Client	FTP Server	FTP	Data Transfer To Client, Port = 2507, size 1102
95	20.670	Client	FTP Server	FTP	Data Transfer To Client, Port = 2507, size 1418
96	20.670	FTP Server	Client	TCP	.A...., len: 0, seq: 57386-57386, ack: 241969, win: 8508,
97	20.717	Client	FTP Server	FTP	Data Transfer To Client, Port = 2507, size 1418
98	20.758	Client	FTP Server	FTP	Data Transfer To Client, Port = 2507, size 1260
99	20.759	FTP Server	Client	TCP	.A...., len: 0, seq: 57386-57386, ack: 244647, win: 8508,
100	20.805	Client	FTP Server	FTP	Data Transfer To Client, Port = 2507, size 1418
101	20.852	Client	FTP Server	FTP	Data Transfer To Client, Port = 2507, size 1418
102	20.853	FTP Server	Client	TCP	.A...., len: 0, seq: 57386-57386, ack: 247483, win: 8508,

FIGURE 8.11 FTP commands and data transfer.

The server initiates the TCP connection for data transfer. For example, in Figure 8.11, the server is setting up a TCP connection in packets 81–83 in response to a file retrieve command from the user. The actual file transfer is in packets 85 and forward.

The TCP port 21 command connection stays open as long as the user is logged into the FTP server and the server doesn't "time-out" the connection due to inactivity. Connections for port 20 file transfers are only active during the transfer. The server terminates the TCP data connection when the transfer is complete.

8.2.4 Telnet

Telecommunications Network Protocol, or simply Telnet (RFC 854, Telnet Protocol Specification), provides general-purpose, character-based communications between a user and host. Characters are sent using an 8-bit byte, with the eighth bit always set to 0.

Telnet is built on the principle of a Network Virtual Terminal, or NVT, which provides a virtual device from which both ends of the connection map their real terminal. For example, a client running Telnet with VT100 emulation will map VT100 to NVT and the server in turn maps NVT to whatever terminal type it supports. Characters that are typed by the user are sent to the server for output to a "printer" (which could be an application). By default, each character typed by the user is echoed back from the server. Earlier this chapter mentioned how typing one character generates an Ethernet packet with some 830 percent overhead to carry that one character to the host.

Characters do not have to be sent one per packet, however. A fast keyboardist working with a Telnet application that waits a few milliseconds before sending a keystroke may get in a few characters per packet. More important, a host application can respond with a full screen of data, such as choice of items making up a menu.

Like FTP, a client also establishes a TCP connection (using the destination Telnet port of 23) with a host before sending Telnet commands. If the host does not have Telnet capability, the TCP connection is rejected.

Once a TCP connection is established, the host negotiates options with the client. The client responds to each option with either a WILL enable the option or WONT enable the option. One such option that Telnet will ask for is the terminal type. Other options will affect the mode of operation: half-duplex, character-at-a-time, line-at-a-time, or linemode. In half-duplex mode, the characters are echoed locally by the client rather than remotely by the server. Character-at-a-time is the default mode in which the server will echo the characters typed by the user. In line-at-a-time or linemode, basically all the character processing including backspacing is done by the client, with the desired characters sent to the server only when the enter key is pressed.

Figure 8.12 shows a series of packets sending user keystrokes to a host. Because the host is echoing each character, the packet returned from the host also contains the TCP acknowledgment. For example, packet 21 is sending the character S over to the host. Packet 22 is the letter S being echoed back to the user. Packet 22 also has the TCP acknowledgment for the TCP sequence

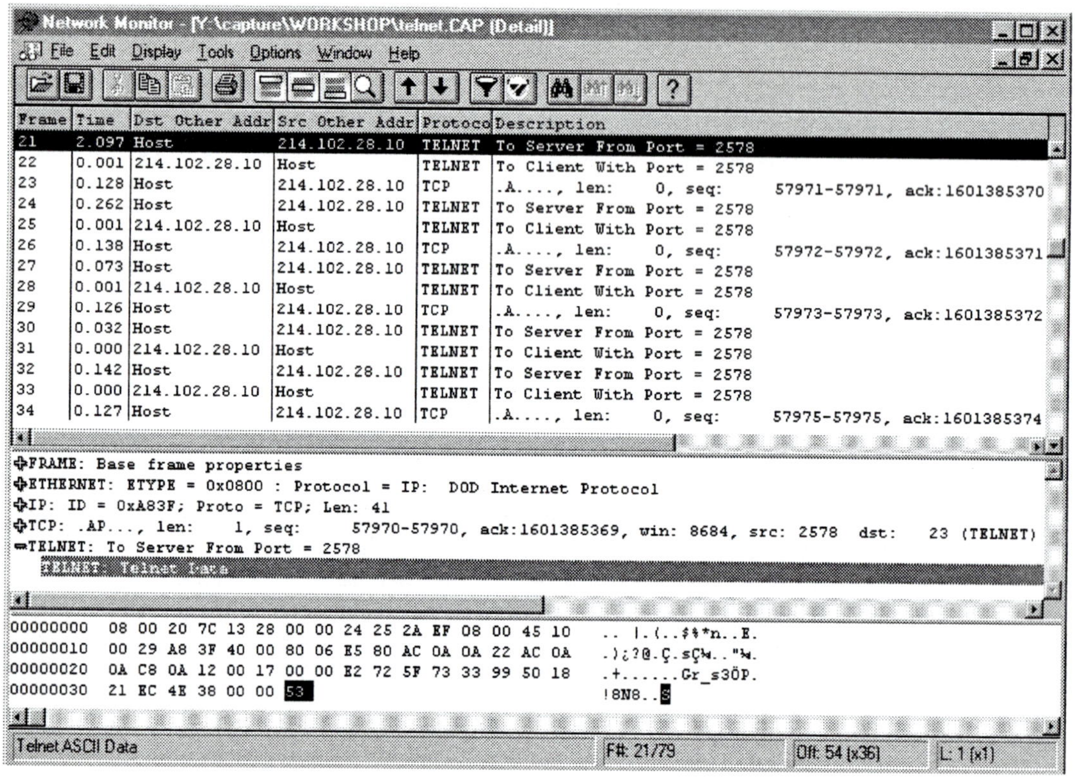

FIGURE 8.12 Sending Telnet keystrokes to a host.

number in packet 21. This piggybacking of TCP acknowledgments along with new application data is an efficient usage of TCP.

Notice, however, packet 23. This packet is an acknowledgment only packet from the user to the host, acknowledging the receipt of the echo character in packet 22. This seems like a waste, but the user is a bit slow in typing in their user name, so TCP times out and sends an ack anyhow. Packets 30 through 33 are actually two rapidly typed keystrokes in succession. Thus packet 32 contains a new keystroke *and* the acknowledgment for the echo character in packet 31.

Echoing Telnet characters can result in a noticeable delay by the end-user such as over a high latency frame relay network or even worse, over a satellite link. An impatient user may type the same character more than once, resulting in the host's receiving duplicate characters. Unlike duplicate TCP segments that are discarded by a host, multiple Telnet segments are received and processed by a host because each character is sent in its own TCP packet with a unique TCP sequence number. Thus, every typed character will be echoed back to the user. If the user doesn't backspace and correct a command before pressing the enter key, that command or data will be erroneously processed by the host.

One of the more popular uses for Telnet is to simply "Telnet into" a remote switch or router for administrative purposes. With the advent of desktop operating systems and client/server architectures, the importance of Telnet as an end-user application has declined.

8.2.5 Sun Network File System (NFS)

The Sun Microsystems NFS protocol (RFC 1094, NFS: Network File System Protocol Specification, and RFC 1813, NFS Version 3 Protocol Specification) provides clients with access to shared files regardless of operating system and transport protocol. NFS uses a number of Sun Remote Procedure Call (RPC) primitives described in RFC 1057 (Remote Procedure Call Protocol Specification). An example of NFS using RPC is shown in Figure 8.13. The RPC primitives operate on top of an eXternal Data Representation (XDR), a common way of representing a set of data types over a network. XDR is documented in RFC 1014 (XDR: External Data Representation Standard).

NFS is transport layer independent. In the IP world, the most popular implementation of NFS is over UDP although TCP is supported as well. Remember that NFS uses RPC. Sun has defined a version of RPC specifically for UDP as well as a version that's transport layer independent.

Because UDP doesn't segment data as does TCP, requests for reading or writing NFS data greater than the underlying IP MTU will result in IP datagram fragments sent by the client or server. In Figure 8.13, the client is writing NFS data in blocks of 8192, resulting in IP fragments. Chapter 4 discussed IP fragmentation in detail.

NFS over TCP provides greater reliability than NFS over UDP. This time, TCP is responsible for segmenting the NFS block. TCP assigns the appropriate sequence numbers and performs error control and flow control via acknowledgments and windowing, as discussed in Chapter 4. Figure 8.14 shows an example of NFS file transfer over TCP.

When using TCP, it's safer and more efficient to assign a larger read or write block size, say, 32,768 instead of 8192 bytes because one dropped TCP segment does not necessarily mean that you need to send all 32,768 bytes over again as was needed with UDP. Instead, the number of bytes that need to be retransmitted depends on how many outstanding TCP segments there are after the last valid TCP acknowledgment.

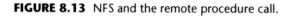

```
Network Monitor - [Y:\capture\NET3\NFS to Versa.CAP (Detail)]
File  Edit  Display  Tools  Options  Window  Help

Frame Time    Dst Other Addr  Src Other Addr  Description
73    0.001   NFS Server      NFS Client      "Write To File" Call
74    0.000   NFS Server      NFS Client      ID = 0xF09; Proto = UDP; Len: 1500, Frag. Offset = 1480 (0x5C8)
75    0.000   NFS Server      NFS Client      ID = 0xF09; Proto = UDP; Len: 1500, Frag. Offset = 2960 (0xB90)
76    0.000   NFS Server      NFS Client      ID = 0xF09; Proto = UDP; Len: 1500, Frag. Offset = 4440 (0x1158)
77    0.000   NFS Server      NFS Client      ID = 0xF09; Proto = UDP; Len: 1500, Frag. Offset = 5920 (0x1720)
78    0.000   NFS Server      NFS Client      ID = 0xF09; Proto = UDP; Len: 940, Frag. Offset = 7400 (0x1CE8)
79    0.001   NFS Client      NFS Server      "Write To File" Reply, Status: Success
80    0.001   NFS Server      NFS Client      "Write To File" Call
81    0.000   NFS Server      NFS Client      ID = 0x1009; Proto = UDP; Len: 1500, Frag. Offset = 1480 (0x5C8)
82    0.000   NFS Server      NFS Client      ID = 0x1009; Proto = UDP; Len: 1500, Frag. Offset = 2960 (0xB90)

ETHERNET: ETYPE = 0x0800 : Protocol = IP:  DOD Internet Protocol
IP: ID = 0xF09; Proto = UDP; Len: 1500
UDP: Src Port: Unknown, (1014); Dst Port: NFS (2049); Length = 8320 (0x2080)
RPC: Call: Network File System(NFS), Procedure 8 (0x8)
  RPC: Transaction ID = 125830266 (0x780047A)
  RPC: Message type = Service call
  RPC: RPC Version number = 2 (0x2)
  RPC: Program Number = Network File System(NFS)
  RPC: Program Version = 2 (0x2)
  RPC: Procedure Number = 8 (0x8)
  RPC: Authentication Credentials
   RPC: Authentication Type = Unix Authentication
   RPC: Authorization Data Length = 32 (0x20)
   RPC: Stamp ID = 924111402 (0x3714D22A)
   RPC: Machine Name = SCOTT
   RPC: UID = 1001 (0x3E9)
   RPC: GID = 333 (0x14D)
   RPC: Additional GID(s)
     RPC: Additional GID = 333 (0x14D)
  RPC: Authentication Verification
   RPC: Authentication Type = No Identity Authentication
   RPC: Authorization Data Length = 0 (0x0)
  RPC: Data: Number of data bytes remaining = 1400 (0x0578)
NFS: "Write To File" Call
  NFS: Procedure = Write To File
  NFS: File Handle = 030000002A00000000000000030000003000000000000006666617374756E30
  NFS: Beginning Offset = 57344 (0xE000)
  NFS: Offset = 57344 (0xE000)
  NFS: Byte Count = 8192 (0x2000)
  NFS: Total Byte Count = 8192 (0x2000)
  NFS: File Data: Number of data bytes remaining = 1280 (0x0500)

00000000  00 00 0E 00 EC B8 00 00 24 25 2A EF 08 00 45 00   ....8+..$%*n..E.
00000010  05 DC 0F 09 20 00 80 11 99 B0 AC 0A 0A 22 AC 0A   ._x. .Ç.Ö|4..."4.
00000020  0A 21 03 F6 08 01 20 80 68 12 07 80 04 7A 00 00   .!.÷.. Ch..ç.z.
00000030  00 00 00 00 00 02 00 01 86 A3 00 00 00 02 00 00   ......äu....
00000040  00 08 00 00 00 01 00 00 00 20 37 14 D2 2A 00 00   ........ 7¶I-*.
00000050  00 05 53 43 4F 54 54 00 00 00 00 00 03 E9 00 00   ..SCOTT......T.

Remote Procedure Call                           F#: 73/737     Off: 42 (x2A)   L: 72 (x48)
```

FIGURE 8.13 NFS and the remote procedure call.

8.2.6 Hypertext Transfer Protocol (HTTP)

The Hypertext Transfer Protocol (RFC 2068, Hypertext Transfer Protocol — HTTP/1.1) is a client-initiated request/reply protocol for accessing Web content. The most popular application that uses HTTP is a Web browser such as

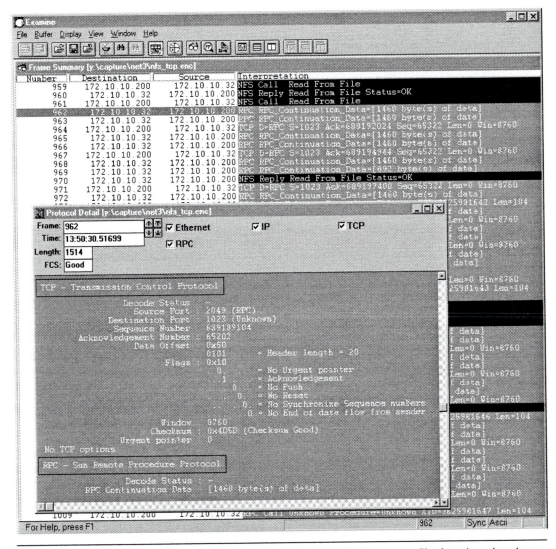

FIGURE 8.14 NFS using TCP. All the TCP data bytes in Frame 962 are pure file data; i.e., there's no RPC header.

Internet Explorer or Netscape Communicator, to download "multimedia" content from Internet and intranet Web servers. Multimedia content is specified using Hypertext Markup Language (RFC 1866, Hypertext Markup Language—2.0), or HTML, a simple language used to create hypertext documents independent of a computing platform. HTML can be used to directly represent simple text and graphics on a display as well as provide the loading of more complex images and applications or Java applets. HTML also provides "hyperlinks" to navigate to other Web pages.

```
Network Monitor - [Y:\capture\NET3\net3browse.CAP [Detail]]                    _ □ ×
File   Edit   Display   Tools   Options   Window   Help                          _ 8 ×

Frame Time   Dst Other Addr   Src Other Addr   Protocol Description
1     0.000                                    ARP_RARP ARP: Request, Target IP: 172.10.10.254
2     0.004                                    ARP_RARP ARP: Reply, Target IP: 172.10.10.34 Target Hdwr Addr: 00
3     0.000 204.248.18.2     Browser User     DNS      0x1:Std Qry for www.net3group.com. of type Host Addr on
4     0.017 Browser User     204.248.18.2     DNS      0x1:Std Qry Resp. for www.net3group.com. of type Host Ad
5     0.009 216.106.128.12   Browser User     TCP      ....S., len:     4, seq:      65464-65467, ack:       0,
6     0.013 Browser User     216.106.128.12   TCP      .A..S., len:     4, seq:     643288-643291, ack:   65465
7     0.001 216.106.128.12   Browser User     TCP      .A...., len:     0, seq:      65465-65465, ack:  643289,
8     0.001 216.106.128.12   Browser User     HTTP     GET Request (from client using port 1133)
9     0.042 Browser User     216.106.128.12   HTTP     Response (to client using port 1133)
10    0.049 Browser User     216.106.128.12   HTTP     Response (to client using port 1133)
11    0.000 216.106.128.12   Browser User     TCP      .A...., len:     0, seq:      65692-65692, ack:  644934,
12    0.006 Browser User     216.106.128.12   HTTP     Response (to client using port 1133)
13    0.030 Browser User     216.106.128.12   TCP      ....S., len:     4, seq:      65466-65469, ack:       0,
14    0.024 Browser User     216.106.128.12   HTTP     Response (to client using port 1133)
15    0.000 216.106.128.12   Browser User     TCP      .A...., len:     0, seq:      65692-65692, ack:  646502,
16    0.048 Browser User     216.106.128.12   HTTP     Response (to client using port 1133)
17    0.002 Browser User     216.106.128.12   TCP      .A..S., len:     4, seq:     643302-643305, ack:   65467
18    0.000 216.106.128.12   Browser User     TCP      .A...., len:     0, seq:      65467-65467, ack:  643303,
19    0.004 216.106.128.12   Browser User     HTTP     GET Request (from client using port 1134)
20    0.042 Browser User     216.106.128.12   HTTP     Response (to client using port 1133)

⊕FRAME: Base frame properties
⊕ETHERNET: ETYPE = 0x0800 : Protocol = IP:  DOD Internet Protocol
⊕IP: ID = 0x8518; Proto = TCP; Len: 267
⊕TCP: .AP..., len:   227, seq:     65465-65691, ack:     643289, win: 8508, src: 1133 dst:    80
⊟HTTP: GET Request (from client using port 1133)
   HTTP: Request Method = GET
   HTTP: Uniform Resource Identifier = /
   HTTP: Protocol Version = HTTP/1.1
   HTTP: Accept = */*
   HTTP: Accept-Language = en-us
   HTTP: Accept-Encoding = gzip, deflate
   HTTP: User-Agent = Mozilla/4.0 (compatible; MSIE 5.0; Windows NT; DigExt; CNETHomeBu
   HTTP: Host = www.net3group.com
   HTTP: Connection = Keep-Alive

00000030  21 3C 53 5D 00 00 47 45 54 20 2F 20 48 54 54 50   !<S]..GET / HTTP
00000040  2F 31 2E 31 0D 0A 41 63 63 65 70 74 3A 20 2A 2F   /1.1..Accept: */
00000050  2A 0D 0A 41 63 63 65 70 74 2D 4C 61 6E 67 75 61   *..Accept-Langua
00000060  67 65 3A 20 65 6E 2D 75 73 0D 0A 41 63 63 65 70   ge: en-us..Accep
00000070  74 2D 45 6E 63 6F 64 69 6E 67 3A 20 67 7A 69 70   t-Encoding: gzip
00000080  2C 20 64 65 66 6C 61 74 65 0D 0A 55 73 65 72 2D   , deflate..User-
00000090  41 67 65 6E 74 3A 20 4D 6F 7A 69 6C 6C 61 2F 34   Agent: Mozilla/4
000000A0  2E 30 20 28 63 6F 6D 70 61 74 69 62 6C 65 3B 20   .0 (compatible;
000000B0  4D 53 49 45 20 35 2E 30 3B 20 57 69 6E 64 6F 77   MSIE 5.0; Window
000000C0  73 20 4E 54 3B 20 44 69 67 45 78 74 3B 20 43 4E   s NT; DigExt; CN

HTTP Protocol Packet Summary              F# 8/57           Oft: 54 (x36)      L: 227 (xE3)
```

FIGURE 8.15   Connecting to a Web server and beginning HTTP.

To understand how HTTP and HTML work together, let's examine what happens when a user opens a browser and specifies an HTTP Uniform Resource Locator (URL) for a Web site. Figure 8.15 shows a series of packet transactions required to locate and load the Net3 Group home page.

The user can access a Web site via its IP address (e.g., http://216.106.128.12/) or by name (e.g., http://www.net3group.com/). Usually the name is given, in which case the browser must find the IP address for www.net3group.com in its ARP cache or perform a DNS query. In the figure, the ARP cache entry for the user's default router has expired, as indicated by the ARP for the router in packet 1. After obtaining the router's DLC address in packet 2, the browser then sends a DNS query for www.net3group.com in packet 3. Packet 4 is the response from the DNS server containing the IP address for www.net3group.com.

Now that the IP address for the Web server is obtained, a TCP connection is attempted with the server's HTTP port (TCP port 80). This is successful as shown in packets 5 through 7. The first HTTP packet (number 8) is then sent from the browser over that TCP connection.

The first HTTP packet contains three key items:

1. The request method (Get or Post)
2. The URL that specifies the requested file
3. The HTTP protocol version

The detail of the highlighted packet in Figure 8.15 shows the details of this packet, an HTTP Get request. The initial URL is a /, meaning the root file (usually called the home page) of that server. If the user doesn't put the / at the end of the URL, as in www.net3group.com, the server adds it automatically. The server also assumes http:// at the beginning of the URL if the user does not specify it. The user could also be more specific in the URL, such as http://www.net3group.com/download.asp in order to go to a specific "page" on the server.

There's some additional information in the first HTTP packet such as the browser version, which happens to be Internet Explorer 5.0 in this case. This allows the Web server to customize responses for that particular browser and, of course, to maintain statistics about which browsers are in use.

One of the interesting things about HTTP packets is that nothing is encoded: all the commands are in plain English. This makes it easy to read HTTP data by looking at the raw packet data, but it also adds a fair amount of overhead to every packet.

The server then responds with the requested data in a TCP stream. The first response packet contains a Response Status (a line of text with the server's HTTP version number and a status code describing the result), the Response Header (date, server-type, MIME-version, and content-type), and the Response Data (the content of the requested file).

When an HTTP text file is being transferred, a browser will crawl through text and establish additional TCP connections for each linked file (such as images) and proceed to download those files. Thus every GIF, JPEG, audio, Java applet, and so on requires a separate HTTP TCP connection to download. The browser maintains several simultaneous TCP connections and usually flashes the status of each download as it happens, such as "58% of logo.gif."

Figure 8.16 shows a detail of packet 19, an HTTP "get" request for an image file using a new TCP connection that was set up in packets 13 (the SYN packet), 17 (the server ACK packet), and 18 (the client ACK packet). This file is now transferred using the client-assigned TCP port number of 1134. The initial HTTP data was transferred using client-assigned port number 1133. As you look beyond packet 19, you can see packets for the two simultaneous TCP conversations being interleaved.

When a file transfer is complete, the server drops the TCP connection, freeing up that TCP connection for a new user. As you can see, it's wise for a Web designer to keep the number of files on any given Web page (especially the home page) at a minimum and keep the size small. This minimizes the chance of running out of TCP ports and making users wait when attempting to connect to the server.

❗

When analyzing HTTP server traffic, you may encounter several simultaneous TCP connections from several clients. To focus on a particular client, you will not only need to filter on that client's IP address but also on a specific TCP port number. This allows you to analyze a TCP connection much more effectively, without having to worry about sequence numbers and other data from other simultaneous HTTP file transfers to that client.

8.3 NetWare Core Protocol (NCP)

Previous chapters have looked at examples of how different layers of protocol come into play when logging in to a NetWare server, such as how a node finds the IPX address of a server. Recall that NCP does not have a separate session layer per se, except to locate a resource (such as a server) using the NetWare Services Advertising Protocol (SAP). After that, the actual session is established by sending a RIP packet to find the next "hop" to the resource, followed by an exchange of NCP packets with that resource. The NCP packet exchanges include a discovery of the end-to-end IPX maximum transmission unit (MTU).

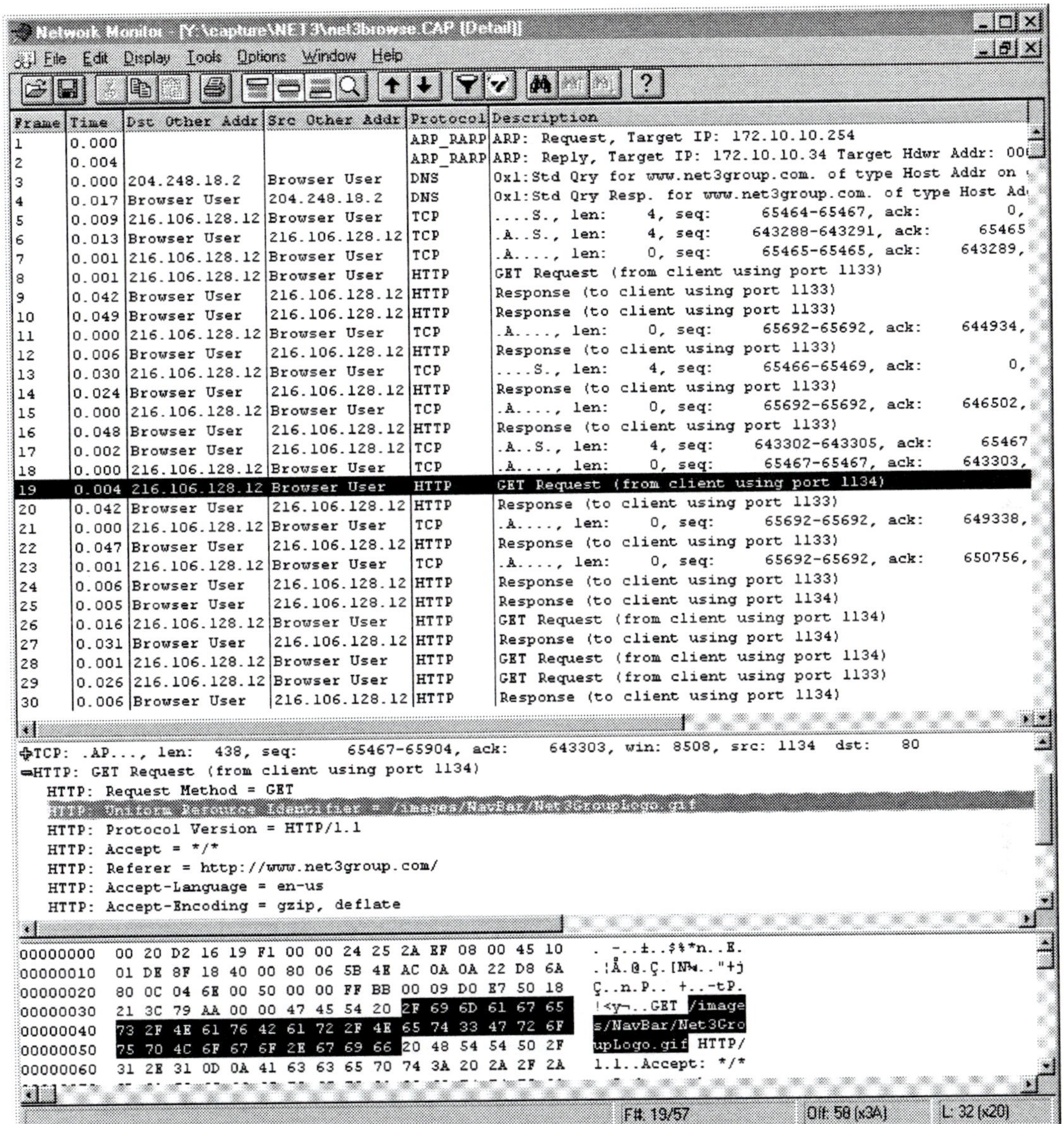

FIGURE 8.16 Downloading an image file using a new TCP connection.

The basic NetWare IPX boot sequence from a client's perspective is as follows:

1. Broadcast a SAP packet to find the "nearest" file server or NDS capable server. One or more SAP responses are received.

2. Pick the first SAP response and broadcast an IPX RIP packet to find a router to the server. One or more routers respond.

3. Pick the first RIP response and send an NCP connect packet request to the server via the router that responded.

4. Get information about the server.

5. Negotiate the Large Internet Packet (LIP) size from the server.

6. If LIP was successful, negotiate Packet Burst; if not, use 576 bytes as the IPX MTU.

7. Connect to server(s) you really want to talk to via bindery look-up in the server you connected to or via a series of NetWare Directory Services (NDS) commands.

8. Send NCP commands to the server(s) to access server resources.

The NetWare Core Protocol is primarily a layer 7 protocol that provides file, print, messenger, and queuing services. Legacy NCP runs directly over IPX, whereas NetWare 5.x and higher can now use TCP/IP. Because NCP over IPX has no session or transport layer, NCP must take care of some of these functions. NCP has its own session connection protocol and adds sequence numbers for packet recovery.

NCP also lacks explicit acknowledgments. For every NCP command there is one reply—by virtue of a reply, the command is acknowledged. If no reply is received, the command is repeated. Some protocol analyzer expert systems will flag this as a "transport retransmission" because NCP is doing double duty as the transport layer.

Figure 8.17 illustrates the NCP packet headers for request and reply NCP packets. The first field is a 16-bit packet type identifier. Table 8.1 lists the six possible values for this field, depending on the packet type (shown in hex).

NCP Request

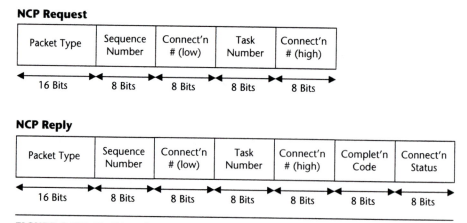

NCP Reply

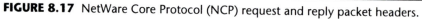

FIGURE 8.17 NetWare Core Protocol (NCP) request and reply packet headers.

TABLE 8.1 Packet Type Definitions

Field Value (hex)	Description
1111	Create service.
2222	NCP request.
3333	NCP reply.
5555	Destroy service connection.
7777	Packet burst.
9999	Server busy reply.

The create service connection, NCP request, and destroy service packets all follow the request header format. The NCP reply and server busy reply packets follow the reply header format.

Figure 8.18 shows an NCP request packet type hex 2222. More details about the request follow the NCP header, which in this case is an NCP "read from file" command. Packet type hex 7777 has a special format, which is covered in more detail later on.

Following the packet type is the sequence number. A request packet contains a sequence number that it expects to see in a reply packet associated with that request. Following the sequence number is the lower 8 bits of the client's connection number with the file server. This connection number is unique inside a file server. Versions of NetWare prior to 3.x could only have 255 client connections. This is now extended to 65,353 maximum theoretical connections with an additional high-order 8 bits of the connection number at the end of the request header. The task number allows a client to have more than one task outstanding with a server.

A reply packet also contains a completion code and connection status. An error-free NCP request responds with a completion code of 0; any other value indicates a problem. Some completion codes have multiple meanings depending on the request packet. Table 8.2 lists examples of completion codes (in hex).

The last field in an NCP reply packet is the 8-bit connection status. A nonzero value indicates that a user attempted to use a connection number that's no longer valid for that user. This can happen if a server times out a user connection and that user subsequently attempts to use the connection without first logging back in.

Because NCP has a packet "window" of one to one, the packet burst protocol was added to improve file transfer efficiency by allowing a "burst" of packets to be sent before the next command is required. This improves efficiency dramatically in WANs by "filling the pipe" with several packets without having to wait for command packets from the client. Efficiency in LANs

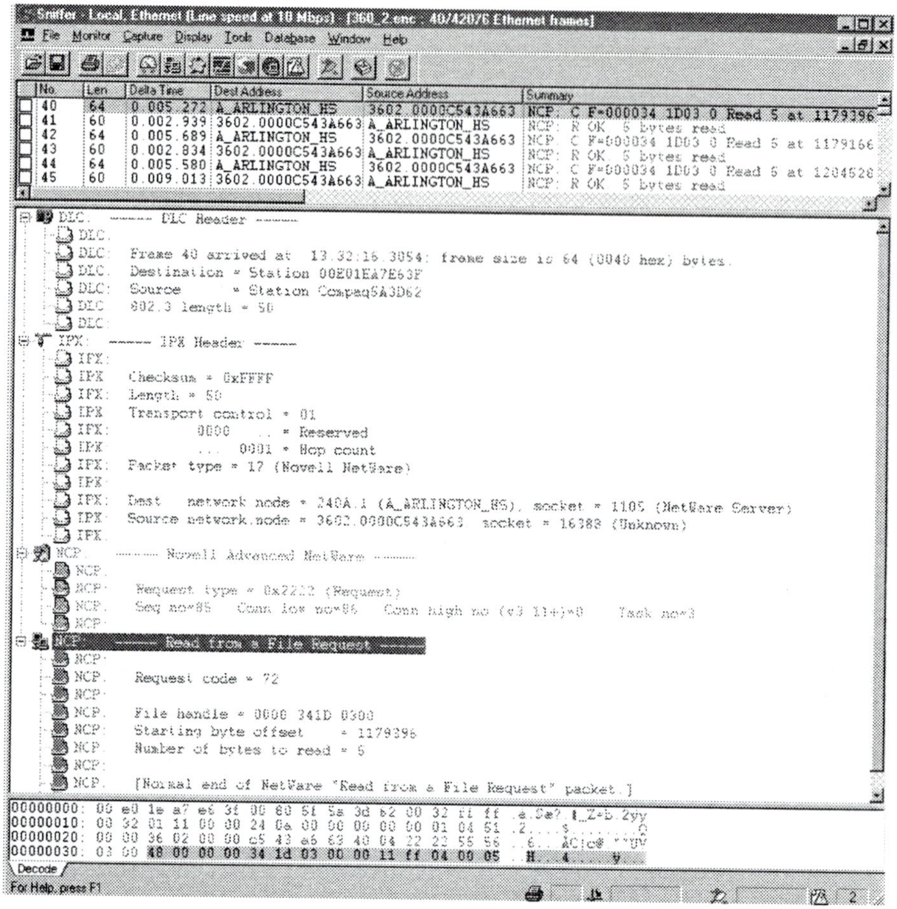

FIGURE 8.18 NCP request packet.

When watching for problems or hacking attempts with NetWare servers, use a protocol analyzer and a pattern match filter to look for a nonzero NCP completion code *or* a nonzero connection status. Both are 8-bit fields at the end of an NCP reply packet, so you can set one pattern match looking for a nonzero 16-bit value beginning at the completion code offset. Your analyzer should decode the completion code (a few of these are listed in Table 8.2) and connection status in order for you to determine the nature of the problem.

TABLE 8.2 NCP Completion Code Examples

Completion Code (hex)	Description
01	Insufficient disk space.
02	Client not logged in.
80	Lock failed. File is already open.
82	Unauthorized to open the file.
83	Possible bad disk sector on the file server.
84	Unauthorized to create the file.
85	Unauthorized to overwrite or delete the file.
87	Unexpected character in the file name.
88	Invalid file handle.
93	Unauthorized to read file.
94	Unauthorized to write file.
D0	Queue error.
D1	No queue rights.
D9	Maximum connections (based on server license) exceeded.
DA	Attempt to log in during a restricted time period.
DC	Account has expired.
DE	Password is incorrect.
DF	Password has expired.
FB	Property does not exist or bad directory handle or request not supported.
FF	Binary failure or unable to complete the request or unable to unlock the file.

is also improved because the number of packets required to transfer a file is reduced. This reduces the packet handling load on switches, routers, servers, etc. Chapter 9 shows just how packet burst can dramatically improve the performance of a file transfer over frame relay.

The packet burst protocol is separate from NCP and has an entirely different packet format. Only the initial burst mode connection request is set up using an NCP packet type of hex 2222. The packet bursting is performed using packet type hex 7777. Figure 8.19 shows the packet burst header. Each field is detailed in Table 8.3.

8.3.1 Case Study: The Network Is Slow

This is one of those typical complaints where the user says "the network is slow." Because the user was complaining about file transfer time, I had the user drag and drop a file from the "slow" file server to the desktop while I captured the packets with a protocol analyzer. Analyzing the trace revealed

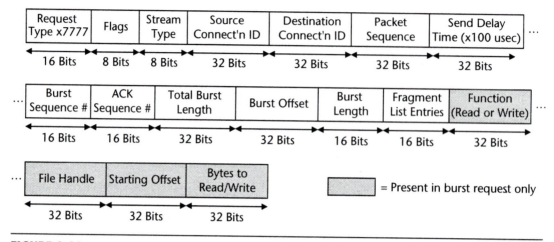

FIGURE 8.19 NetWare packet burst protocol header.

TABLE 8.3 Packet Burst Header Definitions

Field	Description
Flags	8- bits set as follows: x0000000—set to 1 if a system (command) packet; else it's a data packet. 0x000000—set to 1 if requesting a missing fragment list. 000x0000—set to 1 if the last packet in a burst set. 0000x000—set to 1 if the file server is busy. 00000x00—set to 1 to abort a request.
Stream Type	Set to hex 02.
Source Connection ID	Set by the client when requesting a burst mode connection with a server.
Destination Connection ID	Set by the server when acknowledging a burst mode connection.
Packet Sequence	The sequence number within the current burst of packets. The first packet in a burst will have a sequence number of 1.
Send Delay	Delay between consecutive packets in 100-microsecond increments. Normally set to zero, but the sender can adjust the delay if the recipient starts dropping burst packets.
Burst Sequence Number	Sequence number of the burst set.
Acknowledgment Sequence Number	The next burst set sequence expected from the sender.
Total Burst Length	Total amount of data in the burst set.
Burst Offset	The offset of the data in the burst set. Used by the client to reassemble a burst set in the correct order and determine if a packet is missing from the set.
Burst Length	Total amount of data in the current packet.

TABLE 8.3 (continued)

Field	Description
Fragment List Entries	If nonzero, the number of packets to be retransmitted, followed by the burst offset and data length for each missing packet. Checking for a nonzero value with a protocol analyzer is a good way to check your network integrity.

The following fields are present in the burst command packet only:

Function	Read (hex 01000000) or write (hex 02000000).
File Handle	File handle of the file that was open for reading or writing.
Starting Offset	The file offset in bytes for the next burst.
Bytes to Write	The total bytes to be read or written in this burst set.

that the throughput was far below the bandwidth of network segment the user was on despite using the normally efficient packet burst protocol.

Figure 8.20 is a snapshot of the trace containing packet burst read requests and responses. Packet number 1612 is a burst read request for 10,008 bytes at file offset 159704. The data is returned in packets 1613 through 1616 (because this is Token Ring, only a few large packets are required to transfer 10K of data). From the trace, it appears that some of the packets are not making it back to the client, as you can see from packets 1617 and 1623. These are notifications from the client to the server that a packet from the burst set is missing. This is similar to a transport retransmission, except that the client has to request that the packet be resent. Contrast this to TCP, where the client stays silent about missing TCP segments and the sending TCP process times out due to not getting an acknowledgment from the client.

By examining the detail of packet 1617, you can see that the missing fragment offset is 7992 and the amount of data is 2024 bytes. Thus it looks like the previous packet, number 1616, never made it to the client. Also note from the delta time between frames 1616 and 1617 that there was about a 1-second delay before the client realized that it wasn't getting all the packets. Likewise, there's about a half-second delay for the second missing packet notification, the gap between frames 1622 and 1623.

By moving the analyzer to the client segment, I was able to determine that a congested switch was dropping some of the packets. Dropping burst packets clearly adds a significant delay to the file transfer time due to the half-second to 1-second recovery time for each dropped packet.

The problem was due to older layer 2 switches that didn't have adequate memory for each port and the memory couldn't be upgraded. One solution was to reduce the number of users per port. Another was to upgrade the

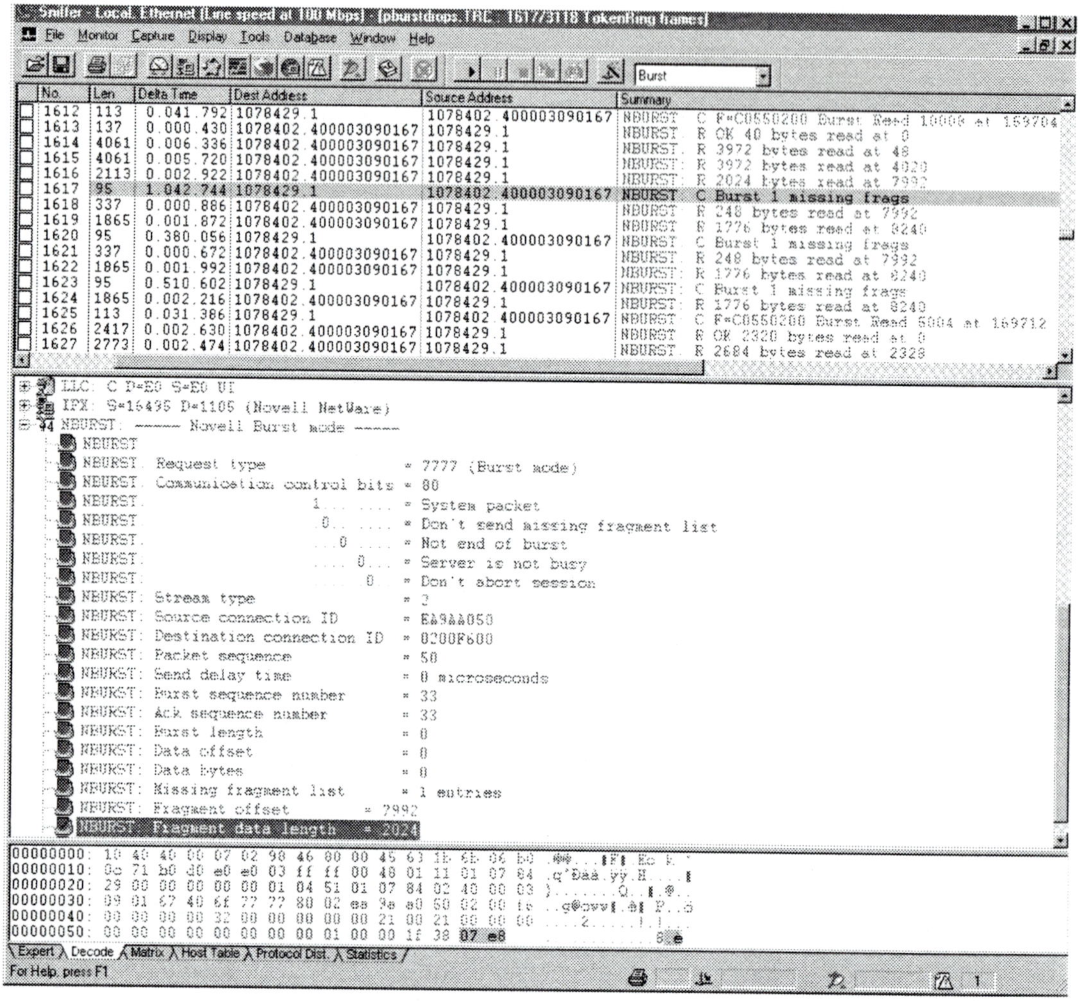

FIGURE 8.20 Packet burst with missing packet requests.

switch. Ironically, I ended up increasing the user's ring speed from 4 Mbps to 16 Mbps to help alleviate the problem short term. Throughput improved primarily due to fewer dropped packets and time-outs to resend the data, not to the increase in user ring speed.

Why would increasing the ring speed result in a *decrease* in dropped packets? Usually more data is being read from servers than written. By increasing the port speed of a user ring, the transmit buffer onto that port could be emptied four times faster, decreasing the likelihood of dropped packets originating from servers on 16 Mbps rings. This goes to show why it's not always better to put servers on faster network segments than the users (another example would be a server on a 100 Mbps Ethernet feeding users on a shared 10 Mbps Ethernet) unless the users have their own dedicated switch ports with adequate memory to buffer momentary packet bursts.

8.3.2 Case Study: The Network Is Slow II

This is another case of a user complaining that the network is slow. Again, an analysis of a file transfer between a user and server revealed throughput problems, but this time the manifestation was entirely different than the previous case.

As before, packet burst was being used to transfer files from a NetWare server. This time there were no missing fragments but a bit set in some of the packet burst system packets coming from the server indicated that the server was busy. Because packet burst is not an NCP protocol, it needs its own way of letting the client know that a duplicate request packet has been received while the first packet is still in the queue waiting to be processed. With NCP commands, the packet type of hex 9999 is used for this purpose. With packet burst, however, one of the flag bits is set in the packet burst header to indicate that the file server is busy with the previous request. Thus, if you are looking only for type "9999" packets to see when NetWare servers are busy, you will miss these critical packets altogether.

To get a feel for just how busy the server was, I captured packets between the server and user and then set a display filter on the server busy bit in the packet burst header. The result is shown in Figure 8.21.

For the first 80 seconds or so of my trace, there are only a few packet burst server busy packets. Then the server appears to get fairly busy as I am now getting busy packets every 60 milliseconds or so. The next step was to figure out why that server was slow in processing the user's packet burst requests. As it turns out, the server in question was the "main" server for hundreds of users and was also maintaining the master NetWare Directory Services (NDS) replica for thousands of users. The server was so busy doing NDS tasks that it didn't have time for much of anything else.

The solution? Ideally I would have liked to have seen the master NDS replica moved to a different server. As an alternative, the platform could be beefed up because it was an old Pentium-based server. My client choose the second route, upgrading the server to a much faster Pentium II and hard drive subsystem, allowing the server to process NDS information and other tasks at a much faster rate. Subsequent analysis showed that users no longer experienced burst busy packets.

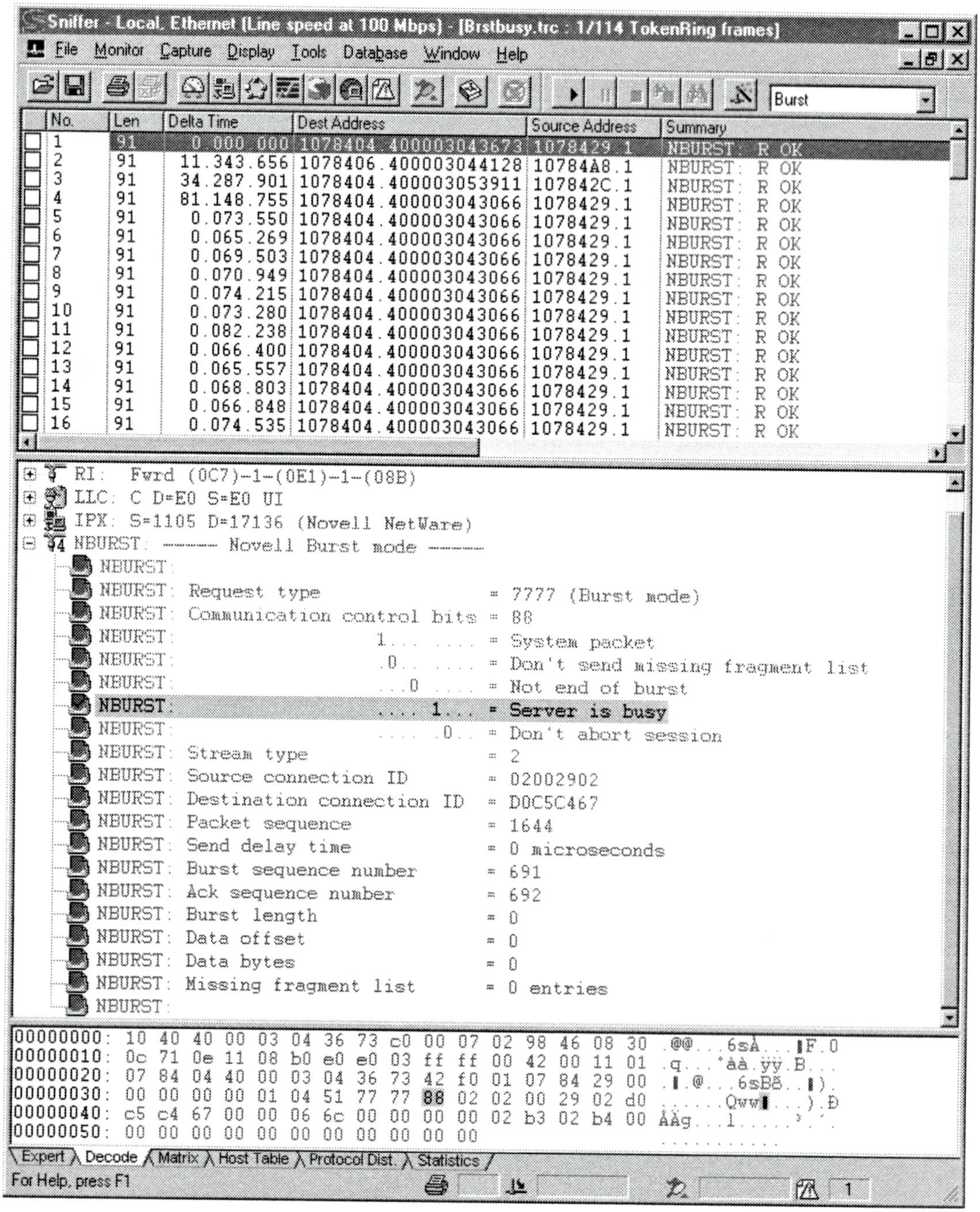

FIGURE 8.21 Packet burst server busy packets.

8.3.3 Case Study: Degraded Login Response Time

It's not untypical for workstations to take a long time to boot and log on to the network in the morning, especially with organizations that have thousands of users. There can be many reasons for this, ranging from hundreds of users waiting for access to a single file that's locked as part of the logon process and can only be accessed by one user at a time, to overwhelming demand for bandwidth. Usually it's something closer to the former rather than the latter.

Response time at one such customer reached into the 20+ minute range, which was unacceptable. It used to take only about 2 to 3 minutes in the past and users were becoming irritated.

A capture of a slow login (one that took over 15 minutes) on one particular client revealed major delays in the processing of dozens of NDS packets out of hundreds of NDS transactions between a server and client during the boot process. Figure 8.22 shows a detail of the classic NetWare type "9999" file server busy packet in response to an NDS packet sent from the client to the server.

Packet 35 is the original NDS request that's being delayed. Note that the client is sending the same packet several times, repeated in packets 36, 38, and 40. The first packet retransmission, packet 36, occurs 1.258 seconds after packet 35. This packet causes an immediate reply from the server acknowledging that it already got the original packet. The workstation figures, okay cool, I'll just wait a bit longer. Another packet (number 38) goes out 2.497 seconds after the server busy packet. Again the server is "busy." This time the client waits 5.029 seconds and tries again, only to be told to wait further. Finally, a response is received in packet 42. Notice how the retry time is increasing exponentially, similar in nature to the TCP protocol when it does not hear an acknowledgment.

By using the analyzer's relative time feature and setting a zero reference point at packet 35, you can easily see how long it took to complete this one NDS operation—13.664 seconds! At first glance, you might assume that the file server's CPU must be pegged based on the server busy packets. Perhaps the problem is similar to the previous case study. As it turned out, the server's CPU wasn't very busy at all. To help figure out the reason behind this mysterious delay, it helps to know a little about how NDS works.

NDS replicates a tree of objects (resources that users can access) and user rights across multiple NDS servers. One server holds the master database or replica, and the others act as backup replicas. On occasion, the master will synchronize with the backup replicas. There are also times when the backup replica servers need to contact the master to make sure the information is really up to the minute when a user logs in. Herein lies the problem.

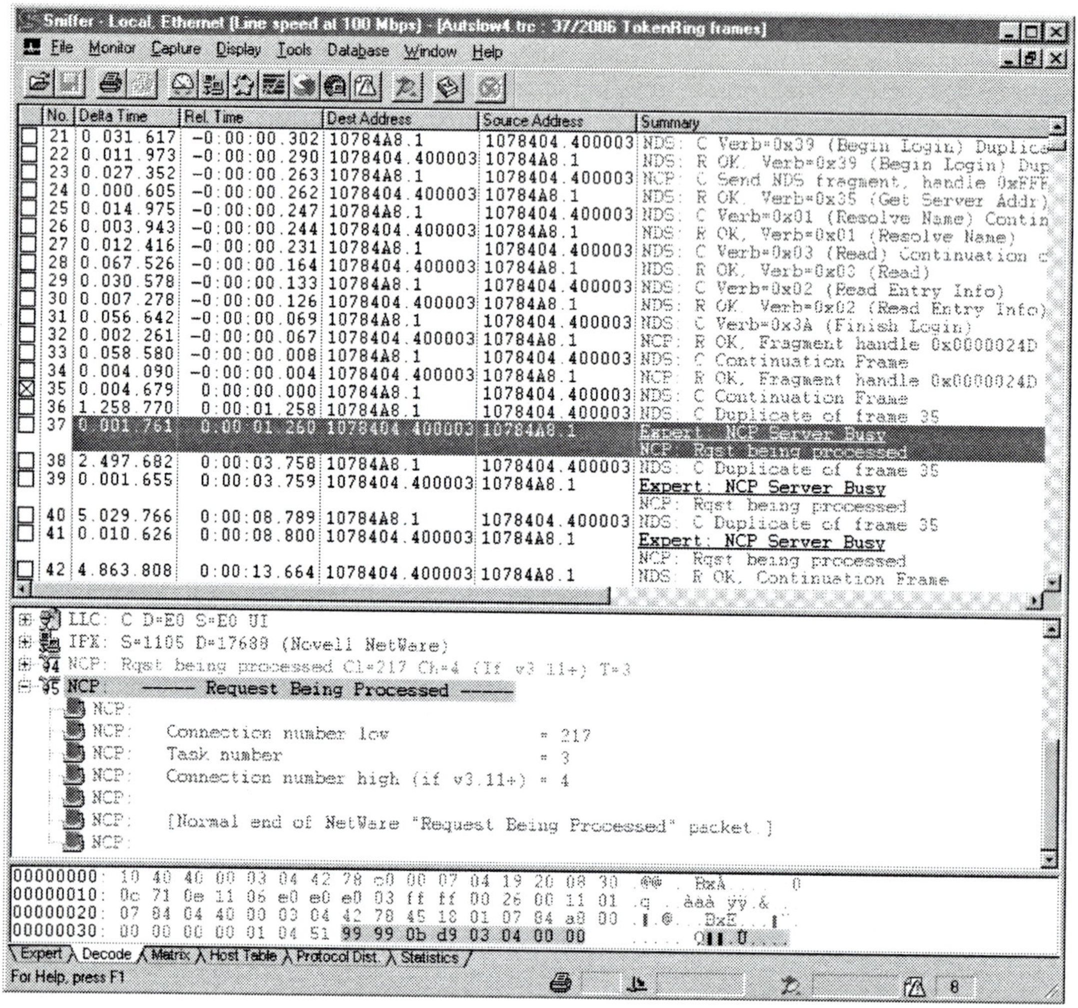

FIGURE 8.22 A busy server?

The NDS server is actually a backup replica that's trying to contact the master replica during the large delay. I could see this by placing an analyzer on the master NDS server's segment. Thus the backup replica was not very busy, but there were times in the morning hours when the master replica became very busy and was unable to respond in a timely fashion to the backup replicas that were authenticating users as they logged on to the network. This problem ties in with the previous case study where the master NDS server was also a busy "main" file server and required a substantial platform upgrade to improve performance. After upgrading the master NDS server's computing platform, the morning logon times returned to the less-than-5-minute range.

8.3.4 Case Study: Dropped Server Connections

Users in this network were experiencing intermittent disconnects from their home server. The problem could not be attributed to any particular application, time or day, or any other event. It appeared to be quite random in nature. These random problems can be difficult to solve because it's not a simple matter of slapping an analyzer on the network, pressing a button, then looking at the trace.

This is one of those instances in which I started by looking for the proverbial needle in a haystack. Because the problem was affecting users corporate-wide and not any workgroup network segment in particular, I began by capturing packets on the Token Ring backbone where the home file server resided. I'd like to note that this particular problem can happen on either Ethernet or Token Ring, but being on Token Ring actually helped solved it.

Every now and then I'd see a "Receiver Congestion" soft error report MAC frame being sent out by the home file server. Recall from Chapter 3 that these frames actually contain error counts over the past two seconds, so I had to look inside the frame with the analyzer to see if more than one receiver congestion error was being reported.

Sure enough, tens of receiver congestion errors were being reported. This means that, periodically, several packets sent to the file server were being dropped. Some Ethernet adapters may also drop packets when heavily loaded, but unlike Token Ring, there's no error reporting mechanism. It definitely would have taken me longer to solve this problem on an Ethernet.

Normally, dropping a few packets now and then is not a big deal because you expect the higher layer protocols to recover. This can be a dangerous assumption, however, depending on the protocol. Therefore my next step was to try to figure out what packets were being dropped and if dropping those packets had anything to do with the end-user disconnect problem.

Finding out what packets are dropped by a Token Ring node is actually easy with a protocol analyzer. By placing the analyzer immediately downstream from the home file server, I was able to watch for receiver congestion reports *and* determine which packets were dropped. I merely had to look at the receiver congestion report frames in the capture buffer and go *backwards* into the buffer approximately 2 seconds. It wasn't long before I had the answer.

Token Ring packets that passed through the home file server without the frame copied bit set were those that were being dropped. Having the analyzer directly downstream from the home server was important. Putting the analyzer immediately before the home server would be a worst-case scenario because packets captured by the analyzer addressed to the home server would never have the frame copied bit set.

After gathering several traces of dropped packets, I saw a pattern begin to emerge. The vast majority of the dropped packets were packets of the Watchdog protocol used to keep NetWare user connections alive. If a server doesn't receive a packet from a user over the past 5 minutes (by default), it sends out a Watchdog packet to "ping" the user to make sure the workstation hasn't been deactivated (e.g., turning it off) without properly logging off. If there is no response, the server goes into a cycle of sending out nine more packets (by default, for a total of 10 Watchdog packets) over 1-minute intervals. By watching for dead connections (no response is received), the server can eventually free up the connection for another user.

Over time, NetWare servers have a tendency to send out all the Watchdog checks at the same time, regardless of when users initially logged in. In this case, the users would log in to the home server and then "attach" to a different server that acted as a 3270 gateway to communicate with a mainframe. That server stayed busy, but the home server was rarely accessed once the user logged on in the morning. Eventually the home server sent out hundreds of Watchdog packets every 5 minutes. This in turn caused hundreds of replies even before the server had a chance to complete sending out its Watchdog packets. The responses overwhelmed the network adapter, causing it to drop packets. Because Watchdog reply packets are not acked by the server, every now and then a user was unlucky in that the server dropped all ten Watchdog replies from that user. This caused the server to think the user was "dead" and time out the connection.

This problem had several potential solutions. One solution was to adjust the Watchdog timers to wait longer before the first Watchdog packet goes out and to try more than ten times. This is really a kludge in that it masks the true problem—a performance problem with the server/NIC—and potentially uses up all the connections at some point because truly dead connections take much longer to time out.

The customer was not ready to upgrade the server hardware just yet, so another solution was arrived at. Rather than place the Watchdog burden on the server, it was placed on each workstation. This was also a bit of a kludge in that it required special software installed in each workstation to "spoof" the Watchdog process by periodically sending an unsolicited Watchdog packet to the server. It was a sufficient solution until the server could be upgraded.

8.4 Server Message Block (SMB) Protocol

The SMB protocol provides layer 7 redirector, messenger, printing, and server functions for OS/2, Windows for Workgroups, Windows 95/98, and Windows NT clients. The redirector converts native operating system calls into SMB calls for a remote server. The messenger provides peer-to-peer services, and the server provides session, file, and print services.

Intel and Microsoft originally developed SMB for Microsoft's Xenix operating system, which Intel dubbed OpenNet. Xenix has long since been taken over by the Santa Cruz Operation (SCO).

Next, Microsoft and IBM jointly developed OS/2 that started mainly as a desktop operating system, and Microsoft developed the Microsoft LAN Manager server. After the IBM/Microsoft split, IBM continued with OS/2 Warp and Microsoft developed NT, both of which are combination desktop/server operating systems that continue to use SMB.

SMB is also supported by many UNIX systems. A popular implementation of SMB for UNIX is called Samba written by Andrew Tridgell. Samba provides DOS and Windows users an alternative to NFS as a way to access UNIX resources.

Microsoft is pushing to standardize SMB by renaming it the Common Internet File System (CIFS) and submitting it to the IETF as Internet Draft "A Common Internet File System (CIFS/1.0) Protocol." One of the motivations for this effort is to provide a common version of SMB that provides interoperability between different network operating systems over the Internet. Currently SMB is an Open Group (formerly X/Open) standard for PC and UNIX interoperability.

8.4.1 SMB Logon and Packet Format

The basic steps required to log on to an NT server, as taken from a protocol analyzer trace of a Windows 95 workstation boot using TCP/IP, are as follows:

1. Renew or get an IP address from a DHCP server or ARP your statically assigned IP address.
2. If Windows Internet Naming Service (WINS, an implementation of NetBIOS naming servers over TCP/IP—see RFCs 1001 and 1002 for more details) is enabled, register your NetBIOS names with a WINS server. Otherwise, broadcast the names to make sure that no one is using them.
3. Broadcast an SMB NETLOGON request to get the name of a server.
4. Get the address of the server from a WINS server or send a broadcast packet if WINS is not configured.

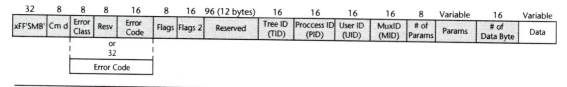

FIGURE 8.23 The SMB packet format.

5. Set up a TCP connection with the server.

6. Set up a NetBIOS session with the server over the TCP connection.

7. Set up an SMB session with the server over the NetBIOS session.

8. Use the SMB session to get the name of a Primary Domain Controller (PDC) or Backup Domain Controller (BDC).

9. Disconnect from the NT server and connect to the PDC or BDC to authenticate shares (mapping of drive letters to server drives). Shares can be automatically mapped (reconnnected) when a user logs on or mapped manually via the Network Neighborhood or via the NET USE command at the command prompt.

The SMB packet format is illustrated in Figure 8.23. The first 4 bytes contain the characters hex FF, followed by ASCII "SMB". The next field is a 1-byte command field containing the requesting or responding operating code, as shown in Table 8.4.

As SMB evolved, more commands were added to improve the efficiency of the protocol. Lacking in the original SMB 1.0 specification, for example, was the ability to daisy chain commands. In Table 8.4, commands that have "ANDX" in them allow subsequent SMB commands to be sent in a single packet. A client redirector usually chains together commands where possible. As an example, packet number 43 in Figure 8.24 contains two SMB commands, "session setup" and "tree connect." Likewise, packet 44 contains two responses in a single packet.

Later versions of SMB also improved file reading and writing efficiency. For example, the "read block raw" and "read block multiplexed" commands allow a client to request a large block of file data (up to 65,535 bytes) from a server. The underlying transport layer, such as TCP, would take care of segmenting the packets into smaller units for use by the network layer.

The latest version of SMB (CIFS) has added commands for bulk file transfer where a client can initiate a file transfer of any size with just one read packet. The client does not have to keep requesting blocks to order to read the file. This allows SMB to compete with FTP over the Internet in terms of efficiency. Once the SMB "read bulk" command starts, the remaining packets are TCP, just like you'd see using FTP over TCP.

TABLE 8.4 SMB Commands

SMD_CMD_CREATE_DIRECTORY	0x00
SMD_CMD_DELETE_DIRECTORY	0x01
SMD_CMD_OPEN	0x02
SMD_CMD_CREATE	0x03
SMD_CMD_CLOSE	0x04
SMD_CMD_FLUSH	0x05
SMD_CMD_DELETE	0x06
SMD_CMD_RENAME	0x07
SMD_CMD_QUERY_INFORMATION	0x08
SMD_CMD_SET_INFORMATION	0x09
SMD_CMD_READ	0x0A
SMD_CMD_WRITE	0x0B
SMD_CMD_LOCK_BYTE_RANGE	0x0C
SMD_CMD_UNLOCK_BYTE_RANGE	0x0D
SMD_CMD_CREATE_TEMPORARY	0x0E
SMD_CMD_CREATE_NEW	0x0F
SMD_CMD_CHECK_DIRECTORY	0x10
SMD_CMD_PROCESS_EXIT	0x11
SMD_CMD_SEEK	0x12
SMD_CMD_LOCK_AND_READ	0x13
SMD_CMD_WRITE_AND_UNLOCK	0x14
SMD_CMD_READ_RAW	0x1A
SMD_CMD_READ_MPX	0x1B
SMD_CMD_READ_MPX_SECONDARY	0x1C
SMD_CMD_WRITE_RAW	0x1D
SMD_CMD_WRITE_MPX	0x1E
SMD_CMD_WRITE_COMPLETE	0x20
SMD_CMD_SET_INFORMATION2	0x22
SMD_CMD_QUERY_INFORMATION2	0x23
SMD_CMD_LOCKING_ANDX	0x24
SMD_CMD_TRANSACTION	0x25
SMD_CMD_TRANSACTION_SECONDARY	0x26
SMD_CMD_IOCTL	0x27
SMD_CMD_IOCTL_SECONDARY	0x28
SMD_CMD_COPY	0x29
SMD_CMD_MOVE	0x2A
SMD_CMD_ECHO	0x2B
SMD_CMD_WRITE_AND_CLOSE	0x2C
SMD_CMD_OPEN_ANDX	0x2D
SMD_CMD_READ_ANDX	0x2E
SMD_CMD_WRITE_ANDX	0x2F
SMD_CMD_CLOSE_AND_TREE_DISC	0x31
SMD_CMD_TRANSACTION2	0x32
SMD_CMD_TRANSACTION2_SECONDARY	0x33
SMD_CMD_FIND_CLOSE2	0x34
SMD_CMD_FIND_NOTIFY_CLOSE	0x35
SMD_CMD_TREE_CONNECT	0x70
SMD_CMD_TREE_DISCONNECT	0x71
SMD_CMD_NEGOTIATE	0x72
SMD_CMD_SESSION_SETUP_ANDX	0x73

TABLE 8.4 (continued)

SMD_CMD_LOGOFF_ANDX	0x74
SMD_CMD_TREE_CONNECT_ANDX	0x75
SMD_CMD_QUERY_INFORMATION_DISK	0x80
SMD_CMD_SEARCH	0x81
SMD_CMD_FIND	0x82
SMD_CMD_FIND_UNIQUE	0x83
SMD_CMD_NT_TRANSACT	0xA0
SMD_CMD_NT_TRANSACT_SECONDARY	0xA1
SMD_CMD_NT_CREATE_ANDX	0xA2
SMD_CMD_NT_CANCEL	0xA4
SMD_CMD_OPEN_PRINT_FILE	0xC0
SMD_CMD_WRITE_PRINT_FILE	0xC1
SMD_CMD_CLOSE_PRINT_FILE	0xC2
SMD_CMD_GET_PRINT_QUEUE	0xC3
SMD_CMD_READ_BULK	0xD8
SMD_CMD_WRITE_BULK	0xD9
SMD_CMD_WRITE_BULK_DATA	0xDA

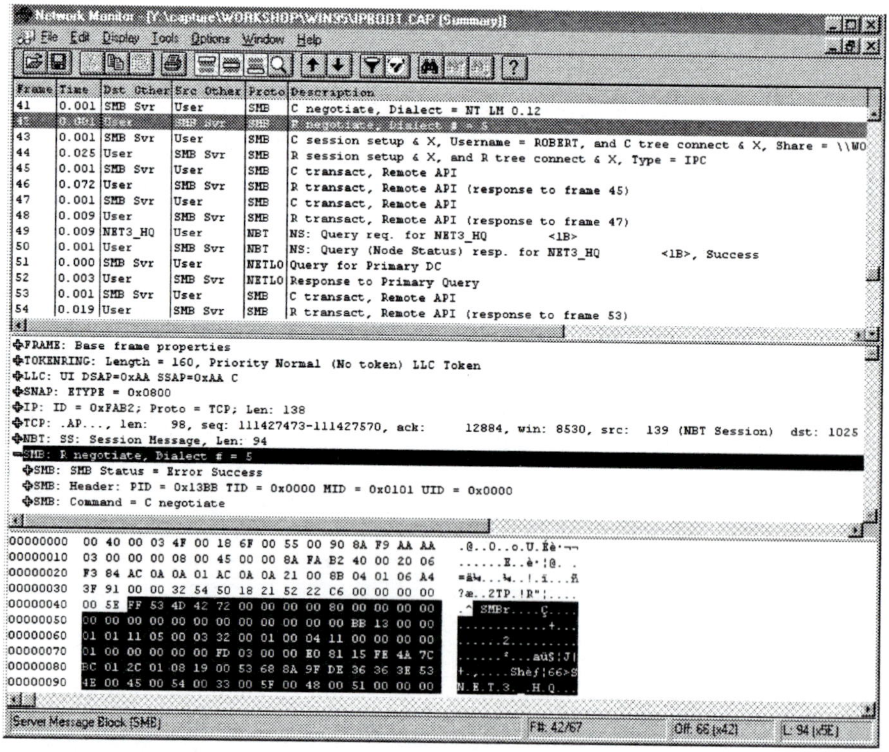

FIGURE 8.24 Daisy chaining SMB commands in a single packet.

TABLE 8.5 Possible SMB Error Classes

Class	Value	Definition
SUCCESS	0	The request was successful.
ERRDOS	1	Error generated by the server operating system.
ERRSRV	2	Error generated by the server network file manager.
ERRHRD	3	Hardware error.
ERRCMD	255	Command was not in the SMB format (optional).

The next field or fields depends on the "dialect" of SMB. Protocol dialects prior to NT LM 0.12 return status to the client using "error class" and "error code" fields. Beginning with the "NT LAN Manager 0.12" (LM NT 0.12) dialect, servers can return 32-bit error information. If the incoming client SMB has bit 14 set in the Flags2 field of the SMB header, the server can return 32-bit information.

The majority of Windows and other clients are still using the error class/ error code fields. The various error classes are listed in Table 8.5.

If the error class code is nonzero, the error code can be consulted for more information. Tables 8.6, 8.7, and 8.8 give the error codes for ERRDOS, ERRSRV, and ERRHRD, respectively. As a general rule, ERRDOS problems are client related, ERRSRV are server limitations or restrictions, and ERRHRD are server hardware problems.

TABLE 8.6 Possible ERRDOS Return Codes

Code	Value	Definition
ERRbadfunc	1	Invalid function.
ERRbadfile	2	File not found.
ERRbadpath	3	Directory invalid.
ERRnofids	4	Too many open files on server.
ERRnoaccess	5	Access denied.
ERRbadfid	6	Invalid file handle.
ERRbadmcb	7	Memory control blocks destroyed.
ERRnomem	8	Insufficient server memory to perform function.
ERRbadmem	9	Invalid memory block address.
ERRbadenv	10	Invalid environment.
ERRbadformat	11	Invalid format.
ERRbadaccess	12	Invalid open mode.
ERRbaddata	13	Invalid data.
ERRbaddrive	15	Invalid drive specified.
ERRremcd	16	Invalid Delete Directory request.
ERRdiffdevice	17	Not same device.
ERRnofiles	18	No more matching File Search files.

TABLE 8.6 (continued)

ERRbadshare	32	Sharing mode conflicts with existing FIDs.
ERRlock	33	Lock request conflict, invalid lock mode, or deadlock.
ERRfilexists	80	File already exists.
ERRbadpipe	230	Pipe invalid.
ERRpipebusy	231	All instances of the requested pipe are busy.
ERRpipeclosing	232	Pipe close in progress.
ERRnotconnected	233	No process on other end of pipe.
ERRmoredata	234	There is more data to be returned.

TABLE 8.7 Possible ERRSRV Return Codes

Code	Value	Definition
ERRerror	1	Nonspecific.
ERRbadpw	2	Bad password.
ERRaccess	4	Client does not have access rights.
ERRinvtid	5	Invalid tree TID command.
ERRinvnetname	6	Invalid network name in tree connect.
ERRinvdevice	7	Invalid printer device.
ERRqfull	49	Print queue full—too many files.
ERRqtoobig	50	Print queue full—out of space.
ERRqeof	51	EOF on print queue dump.
ERRinvpfid	52	Invalid print file FID.
ERRsmbcmd	64	Command not recognized by server.
ERRsrverror	65	Internal server error.
ERRfilespecs	67	Invalid values in FID and/or pathname.
ERRbadpermits	69	Path access permissions not valid.
ERRsetattrmode	71	Set File Attribute mode is invalid.
ERRpaused	81	Messaging is paused.
ERRmsgoff	82	Not receiving messages.
ERRnoroom	83	No room to buffer message.
ERRrmuns	87	Too many remote user names.
ERRtimeout	88	Operation timed out.
ERRnoresource	89	No resources currently available.
ERRtoomanyuids	90	Too many UIDs active on this session.
ERRbaduid	91	The UID is not valid on this session.
ERRusempx	250	Temp unable to support Raw, use MPX mode.
ERRusestd	251	Temp unable to support Raw, use standard read/write.
ERRcontmpx	252	Continue in MPX mode.
ERRnosupport	255	Function not supported.

TABLE 8.8 Possible ERRHRD Return Codes

Code	Value	Definition
ERRnowrite	19	Attempt to write on write-protected disk.
ERRbadunit	20	Unknown unit.
ERRnotready	21	Drive not ready.
ERRbadcmd	22	Unknown command.
ERRdata	23	Data CRC error.
ERRbadreq	24	Bad request structure length.
ERRseek	25	Seek error.
ERRbadmedia	26	Unknown media type.
ERRbadsector	27	Sector not found.
ERRnopaper	28	Printer out of paper.
ERRwrite	29	Write fault.
ERRread	30	Read fault.
ERRgeneral	31	General failure.
ERRbadshare	32	An open conflicts with an existing open.
ERRlock	33	Lock request conflict, invalid lock mode, or deadlock.
ERRwrongdisk	34	Wrong disk in drive.
ERRFCBUnavail	35	No FCBs available to process request.
ERRsharebufexc	36	A sharing buffer has been exceeded.

When watching for NT or any SMB server problems or hacking attempts, use a protocol analyzer and a pattern match filter to look for a nonzero 32-bit value following the SMB command code. Your analyzer should decode the error information in detail in order for you to determine the nature of the problem.

This brings us to the 8-bit flags field in the SMB header. Reading from right to left (least to most significant), each bit is defined in Table 8.9.

TABLE 8.9 Flags Field Definitions

Bit	Description
0	Reserved for obsolete commands.
1	Reserved.
2	Reserved.
3	If set to 1, pathnames are case insensitive.
4	Reserved.
5	Reserved for obsolete commands.
6	Reserved for obsolete commands.
7	SMB is a response to a client request (this is how a protocol analyzer figures out SMB commands from responses).

TABLE 8.10 Flags2 Field Definitions

Bit	Description
0	Client understands long file names.
1	Client understands extended attributes.
2	Security signature—if set, the SMB is integrity checked.
3	Reserved.
4	Reserved.
5	Reserved.
6	If set, any pathname in the request is a long file name.
7	Reserved.
8	Reserved.
9	Reserved.
10	Reserved.
11	If set, the client is aware of extended security.
12	If set, use the Distributed File System to resolve pathnames.
13	If set, client is permitted to read if client doesn't have read permission but does have execute permission (using for paging I/O).
14	If set, the error code is a 32-bit status.
15	If set, the SMB data type string is in UNICODE; otherwise, it is in ASCII.

The next field, the 16-bit Flags2 field, contains additional flags. From left to right, the bits are defined in Table 8.10.

The Tree ID, or TID, field represents an authenticated connection to server resource. When a client disconnects from the server using an SMB tree "disconnect" command, the server closes any files opened with that TID over the connection.

The Process ID, or PID, field tells the server which process from a client opened a file. The interpretation of a process is up to the client application and the client sets the PID.

The server assigns a value to the User ID, or UID, field after a user authenticates to the server.

The Multiplex ID, or MID, field allows multiplexing of a single client and server connection among multiple client processes and threads. The client is not allowed to have multiple outstanding requests to a server with the same MID.

The number of parameters field includes the number of 16-bit words for a given SMB command. This is followed by the actual parameters for the SMB command.

The final field is a 16-bit value to indicate the number of data bytes (such as part of a file) that follow the SMB header.

Network Monitor

File Edit Display Tools Options Window Help

Y:\capture\WORKSHOP\WIN95\NBXFER2.CAP [Summary]

Frame	Time	Dst MAC Addr	Src MAC Addr	Dst Other Addr	Src Other Addr	Proto	Description
46	0.001	3COM 26B37E	WestDgEC4A8E			SMB	R open & X, File = \WOODSTOCK DRIVEC\WINDOWS
47	0.001	WestDgEC4A8E	3COM 26B37E			SMB	C lock & X, FID = 0x1801, Unlocks = 0 (0x490
48	0.001	WestDgEC4A8E	3COM 26B37E			SMB	C close file, FID = 0x1801
49	0.001	WestDgEC4A8E	3COM 26B37E			SMB	R close file
50	0.043	3COM 26B37E	WestDgEC4A8E			NETBI	Data Ack (0x14): LSN = 0x26, RSN = 0x37
51	0.000	WestDgEC4A8E	3COM 26B37E			SMB	R open & X, FID = 0x2000, File Size = 0x14f5
52	0.001	3COM 26B37E	WestDgEC4A8E			NETBI	Data Ack (0x14): LSN = 0x26, RSN = 0x37
53	0.006	WestDgEC4A8E	3COM 26B37E			SMB	C read block raw, FID = 0x2000, Read 0xf000
54	0.002	WestDgEC4A8E	3COM 26B37E			NETBI	Data First Middle (0x15): LSN = 0x37, RSN =
55	0.001	WestDgEC4A8E	3COM 26B37E			NETBI	Data First Middle (0x15): LSN = 0x37, RSN =
56	0.001	WestDgEC4A8E	3COM 26B37E			NETBI	Data First Middle (0x15): LSN = 0x37, RSN =
57	0.002	WestDgEC4A8E	3COM 26B37E			NETBI	Data First Middle (0x15): LSN = 0x37, RSN =
58	0.001	3COM 26B37E	WestDgEC4A8E			LLC	RR DSAP=0xF0 SSAP=0xF1 R N(R) = 0x65 FINAL
59	0.001	WestDgEC4A8E	3COM 26B37E			NETBI	Data First Middle (0x15): LSN = 0x37, RSN =

NetBEUI

Y:\capture\WORKSHOP\WIN95\IPXFER.CAP [Summary]

Frame	Time	Dst MAC Addr	Src MAC Addr	Dst Other Addr	Src Other Addr	Proto	Description
37	0.001	3COM 26B37E	WestDgEC4A8E	1000.0020AF26B37E	0.0000C0EC4A8E	SMB	R open & X, File = \WINNT\SYSTEM32\SHELL32.D
38	0.000	WestDgEC4A8E	3COM 26B37E	1000.0000C0EC4A8E	1000.0020AF26B37E	SMB	R open & X, FID = 0x8000, File Size = 0x137d
39	0.002	3COM 26B37E	WestDgEC4A8E	1000.0020AF26B37E	0.0000C0EC4A8E	SMB	C seek, FID = 0x8000, Offset = 0
40	0.000	WestDgEC4A8E	3COM 26B37E	1000.0000C0EC4A8E	1000.0020AF26B37	SMB	R seek, New offset = 1277200
41	0.007	3COM 26B37E	WestDgEC4A8E	1000.0020AF26B37E	0.0000C0EC4A8E	SMB	C read block mpx, FID = 0x8000, Read 0x3728
42	0.001	WestDgEC4A8E	3COM 26B37E	1000.0000C0EC4A8E	1000.0020AF26B37	SMB	R read block mpx, Read 0x584 of 0x3728
43	0.002	WestDgEC4A8E	3COM 26B37E	1000.0000C0	020AF26B37	SMB	R read block mpx, Read 0x584 of 0x3728
44	0.001	WestDgEC4A8E	3COM 26B37E	1000.0000C0	020AF26B37	SMB	R read block mpx, Read 0x584 of 0x3728
45	0.001	WestDgEC4A8E	3COM 26B37E	1000.0000C0EC4A8E	1000.0020AF26B37	SMB	R read block mpx, Read 0x584 of 0x3728
46	0.001	WestDgEC4A8E	3COM 26B37E	1000.0000C0EC4A8E	1000.0020AF26B37	SMB	R read block mpx, Read 0x584 of 0x3728
47	0.002	WestDgEC4A8E	3COM 26B37E	1000.0000C0EC4A8E	1000.0020AF26B37	SMB	R read block mpx, Read 0x584 of 0x3728
48	0.001	WestDgEC4A8E	3COM 26B37E	1000.0000C0EC4A8E	1000.0020AF26B37	SMB	R read block mpx, Read 0x584 of 0x3728
49	0.001	WestDgEC4A8E	3COM 26B37E	1000.0000C0EC4A8E	1000.0020AF26B37	SMB	R read block mpx, Read 0x584 of 0x3728
50	0.002	WestDgEC4A8E	3COM 26B37E	1000.0000C0EC4A8E	1000.0020AF26B37	SMB	R read block mpx, Read 0x584 of 0x3728

IPX

Y:\capture\WORKSHOP\WIN95\IPXFER.CAP [Summary]

Frame	Time	Dst MAC Addr	Src MAC Addr	Dst Other Addr	Src Other Addr	Proto	Description
37	0.006	3COM 26B37E	WestDgEC4A8E	172.10.10.69	172.10.10.30	SMB	R open & X, File = \WINNT\SYSTEM32\SHELL32.D
38	0.001	3COM 26B37E	WestDgEC4A8E	172.10.10.69	172.10.10.30	SMB	C lock & X, FID = 0x500f, Unlocks = 0 (0x630
39	0.001	3COM 26B37E	WestDgEC4A8E	172.10.10.69	172.10.10.30	SMB	C close file, FID = 0x500f
40	0.001	3COM 26B37E	WestDgEC4A8E	172.10.10.69	172.10.10.30	SMB	R close file
41	0.116	3COM 26B37E	WestDgEC4A8E	172.10.10.69	172.10.10.30	TCP	.A...., len: 0, seq: 376131-376131, ac
42	0.001	WestDgEC4A8E	3COM 26B37E	172.10.10.30	172.10.10.69	SMB	R open & X, FID = 0xa809, File Size = 0x137d
43	0.011	3COM 26B37E	WestDgEC4A8E	172.10.10.69	172.10.10.30	SMB	C read block raw, FID = 0xa809, Read 0xf000
44	0.002	WestDgEC4A8E	3COM 26B37E	172.10.10.3	172.10.10.69	NBT	SS: Session Message, Len: 61440
45	0.002	WestDgEC4A8E	3COM 26B37E	172.10.10.3	172.10.10.69	NBT	SS: Session Message Cont., 1460 Bytes
46	0.001	WestDgEC4A8E	3COM 26B37E	172.10.10.30	172.10.10.69	NBT	SS: Session Message, Len: 35669
47	0.001	3COM 26B37E	WestDgEC4A8E	172.10.10.69	172.10.10.30	TCP	.A...., len: 0, seq: 376186-376186, ac
48	0.000	WestDgEC4A8E	3COM 26B37E	172.10.10.30	172.10.10.69	NBT	SS: Session Message Cont., 1460 Bytes
49	0.001	WestDgEC4A8E	3COM 26B37E	172.10.10.30	172.10.10.69	NBT	SS: Session Message Cont., 1460 Bytes
50	0.001	3COM 26B37E	WestDgEC4A8E	172.10.10.69	172.10.10.30	TCP	.A...., len: 0, seq: 376186-376186, ac

TCP/IP

Server Message Block (SMB)   F#: 37/1055   Off: 47 (x2F)   L: 122 (x7A)

FIGURE 8.25 SMB operating over three different protocol stacks.

The SMB application layer protocol is designed to run over virtually any protocol stack. In Windows 95/98/NT environments, you can choose from TCP/IP, IPX, or NetBEUI. The command structure for every SMB packet is identical in each case.

Figure 8.25 shows an SMB open file request followed by several read requests from an NT server for three different underlying protocol stacks. In the case of NetBEUI, you can see file data being returned in a series of NetBIOS session datagram packets. These packets are embedded directly

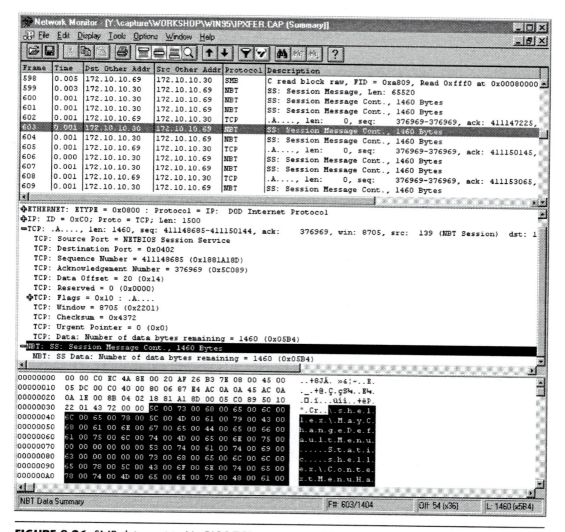

FIGURE 8.26 SMB data sent to NetBIOS TCP source port 139 immediately follows the TCP header.

into a layer 2 LLC frame. Because there's no network layer, these packets would have to be bridged or switched in a large infrastructure.

For IPX, the data is returned as a series of SMB headers embedded in IPX datagrams. The reason for the SMB header in every IPX packet is that there's no session or transport layer—SMB is running directly over the network layer.

In the case of TCP/IP, SMB allows a NetBIOS session to take care of the read responses. In Figure 8.25, NetBIOS over TCP is decoded in the protocol column as "NBT." There is actually no NetBIOS overhead in transferring data.

As seen in Figure 8.26, a data packet returned from a server merely has a TCP port number to identify NetBIOS to the application—there's no NetBIOS header.

❗

A neat trick is to use a protocol analyzer to capture packets prior to an NT server's going down and automatically stopping the capture. Start by using the following batch file:

```
:TOP
NET VIEW \\A_SERVER
If errorlevel 1 GOTO FAIL
GOTO TOP
:FAIL
PING 10.10.10.10
```

Simply run this batch file on the same network segment as the analyzer and server (or on the analyzer itself if the analyzer is Windows-based) and set a trigger to stop the capture when the bogus destination IP address of 10.10.10.10 is seen in a packet. There are variations on this trick. You could also use the NET SEND command instead of PING and do a pattern match trigger on the message. For example, NET SEND SCOTT "Server is Down." Send the message once manually and capture it with your protocol analyzer to get the offset for the text "Server is Down." One caveat: Analyze the network during batch file operation to ensure that the file doesn't chew up a large amount of your bandwidth; note that the looping in the batch file is without delay. I ran this file on a fast NT workstation connected to a 100 Mbps Ethernet segment and it only used about 1 percent of the Ethernet—not too bad.

8.4.2 Case Study: Poor Response Time

This is another one of those troubleshooting efforts that began with the typical "the network is slow" complaint from an end-user. A salesperson would take an order from a customer, enter it into their workstation, and send the order to a mainframe for processing. In some cases, the response time was in the several tens of seconds range, during which the customer was on hold.

Without any further information about the problem, you might blame the problem on the mainframe. Needless to say, mainframes are very expensive to upgrade, so before I would do that, I'd analyze the problem in detail.

The first step was to analyze how the user communicated with the mainframe. In this case, the user was on a remote LAN connected to a router that communicated via a high-speed (4 Mbps) leased line to a router attached to a backbone where a 3745 front-end processor resided that attached the backbone to the mainframe. Now the potential problem areas include the remote

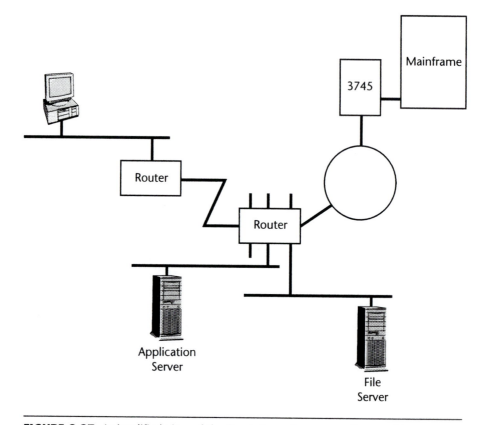

FIGURE 8.27 A simplified view of the "mainframe" response time problem.

workstation, the remote LAN, the remote router, the leased line, the local router, the backbone, or the mainframe. Before breaking out the protocol analyzer and looking for problems on one of the interleaving networks, I decided to gather additional information about the nature of the application. In this case, having done my homework paid off handsomely.

As it turned out, the mainframe was not the end of the application. The mainframe communicated over a local LAN to a custom application server that verified the order. The application server in turn communicated to an SMB file server (OS/2) where the actual data was stored. Figure 8.27 shows a simplified view of the situation. Even though the potential problem areas had expanded, I had more choices of where to begin my analysis.

Because I was already on site at the corporate campus, I chose to begin the analysis right in the middle of the network between the remote user and the end file server. By placing the analyzer on the application server's segment, I was able to capture data to and from the mainframe/application server as well as to and from the application server/file server. This gave me the most analysis "bang for the buck" to begin with.

I didn't have to wait long for the problem to begin to show itself. There were occasions when the application server waited 10 seconds or more for a reply from the file server. Could the file server really be taking this long to reply?

To answer that, I moved the analyzer to the file server's segment and captured sufficient packets to look at a number of "delayed responses." The file server was actually responding with two packets: one immediately, and one about 10 seconds later. This meant that the first packet never made it back to the application server: a router that connected the application and file server segments together was dropping packets causing the upper layer protocols to time out and recover.

The protocol in use was SMB over NetBIOS over LLC. Because there is no transport layer for recovery, the recovery is done by SMB. Whenever the application server didn't acknowledge data from the file server, the file server's SMB process would resend the packet. Unfortunately someone had changed the default SMB retry timer on all of the file servers to 10 seconds, thinking it would cut down on the number of SMB retransmission packets (the default value is 1 second).

Unfortunately the effect was to merely delay the response time to the end-user by 10 or 20 seconds and not cut down on the number of retransmissions! Throughout the day, the network was quite busy and a packet being resent in 1 second had about the same chance of being dropped as a packet that was resent in 10 seconds. The short-term solution was to lower the retransmission timer. Longer term, the busy router needed attention.

There were several reasons why the router was dropping packets during heavy peak loads, including inadequate buffer memory and issues surrounding packet queuing and prioritization. Possible solutions include to better tune and optimize the existing router, upgrade the router's memory or processor, or install a second router to share the load. Time was of the essence and the customer didn't feel that additional memory was feasible with their particular router configuration, so a second router was installed. This offloaded the busy router and packet drops were far less frequent.

8.4.3 Case Study: Poor Throughput

This case study began with yet another "the network is slow" complaint from an end-user. This time, the issue was throughput, not response time. The user noticed that transferring files from an NT file server would sometimes be very quick—a one megabyte file in a second or two—and sometimes be very slow, taking several seconds. The effective throughput was about 90 Kbytes per second, well below the theoretical maximum of 1250 Kbytes/second of the Ethernet the user was on. The problem appeared to be random in nature and could happen at any time of the day. When the problem occurred, it was repeatable for up to several minutes to an hour or so.

The next time the user experienced the problem, I used a protocol analyzer to capture a trace of the user dragging and dropping a file from the file server to their desktop. A snapshot of what I observed is shown in Figure 8.28. Notice that every time the user requests a block of data from the server there's a delay before the first packet of that block is received. The remaining packets in the block are received with little delay.

For example, after the SMB "read block multiplexed" request to read 14,120 bytes of data in packet 15, there's a delay of 112 milliseconds before packet 16 is returned from the server. Similar delays are experienced after the other SMB read request packets. Either there's a large amount of latency between the workstation and server or something else is going on.

From the detail of a server response packet in Figure 8.28, you can see that SMB is running over IPX. Having an IPX hop count of 0 tells me that there's no router between the user and the server because the analyzer captured the packet on the same segment as the user. The server and user also have the same IPX network number, hex 1000. (This can happen with an NT server. With a NetWare server, the server uses its unique internal IPX network number in the reply packet, not the cable number.)

With no hops, chances are the server is not located on a remote WAN. It could, however, be on the other side of a switch implementing transparent bridging. Consulting the network documentation, I discovered that the user and file server were connected to the same physical Ethernet segment! By taking a closer look at the trace, you can see how consistently the packets are returning to the workstation (by observing the delta time between the response packets). This tells me that there's very little contention (other traffic) on the Ethernet. Therefore I concluded that something must have been happening at the server to affect the response time.

Going to the server and looking at the NT task manager, I saw nothing obvious that was chewing up CPU cycles. There were no major applications running in the background, such as an SQL database or a router. Maybe it was a slow hard drive, but I've never seen a server consistently take one-tenth of a second (100 milliseconds) to read data from the hard drive and transmit it to the network.

After not finding any immediate problem at the server, I had the user transfer another file. This time, the file transfer was approximately 900 Kbytes/second or a factor of ten faster. Thinking back, it dawned on me that there was an application running on the server as we approached it—the 3D pipes screen saver. This application uses Open GL graphics drivers that tend

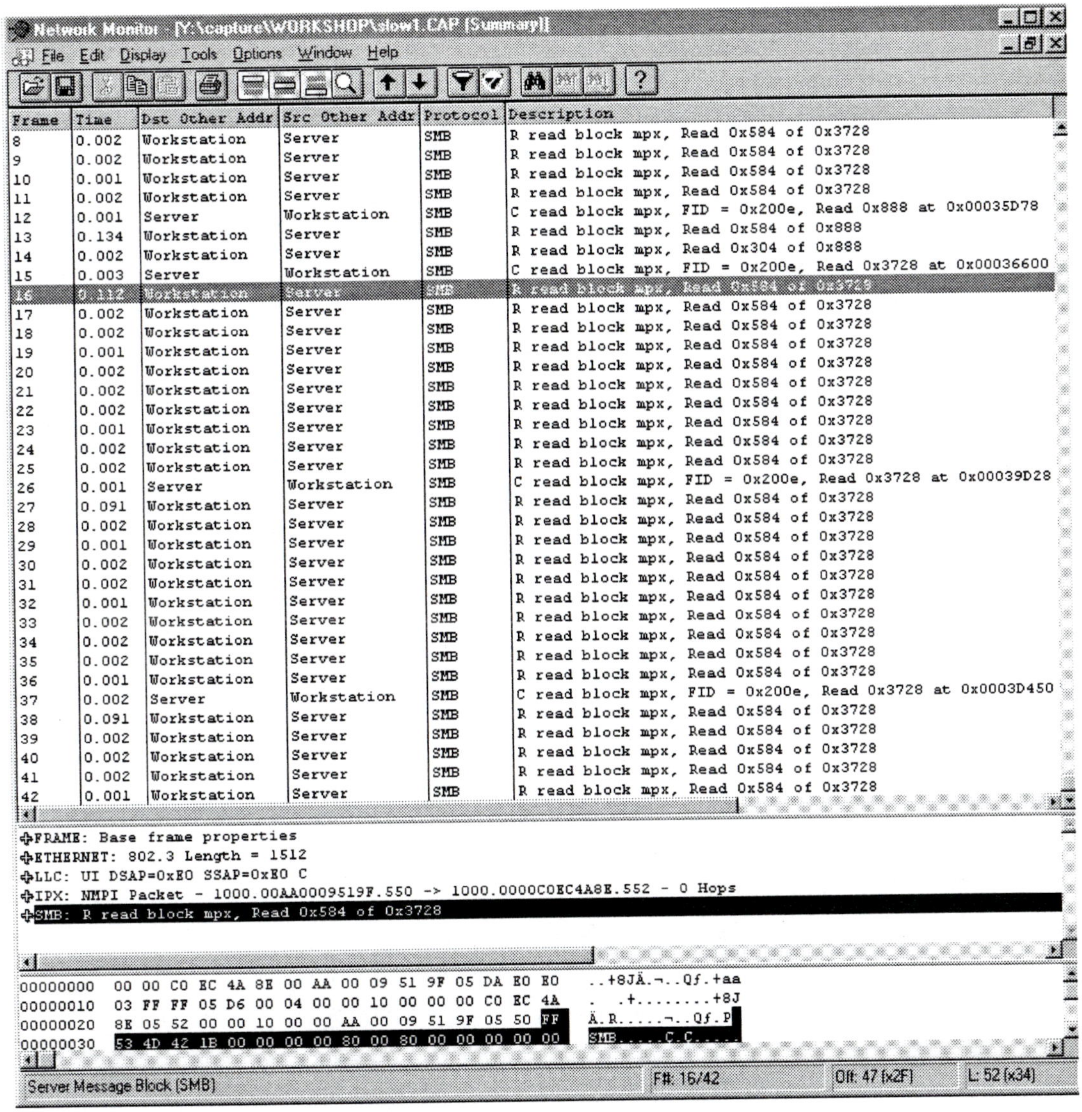

FIGURE 8.28 Long server response time affects file transfer throughput.

to chew up a lot of CPU time. Apparently a certain NT administrator thought it was a cool screen saver. Whenever it kicked in, user response time suffered, primarily on file transfers.

The solution? Simply change the screen saver to a blank screen. The server was also NT 3.51. The impact is not as severe on NT 4.0, but do not run complex screen savers on your servers!

I once wrote a column in a major networking magazine about my experience with this problem called something like "The World's Easiest Server Optimization!" In essence, all it took was one keystroke to increase the throughput by a factor of ten. Longer term, of course, I changed the screen saver.

In Chapter 9, I'll revisit this problem and explain how you can analyze the throughput in detail. I'll also take a look at how to measure the response time of not only a server, but a client as well.

8.4.4 The MS Browser Protocol

In a Microsoft SMB server environment, the user must either know the name of the server or browse the network using the Network Neighborhood feature of Windows 95/98/NT. When a server name is known, the user can type in the NET USE command to map a server's drive to a local drive.

SMB has strong ties to NetBIOS with its naming scheme. An SMB server such as Windows NT can have up to a 16-character name, with the sixteenth character reserved for identifying the function of the name (refer to Chapter 6 for more details about NetBIOS name functions). Access in a network resource is as simple as specifying \\<network name><16th>\path in the NET USE command.

Alternatively, the user can select a server from the Network Neighborhood. The Microsoft Browser protocol (not to be confused with an Internet browser) keeps track of the servers that are shown to the user in the Network Neighborhood or when using the NET VIEW command. NT servers and Windows workstations with sharing enabled will be listed. A workstation or server can play one of the following roles in the MS Browser protocol:

1. Non-Browser servers are those that do not maintain browse lists but announce themselves periodically to the Master Browser.
2. Potential Browsers can become a Browser server if needed.
3. Backup Browsers maintain a browse list of servers and domains that are retrieved from the Master Browser.
4. Master Browsers receive server and domain announcements, send browse lists to Backup Browsers, respond to clients requesting a browse list, promote Potential Browsers to Backup Browsers, and announce the domain to inform the Master Browsers of other domains.
5. Preferred Master Browsers are Backup Browsers with a bias to become the Master Browser in the event of a Browser election.
6. A Domain Master Browser is the PDC of a domain and has the highest priority in becoming the Master Browser.

There is at least one Master Browser on a workgroup/domain and one Backup Browser for every 32 workstations and servers in that workgroup/domain. For TCP/IP browsing, there is one Master Browser for every IP subnet. For IPX and NetBEUI, there is only one Master Browser for the entire workgroup/domain.

If a Master Browser can't be found such as when a user clicks on the Network Neighborhood, an election takes place to elect a new Master Browser. These elections take place using the special NetBIOS name of <domain><1E>, where <1E> is the sixteenth NetBIOS character, using subnet broadcasts. From highest to lowest, the following operating systems have priority in becoming the Master Browser: PDC, NT Server, Windows 95/98, Windows for Workgroups.

> **!**
>
> When having intermittent resource list problems with the Network Neighborbood, set your analyzer to look for NetBIOS names with a suffix character of <1E>. Reasons for forced browser elections include that a client cannot find the Master Browser at startup; that a client detects that a Master Browser has disappeared; or an NT server starts (i.e., a preferred Master Browser) on the network.

Servers, including workstations that are sharing resources, announce their presence every 12 minutes to the NetBIOS name of <domain> with a sixteenth-character suffix of <1D> in an IP subnet broadcast. The Master Browser uses these broadcasts to build the browse list. The Master Browser also maintains lists of other domains with their associated Master Browsers.

Because a failed server stops announcing itself, it will eventually be removed from a browse list. This could take as long as 51 minutes: three 12-minute announcement cycles plus up to 15 minutes for the backup browsers to retrieve the updated browse list from the Master Browser. Thus a user may see a server in the Network Neighborhood for up to 51 minutes after it "died."

When a browse list request is made from a client, a "Get Backup List Request" is sent to the Master Browser, which returns a list of Browser servers for the local subnet (for IP; with IPX and NetBEUI, a list of Browser servers is returned that services all of NetBEUI or IPX). The client then selects three browsers from the list and stores them for future use. When a client browse list is required, the client contacts one of the three browse servers.

8.4.5 Case Study: Non-broadcast Packet Storm Melts Network

The topology of the network in this case study consisted of a hundred or so Token Ring segments interconnected by workgroup switches and backbone routers. Users were migrating from older versions of Windows to Windows

NT 4.0, with well over 2000 workstations recently converted or newly deployed and more on the way. During this migration, users began experiencing intermittent problems such as dropped printer connections.

Using two protocol analyzers, I captured packets simultaneously on both the printer server and user rings and discovered that packets were being dropped by workgroup switches. Even though the higher layer protocols attempted to recover, successively dropped packets for each recovery attempt led to print time-outs and disconnects from print queues located on file servers. But was the switch to blame?

During this time, I also noticed something very peculiar: A large number of NetBIOS "Name Recognized" packets from all over the campus were sent via source routing back to a given workstation. These packet storms were not "broadcast storms" and did not originate from one source, making the problem somewhat difficult to diagnose.

By watching a number of rings longer term, it was determined that this phenomenon was occurring every few minutes, but each time the burst was sent to a different workstation. The NetBIOS "Name Recognized" packet contained the name "NTCORP," the main domain name that most of the users were members of. The sixteenth character of the name (also called the name suffix; see Chapter 6) was hex 1E, a group name used to elect a Master Browser.

In one such trace during this flood of packets, I was fortunate to discover that a workstation had broadcast a "Find Name" of NTCORP with a suffix of hex 1D, which is used to access a Master Browser. The Primary Domain Controller, which functions as a Master Browser by default master election criteria, responded. According to my analyzer, the workstation then attempted what looked like a \MAILSLOT\BROWSE SMB connection with a "Get Backup List Request" to the Master Browser, but the Master Browser never responded.

> **❶**
>
> Sometimes it takes more than one protocol analyzer to realize what's going on inside a trace. My first analyzer decoded the workstation packet sent to the Master Browser as an SMB "\MAILSLOT\BROWSE" packet with no further detail. Converting the file to a different protocol analyzer revealed that the packet was a "Get Backup List Request" to the Master Browser.

Not seeing a response from the Master Browser caused the workstation to subsequently send out a "Find Name" of NTCORP with the suffix 1E. Further, the "Find Name" was broadcast as an IPX Type 20 (also known as an IPX WAN broadcast; refer to Chapter 4 for more details). Luckily there were no routers running in parallel, so there was never a problem of more than one Type 20 packet appearing on each remote segment.

On the down side, every NT workstation is a "potential browser" by default, and responds to the hex 1E elect Master Browser request, generating well over 6000 return packets! Why 6000? Call it classic NetBIOS broadcasting—in the Microsoft implementation, the workstation sends out 3 "Find Name" requests. The broadcasts were source routed to the 2000 or so NT workstations (in an Ethernet layer 2 switched environment, they would be forwarded to all ports) and thus 2000 $\times$ 3, or 6000, packets were returned.

What I was seeing was part of the Microsoft "Browse" (not to be confused with Internet browsing) or MS Browse protocol at work. When using IPX, a workstation first locates the Master Browser using the NetBIOS "Find Name" hex 1D IPX broadcast, then asks for a list of backup browsers (usually requesting up to four because the Master Browser maintains a list of one backup browser for every 32 workstations in a domain). The workstation then establishes a session with a backup browser server to retrieve the actual resource information that appears in the user's Network Neighborhood.

The problem with this network was that sometimes the Master Browser never responded to the "Get Backup List Request" packets, causing the workstation to broadcast the "Elect Master Browser" packet (see Figure 8.29) which in turn caused the 6000+ packet response. These response storms were overwhelming the switches, causing them to drop packets. With enough successive "response storms," other packets were caught in the storm and dropped, with some unlucky users losing their print connections. Having identified the root of the problem, I now had to complete the analysis and come up with potential solutions.

At the end of the response packet storm, the workstation sent out an MS Browse "Force Election" packet. Immediately following this packet were yet another burst from hundreds of NT workstations (that are potential browsers) participating in the Master Browser election process. Eventually the Primary Domain Controller (PDC) wins the election and the network settles down for a while.

Several solutions were possible such as removing the NWLINK driver from the NT workstations and relying instead on Novell's Client32 for IPX (because there were still NetWare services the NT workstations had to access). Client32 does not broadcast NetBIOS packets like NWLINK. Another solution was to prevent NT workstations from being potential browsers (via a registry setting) and thus not participate in the browser elections.

My solution depended on another important piece of information about the MS Browse protocol. Microsoft documents the fact that each IP subnet has its own Master Browser. What they don't say is that for IPX, there is one Master Browser for *all* of IPX. For both protocols, there is a backup browser for every 32 workstations, but bear in mind that a workstation will always first request a list of backup browsers from the Master Browser.

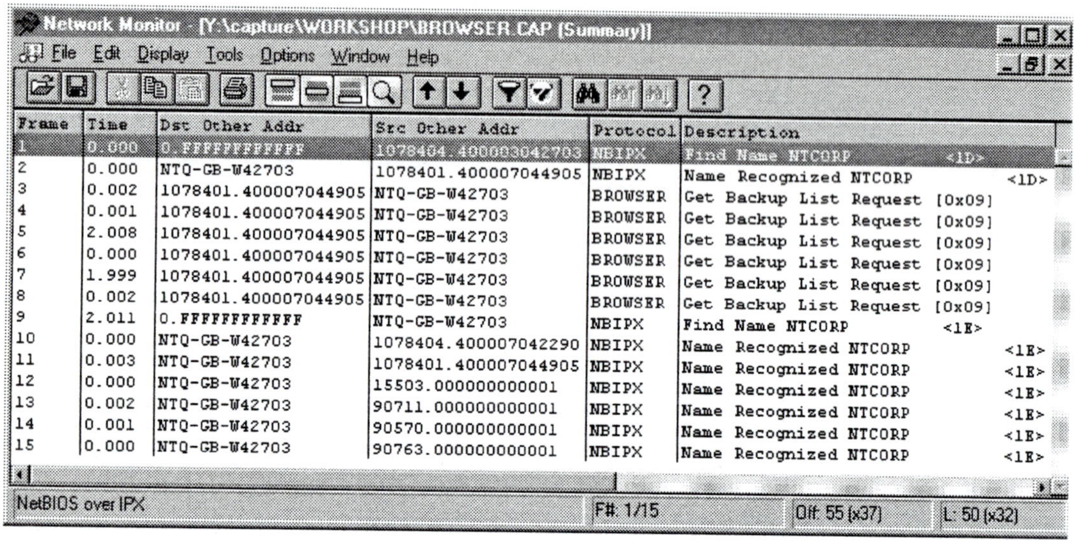

FIGURE 8.29 MS Browse problem.

In my client's network, the PDC was overwhelmed acting as *the* Master Browser for IPX. Because the PDC was located on the "far" side of the backbone and it was determined that no IPX resources needed to be accessed over the backbone, IPX Type 20 WAN broadcasts were simply filtered out at the router. This forced a Backup Domain Controller (BDC) located on the "near" side of the router to function as a Master Browser. Subsequent packet traces showed that the BDC responded just fine to IPX browse requests and the users no longer had the brief, but intense browse response packet storms. Not only that, but the users were no longer dropping their print connections.

This case study clearly shows how different application layer protocols can behave differently, depending on the underlying protocol stack. In this case, the nature of Microsoft's support for IPX resource browsing doesn't scale the same way as IP. With IP, each subnet has its own Master Browser. This is why I didn't want to turn off master browsing capability at every NT workstation. Then a BDC would be mandatory on each IP subnet in order for users to be able to browse the network in their Network Neighborhood. I could have left a couple of NT workstations with master browse capability turned on, but what if these machines were inadvertently turned off?

Another important lesson from this case study is that many network analysis tools out there are overly bent on looking for "broadcast storms" rather than serious problems like periodic "response storms" that are harder to detect and resolve.

Chapter   **9**

Measuring and Analyzing Throughput and Latency

9.1 Introduction

"The network is slow!" Sound all too familiar? This is probably the number one complaint I hear from end-users, second only to "The network is broken." Sometimes it seems that everything is blamed on the network. My favorite is the perennial question "Where's the 'any' key?" I also noted in the very first chapter that many of the problems that we diagnose with our analyzers can be traced back to the end-user's application or operating system.

This chapter will be teaching you powerful techniques for troubleshooting problems related to throughput and latency. At the same time, these techniques can be applied to establish performance baselines.

9.2 Characterizing the Application

More often than not your first task as a network analyst is to prove or disprove the user's complaint that the "network is slow." One way to start is to characterize the user's application to get an idea if you should focus your analysis efforts on latency, throughput, or a combination of the two.

Most applications fall into one of three categories: terminal emulation, client/server, or file transfer.

In the case of *terminal emulation,* the application can be characterized as generating small packets and having low output. With Telnet, for example, characters are sent to a host and echoed back by default. The packet output from the client is limited by how fast the user can type. In some cases, the user will send a line or a screen of text to the host, such as with 3270 terminal emulation. Your goal is optimize the network for minimal round-trip delay so that the network is not contributing significantly to the user-perceived response time. Leave that up to the host!

With *client/server*, small to medium packets are the norm with moderate output, depending on the complexity of the commands sent to the server and the amount of data returned to the client. These variables are greatly affected by the client/server architecture. The three major architectures are peer-to-peer, in which the client and server are interchangeable, two-tier, and three-tier. Figure 9.1 illustrates examples of two-tier and three-tier client/server architectures.

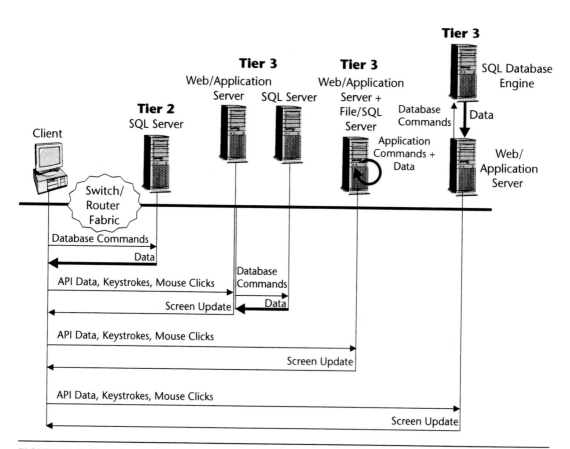

FIGURE 9.1 Two-tier and three-tier client/server architectures.

In a two-tier architecture, the client typically sends SQL commands to a SQL server, such as an Oracle, DB/2, Sybase, Informix, or Microsoft SQL Server. The server executes the SQL statements and returns data to the client. The client application then processes the data.

With a three-tier architecture, a client connects to an application server, which receives keystrokes and mouse clicks from the user. The application server interfaces with a SQL server or another application, which can coexist on the same machine, a computer connected over a high-speed pipe (such as Fibre Channel) or proprietary backbone, or a computer located elsewhere on the network. The application server processes the data and sends data in the form of screen updates back to the client.

Examples of three-tier architectures include SAP and WinFrame (or NT Terminal Server), also known as "thin clients." The former is built around a back-end database, whereas the latter is a way to turn an NT into a multiuser application processor and run off-the-shelf applications like Word and Excel for multiple users on one NT server. The applications become three-tier in a sense because the application and data are separated from the user. With SAP, clients communicate to an application server that runs in a machine such as an IBM RS/6000 that is tightly coupled to a database engine running on a separate RS/6000.

Although three-tier applications may be more expensive to implement in terms of initial capital investment, the bandwidth required to support clients is substantially lower. Unlike two-tier applications, all of the SQL commands and data stay local to the application server/database engine. This also makes three-tier applications more resilient to high latency networks such as frame relay. You'll discover why a bit later in this chapter.

The third major application area is *file transfer*. These applications are characterized by medium to large packets and high output. In this case, the goal is to optimize the application to use the MTU of the underlying network for maximum packet size. This minimizes the protocol overhead per packet and reduces the number of packets that switches, routers, and servers have to handle to transfer bulk data. Examples of applications include file transfers using FTP, NCP, and SMB protocols that were explored in Chapter 8.

9.3 Areas of Latency in WANs and LANs

Latency is essentially the amount of delay or time in getting a packet from point A to point B. The response time is the *round-trip* delay, or latency. Figure 9.2 represents various components in a network that contribute to latency.

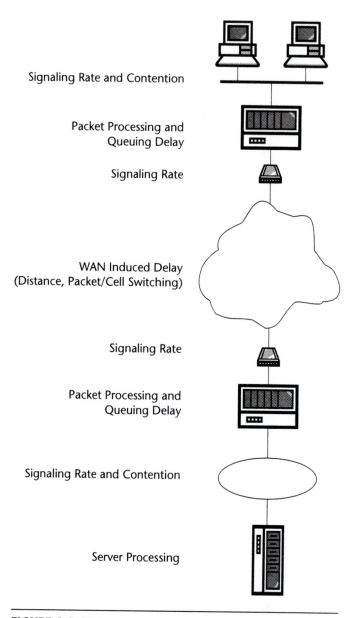

FIGURE 9.2 Various sources of latency or delay in a network.

If you are on a shared LAN (i.e., you do not have your own dedicated switched connection), there may be some delay due to waiting your turn to transmit the packet on the LAN. Once you are on the LAN, there is some amount of transmission delay, depending on the packet size and speed of the

LAN. From there, your packet may enter a switch or a router, in which there may be some further packet processing delay (such as filtering or looking up the destination address) and queuing delay if many packets are trying to get to one output port or the output port is slower than the input port.

In Figure 9.2, your next link is over a WAN. Here you induce further delay due to the transmission speed of the WAN, propagation delay due to the potentially large distance the packet has to travel geographically, and any cell or frame switching delay in the "cloud." Cell switching is faster when hopping over more than two switches because once the frame is turned into cells at the edge of the network, the cells can be immediately forwarded independently of each other. For example, if cell switch B sits between cell switches A and C in a network, switch B does not have to wait for the entire frame from A before forwarding to C as would be the case with frame relay.

Of course, if your WAN is a leased line, you don't have to worry about cell or frame switching delay—just the propagation delay.

Once the packet reaches the server, there may be additional delay due to server processing time. Here you get into issues of the server platform (operating system and hardware) and other processes/applications that are running concurrently. On its way back to the client, the first packet that the server returns will experience a similar delay as the original command packet from the client.

9.4 The "Latency Wedge"

If you were to visualize the round-trip delay of a command/reply packet pair at various points in your network, you would see something I've coined a "latency wedge," as illustrated in Figure 9.3. You can get a more precise picture by calculating the theoretical delay by hand, or better yet, by using a protocol analyzer.

In Figure 9.4, I used a spreadsheet to input and compute the round-trip delay over a frame relay that had 30 milliseconds of distance and switching delay (these number can be obtained from your frame relay provider, or you can measure it yourself by pinging between two routers at the opposite edges of a frame relay circuit, taking the best response time, and dividing by 2). A 30-millisecond one-way delay is typical for a regional frame relay; 5 milliseconds might be typical within a city and 60 or so milliseconds one-way across the United States.

In Figure 9.4, the first calculation is for a small 64-byte command packet followed by a small reply 64-byte packet, such as a Telnet character echo. The

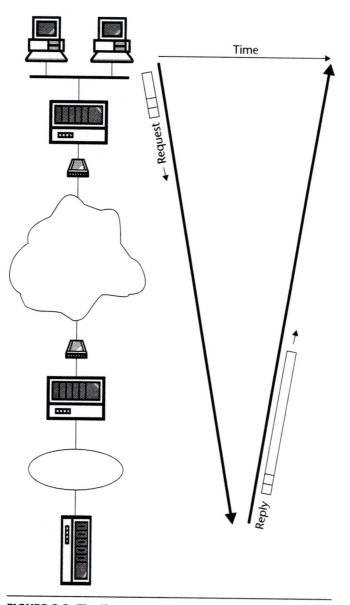

FIGURE 9.3 The "latency wedge."

second calculation is for a small 64-byte command packet followed by a larger 1024-byte packet.

The total round-trip delay is about 69 milliseconds for the first case compared to 130 milliseconds for the second. If you never did this exercise on

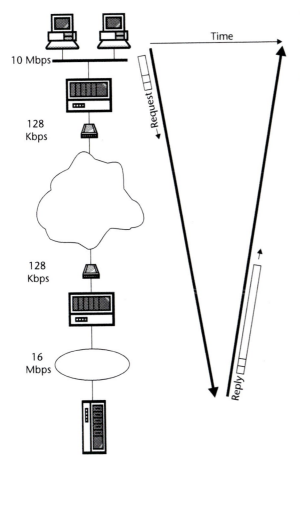

Round-Trip Latency Calculation (in milliseconds)

64-Byte Request Packet

10 Mbps Ethernet	0.051
Router Processing & Queuing Delay	0.010
128 Kbps Serial	4.000
WAN Induced Delay	30.000
Router Processing & Queuing Delay	0.010
16 Mbps Token Ring	0.032

64-Byte Reply Packet

Server Processing	1.000
16 Mbps Token Ring	0.032
Router Processing & Queuing Delay	0.010
128 Kbps Serial	4.000
WAN Induced Delay	30.000
Router Processing & Queuing Delay	0.010
10 Mbps Ethernet	0.051
Total (milliseconds)	69.206
Total (seconds)	0.069

Round-Trip Latency Calculation (in milliseconds)

64-Byte Request Packet

10 Mbps Ethernet	0.051
Router Processing & Queuing Delay	0.010
128 Kbps Serial	4.000
WAN Induced Delay	30.000
Router Processing & Queuing Delay	0.010
16 Mbps Token Ring	0.032

1024-Byte Reply Packet

Server Processing	1.000
16 Mbps Token Ring	0.512
Router Processing & Queuing Delay	0.010
128 Kbps Serial	64.000
WAN Induced Delay	30.000
Router Processing & Queuing Delay	0.010
10 Mbps Ethernet	0.819
Total (milliseconds)	130.454
Total (seconds)	0.130

FIGURE 9.4 Computing latency on paper.

paper, you might assume that if you double your frame relay bandwidth you might halve the response time.

Suppose you double your frame relay to 256 Kbps and recompute. Figure 9.5 shows the results. You've cut only 4 milliseconds off your small packet response time and 34 milliseconds off your larger packet response time. So it didn't help your terminal emulation or three-tier application too much, but it did help with your file transfer.

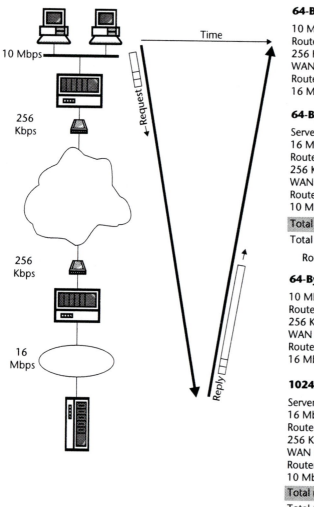

Round-Trip Latency Calculation (in milliseconds)

64-Byte Request Packet

10 Mbps Ethernet	0.051
Router Processing & Queuing Delay	0.010
256 Kbps Serial	2.000
WAN Induced Delay	30.000
Router Processing & Queuing Delay	0.010
16 Mbps Token Ring	0.032

64-Byte Reply Packet

Server Processing	1.000
16 Mbps Token Ring	0.032
Router Processing & Queuing Delay	0.010
256 Kbps Serial	2.000
WAN Induced Delay	30.000
Router Processing & Queuing Delay	0.010
10 Mbps Ethernet	0.051
Total (milliseconds)	65.206
Total (seconds)	0.065

Round-Trip Latency Calculation (in milliseconds)

64-Byte Request Packet

10 Mbps Ethernet	0.051
Router Processing & Queuing Delay	0.010
256 Kbps Serial	2.000
WAN Induced Delay	30.000
Router Processing & Queuing Delay	0.010
16 Mbps Token Ring	0.032

1024-Byte Reply Packet

Server Processing	1.000
16 Mbps Token Ring	0.512
Router Processing & Queuing Delay	0.010
256 Kbps Serial	32.000
WAN Induced Delay	30.000
Router Processing & Queuing Delay	0.010
10 Mbps Ethernet	0.819
Total (milliseconds)	96.454
Total (seconds)	0.096

FIGURE 9.5 Recomputing latency after doubling the WAN bandwidth.

9.4.1 Case Study: The Slow Remote

Around the time frame relay started to deploy, I was called out to troubleshoot a performance problem between a remote site and headquarters. A two-tier client/server application was developed using a popular human resources application, which consisted of a database package, middleware, and APIs for interfacing to a higher level language such as Visual Basic. The application ran great within the local headquarters infrastructure and okay at a remote site connected via a leased line, but it failed miserably at a remote site over frame relay—the response time was in the tens of seconds. Doubling the frame relay CIR from 128 to 256 Kbps showed little improvement. Because frame relay was already being rolled out in lieu of leased lines due to the "lower cost" of the bandwidth, something had to be done about the response time.

Because the problem was only at the remote site, it seemed like a logical place to start the analysis. Unfortunately my analyzer at the time did not have SQL decodes, so it was difficult to figure out just what the user was doing when looking at a trace. All I could see were TCP/IP packets going back and forth between the client and SQL server, so I resorted to the following trick:

> ❗
>
> When your analyzer doesn't decode certain application layer protocols such as SQL transactions or proprietary applications, go out to the end-user—get out of the (wiring) closet!—and place your analyzer right next to the end-user. Find a tap on the same hub as the user or temporarily use a pocket hub. Set a capture filter on the workstation's DLC address and begin capturing. During the queries, write down the beginning and ending packet numbers that your analyzer says it has captured. This way you can later go into the display buffer and analyze the number, size, and delay characteristics of all the packets for a given transaction such as when the user clicked on the "next record" button.

Having done so, I noticed small command/response packets with a consistent 70- to 80-millisecond delay between them. It appeared that most packet exchanges required waiting on a single packet. Looking at the ASCII in the TCP data gave me a further clue—most of the one-to-one packet exchanges were SQL statements being sent, then acknowledged by the SQL database server. Because many of the "simple user clicks" required hundreds of SQL statements to be executed, the response time was horrific.

Think about it for a moment. If the round-trip delay was 100 milliseconds (or 1/10 of a second) due to distance and switching no matter what the bandwidth, the most SQL commands the client could send would be 10 per second! If it took, say, three hundred SQL statements and/or packet exchanges to get actual data down from the server, the minimal delay would be 300 packets/10 packets per second, or 30 seconds. This was the essence of what was happening. On a LAN with little delay, dealing with 300 packets is usually not a huge deal.

At the time, none of the solutions to this problem were appealing, including completely rewriting the application for a three-tier platform from a different vendor, going back to leased lines at three times the monthly cost of frame relay, rewriting the application to bypass the human resources "middleware" to improve the efficiency, or beating on the vendor of the human resources software. We beat on the software vendor and their response was basically, "Huh? We didn't design it for WANs." Three years later, the vendor comes out with a three-tier solution. Surprise, surprise. Meanwhile, the remote users had to suffer for a while.

9.5 Analyzing Latency

The general technique for analyzing network latency using a protocol analyzer can be summarized as follows:

1. Analyze from the workstation segment for the overall round-trip delay.
2. Filter on a selected source/destination network address pair.
3. Pick packet pairs for analysis such as ping packets, client command/server response packets, or LLC polls.
4. Use the delta time on the reply packet in your analyzer's summary display.
5. For accuracy, use packets close to or smaller than 64 bytes. Remember that you are not trying to measure the bandwidth at this point.
6. Take several dozen samples!

By taking several samples, you can establish a baseline even when the network is fairly busy because the sample with the *lowest* delta time is probably the closest to your best case response time.

Next, compute the average delta time over several samples. The difference between the average time and the best case time depends on the contention for all network components between the client and server. By computing this weekly at a set time (such as 10:00 A.M. every Monday morning), you can establish long-term baselines and trending.

This is a very powerful baseline. Shifts in the best case response time may indicate a change in your network infrastructure. In one case, a frame relay provider changed the path for a given Permanent Virtual Circuit (PVC), resulting in a *higher* best case response time. On the other hand, a steady best case time but an increase (or decrease) in the average response time may indicate a shift in network users or applications.

Network Monitor - [c:\Capture\workshop\FRPING.CAP [Summary]]

File Edit Display Tools Options Window Help

Frame	Time	Dst MAC Addr	Src MAC Addr	Protocol	Description
5	0.081	Cisco 014E8F	3COM 003830	ICMP	Echo, From 158.48.160.20 To 158.48.16.02
6	0.065	3COM 003830	Cisco 014E8F	ICMP	Echo Reply, To 158.48.160.20 From 158.48.16.02
13	0.959	Cisco 014E8F	3COM 003830	ICMP	Echo, From 158.48.160.20 To 158.48.16.02
14	0.065	3COM 003830	Cisco 014E8F	ICMP	Echo Reply, To 158.48.160.20 From 158.48.16.02
23	1.017	Cisco 014E8F	3COM 003830	ICMP	Echo, From 158.48.160.20 To 158.48.16.02
24	0.070	3COM 003830	Cisco 014E8F	ICMP	Echo Reply, To 158.48.160.20 From 158.48.16.02
31	0.957	Cisco 014E8F	3COM 003830	ICMP	Echo, From 158.48.160.20 To 158.48.16.02
32	0.063	3COM 003830	Cisco 014E8F	ICMP	Echo Reply, To 158.48.160.20 From 158.48.16.02
39	0.960	Cisco 014E8F	3COM 003830	ICMP	Echo, From 158.48.160.20 To 158.48.16.02
40	0.061	3COM 003830	Cisco 014E8F	ICMP	Echo Reply, To 158.48.160.20 From 158.48.16.02
47	1.019	Cisco 014E8F	3COM 003830	ICMP	Echo, From 158.48.160.20 To 158.48.16.02
48	0.067	3COM 003830	Cisco 014E8F	ICMP	Echo Reply, To 158.48.160.20 From 158.48.16.02
57	0.960	Cisco 014E8F	3COM 003830	ICMP	Echo, From 158.48.160.20 To 158.48.16.02
58	0.063	3COM 003830	Cisco 014E8F	ICMP	Echo Reply, To 158.48.160.20 From 158.48.16.02
65	0.962	Cisco 014E8F	3COM 003830	ICMP	Echo, From 158.48.160.20 To 158.48.16.02
66	0.068	3COM 003830	Cisco 014E8F	ICMP	Echo Reply, To 158.48.160.20 From 158.48.16.02
73	1.011	Cisco 014E8F	3COM 003830	ICMP	Echo, From 158.48.160.20 To 158.48.16.02
74	0.076	3COM 003830	Cisco 014E8F	ICMP	Echo Reply, To 158.48.160.20 From 158.48.16.02
81	0.952	Cisco 014E8F	3COM 003830	ICMP	Echo, From 158.48.160.20 To 158.48.16.02
82	0.070	3COM 003830	Cisco 014E8F	ICMP	Echo Reply, To 158.48.160.20 From 158.48.16.02
89	0.955	Cisco 014E8F	3COM 003830	ICMP	Echo, From 158.48.160.20 To 158.48.16.02
90	0.065	3COM 003830	Cisco 014E8F	ICMP	Echo Reply, To 158.48.160.20 From 158.48.16.02
97	1.014	Cisco 014E8F	3COM 003830	ICMP	Echo, From 158.48.160.20 To 158.48.16.02
98	0.064	3COM 003830	Cisco 014E8F	ICMP	Echo Reply, To 158.48.160.20 From 158.48.16.02
105	0.963	Cisco 014E8F	3COM 003830	ICMP	Echo, From 158.48.160.20 To 158.48.16.02
106	0.064	3COM 003830	Cisco 014E8F	ICMP	Echo Reply, To 158.48.160.20 From 158.48.16.02
113	0.960	Cisco 014E8F	3COM 003830	ICMP	Echo, From 158.48.160.20 To 158.48.16.02
114	0.073	3COM 003830	Cisco 014E8F	ICMP	Echo Reply, To 158.48.160.20 From 158.48.16.02

Look for the minimum, maximum, and average response time.

FIGURE 9.6 Analyzing frame relay latency using PING.

For consistency, you may choose to run a simple application like PING to gather your data. At one site I set up a PING from a workstation on the same segment as a router servicing the frame relay and pinged simultaneously to several remote routers. About an hour's worth of packets were captured from the workstation's segment and saved for later analysis. By repeating this baseline at a later date, I was able to spot a shift in one of the frame relay PVCs as mentioned above.

Figure 9.6 shows a snapshot of a PING over frame relay trace. A capture filter was set on the workstation's IP address while the workstation was pinging for several minutes to several remote routers. By filtering on a specific router in the capture buffer display, I was able to characterize the response time during this capture. The consistency of the response time (around 60 to 70 milliseconds) in this particular trace told me that I pretty much had the

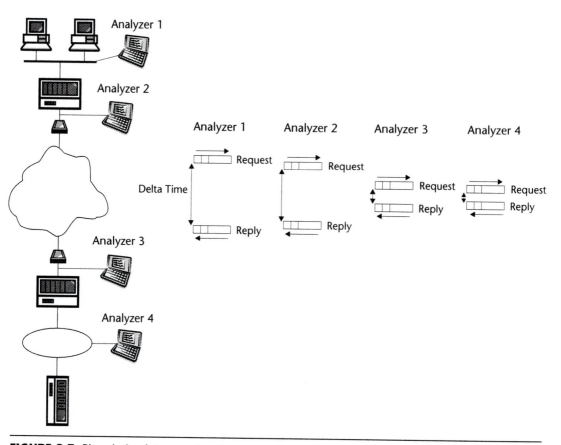

FIGURE 9.7 Pinpointing latency using the protocol analyzer.

frame relay to myself. In a heavily loaded network, you would see greater fluctuations in response time.

To further pinpoint the latency, you can move your analyzer around or use multiple protocol analyzers, as shown in Figure 9.7. By once again examining the best delta times between a command and reply packet, you can get a good feel for where the latency bottleneck is. In Figure 9.7, the biggest drop is between analyzers 2 and 3, placed on either side of a WAN.

9.6 Analyzing Throughput

Users may also complain that "the network is slow" when the hourglass stays up for a long time after they drag and drop a file from a server to their desktop, or vice versa. Once again, you need to analyze the file transfer to see just how bad (or good) the throughput really is.

One of the first things I do in this situation is to mentally compute what the maximum theoretical throughput might be under ideal conditions. If the user is on a 10 Mbps Ethernet, I'll take that bandwidth and divide by 8 bits/byte to end up with 1,250,000 bytes per second, or just over a megabyte per second. Next, I'll take a snapshot of the throughput using the following generalized steps:

1. Use any segment along the path between the workstation and server. The overall throughput will not be higher than the slowest link between user and server, so it really doesn't matter where you start the analysis.
2. Filter on a selected source/destination network address pair.
3. Use cumulative time and cumulative bytes in the summary display. If this is not possible with your analyzer (talk to your vendor!), use absolute time and look at the file read or write offsets as an alternative to computing how many bytes were transferred over time.
4. Use a file transfer for analysis such as FTP, NFS, NCP, Packet Burst, or SMB.
5. For accuracy in determining the average and best possible throughput, use packets close to the maximum MTU of the underlying network segment.
6. Take several samples over a handful of packets.

The last step is important. To put it another way, compute the throughput over 20 to 30 consecutive packets at a time to see what the best case throughput is during those short intervals. Taking the entire interval from the file open to the file close will give you the overall average throughput.

Just like computing latency, the difference between the best case "burst" and the average depends on the contention for all network components between the server and workstation. Perform this exercise weekly at a given time for long-term trending.

Let's say you analyze a file transfer from the user on the 10 Mbps Ethernet segment and determine that the average throughput is around 150 Kbytes per second. Because this is slower than our theoretical maximum of 1250 Kbytes per second by almost a factor of ten, the user may have a valid complaint. If our shorter interval best case throughput were 800 Kbytes per second or so, I might suspect heavy utilization by many users for a network resource such as a LAN segment or server.

On the other hand, if the short interval best case was only 160 Kbytes per second, I might suspect a smaller pipe somewhere in the network. If I consult the network documentation and see that there's a full T1 somewhere between the user and server, 160 Kbytes per second is actually pretty good. In rough numbers, 160 Kbytes/second * 8 bits/byte = 1.2 Mbits per second, or about 78% of a 1.544 Mbps T1. If users are constantly complaining about this level of performance for remote file transfer, one solution is to increase the WAN bandwidth, depending on how often large files need to be remotely transferred. You can also set the user's expectation that remote file transfers are not going to go as quickly as local ones.

The client itself could also be the culprit in low throughput problems. You can determine this by using the following tip.

> **!**
>
> When analyzing low throughput, don't rule out the client. Although much of the focus is on analyzing the response time by studying command and response packets, a similar technique can be applied for analyzing the client. Instead of command and response packets, focus on the delta time from the last response packet from a server and the next command packet from the client. This gives you some indication of how long the client is taking to process the information it received from the server.

I once encountered a situation in which the user increased their TCP window size to 64 Kbytes, allowing an NT server to blast back up to 64 Kbytes of data before a TCP acknowledgement with an open window was required from the workstation. Unfortunately the user had a rather slow hard drive, and the TCP window could not be opened back up until a 64 Kbyte block of data was written to the hard drive. This had the effect of a very fast burst from the server, then a wait, a very fast burst from the server, then a wait, and so on. Although the peak throughput was nearly the bandwidth of Ethernet, the average throughput was less than half. By lowering the window size to a more reasonable number such as 16 Kbytes, the average actually improved because there was more overlapping in simultaneous reading and writing between the server and client. Sometimes there's something to be said for attempting to "over-optimize" your network!

9.6.1 A Case Study Revisited

Remember the case study in Chapter 8 about the "one keystroke" optimization, the screen saver problem? Figure 9.8 shows another view, this time with an analyzer showing us the cumulative (or relative) time and cumulative bytes. As you can see from frames 58 to 93, we've only transferred about 48 Kbytes in about a half second, or about 96 Kbytes per second. As we learned

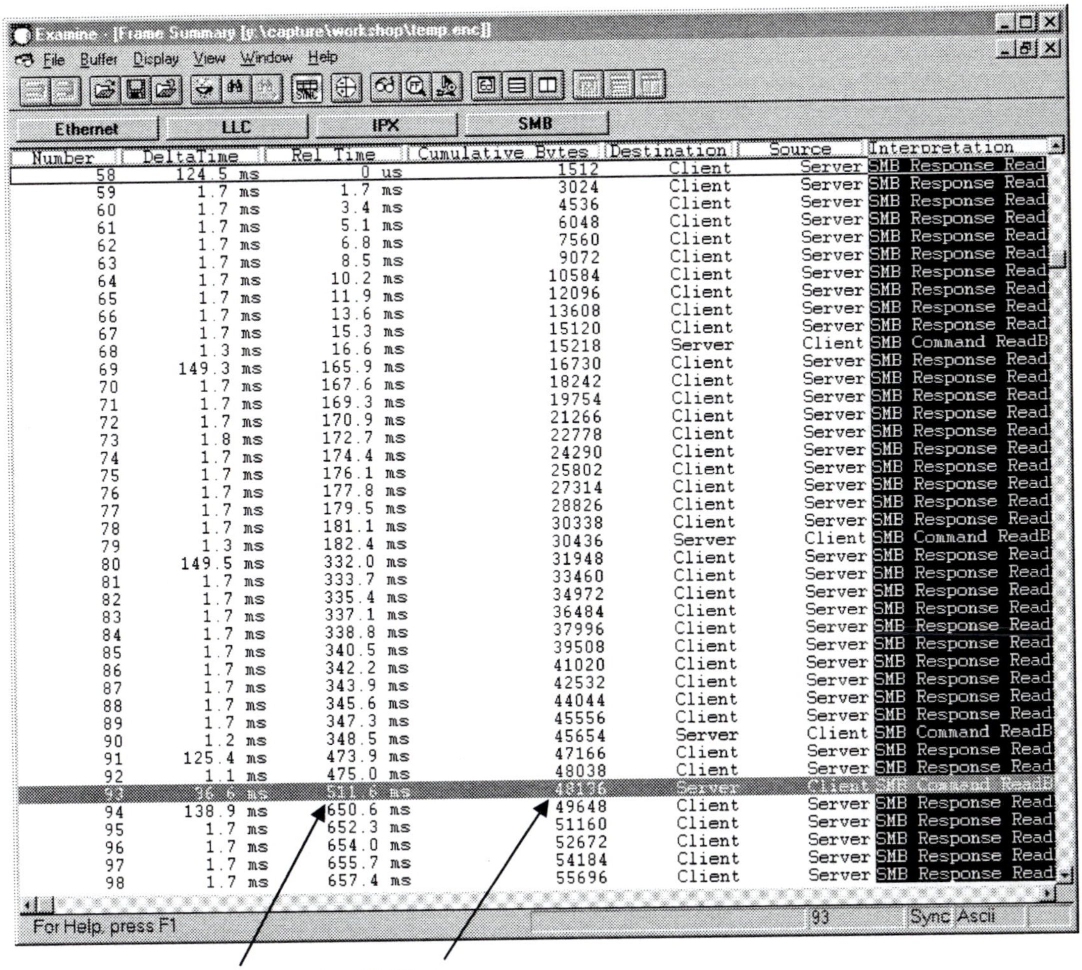

About 1/2 second to transfer 48 Kbytes.

FIGURE 9.8 Analyzing throughput.

from the case study, the cause was slow response from the server, as evidenced by the large delta time between a read request from the client and the first packet to return from the server.

9.6.2 Case Study: The Slow Remote II

Once again I encountered a situation where the customer was not getting the expected throughput over a frame relay circuit. Increasing the frame relay

SUMMARY	Rel Time	Bytes	CumByt	Dest	Source	Summary
M 460	0.000	73	73	Svr	WS	NCP C F=9297 0000 Read 1024 at 44032
461	0.184	1087	1160	WS	Svr	NCP R OK, 1024 bytes read
462	0.185	73	1233	Svr	WS	NCP C F=9297 0000 Read 1024 at 45056
463	0.371	1087	2320	WS	Svr	NCP R OK, 1024 bytes read
464	0.372	73	2393	Svr	WS	NCP C F=9297 0000 Read 1024 at 46080
465	0.571	1087	3480	WS	Svr	NCP R OK, 1024 bytes read
466	0.572	73	3553	Svr	WS	NCP C F=9297 0000 Read 1024 at 47104
467	0.756	1087	4640	WS	Svr	NCP R OK, 1024 bytes read
468	0.757	73	4713	Svr	WS	NCP C F=9297 0000 Read 1024 at 48128
469	0.948	1087	5800	WS	Svr	NCP R OK, 1024 bytes read
470	0.948	73	5873	Svr	WS	NCP C F=9297 0000 Read 1024 at 49152
471	**1.134**	1087	**6960**	WS	Svr	NCP R OK, 1024 bytes read
472	1.135	73	7033	Svr	WS	NCP C F=9297 0000 Read 1024 at 50176
473	1.320	1087	8120	WS	Svr	NCP R OK, 1024 bytes read
474	1.321	73	8193	Svr	WS	NCP C F=9297 0000 Read 1024 at 51200
475	1.513	1087	9280	WS	Svr	NCP R OK, 1024 bytes read
476	1.514	73	9353	Svr	WS	NCP C F=9297 0000 Read 1024 at 52224
477	1.696	1087	10440	WS	Svr	NCP R OK, 1024 bytes read
478	1.696	73	10513	Svr	WS	NCP C F=9297 0000 Read 1024 at 53248
479	1.881	1087	11600	WS	Svr	NCP R OK, 1024 bytes read

FIGURE 9.9 Analyzing throughput—"ping pong."

CIR from 128 to 256 Kbps did little to improve it. The local workstations in this situation were DOS-based NetWare clients transferring files from a remote NetWare server.

By capturing a trace on the same segments as the local users, I could see how the latency in the frame relay was throttling the throughput due to the DOS client's use of the NCP protocol to read files.

Chapter 8 noted that NCP has a packet window of one-to-one, which allows only one reply packet for each command packet. This meant that the client was limited to asking for only one packet at a time from a file, as illustrated in Figure 9.9. Because the round-trip delay factored in for every command/reply pair, the overall throughput was restricted. In Figure 9.9 the throughput is only around 6 Kbytes in 1 second. This converts to 48 Kbps, far short of the 256 Kbps of our frame relay.

This is one reason why Novell developed the packet burst protocol—to improve file transfer efficiency by allowing a "burst" of packets to be sent before the next command is required. This allows a WAN pipe to be filled with several packets without having to wait for the next command packet from the client, as shown in Figure 9.10. By merely upgrading the DOS client from a shell to a VLM and verifying that the server was packet burst capable (it was), I was able to substantially improve the file transfer.

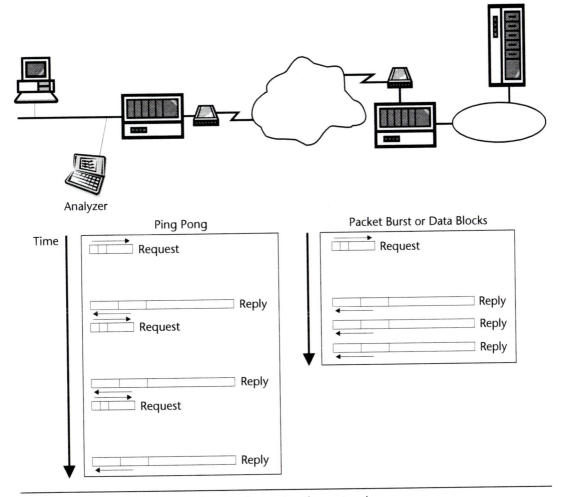

FIGURE 9.10 Maximizing throughput by improving the protocol.

Figure 9.11 shows the result. Now the customer is achieving 19 Kbytes per second over the same 256 Kbps circuit, about a 3× improvement from before. The frame relay bandwidth is now much more efficiently utilized.

Analyzing throughput and latency throughout your network will help you gain a better understanding of the limits of your infrastructure. Numbers that come up short require detailed network analysis to determine where the problem or bottleneck is. In some cases, you will discover high utilization or contention for critical network resources such as backbones, switches, or

SUMMARY	Rel Time	Bytes	CumByt	Dest	Source	Summary
M 473	0.000	113	113	Svr	WS	NCP C F=9797 Burst Read 22712 at 87736
474	0.417	1509	1622	WS	Svr	NCP R OK 1412 bytes read at 0
475	0.463	1509	3131	WS	Svr	NCP R 1420 bytes read at 1420
476	0.512	1509	4640	WS	Svr	NCP R 1420 bytes read at 2840
477	0.560	1509	6149	WS	Svr	NCP R 1420 bytes read at 4260
478	0.607	1509	7658	WS	Svr	NCP R 1420 bytes read at 5680
479	0.658	1509	9167	WS	Svr	NCP R 1420 bytes read at 7100
480	0.705	1509	10676	WS	Svr	NCP R 1420 bytes read at 8520
481	0.754	1509	12185	WS	Svr	NCP R 1420 bytes read at 9940
482	0.809	1509	13694	WS	Svr	NCP R 1420 bytes read at 11360
483	0.856	1509	15203	WS	Svr	NCP R 1420 bytes read at 12780
484	0.904	1509	16712	WS	Svr	NCP R 1420 bytes read at 14200
485	0.954	1509	18221	WS	Svr	NCP R 1420 bytes read at 15620
486	**1.005**	1509	**19730**	WS	Svr	NCP R 1420 bytes read at 17040
487	1.053	1509	21239	WS	Svr	NCP R 1420 bytes read at 18460
488	1.101	1509	22748	WS	Svr	NCP R 1420 bytes read at 19880
489	1.155	1509	24257	WS	Svr	NCP R 1420 bytes read at 21300
490	1.156	113	24370	Svr	WS	NCP C F=9797 Burst Read 19600 at 110448
491	1.344	241	24611	WS	Svr	NCP R OK 144 bytes read at 0
492	1.421	1122	25733	WS	Svr	NCP R 1033 bytes read at 152

FIGURE 9.11 Reanalyzing throughput—"packet burst."

routers. In other cases, you may see that the protocols are not working efficiently for a given application such as terminal emulation, client/server, or file transfer over a given topology, including a high-speed LAN or a highly latent WAN. Finally, as LAN technology gets faster and cheaper, you may discover that the client or server platforms themselves are simply unable to react fast enough to fully use the bandwidth. Then you get into platform issues such as processor, memory, bus, disk subsystems, and operating systems. For that, I'll leave it to you to delve into another book that deals with these kinds of issues in more detail.

Resources and References

Up-to-date links for numerous network analysis resources available on the Internet may be viewed via http://www.net3group.com/.

Links to the online Internet Requests for Comments (RFCs) may be found at the Internet Engineering Society, http://www.ietf.org/.

If your Network contains Ethernet, Token Ring, and/or uses LLC, you have no excuse not to have a copy of the IEEE 802.3, 802.5, and/or 802.2 standards, respectively. Point your browser to http://www.ieee.org for more details on obtaining a copy of these standards.

The following books and documents (listed by title) are highly recommended and are part of my personal library:

The Basic Guide to Frame Relay Networking, by the Frame Relay Forum, 1998.

> Need to come up to snuff in a hurry on frame relay? This little book contains all you need to know in less than 80 pages. Best of all, it's free for the asking from the Frame Relay Forum (http://www.frforum.com).

Computer Networks, Third Edition, by Andrew S. Tanenbaum, Prentice-Hall, 1996, ISBN 0133499456.

> A classic book on networking covering a wide variety of networking technologies.

DNS and BIND, Third Edition, by Paul Albitz and Cricket Liu, O'Reilly and Associates, 1998, ISBN 1565925122.

> One of my favorites covering the Domain Name System including a good discussion of the nslookup debugging tool for DNS.

Gigabit Ethernet: Technology and Applications for High-Speed LANs, by Rich Siefert, Addison Wesley Longman, 1998, ISBN 0201185539.

> Need to go fast? Then this is the book for you. Good in-depth technical coverage of technology behind the IEEE 802.3z 1000 Mbps MAC standard.

Interconnections: Bridges, Routers, Switchers, and Internetworking Protocols, Second Edition, by Radia Perlman, Addison Wesley Longman, 2000, ISBN 0201634481.

The book that explains how bridging (spanning tree) and routing protocols work. From the author of the spanning tree algorithm.

Internetworking Technologies Handbook, Second Edition, by Merilee Ford, H. Kim Lew et al., Cisco Press, 1998, ISBN 1578701023.

A great book for starting from ground zero. Introductory level material for virtually every LAN and WAN technology and protocol in use today, including sections on QoS, security, and network management.

ISDN and Broadband ISDN with Frame Relay and ATM, Fourth Edition, by William Stallings, Prentice-Hall, 1998, ISBN 0139737448.

The title pretty much says it all. The fourth edition has added coverage for DSL technologies.

Novell's Guide to LAN/WAN Analysis, by Laura A. Chappell, IDG Books Worldwide, 1998, ISBN 0764545086.

The *only* book dedicated to analysis of Novell's IPX/SPX and related protocols, including SAP, IPX RIP, and NCP.

OSPF: Anatomy of an Internet Routing Protocol, by John T. Moy, Addison Wesley Longman, 1998, ISBN 0201634724.

IP RIP is giving way to the Open Shortest Path First (OSPF) protocol and this book provides extensive coverage of OSPF and makes comparisons to RIP where applicable.

Protocols for X/Open PC Interworking: SMB Version 2, by The Open Group, 1992, ISBN 1872630456.

This is the officially published document on the Server Message Block protocol. For embellishments added by Microsoft for the Common Internet File System (CIFS) protocol, refer to the internet draft: draft-leach-cifs-v1-spec-01.txt.

The Simple Book: An Introduction to Networking Management, Revised Second Edition, by Marshall T. Rose, Prentice-Hall, 1996, ISBN 0134516591.

Written by the chairman of the SNMP working group, this book is probably the clearest and even entertaining text written about SNMP. Contains interesting opinions and insights about network management and of course, SNMP (through v2) in particular.

TCP/IP Addressing: Designing and Optimizing Your IP Addressing Scheme, by Buck Graham, AP Professional, 1997, ISBN 0122946308.

TCP/IP Illustrated, Volume I: The Protocols, by W. Richard Stevens, Addison Wesley Longman, 1994, ISBN 0201633469.

If there's *one* book to buy for learning details on TCP/IP, this is the one. Generous examples of TCP/IP and related protocols and trace dumps, too.

Troubleshooting IBM LAN/ATM Campus Networks, by IBM International Technical Support Organization, 1997, part number SG24-2105-00.

This 500+ page ATM document describes ATM concepts, ATM networking models, LAN Emulation (LANE), and ATM problem determination guidelines and isolation. Available as part of the IBM Red Books.

Troubleshooting TCP/IP, Third Edition, by Mark A. Miller, IDG Books Worldwide, 1999, ISBN 0764570129.

Be prepared to wade through a lot of text on TCP/IP, but Mark does include some interesting case studies. We need more books like this that chronicle our troubleshooting experiences.

Hex-Decimal-Binary Conversion Table

Hex	Dec	Binary	Hex	Dec	Binary	Hex	Dec	Binary	Hex	Dec	Binary
00	0	00000000	40	64	01000000	80	128	10000000	C0	192	11000000
01	1	00000001	41	65	01000001	81	129	10000001	C1	193	11000001
02	2	00000010	42	66	01000010	82	130	10000010	C2	194	11000010
03	3	00000011	43	67	01000011	83	131	10000011	C3	195	11000011
04	4	00000100	44	68	01000100	84	132	10000100	C4	196	11000100
05	5	00000101	45	69	01000101	85	133	10000101	C5	197	11000101
06	6	00000110	46	70	01000110	86	134	10000110	C6	198	11000110
07	7	00000111	47	71	01000111	87	135	10000111	C7	199	11000111
08	8	00001000	48	72	01001000	88	136	10001000	C8	200	11001000
09	9	00001001	49	73	01001001	89	137	10001001	C9	201	11001001
0A	10	00001010	4A	74	01001010	8A	138	10001010	CA	202	11001010
0B	11	00001011	4B	75	01001011	8B	139	10001011	CB	203	11001011
0C	12	00001100	4C	76	01001100	8C	140	10001100	CC	204	11001100
0D	13	00001101	4D	77	01001101	8D	141	10001101	CD	205	11001101
0E	14	00001110	4E	78	01001110	8E	142	10001110	CE	206	11001110
0F	15	00001111	4F	79	01001111	8F	143	10001111	CF	207	11001111
10	16	00010000	50	80	01010000	90	144	10010000	D0	208	11010000
11	17	00010001	51	81	01010001	91	145	10010001	D1	209	11010001
12	18	00010010	52	82	01010010	92	146	10010010	D2	210	11010010
13	19	00010011	53	83	01010011	93	147	10010011	D3	211	11010011
14	20	00010100	54	84	01010100	94	148	10010100	D4	212	11010100
15	21	00010101	55	85	01010101	95	149	10010101	D5	213	11010101
16	22	00010110	56	86	01010110	96	150	10010110	D6	214	11010110
17	23	00010111	57	87	01010111	97	151	10010111	D7	215	11010111
18	24	00011000	58	88	01011000	98	152	10011000	D8	216	11011000
19	25	00011001	59	89	01011001	99	153	10011001	D9	217	11011001
1A	26	00011010	5A	90	01011010	9A	154	10011010	DA	218	11011010
1B	27	00011011	5B	91	01011011	9B	155	10011011	DB	219	11011011

Hex	Dec	Binary	Hex	Dec	Binary	Hex	Dec	Binary	Hex	Dec	Binary
1C	28	00011100	5C	92	01011100	9C	156	10011100	DC	220	11011100
1D	29	00011101	5D	93	01011101	9D	157	10011101	DD	221	11011101
1E	30	00011110	5E	94	01011110	9E	158	10011110	DE	222	11011110
1F	31	00011111	5F	95	01011111	9F	159	10011111	DF	223	11011111
20	32	00100000	60	96	01100000	A0	160	10100000	E0	224	11100000
21	33	00100001	61	97	01100001	A1	161	10100001	E1	225	11100001
22	34	00100010	62	98	01100010	A2	162	10100010	E2	226	11100010
23	35	00100011	63	99	01100011	A3	163	10100011	E3	227	11100011
24	36	00100100	64	100	01100100	A4	164	10100100	E4	228	11100100
25	37	00100101	65	101	01100101	A5	165	10100101	E5	229	11100101
26	38	00100110	66	102	01100110	A6	166	10100110	E6	230	11100110
27	39	00100111	67	103	01100111	A7	167	10100111	E7	231	11100111
28	40	00101000	68	104	01101000	A8	168	10101000	E8	232	11101000
29	41	00101001	69	105	01101001	A9	169	10101001	E9	233	11101001
2A	42	00101010	6A	106	01101010	AA	170	10101010	EA	234	11101010
2B	43	00101011	6B	107	01101011	AB	171	10101011	EB	235	11101011
2C	44	00101100	6C	108	01101100	AC	172	10101100	EC	236	11101100
2D	45	00101101	6D	109	01101101	AD	173	10101101	ED	237	11101101
2E	46	00101110	6E	110	01101110	AE	174	10101110	EE	238	11101110
2F	47	00101111	6F	111	01101111	AF	175	10101111	EF	239	11101111
30	48	00110000	70	112	01110000	B0	176	10110000	F0	240	11110000
31	49	00110001	71	113	01110001	B1	177	10110001	F1	241	11110001
32	50	00110010	72	114	01110010	B2	178	10110010	F2	242	11110010
33	51	00110011	73	115	01110011	B3	179	10110011	F3	243	11110011
34	52	00110100	74	116	01110100	B4	180	10110100	F4	244	11110100
35	53	00110101	75	117	01110101	B5	181	10110101	F5	245	11110101
36	54	00110110	76	118	01110110	B6	182	10110110	F6	246	11110110
37	55	00110111	77	119	01110111	B7	183	10110111	F7	247	11110111
38	56	00111000	78	120	01111000	B8	184	10111000	F8	248	11111000
39	57	00111001	79	121	01111001	B9	185	10111001	F9	249	11111001
3A	58	00111010	7A	122	01111010	BA	186	10111010	FA	250	11111010
3B	59	00111011	7B	123	01111011	BB	187	10111011	FB	251	11111011
3C	60	00111100	7C	124	01111100	BC	188	10111100	FC	252	11111100
3D	61	00111101	7D	125	01111101	BD	189	10111101	FD	253	11111101
3E	62	00111110	7E	126	01111110	BE	190	10111110	FE	254	11111110
3F	63	00111111	7F	127	01111111	BF	191	10111111	FF	255	11111111

Glossary

AppleTalk   Apple Computer's proprietary networking protocol

AC (Access Control) Field   Used in the header of a Token Ring frame to distinguish a frame from a token and to provide prioritization

ack   Abbreviation for acknowledgment; a message sent back from the recipient of a packet confirming its receipt

API (Application Programming Interface)   A well-defined interface for applications to call a set of services, for example, the Windows Socket (Winsock) API for TCP/IP

ARP (Address Resolution Protocol)   A broadcast packet used to obtain a DLC address for a given IP address; typically used by routers to find workstations on a subnet and by workstations to find their default gateway (also known as router)

Bandwidth   Maximum rate of data flow for a given media type; usually measured in bits per second (bps)

Beacon   The Token Ring process that occurs when a station detects a ring failure (long-term signal loss); the station transmits a beacon frame to alert other stations of the failure

BOOTP (BOOTstrap Protocol)   Used by diskless client machines to obtain startup information, including an IP address, from a server

BPDU (Bridge Protocol Data Unit)   Used by a bridge implementing the spanning tree algorithm to advertise information about itself and the Root Bridge

Bridge   A device that connects two networks and operates at the data link layer

Broadcast   A packet destined for all stations on the network or subnet

Burst Error   A brief signal loss in a Token Ring

Checksum   Used to detect errors in specifying the type of data during the transmission of data; typically used in protocol headers and computed by treating the data as a series of octets and finding their sum

Collision   Occurs when two stations start transmitting on Ethernet at about the same time, resulting in garbled information

Contention Factor   Loss time or throughput due to network resources (bandwidth, routers, servers, etc.) being used by multiple clients

CRC (Cyclic Redundancy Check or Code)   Used to detect errors in data on the local media that occur during transmission; computed by treating binary data as a polynomial with 0 or 1 coefficients and dividing it by a special preset polynomial; the remainder is taken as the CRC (32 bits on LANs)

CSMA/CD (Carrier Sense Multiple Access with Collision Detection)   A method of dealing with contention on a broadcast network; stations listen for a quiet network (no carrier signal) before attempting to transmit. If a station's transceiver detects a collision while transmitting, it will back off and retry.

CSU (Channel Service Unit)   A digital interface device provided by a communication carrier (*see also* DSU)

Datagram   A self-contained packet; no connection or setup is required

Data Link Layer   Layer 2 of the OSI reference model; provides synchronization, hardware addressability, and error control over a physical link

DECnet   Digital Equipment Corporation's proprietary network protocol

DLC (Data Link Control)   The layer of protocol that controls access to the physical media

DNS (Domain Name Service)   A way for a node to retrieve an IP address associated with a domain name, such as www.net3group.com

DSU (Digital Service Unit)   A digital transmission device that connects a Channel Service Unit (*see* CSU) to a computer or router

Echo   A protocol that echoes information from a sent packet back to the sender

EGP (Exterior Gateway Protocol)   Used to advertise IP addresses of networks known to a particular gateway or router to other gateways or routers

Ethernet   A contention-based broadcast media network that formed the basis for the IEEE 802.3 CSMA/CD standard; invented by Xerox and formalized by Dec/Intel/Xerox (DIX)

Ethertype   A 16-bit value that follows the DLC destination and source addresses in a packet and that identifies the protocol above the DLC layer

Fragment   The first part of a packet left over after experiencing a collision beyond the Ethernet preamble

Frame   The block of data containing a Protocol Data Unit (PDU) transmitted at the data link layer; used interchangeably with the term "packet," although some liken frames to the DLC layer and packets to everything above that (*see also* Packet)

Frame Copied Error   An error that is reported on Token Ring when a station receives a frame addressed to it, but the frame-copied bit at the end of the frame was already set by an upstream station

FTP (File Transfer Protocol)   A popular protocol in IP networks used to transfer bulk data; operates over the TCP protocol

Functional Address   On Token Ring networks, subset of a broadcast address that denotes a special service

GGP (Gateway-to-Gateway Protocol)   Used by gateways to communicate routing information

Hop Count   A network layer metric that denotes the number of routers a packet has passed through

ICMP (Internet Control Message Protocol)   Used by IP for reporting routing errors and to handle control messages (such as Ping)

IEEE (Institute of Electrical and Electronics Engineers)   A professional engineering organization responsible for many of the LAN standards, including the 802.3 CSMA/CD, 802.4 Token Bus, and 802.5 Token Ring standards; also responsible for the 802.2 Logical Link Control (LLC) standard and for assigning OUIs

IGMP (Internet Group Management Protocol)   Used by hosts to send multicast membership information to local routers

IGP (Interior Gateway Protocol)   The protocol used by collaborating routers on an autonomous system to convey network reachability and routing information (*see also* RIP)

IGRP (Internet Gateway Routing Protocol)   A proprietary IGP used by Cisco routers

Internal Error   Reported by Token Ring stations when an error occurs on the adapter itself

IP (Internet Protocol)   A connectionless, best-effort network layer protocol that uses 32-bit addressing

IPX (Internetwork Packet Exchange)   The network layer protocol used by NetWare, with 80-bit addressing

ISO (International Organization for Standardization)   International institution that drafts and specifies standards for network protocols; best known for its seven-layer OSI reference model

Jabber   An Ethernet packet transmitted beyond the 1518-byte maximum allowable length

Kbps   Kilo (thousand) bits per second

LAN (Local Area Network)   Any network topology designed to span short distances at high speeds and low latency; Ethernet, Token Ring, and FDDI are such examples

LAT (Local Area Transport)   DEC's proprietary virtual terminal-to-host protocol; operates directly over the DLC layer with no intervening network layer protocol

Latency   The amount of delay from the beginning of a packet transmission to its reception by the destination

LAVC (Local Area Vax Cluster)   A proprietary DEC protocol that provides the means for the System Communication Architecture (SCA) to operate over Ethernet

Line Error   In Token Ring, a bit error that causes the CRC to fail

LLC (Logical Link Control)   The IEEE 802.2 standard; a sublayer of the data link layer that utilizes MAC services to support media-independent services to the network layer

Long Packet Error   In Ethernet, a packet that exceeds the maximum of 1518 bytes (including the CRC); also called a Jabber

Lost Frame Error   In Token Ring, a frame that didn't complete the path around the ring

MAC (Media Access Control)   An IEEE reference to the sublayer used to access a physical medium; the term "MAC address" is synonymous with DLC address

MAC Frames   Frames that provide error recovery and management of Token Ring networks

MAN (Metropolitan Area Network)   A high-speed network usually spanning a city; the size of this network falls between a LAN and a WAN

Mbps   Mega (million) bits per second

MTU (Maximum Transfer Unit)   The largest possible data unit size allowed for a given conversation between nodes

Multicast   A subset of a broadcast meant for a group of nodes

NACK or NAK   Abbreviation for negative acknowledgment (*see also* ack)

NAUN (Nearest Active Upstream Neighbor)   In Token Ring, the station that is repeating the signal to the receiving station

NCP (Network Core Protocol)   NetWare's file and print services protocol

NetBEUI (NetBIOS Extended User Interface)   NetBIOS over LLC; used by IBM and Microsoft

NetBIOS (Network Basic Input Output System)   A standard interface for session and datagram services on a PC network

Network Layer   Layer 3 of the OSI reference model; adds datagram (connectionless) services, end-to-end addressability, and routing

NFS (Network File System)   A distributed file system protocol developed by Sun Microsystems

Novell Raw   A DLC encapsulation type (an IEEE 802.3 frame length field but missing the LLC header that should follow) unique to Novell

OSI (Open Systems Interconnection)   A reference to ISO protocol standards for the interconnection of dissimilar computers; often referenced for comparing non-ISO protocols

OSPF (Open Shortest Path First)   A routing protocol based on network-wide link state information

OUI (Organizationally Unique Identifier)   The first 3 bytes of a 48-bit adapter address that are uniquely assigned by the IEEE to networking hardware vendors

Overhead   The extra control, error handling, and routing or switching information added to user data for transmission in the form of headers and trailers

Packet   The data unit used by the network layer to communicate with peers; more loosely defined by any block of data sent across a network (*see also* Frame)

Packet Burst   A NetWare protocol that improves bulk data efficiency by not requiring a request packet for every reply packet

Payload   The amount of data that a certain layer of protocol can send

Peer   Communication between the same layer of protocol in a network

Physical Layer   Layer 1 of the OSI reference model; the transmission of a bit stream over a physical medium along with the access technique for the physical medium

PING (Packet INternet Groper)   The ICMP echo message and its reply

Port   The abstraction used by Internet transport protocols to distinguish among multiple simultaneous connections to a single host

Preamble   In Ethernet, a 64-bit pattern of alternating 1s and 0s, ending in two 1s, used to synchronize transceivers and indicate the start of data

Protocol   A formal set of rules governing communications between peers; may define or negotiate such elements as acknowledgment algorithms, addressing, and MTU

RARP (Reverse Address Resolution Protocol)   Used by diskless nodes at startup to request an IP address from a server to bind their DLC address to (*see also* ARP)

Receiver Congestion Error   A reported Token Ring adapter problem; the adapter recognizes its destination address in a frame but is unable to buffer the frame due to a lack of adapter memory resources

Ring Purge   A frame sent by the Active Monitor on a Token Ring for the purposes of testing for completeness around the ring and generating a new token; most often occurs whenever a token or frame is lost

RIP (Routing Information Protocol)   A protocol used to advertise routing information within an autonomous network; often called a distance vector protocol because vectors consisting of network identifiers and hop counts (the distance) are provided

RPC (Remote Procedure Call)   A network API for an application to call a service across a network

Router   A device that connects two or more network segments and forwards packets based on network addresses and a set of one or more metrics

Runt/Short Error   On Ethernet, packets whose CRC is all right, but the length is less than the 64-byte minimum for both the Ethernet and IEEE 802.3 specification

SAP (Service Access Point)   The point at which services provided by a protocol layer are made available to a higher layer

Session Layer   Layer 5 of the OSI reference model; establishes a dialog based on a logical name rather than an address

Sliding Window   A method of flow control where the receiving side of a connection gives the transmitting side information (i.e., a window) about how much data it is willing to accept; used by TCP and other transport protocols

SMTP (Simple Mail Transport Protocol)   A protocol that provides electronic mail services for the Internet

SNA (System Network Architecture)   The proprietary IBM networking architecture

SNAP (SubNetwork Attachment Point)   A small header attached to data, specifying the type of data, when sending across a network that doesn't have self-identifying frames

SNMP (Simple Network Management Protocol)   An Internet management protocol used to monitor network events and set configuration parameters

Spanning Tree Algorithm   Used by bridges to prevent loops in a topology; invented by DEC and now an IEEE 802.1d standard (the DEC and IEEE methods are not compatible)

SPX (Sequenced Packet Exchange)   A transport protocol that provides connection-oriented services over IPX

SPX II   An improvement over SPX, allowing for larger packets and a burst-like mechanism

TCP (Transmission Control Protocol)   A connection-oriented, transport layer protocol that provides reliable, full-duplex communication between processes on separate stations over IP

TELNET   TCP/IP virtual terminal protocol; allows a user to log on to a remote host and interact as if directly connected to that host

Throughput   Rate of data flow achieved; usually measured in bits per second (bps)

Token Error   On Token Ring, an error reported by the Active Monitor for corrupted or lost tokens

Token Ring   An IEEE 802.5 standard where stations are connected in daisy-chain fashion, completing a loop; a station can transmit only when it possesses the token; originally developed by IBM

Transmit Abort Error   Reported by a Token Ring station that ends a packet transmission prematurely

Transport Layer   Layer 4 of the OSI reference model; provides reliable transfer of information between two end nodes by implementing error recovery and flow control

TTL (Time To Live)   A field inside the IP network layer header used to avoid looping packets. The time to live counter is decremented each time it passes through a router; if the counter reaches zero, the packet is discarded. The counter is also decremented at receiving workstations while waiting for packet fragments to complete an IP datagram.

UDP (User Datagram Protocol)   A transport layer protocol that sits on top of IP and provides port multiplexing for higher layer protocols; unlike TCP, UDP is a connectionless datagram service without acking or guaranteed delivery

Vines (Virtual Network System)   The proprietary Banyan networking protocol

WAN (Wide Area Network)   Any physical network that spans a large geographic area, such as countries or continents

XNS (Xerox Network Systems)   A collection of protocols developed by Xerox; these were the protocols from which IP and IPX were derived.

Index

The CD that accompanied this book has been replaced by a web site that can be found at the following address: http://www.awprofessional.com

Note that all references to the CD in the book now pertain to the web site.